The
WINE
DRINKER'S
Handbook

The WINE DRINKER'S Handbook

SERENA SUTCLIFFE

MASTER OF WINE

DAVID & CHARLES
Newton Abbot London

TO
AMANDA AND BILL
MY FAVOURITE
WINE DRINKERS

A Marshall Edition
Edited and designed by
Marshall Editions Ltd
71 Eccleston Square
London SW1V 1PJ

Editor **Penny David**
Art Editor **Heather Garioch**
Picture Editor **Zilda Tandy**
Editorial Assistants **Gwen Rigby,
  Helen Armstrong**
Art Assistant **Elizabeth Cooke**

Printed and bound in Belgium
by Brepols SA

First published 1982 by
David & Charles (Publishers) Ltd
Brunel House   Newton Abbot   Devon
in conjunction with Pan Books Ltd

ISBN 0 7153 8390 6

© Marshall Editions 1982

CONTENTS

ACKNOWLEDGEMENTS
The author wishes to thank the following writers for their contributions
to *The Wine Drinker's Handbook:*
Ian Jamieson MW (Germany), Bill Gunn MW (Central and Eastern Europe,
The Eastern Mediterranean and Other regions), David Stevens MW (South Africa),
Anders Ousback (Australia and New Zealand) and Dr Steve Taylor (Wine and health),
and also to acknowledge the advice and help of Dr Ralph Hutchinson (North America).

PREFACE

I love wine, and want you to feel the same. But with the world's wines available to us in such profusion, how can the drinker make the most pleasurable choices among the bewildering array of labels?

We have tackled the problem in two ways. First, *The Wine Drinker's Handbook* examines the liquid in question according to taste and type. In this book 'wine' is the freshly fermented product of the grape, which may be fortified but is not distilled. 'The range of wine' groups the different types taking into account subjective taste, which is what *you* feel about the wine, constant criteria such as colour, sweetness and strength, and objective facts such as where the wines come from and what grapes make them. These are the pages in which to find inspiration, to encounter new names for familiar types of wine, and to focus on taste sensation.

'The wine producers' paints in broad brushstrokes the background to the wines, so that you get the feel of each country's wine-making traditions and attitudes. Here is the information to deepen your understanding of subtleties of flavour, longevity and price. Distinctions between wines of similar or adjacent regions are clarified; foibles of local naming and labelling are indicated; good names to look for, on the spot and on imported bottles at home, are recommended.

Then, having made your choices, the third section contributes practical ideas and advice to enhance enjoyment of your drinking. How to choose, store and serve wine to its – and your own – full benefit is basic information that you need whether you drink the odd bottle casually at home, patronize a restaurant locally or abroad, or are planning to entertain on a grand scale.

Finally comes a back-up section of facts and formulae, from the size of a Bordeaux barrel to pronunciation hints, glossaries and vintage notes. Here too are measurement and temperature equivalents: throughout the book, quantities are given in metric measures, since this is how most wine is now made.

Santé!

Serena Sutcliffe

JUNE 1982

6

GROWING THE GRAPES

Fine wine cannot be made with poor grapes, just as good dishes cannot be produced from poor ingredients. On the other hand, ripe grapes of a good variety can still make mediocre wine if the wine-making process is not carefully done, so the two skills of viticulture and vinification are complementary – both need to be good if a fine wine is to emerge.

Choosing the grape variety is a science in itself. The choice will depend on the soil, site, exposure, overall climate and micro-climate of the vineyard. The variety will also have to 'marry' well with the root-stock chosen, as in most countries of the world producing fine wines, European grape varieties *(Vitis vinifera)* are grafted on American root-stocks to avoid the blight of phylloxera, which devastated most European vineyards in the late nineteenth century.

In some areas of the world, the choice of grape variety will be narrowed down to those permitted by law. For example, in Burgundy, a grower may use only the Pinot Noir or the Gamay for his red wines, and the Chardonnay or the Aligoté for his whites. If you want to make red Hermitage in the Rhône, you have to use the Syrah, and if you want to make Vouvray in the Loire, you have to use the Chenin. But, in some more recently established wine-growing areas of the world, such as California, the choice of grape variety is entirely personal and will be based on the conditions prevailing in each vineyard.

Certain grape varieties like certain soils. Thus, Cabernet Sauvignon, the noble red grape of the Médoc in Bordeaux, does particularly well on gravel, which gives very good drainage. Merlot, which predominates in the St Emilion and Pomerol districts of Bordeaux, is better suited to soil where there is a high clay content, where the Cabernet Sauvignon does not ripen well. Chardonnay and Sauvignon like basically chalky, limestone soil, while Riesling does well in slate, and also in loess and loam combination soils. The Chenin likes the limestone tufa around Saumur and Vouvray, and Pinot Noir produces great wines on marl.

On the other hand, it has been found that in certain wine-growing areas, for instance California and Australia, grape varieties can adapt well to rather different soil from that which suits them in Europe, and that in such places, climate is often more important than soil.

Fixed ideas about which grape varieties suit which climates can also be questioned nowadays. The Rhine Riesling produces superlative wines of great style in the Rhine and Mosel of Germany, areas hardly renowned for the heat of their climate. But now, enormously aided by the trained hand of man, remarkably elegant, and often superripe, Riesling is made in California and Australia. It would appear that Pinot Noir does not adapt too well to great heat, but Chardonnay makes excellent wines in areas as disparate as the Côte de Beaune, the Napa, Sonoma and Alexander Valleys in California, and the Hunter Valley in Australia.

Man will never learn to control the weather, just as he cannot control the sea, but there are ways in which its effects can be moderated or mitigated. In certain dry vineyard areas of the world, and where laws permit, irrigation is used to compensate for the rain which would ideally have fallen – California and Argentina are areas where irrigation is used to produce quality wines.

Damage by frost can be largely averted if spraying apparatus is installed, covering the vines with water, which then freezes and protects them – this system is used on the *grands crus* slope of Chablis. Heating apparatus can also be used among the vines, but this is less effective and more difficult to operate. Hail, always very localized, is a great menace in certain areas (Burgundy and the Veneto in Italy suffer from it), but it can be encouraged to fall as rain if light aeroplanes fly through the storm clouds to break them up.

The choice of site and aspect for a vineyard is very important. Frost is at its most severe on valley floors and near woods. Water in the vicinity, in the form of a lake or river, can raise the ambient temperature and help to prevent frost. Hills and mountains provide protection and shelter from winds, and help to give a favourable micro-climate – especially important in a northern vine-growing country such as Germany. When the maximum must be gained from the sun, south-facing slopes are chosen.

In areas where ripening can be a problem (Germany, England), some new grape variety crossings have been developed. These are *not* hybrids, but crossings of *Vitis vinifera*. They can be developed to resist frost, to ripen earlier, or to attain higher sugar levels.

Once the grape variety is chosen, the method of training the vine is decided upon. Here, terrain, soil and climate are taken into account. In cool or more temperate areas, vines are often trained nearer the ground so that they can benefit at night from the heat amassed in the soil during the day. But they must not be too low if the area runs the risk of frost. High training (often on a pergola system) is used in hot areas, such as Puglia in the heel of Italy, and it also allows other crops to be grown underneath, e.g. in the Minho region of Portugal, where Vinho Verde is made. If the slope of the vineyard is very steep, vines are often trained around stakes. In areas where high winds are likely, vines tend to be trained like bushes, and not along wires. But certain grape varieties, which can be grown almost anywhere, need the system of training along wires – the Cabernets, Merlot, Pinot Noir and Chardonnay fall into this group.

The same principles apply to pruning vines as to any garden pruning. It should be done during the time of the year when the vine is dormant – never when the sap is rising. Very productive grape varieties, in favourable climates, will need more restrictive pruning than shy-bearing varieties, if fine wine is the aim. Old vines usually need to be gently handled, since they produce less anyway, while a robust young vine will need restraining.

Great care has to be taken in the vineyard during the growing season. All the procedures of good gardening apply, such as correction of soil imbalances, cleanliness and the use, or not, of fertilizer. Good drainage must be organized, and the soil has to be kept clear of too much vegetation and properly aired. With too much leaf growth, the air circulation lessens and rot can set in if the weather is humid. It is possible now to spray against different kinds of rot, but the timing must be right to prevent its onset; there are also sprays against insects like moth and red spider. The only kind of rot which is desirable is 'noble rot' *(pourriture noble* in French, *Edelfäule* in German, Latin *Botrytis cinerea)*, and then it produces those glorious, late-harvested sweet white wines such as Sauternes/Barsac and Rieslings from Germany and California only if the rot atttacks when the grapes are ripe.

The last crucial stage of vineyard work is picking. This can be done manually or by machine. Mechanical harvesting has improved dramatically over the last decade, and is now much more delicate and less harmful both to the grapes and the vine than it was when first developed. Obviously, when vineyards are in very big parcels, machine picking is the logical method to use, and even traditional areas such as Bordeaux are now seeing its arrival. However, individually picked bunches, with several pickings through the vineyard (Sauternes), or even individually picked grapes *(Beerenauslese* wines) are processes which seem likely to remain in human hands for the moment. Steep slopes, also, have to be picked by hand.

A great improvement has been seen in recent years in the timing of the vintage. This depends on the kind of wine to be made (earlier for dry wines, later for sweet wines) and on the grape variety and the weather conditions of the year. The right balance between sugar and acidity must be struck. People used sometimes to wait for the grapes to attain maximum sugar, which would occasionally give an overripe taste and a flabbiness to the wine produced. This is because the acidity decreases in the grape as the sugar increases – the art (some call it a science) is in finding harmony and being able to pick as quickly as possible when the grape is at its apogee.

When the grapes are delivered to the winery for vinification, the responsibility of the grower, or viticulturist, ends. Now it is over to the wine-maker.

MAKING THE WINE

Vinification is more the domain of man than is viticulture. While the grower can only modify, adapt and mitigate certain conditions of soil, climate and site, the wine-maker has real control. Enormous advances have been made in the science of oenology in the last 15 years, and people are now trained at university to make wine, rather than simply learning from the experience and example of their elders. Technical training is of vital importance in vinification, especially in less than ideal conditions – both hotter countries and regions whose climate is at the colder limits of wine-making.

Before harvested grapes have gone through their fermentation, they are termed 'must'. Grape must is sugary juice, and it is this sugar which is converted into alcohol and carbon dioxide during the process of fermentation. This often starts spontaneously with the natural yeasts found on the skins of the grapes, but some wine-makers, e.g. in California, add cultivated yeasts for a more easily controlled fermentation.

Controlling the temperature during fermentation is of paramount importance, since it allows the length of the process to be manipulated. If the temperature is low, the fermentation will go on longer and more gradually, which gives a better bouquet to the wine, more flavour and fullness to the taste, and a 'long finish'. If temperatures go too high, there is a risk of the fermentation getting out of control and producing harmful bacteria and even a vinegary wine.

Fermentation can take place in open or closed containers of varying size and material. Fine red and white wines can be fermented in oak barrels, which impart a certain flavour and richness, but superb wines are also fermented in stainless steel or concrete vats, often lined with enamel or glass. The container is less vital than temperature control and cleanliness.

The colour is given to wine by the skins. It is possible to make a white wine from black grapes (Champagne is an example), but extreme care must be taken that the skins are not in contact with the fermenting juice. Normally, of course, the wine-maker wants red wine from red grapes and most of the colour

from the grapes is usually extracted in the first days of fermentation, when the transformation of sugar into alcohol and carbon dioxide is fastest.

There is a difference of sequence between red and white wine-making. Red grapes are fermented and then pressed; white grapes are pressed and the juice fermented. Red grapes are often lightly crushed and de-stemmed before fermentation, but sometimes a proportion of the stems is retained in order to give extra tannin to the resultant wine. White grapes are usually not de-stemmed before pressing (unless they are picked by machine) because the stems help the juice to drain out of the press more easily. One of the improvements in white wine-making has been the development of modern horizontal presses. These are preferable to the old vertical type because the pressing action is less violent and the pressure can be accurately controlled.

A special form of fermentation is used in order to produce particularly light, scented red wines which are not intended for keeping. Called carbonic maceration, it involves putting whole grapes into a closed vat in a carbonic gas atmosphere. Some fermentation takes place within the grape itself, while at the same time fermentation occurs in the juice running out of the crushed grapes at the bottom of the vat. The whole maceration/fermentation process can be as short as five days, or as long as ten, but the result will be a fresh, fruity wine, meant for young drinking. The colour of these wines is never dense, but clear red, and the bouquet could be most accurately descibed as fresh grape aroma.

One of the dangers to both red and white wine (but more immediately noticeable in white wine) is oxidation. For this reason, care must be taken at all stages of the vinification process that wine is not overly exposed to the air, so judicious amounts of sulphur dioxide are added at intervals during vinification.

Sometimes the natural sugar in the grape does not give quite enough alcohol to make a well-balanced wine, or a wine that will keep well. In some wine-growing regions around the world, chaptalization is permitted to correct this. Chaptalization is simply the addition during fermentation of some extra sugar, which is then converted into alcohol. The wine must have attained a minimum alcohol level before the process is allowed. In Italy, chaptalization with sugar is forbidden, but the addition of concentrated must to raise the alcohol level is allowed. In hot countries, the problem can be the reverse, for excessive sunshine can give overripeness and too much sugar, resulting in wines that are top-heavy in alcohol. Picking earlier can solve this problem. It is a misconception that a chaptalized wine is sweet – the sugar is converted into alchohol. But the process slightly lowers the fixed acidity of a wine which can make it taste softer and more supple.

After fermentation, both red and white wine can be put into wooden barrels, usually oak, or into vat. Certain grape varieties are particularly suited to ageing in oak cask – Cabernet, Shiraz or Syrah and Chardonnay are examples. Nebbiolo, Barbera and Sangiovese are usually aged in wooden vats, rather than the much smaller barrels. Grape varieties such as Sauvignon and Riesling often see no wood at all, but are kept in glass-lined vats. As the wine matures, care must be taken to see that air does not impair the quality. For this reason, casks are 'topped up' so that there is no ullage, and vats have a covering of carbon dioxide or inert gas to prevent oxidation.

Nearly all red wines, and some white wines, go through a secondary fermentation, either concurrently with alcoholic fermentation, or afterwards. In this malolactic fermentation, the rather green, appley malic acid is converted into the milder lactic acid and carbon dioxide gas. In some white wines (particularly those from hot countries) malolactic fermentation is not desirable, as malic acidity gives welcome freshness. It is often not possible to organize exactly when the malolactic fermentation will take place, but it can be encouraged or discouraged.

If a red wine is left in cask for some years, it will have to be 'racked' periodically to prevent it from going stale. This is simply the process of transferring wine from old lees in one cask to another clean cask. White wine should be racked with extreme care, and as infrequently as possible, to guard against air contact.

The care of the wine before bottling is called, in French, élevage. It may be necessary to clarify the wine to remove solid matter. Egg white is used on very fine red wines; gelatine, fish glue or isinglass for white wines. Sometimes a wine is refrigerated to precipitate tartrates.

The right moment must be chosen for bottling each wine. Some fresh white wines and light reds like Gamay are bottled a few months after they are made, but a top red Bordeaux might spend two years in cask before bottling; Château Yquem will have three years of cask age, and Brunello di Montalcino will spend four to five years in wood. Some types of wine need bottle ageing as well to reach their full potential – top Bordeaux and Burgundy, top sweet white wines, great Chardonnay are examples. Fruit, acidity and tannin are necessary in good balance to make a red wine suitable for ageing; however, excessive tannin will make a wine become too dry as it ages. In white wines there should be fruit, acidity and 'fat' or fullness.

The bottling process should be carried out in very clean conditions; generally some filtering is necessary beforehand so that the wine will be star-bright. But fine, deep red wines will throw a deposit over the years, usually of colouring matter, and Vintage Port will form a 'crust'. All quality wines are bottled under cold conditions, but some mass-produced wines are given a 'flash pasteurization' before bottling to give complete stability. This need not harm a wine, but it does prevent great development.

Wines can obviously be 'made to a price', like anything else. When maximum care is taken during every stage of the wine-making process, the final price will inevitably be higher than for a mass-produced, simply handled, quickly sold, basic quaffing wine. When a wine is made in bulk, held in vat for only a few months, with little individual treatment (no topping up, racking, etc) and sold quickly without years of ageing to finance, it should be cheap.

11

DESCRIBING THE TASTE

The basic sequence when tasting is: look, smell, taste. Note colour and clarity first, scent or bouquet next, and finally the effect on the palate.

Appearance For serious wine tasting, have your glass no more than one-third full. Hold it by the stem, and tilt it against a white background to look at the hue of the wine at the rim. If the rim of a red wine is deep purple, the wine will almost certainly be very young; as a wine ages, the colour becomes more 'bricky', passing from purple, to crimson, to almost tawny when very old. To judge the depth of colour, put the glass down and look straight into it. If you cannot see the base of the bowl, you have a very deep-coloured wine.

Wine should always be 'bright', not cloudy or murky, whether white or red, although shade of colour in white is not as important as in red. 'White' wine which is deep yellow could be oxidized, although very old Sauternes can go dark amber and still taste marvellous.

Smell Pick up the glass, swirl the wine around to give it air and enable it to 'breathe', and smell it. It is better to put your nose in several times, noting your impressions, than to put your nose into the glass and leave it there – the senses become dulled with over-exposure. The wine should smell clean and appetizing.

An off-odour that lasts for a few minutes after the wine has been opened is 'bottle stink', the consequence of being trapped, perhaps for years, in the bottle. If the wine seems to smell corky, let it stand in the glass; if it is genuinely corky, the smell will get worse rather than disappearing.

A straightforward, fruity aroma will come from a young wine, a more complex bouquet from a developed wine. Try and describe the smell – is it floral or spicy? Is it light and ephemeral, or

---

The words for wine

Do you *need* words to describe wines? Don't they speak for themselves? Maybe, but you still need some vocabulary to recommend a wine to a friend, or to tell a wine merchant what you like.

When beginners start to taste wine seriously, they don't know what to look for or how to describe what they find. They lack the tools of the trade, and, looking at notes months later, may find that they have used the same vague description for quite different wines.

Gradually, all wine tasters develop a vocabulary to record their impressions. Some of this is borrowed, some self-created. Ask more experienced tasters to describe a wine and see how their words fit your impressions. If you find a word leaping to mind when you smell or taste a wine, use that as 'your' word. For instance, a taster might associate Pinot Noir wines as produced in Burgundy with a 'farmyard' nose – a trigger word which will always help pinpoint that particular smell.

Most words used in wine description are simple to understand. A wine that smells 'yeasty' – an aroma instantly recognizable from bread – is just that: it can mean that the wine is still fermenting and unstable. If a wine is 'sulphury', the slightly prickly sensation indicates that the sulphur dioxide used to give it stability has been a little overdone, or that the wine is young.

Many descriptions become clearer if you think of their opposites: a 'flabby' wine is the opposite of fresh and crisp; if a wine is 'tough', it is the opposite of soft and supple – tough wines have tannin, soft wines do not; a 'musty' wine is the opposite of a clean, fresh wine: this can be caused by badly maintained casks or a faulty cork, and will wear off; a 'sappy' wine is a young wine, the opposite of a tired wine which is past its best; a wine with finesse is the opposite of a common, coarse-tasting wine. Words like harsh, heavy, light, luscious, mellow, spicy, delicate, fruity and thin explain themselves.

It is when description gets into the realm of words such as dumb, flinty, silky and velvety that the critics begin to get out their red pencils. But these are good descriptions for definite sensations. 'Dumb' means that it does not 'speak', that the nose is closed and undeveloped, nearly always because the wine has not had time to develop bouquet. 'Flinty' describes a certain pungent smokiness in a wine smell.

Oddly enough, the simple descriptions of sweet and dry can cause the most trouble. What is sweet to one person is only medium-sweet to another and what is slightly sweet

intense and persistent? What does it smell *of*? Record your immediate impressions, your personal 'trigger' words: some suggestions are below.

Taste After you have really enjoyed the smell of the wine, which can be a great part of the pleasure of wine-drinking, taste it. Take a good mouthful, and push it all around your mouth. Notice how it tastes as it rolls in over the tongue, passing some of your keenest tastebuds. Let the wine go right into the sides of your mouth, and, if it helps, make 'slurping' noises, as professionals always do. They are letting in air to give the wine more chance to show all its qualities, which will include sweetness, acidity, tannin and flavour. If the juices at the side of your mouth really start to run, the wine probably has marked acidity; if this is unpleasant, it is astringent. If the roof of your mouth dries, or puckers up, the wine probably contains considerable tannin. A wine should never be sour or bitter, but excessive tannin in a young wine can be described as slight bitterness.

You won't miss anything if you spit out – there are no taste buds in the throat – but spitting out will enable you to taste several wines without being influenced by alcoholic intake.

The more wines you drink, the more recognition becomes possible if you concentrate. With practice, nearly anyone can learn to recognize a wine they have had before, but this is a 'party trick'. It is more useful to learn to recognize what you like.

Learning to judge the quality in a wine is harder. Listening to someone who really knows an area can be instructive. Or you can take a wine, which you know is really good of its type, as a yardstick by which to measure others, and develop an idea of what should be attained.

to one is dry to another. Residual sugar can be measured, but the other components in a wine can disguise the sugar so that you can perceive one wine to be drier than another and be proved wrong. The level of acidity in a wine distorts your judgement: if there is a low acidity level, the wine appears softer, and often sweeter, while if the acidity is high you are inclined to judge the wine drier.

Words associated with acidity – green, appley, unripe, raw – are more likely to fit young wines, or wines made from grapes that were not ripe. If a wine is astringent or hard, it will probably have high acid, but also a lot of tannin. When wine with tannin is young, it has a drying, rasping feel to it which softens with age.

Certain descriptions are used almost universally. Muscat d'Alsace is said to smell of cats; Cabernet Sauvignon-dominated wines smell of blackcurrants, while Sauvignon Blanc smells of blackcurrant leaves; fine, mature Clarets often have a nose reminiscent of cedarwood. Wines matured in oak can have a vanilla nose and flavour, while a flowery nose is epitomized in a Mosel or a Nahe wine. A peppery nose can be found on young reds from the Syrah grape, and nuttiness from a true Amontillado Sherry or a mature, great white Burgundy.

Other terms that are heard when tasters get together are: 'earthy', or, in French, *goût de terroir*, which means that there are specific smells and flavours given by the soil on which the wine was produced. 'Fat' implies high glycerine and a full-bodied wine, rich in texture and flavour (rich does not mean sweet here). 'Elegant' implies balance and harmony between component parts of the wine – it will probably be a wine of breed, and is more often white than red.

'Finish' refers to the end-taste of a wine. 'Weight' is a wine's body – the flavour and texture of a wine with a lot of body will probably remain in the mouth, and 'length of palate' is a professional term denoting how long a taste remains in the mouth after elimination. A simple wine will disappear from memory rather quickly, while a great wine's flavours will linger on the palate.

'Volatile acidity' or 'acescence' is a slightly vinegary smell and taste caused by an excess of acetic bacteria. As with all technical faults in wine, it is most easily understood when someone experienced points it out.

The more wine you taste and drink, the wider your vocabulary will become. You need not subscribe to the school of wilder tasting descriptions (sweaty saddles, dank dogs and badgers' sets) – but wine has such varied tasting sensations that picturesque language is, happily, almost unavoidable.

PART ONE: THE RANGE OF WINE

Classifying wines according to taste is both a party game and a serious challenge. Fixing in words those elusive taste impressions brings flights of fancy abruptly to earth, but you do need some idea what to expect when you buy a bottle. This section transcends national barriers and stereotypes and shows the immense choice within each broad group of tastes. The wines themselves do not make the task easy: they resist compartmentalization by changing character or sweetness with the different vintages. For these and other reasons – such as their age – some wines fall into two different groupings.

Nevertheless, many wines do have distinct tastes, often conferred by the grape varieties which make them. Some emphasis is thus given to this raw material of wine: grape varieties are featured in the wine groupings where they play a principal part, e.g. Sémillon in the very sweet white wines – but this does not preclude the same variety from sometimes making dry wines.

Where grape variety tastes are particularly dominant (aromatic whites and assertive reds), the wines are subdivided accordingly. Otherwise, they are described geographically – always within the general heading of their particular taste.

The categories cover every wine taste you may encounter. Still table wines range from the different types of white (from aromatic and dry, right up to exceptionally sweet dessert wines), to reds of increasing weight and body, with the assertive styles in their separate category. Rosés in all their variety are followed by sparkling wines, among them true Champagne, and then by fortified wines, with the classic Sherry, Port and Madeira.

The cosmopolitan choice within each taste category makes possible great variety in your drinking and enables you to find a wide range of wines wherever you are. With this part of the book, the 'theory' of wine is unimportant. If you decide you want to drink, say, a powerful red wine, look under this heading to find the possibilities. The section will uncover a host of wines of similar type, among which you are bound to find something delicious.

The suggestions concluding each wine grouping brim over with ideas for both tastings and meals.

AROMATIC WHITES

Wines made from aromatic grape varieties are among the most seductive weapons in the wine-lover's armoury. Serve a slightly chilled Gewürztraminer or Muscat when people drop in for drinks, or as a less usual combination with a first course, for sure success.

The grape varieties that make aromatic wines tend to keep their characteristic aroma even with bottle age, whereas often, with less aromatic grape varieties, the initial fruit aroma which is there when the wine is young develops with bottle age into a more complex bouquet.

Some aromatic white wines can be described as spicy (Gewürztraminer, Pinot Gris), while others are more pungent (Sauvignon, smelling of black-currant leaves, and Muscat from Alsace with its 'catty' smell).

The wines are often labelled according to the grape variety, especially in Alsace, California and north-east Italy, so that you know immediately what you are getting – although certain variations in sweetness of Gewürztraminer, for example, may be expected. Most aromatic white wines are, however, completely dry: French Sauvignon, for instance, is sometimes searingly so.

Dry aromatic wines are not particularly expensive, and many are very reasonably priced. If, however, you come across the rare sweet ones from late harvests (examples are exceptional Gewürztraminers from California and Alsace, and the occasional Ruländer Auslesen from Germany), they will be expensive, as the yield from these very ripe and often botrytized grapes is tiny.

When to drink these wines

Aromatic whites lend themselves to all sorts of exciting food-and-wine combinations. A Pinot Grigio goes beautifully with *antipasto*, with its assortment of tastes which can include fish, meat and vegetable dishes. A French Sauvignon goes well with a rich *pâté*, its acidity cutting through the full, slightly gamy taste. Pinot Gris, or Tokay d'Alsace, is delicious with a chicken dish, particularly if a delicate white sauce is made of the same wine.

Smoked fish – salmon, eel, trout or mackerel – goes well with aromatics, for a challenging meeting of tastes in the mouth. And if you are not drinking schnapps or aquavit with your gravadlax, try Gewürztraminer.

Prosciutto with melon or ripe figs is lovely with Pinot Grigio, if the ham is top-quality, delicate San Daniele or Parma. Try Gewürztraminer if the ham is saltier.

The aromatic whites are really the best – if not the only – wines to go with Chinese or mild Indian food from the north of that country. Southern, hotter Indian food calls for lager. All but the hottest Hunan or Szechwan Chinese dishes respond beautifully to Gewürztraminer, particularly, and probably best of all to the wines from Alsace – but this theory needs constant testing. Muscat loves the Chinese connection, too.

Remember that the softer styles, with a touch of residual sugar, are delicious as aperitif drinking without food. And the most pungent aromatic wines are often difficult to follow, as they mask the subsequent wine – particularly if it is delicate and subtle. So, either stick to the same wine throughout the meal, or go straight on to a red from your aromatic white instead of having two white wines.

Gewürztraminer

This wine is dry when it is from ALSACE except, very occasionally, when there is such a ripe year that *vendange tardive* (late-harvest), or Sélection de Grains Nobles wines are made.

In Trentino and Alto Adige in north-eastern ITALY, where the grape is also called the Traminer Aromatico, the wine is dry, but less intensely scented than an Alsatian Gewürztraminer. It has great charm and intriguing style, however.

ESTATE BOTTLED

GOLD SEAL VINEYARDS

Gewürztraminer

NEW YORK STATE WHITE WINE

Produced and bottled at the Winery by Gold Seal Vineyards Hammondsport, New York *Charles Fournier* Alcohol 11.9% by Volume

Gewürztraminer in CALIFORNIA is, again, not as pungently spicy as in Alsace. When made at a winery like Joseph Phelps or Chateau St Jean, it is elegant, stylish and grapy, and the Paul Masson Pinnacles Selection Gewürztraminer is also highly recommended for its soft, tempting drinkability. Both Joseph Phelps and Chateau St Jean make late-harvest Gewürztraminer, which in the higher sugar levels can be deep amber in colour. The richest examples can be somewhat over-powering, but they are undoubtedly wines of great intensity. Clos du Bois in Sonoma produces off-dry Gewürztraminer, but when the residual sugar is only around one per cent, the wine is fine with savoury food, as well as on its own. Firestone Vineyard in the Santa Ynez Valley makes dry Gewürz-traminer, as well as late-harvest.

Gewürztraminer in GERMANY is mostly concentrated in the Rheinpfalz, logically enough, as this is the area over the border from Alsace. Here the taste is full of fruit, and with the earthy undertones always characteristic of the Pfalz wines, whatever the grape variety.

In AUSTRIA, the Gewürztraminer is nearly always soft, with some sweetness. An area in which to find typical examples is the western Burgenland, where the name of the old town of Rust often appears on wine labels. The lake of Neusiedlersee is the hub of a very warm and dry micro-climate, and so the grapes ripen well and produce wines of good sugar content.

Muscat

So far, in only two places in the world is Muscat vinified to make dry, light table wine: in Milawa, Victoria, AUSTRALIA, a family firm, Brown Bros, make a speciality of it. Their Muscat is pretty, fruity and charming. They also make a late-picked variety, which is sweeter, but very far from cloying.

In the second, ALSACE, the Muscat is far more pungent, with a marked 'catty' nose and great aromatic flavour. Nearly all the good Alsace houses have a Muscat on their list, but in some years it is very scarce. Less than 4 per cent of all grapes grown in Alsace are Muscat, and it is also a grape variety that suffers from flowering problems, so that tiny yields can ensue. In 1980, for example, the Muscat was virtually wiped out by poor weather at flowering time.

Misket from BULGARIA is not a million miles from Muscat d'Alsace in its sheer force of character and heady scent.

Dry Muscat, or Muscat Trocken, wines can sometimes be found in GERMANY, e.g. at the Bürklin-Wolf estate in the Rheinpfalz.

Moscato wines in ITALY are usually sweet, sometimes sparkling (Asti and Moscato Spumante), but often made as dessert wines.

Muscat grapes are also responsible for many of the world's fortified wines.

Shipped by AVERY'S of BRISTOL Ltd. Park St. BRISTOL

ALSACE

APPELLATION ALSACE CONTRÔLÉE

DEPUIS 1639

MUSCAT "HUGEL"

CUVÉE TRADITION 700 ml ℮

MISE EN BOUTEILLE PAR HUGEL ET FILS·RIQUEWIHR·ALSACE·FRANCE

PRODUCT OF FRANCE   BOTTLED IN FRANCE

Pinot Gris

This versatile grape variety does well in Germany, Alsace, Austria and Italy. As it changes its name from country to country, and even within Alsace, it may not always be appreciated that these are one and the same grape.

As Pinot Grigio, it makes some of the most delicious and interesting dry white wines in ITALY today. The grape is concentrated in the north-east, especially in Friuli-Venezia Giulia and in Alto Adige. The most individual examples probably come from the Collio, west of Gorizia in Friuli. Here, estates make lovely scented wines with a long, fruity taste.

If you see one with a pinkish hue to it, don't send it back, but count yourself lucky. The Pinot Grigio, like the Gewürztraminer, has a pinkish tinge to the skin (the Gewürztraminer can look almost red when really ripe), and if the skins are left in contact with the juice for a time, the resultant wine will have some colour, but also extra fragrance and flavour. American wine-makers call this 'skin contact', and very exciting it sounds, too. Unfortunately, not many producers do this now – the public tends to want their white wines too white.

In ALSACE, Pinot Gris – synonymous with Tokay d'Alsace – is often the dark horse of the region, as people are first attracted by more widely planted, better-known grapes.

But Pinot Gris has a lovely, full, even earthy character, and is definite enough in taste to be excellent with food, including white meat. It needs to be made from ripe grapes, and the really rich wines age beautifully. Tokay d'Alsace can have a wonderful, smoky bouquet and taste to it, much prized by the Alsatians themselves.

The Ruländer in GERMANY needs maximum warmth and sun, and is mostly planted in the Rheinpfalz and in south Germany, where the wines are fuller and have less acidity than in the rest of Germany. The Ruländer has a 'broad' taste, and can easily attain *Spätlese* and even *Auslese* quality – when it is definitely sweet.

Sauvignon

The Sauvignon is at its most aromatic, pungent and forceful in FRANCE, particularly in the areas of Sancerre and Pouilly-sur-Loire. Sancerre and Pouilly Blanc Fumé (the Blanc Fumé is another name for the grape, used here and by some Californians), have such a marked taste that they are two of the easiest wines to recognize in blind tastings. The acidity is high, and this projects the bouquet and flavour right into the nose and mouth of the drinker.

Other wines of this area are also made from Sauvignon and share these characteristics: Reuilly, Quincy and Menetou-Salon. Near Poitiers, in an isolated wine area in the midst of grain production, the Sauvignon du Haut-Poitou is remarkably like a Sancerre.

Sauvignon de Touraine can come from anywhere in this area of the Loire valley, and resembles a lesser Sancerre, delicious when drunk young.

Other wines in France made – or largely made – from the Sauvignon share its pronounced character, but to a lesser degree. Sauvignon may not always appear on the label – dry white Entre-Deux-Mers, for example, is nowadays a Sauvignon-dominated wine, but tastes nothing like Sancerre. It could thus fall into either category: dry white aromatic, or light, dry white. Certainly the aromatic flavour here will not be as pronounced as it is with a Sancerre or a Pouilly Blanc Fumé.

Don't forget the Sauvignons of CENTRAL EUROPE, which sometimes go under the name of Muskat Silvaner.

Sauvignon in CALIFORNIA is a different thing altogether. Europeans often judge these wines badly because they do not have the pronounced flavour and 'attack' of the better-known French wines. But Californian Sauvignon has a quality and character all of its own, and stands solidly on its own merits. One important difference is the lower acidity, which makes the Californian wines fuller and somehow 'grapier'.

Within California, some wine-makers age their wines for a limited time in wood while others do not. The wines which have had some contact with wood are usually 'bigger', and rounder than those which have not.

Mondavi's Fumé Blanc is justly famous, now quite rich and full – serious wine for drinking with food. It is actually blended with a small proportion of Sémillon, which contributes to the vinous body, as does the partial fermenting and ageing in French barrels – quite a different practice from, say, the Ladoucette Pouilly Blanc Fumé.

Sterling Vineyards also have a noted Sauvignon Blanc, which is of the fuller, more firm style. Joseph Phelps makes an elegant, fruity style, the Chateau St Jean Fumé Blanc has some wood-ageing, while Dry Creek Vineyard in Sonoma perhaps makes the most 'French' of the Californian Fumé Blancs. San Martín makes a pretty, light, elegant Fumé Blanc from San Luis Obispo grapes, while Almadén's Sauvignon Blanc from Monterey is outstanding – a lovely, fat, earthy wine. The Sauvignon Blanc of Spring Mountain Vineyards has some wood-ageing, but in large German ovals, while the Paul Masson Pinnacles Selection has a delicate Fumé Blanc.

GRAPE VARIETIES

GEWÜRZTRAMINER
The German *gewürz* means spicy, and wines made from this grape variety have a distinct spicy aroma. It is known as Traminer Aromatico in north-eastern Italy (after the village of Tramin or Termeno in Alto Adige, where it is said to originate).

PINOT GRIS
The wines are characterized by an aromatic, flowery flavour. The grape is known generally in France as Pinot Gris, but some Alsatians call it Tokay d'Alsace. It is Ruländer in German-speaking countries, Pinot Grigio in Italy.

SAUVIGNON
With an aroma reminiscent of blackcurrant leaves, the wines have a crisp, green taste in France and a fuller, smoky taste in California. The grape may be called Sauvignon Blanc in California; Blanc Fumé is an alternative name used in both California and Pouilly-sur-Loire. Muskat Silvaner is a synonym in Central Europe.

Other aromatic wines

Wines made from the Viognier, that strange white grape of the northern Rhône which makes Condrieu and Château Grillet, smell of may-blossom when young. Other attributes are honey-like aromas and many subtle 'layers' of taste.

As for Retsina, some people consider that the smell and taste are reminiscent of moth-balls. Here it is not the grape which gives the aromatic quality, but the pine resin used during the wine's fermentation. Retsina is an acquired taste, but if you learned to love it on Greek holidays, it will always be a nostalgic wine, drunk with red mullet, kebabs or moussaka – and always to be drunk very well chilled indeed.

Germany has developed crossings of grape varieties which are often pungently aromatic. A prime example is the Scheurebe,

which is extremely 'catty' and rather coarse when dry or nearly dry, but becomes very interesting and luscious if picked with a higher sugar level, such as *Auslese* or even *Beerenauslese*.

The Morio-Muskat, a crossing of Weissburgunder and Silvaner, is also markedly aromatic and spicy, and is found mainly in the Rheinhessen and Rheinpfalz. Even a small proportion of this grape variety in a wine makes its presence in the bouquet immediately noticed.

VIN BLANC
DE
CHATEAU-GRILLET
APPELLATION CONTROLÉE

1971

MISE EN BOUTEILLE AU CHATEAU
NEYRET-GACHET
PROPRIÉTAIRE DE CHATEAU-GRILLET PRÈS CONDRIEU, RHONE

SUGGESTED TASTINGS

Taste a simple Gewürztraminer from Alsace against a softer and probably sweeter Austrian version.

Taste a Traminer Aromatico from Alto Adige against one of the drier Californian Gewürztraminers from David Bruce, Davis Bynum, Chateau St Jean, Louis Martini, Matanzas Creek or Stony Hill: look for fruit and elegance.

Try a *vendange tardive* Gewürztraminer from Alsace against a sweeter Californian wine: Veedercrest Late Harvest, Parsons Creek Winery or Wente Brothers Selected Bottling. Among the 'sweet and sticky' brigade, try an Alsatian Sélection de Grains Nobles 1976 against one of California's ripest: Almadén Charles Le Franc Late Harvest from the Paicines Vineyards or Chateau

St Jean Robert Young Vineyards Individual Bunch Selected Late Harvest.

Taste a Pinot Grigio from Alto Adige (perhaps from the excellent wine firm of Santa Margherita) against one from the Friuli (perhaps the Collio district).

Taste a Sancerre against either a Sauvignon du Haut-Poitou or a Sauvignon de Touraine, to see nuances of Sauvignon flavour in France.

Do a graduated tasting of Californian Sauvignon/Fumé Blancs, starting with a lighter flowery/smoky type (Beringer, Inglenook, Parducci) and going on to one of the bigger, firmer possibly wood-aged versions (Santa Ynez Valley or Zaca Mesa Winery).

LIGHT DRY WHITES

Today, this is probably the most widely appreciated category of wine in the world. Gone are the days when people wanted the word Dry on the label but something sweet in the bottle.

The description 'light' refers both to the alcoholic content and to the texture and weight of the wine. Although some wines of this type are 12 per cent alcohol, many are less – German wines, for instance, are 2-3 per cent less. Anything over 12 per cent tends to taste 'heavier' and be more of a mouthful, and is most definitely not within this category. 'Light' refers also to the sensation in the mouth, which is sprightly and refreshing rather than full, round or overpowering in either texture or flavour.

Some wines even have a touch of natural *spritz* or carbon dioxide gas (CO_2) in them when young. Whereas heavier wines have a real feeling of volume, and one can almost sense them coating the mouth, light dry whites score on fresh fruitiness and sheer drinkability: they are what the French call *gouleyant* wines.

Since, with few exceptions, they are bottled very young – often only a few months after they have been made – little capital investment is tied up in maturing these wines in either cask or bottle, and the prices are consequently low or at least reasonable. In fact, since the influence of wood in a cask would not suit such light-textured, fruity wines destined for young drinking, the majority of these wines do not see wood at all, but spend their brief life before bottling in vat: glass-lined concrete or stainless steel is the norm.

When to drink these wines
These are 'anytime' wines, to have to hand and to serve freely. They go well with mussels and whitebait, hors d'oeuvres and salads, sardines and fish and chips. Order a bottle next time you are studying the menu in a restaurant – it will help to pass the time most agreeably until the first course arrives, and will probably go well with your choice as well. It substitutes for heavier aperitifs: light dry white wine is the enemy of the double Martini!

France
Certain grape varieties are better suited to making delicate, dry white wines than others. Muscadet from near Nantes, where the river Loire meets the sea, is an archetypal example of a grape variety making a light white wine, to which it gives its name.

You will find more Muscadet de Sèvre-et-Maine than any other, for 85 per cent of the total volume comes from this area, between two tributaries of the Loire.

Muscadet *sur lie* means that the wine has been bottled directly off its lees, which impart a particularly fruity flavour and sometimes a touch of CO_2, giving a slight prickle on the palate. Muscadet will never be very alcoholic because French AC law says that it must never be more than 12 per cent; this is the only AC to have an upper alcohol limit.

Chasselas, which, when grown at Pouilly-sur-Loire, makes wine of the same name (not to be confused with Pouilly Blanc Fumé, made in the same area but from Sauvignon, is light). Pinot Blanc from Alsace will also be dry, light and a very good buy. Riesling as produced in Alsace (here it is always Rhine Riesling) in good, but not great, years will also be light and dry, but with, perhaps, a more assertive taste and length on the palate than many wines in this category.

Chardonnay in some of its forms makes excellent light dry wine. In France, the lighter white Burgundies fall into this category – Mâcon Blanc, Mâcon-Prissé, Mâcon-Lugny and Mâcon-Viré. Other wines from the Mâconnais, with slightly more body, are St Véran, Pouilly-Loché, Pouilly-Vinzelles and Pouilly-Fuissé itself, the latter sometimes too expensive, so try the lesser-known names. Straight Chablis from a light year would also fall into this category, but from a good year, the wine would have more body and be medium-weight. Coteaux Champenois, the still white wines from Champagne, make light drinking.

Some grape varieties make delicious light dry white wine, if the year has enough sun, otherwise they can be too acid. Aligoté from Burgundy falls into this category. The

Italy
Even a decade ago, it was less easy to find light dry white wines in Italy than it is now. This is because the vinification methods rather than the grape varieties have changed. The great enemy of fresh-tasting white wine is oxidation, and once this problem was conquered, Italy soon became an unbeatable source of supply. Now that grapes are picked earlier and wines bottled earlier, a transformation has taken place from heavy, yellow brews to refreshing, straw-coloured wines. Just occasionally, the transformation has gone too far, and the light white wines are too neutral, with no regional taste at all to identify them; but on the whole, the change has been greatly for the better.

Soave, from the Veneto and near the city of Verona, is the light dry wine *par excellence*. Made from Garganega and Trebbiano grapes, it is straw-coloured, fresh-tasting and delicious young. After Lambrusco, it is the largest-selling Italian wine in the United

States, so it clearly appeals to a huge number of people. Bianco di Custoza and Gambellara are two other light dry whites to enjoy without leaving the Veneto.

In the Marches, there is tempting Verdicchio from the grape of the same name, light but with an identifiable taste that could be almonds or a purely regional *goût de terroir*. From Tuscany comes Vernaccia di San Gimignano, made from the Vernaccia grape – a prime example of an ugly duckling which used to be oxidized, changing into a swan of refreshing fruitiness.

In Sardinia there is light and cheap Vermentino and Torbato, often with no more than 10.5 per cent alcohol; but it is safer to buy these from the firm of Sella and Mosca, since some producers of Sardinian whites are still practising the 'old style' of wine-making. Trebbiano from anywhere in Emilia-Romagna is delicious when only months old, and Riesling Italico from north-east Italy, as a whole, is light and flowery.

Spain and Portugal

The Penedès area of Catalonia seems the region best equipped to join the light-and-dry bandwagon, and many of the most reasonable wines from Torres, such as Viña Sol, as well as Masía Bach dry white, fulfil the modern demand for fresher wines. The more expensive wines from here have more body

and, therefore, fall into a different category.

In Portugal, Vinho Verde is the fresh, enticing wine for easy drinking, but check to see if your exported Vinho Verde has been sweetened for foreign markets before you buy. Aveleda now produce a totally dry Vinho Verde, which is how you will find it on its home territory.

Central Europe

In **Austria,** the driest wines, and also those with more acidity, tend to come from around Vienna, and many of them are made from the indigenous Grüner Veltliner grape. When one is in the wine gardens of the city, nothing is more delicious than drinking the *Heurige*, or new wine – fresh, and with bouncing acidity and the prickle of recent fermentation.

An attractive Chasselas wine is Fendant, which is the name for the grape variety in the Valais region of **Switzerland.** It is often no more than 9 per cent alcohol, and can be marvellous quaffing wine, with absolutely no after-effects. In the Vaud, the Chasselas becomes the Dorin, but remains delicious.

The best dry whites in **Yugoslavia** come from Slovenia, where the Beli Burgundec, or Pinot Blanc, is drier than the Laski Riesling, or Wälschriesling, with the local Sipon grape variety making the driest white of all.

Germany

Riesling in Germany nearly always has a touch of sweetness to match the acidity, unless the wine is labelled *Trocken* or *Halbtrocken* – the latter is just a touch less dry analytically, but very often this cannot be detected on taste. Some of the most successful *Trocken* or *Halbtrocken* wines come from the Rheinpfalz and Franconia, where they seem to avoid the somewhat 'lean' character often evident in totally dry wines from other parts of Germany.

As a general rule, also, it is best to go for a top estate or really respected wine shipper when looking for this type of wine, since less scrupulous producers seem to think that dry equals the lowest quality of wine, which is a disaster for the drinker. In fact, when a wine is made with no masking *Süssreserve*, the basic quality must be very good. It is highly likely that the best *Trocken* wine will also have *Spätlese* or *Auslese* on the label. As these words usually denote sweetness, this might seem an anomaly, but it means that the grape musts had these higher Oechsle readings, which then became dry by fermentation – thus the wine has more body with its dry character.

Many of these wines will be made from Riesling, but good dry German wines also come from varieties such as the Silvaner, Müller-Thurgau and Weissburgunder (Pinot Blanc).

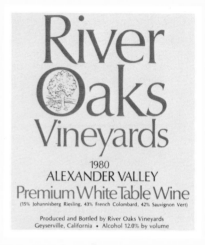

1980
ALEXANDER VALLEY
Premium White Table Wine
(15% Johannisberg Riesling, 43% French Colombard, 42% Sauvignon Vert)

Produced and Bottled by River Oaks Vineyards
Geyserville, California • Alcohol 12.0% by volume

USA

For a light Chardonnay in California, the drinker must look for a 'lightly oaked' wine – one which has seen hardly any barrel-ageing – or for a wine that has never been in contact with wood. As a guide, Chardonnay varietals which are reasonable in price are unlikely to have been stored in barrel for long, although there are obviously exceptions to this rather general rule.

Perhaps the Californian consumer should push for some indication of oak-ageing on the back-label, especially with Chardonnay; it would certainly give an indication as to the relative 'weight' of the wine. A Chardonnay aged in vat will probably lack the richness and some of the forceful flavour of a wine which has been in contact with wood, particularly new oak.

A few wineries in California make a fuller style of Pinot Blanc than that which comes from Alsace. There are some totally dry, or almost totally dry, Johannisberg Rieslings in California which are flowery, delicious fruity drinks. Smith-Madrone make a very good example.

'Light wines'

Recently, 'light wines' which have been produced in America seem to be highly successful. Such a wine is slightly below the norm in alcoholic content and has about 25 per cent fewer calories.

The methods for making 'light wine' vary: most wine-makers pick the grapes at a lower

GRAPE VARIETIES

SYLVANER

Found in Alsace, Germany (where it is spelt Silvaner) and the Südtirol/Alto Adige region of north-east Italy, Sylvaner makes fragrant, fruity wines for young drinking. Delicious in Alsace, the wines are perhaps at their most distinguished in the Alto Adige, especially as made by the historic Abbazia Novacella. In Germany, this is the third most widely planted grape variety, and it can occasionally make sweet, late-harvest wines. It does especially well on the slopes facing the Rhine at Nierstein and Oppenheim in Rheinhessen, and in Franconia. In California this grape is sometimes known as Franken Riesling.

MUSCADET

Light, fresh and bone-dry, Muscadet is perfect with seafood, especially mussels and oysters. Grown around Nantes in the Loire region of France, the grape came originally from Burgundy, where it was called the Melon de Bourgogne. It has given its name to the wine, which should always be drunk young.

ALIGOTÉ

The secondary white grape variety of Burgundy after the noble Chardonnay, Aligoté makes brisk-tasting dry white wines, with good definite taste in ripe years, but sometimes too much acidity in poor years. It is grown particularly on the Côte Chalonnaise, where the village of Bouzeron is noted for its production.

If your bottle of Aligoté is too acid for your taste, add a drop of cassis (blackcurrant liqueur) and make a Kir, the famous Burgundian aperitif.

TREBBIANO

This makes soft, dry white wines which should always be drunk young. The Ugni Blanc of southern France is the same grape variety. In Italy, it is the basic white grape variety of Tuscany, Umbria and Emilia-Romagna, and also makes appearances farther south, such as in Lazio. It is responsible for such white wines as Orvieto from Umbria, Trebbiano di Romagna and Trebbiano d'Abruzzo.

---

sugar level, before they are fully ripe, which effectively lowers the ultimate alcohol level. Others pick the grapes fully ripe, and then remove some of the alcohol (and thus the calories) by evaporation. Still others use a combination of both methods, a practice which leaves the wines with more taste and body.

Large companies in America which are marketing these wines include: Taylor California Cellars, Beringer (Los Hermanos label), Sebastiani, Paul Masson and Almadén. Of course, some of the labels are anathema to Europeans: the name Light Chablis is bound to offend purists. Some consider that the rosé is the best 'light wine', with alcohol at a little over 8 per cent and a touch of sweetness.

These wines do make good aperitifs; the low alcohol leaves one fresh for the meal ahead, and clearly they are suited to outdoor living and warm climates. People on a diet find them a boon, but should remember that two glasses of 'light wine' more than equal one glass of 'normal' wine. Novices, too, often find them a delicious introduction to wine-drinking.

Trefethen
VINEYARDS

NAPA VALLEY 1981
WHITE RIESLING

GROWN, PRODUCED & BOTTLED BY
TREFETHEN VINEYARDS
NAPA, CALIFORNIA, U.S.A.

ALCOHOL 12.5% BY VOLUME
RESIDUAL SUGAR 0.7% BY WEIGHT

In **Australia,** look out for some indication on the label as to whether a wine is Dry or not, for many have a touch of sweetness. But wines like the Barossa Valley company Kaiser-Stuhl's Green Ribbon dry Rhine Riesling, and the dry whites from Barossa's Yalumba company, are excellent examples.

In **South Africa,** a wine made from the Colombar, and marked as such on the label, will be dry and crisp, with a fairly high acid level. Wines labelled Riesling will also be dry and fresh, although not Germanic tasting.

England produces some light dry wine, without perceptible sweetening, but look out for an indication of Dry on the label: Lamberhurst Priory and Elmham Park indicate this, for example. Some grape varieties make the wines almost aromatic.

The rest of the world

New Zealand is now making light dry white wines, rather Germanic in style. Provided the wine has not been the subject of too much back-blending – the addition of sweet reserve – it will be a most eligible entrant to this category of wine. Something like the Montana Marlborough Riesling Sylvaner, at 11 per cent alcohol, fits the bill perfectly.

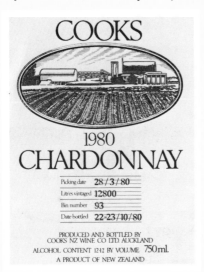

SUGGESTED TASTINGS

Contrast two wines from the Mâconnais e.g. a Mâcon-Lugny and a Pouilly-Vinzelles, and see if you can see a difference other than in price.

Do a round-Italy trip, with a Soave, a Verdicchio and a Vernaccia di San Gimignano vying for the honours.

Compare two Chasselas wines: Pouilly-sur-Loire and a Fendant from the Valais region of Switzerland.

Taste a dry English wine against a German *Trocken* or *Halbtrocken*.

Try a Coteaux Champenois against one of the lighter Californian Chardonnays (no oak or lightly oaked): e.g. the Caves Laurent Perrier Blanc de Blancs produced by Almadén.

Put up an Australian dry white against one from New Zealand or South Africa.

Compare a Portuguese Vinho Verde with a Galician white – which you will probably find only locally. Made just over the border from one another, they are often very similar. In the Minho, the best Vinho Verde comes from the Alvarinho grape, called the Albariño in Galicia.

MEDIUM-BODIED DRY WHITES

Defining the relative 'body' of a wine is a tricky business, with nuances and personal viewpoints obscuring absolute borderlines. But there certainly is a band of white wines which cannot be described as light and which are far from being full-bodied. It is sometimes complicated because what seems at first glance to be more or less the same wine can appear in two categories. This is largely a question of vintage, with some years being much more 'weighty' than others. Sometimes the grouping depends on the age of the wine. On rare occasions, it is due to the influence of the wine-maker, whose methods of vinification take this particular wine out of the category in which you would normally expect to find a wine of this type.

The wines that just get into the medium-bodied category are scarcely out of the 'light and dry', but enter this group because of a more forceful flavour as well as a touch more body. At the other end of the medium-bodied category are those wines that are rather 'round', fairly 'fat', with good body and texture. They are just not massive enough, mouth-enveloping enough, to fall into the 'full-bodied, dry' category.

Sometimes this slight difference can be due to the greater or lesser use of oak: one wine of roughly similar taste to another can become much more full-bodied if it is kept in barrel for a slightly longer time.

This type of wine comes in quite a wide range of prices, and justifiably so. A dry white Rioja, for example, however well-made, will not be intrinsically as fine a wine, or as individually vinified, as some of the estate Californian Chardonnays or white Burgundies. It is up to you as the drinker to decide how much you want to pay, whether the wine is right for the occasion (do not waste a really fine wine at a casual party, for example), and whether you really enjoy the 'better' wine enough to warrant paying more.

When to drink these wines
This rather depends on at which end of this wide category the wine falls. A simple, straightforward Orvieto or white Dão would be marvellous with a buffet, *antipasto* of fish, a plate of prawns, or prosciutto and melon.

On the other hand, white Burgundies and Californian Chardonnays of this weight would better complement shad, cod, halibut or turbot. These are wines to go with good, classic fish dishes, as they are too 'serious' to be quaffed light-heartedly as an aperitif.

GRAPE VARIETY

CHARDONNAY
Perhaps the noblest grape variety for making dry white wines, its character can vary from rich, fat and buttery wines suitable for bottle-ageing to lighter and fresher wines made without wood and intended for young drinking.

Chardonnay is not now considered to be part of the Pinot family of grapes. It is found in Burgundy, California, Central Europe and Australia, but appears nearly everywhere that people are striving towards making fine white wine. It is also one of the two most important grape varieties in the making of Champagne.

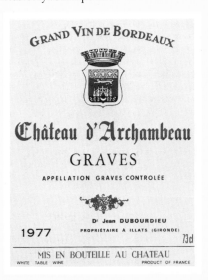

GRAND VIN DE BORDEAUX

Château d'Archambeau

GRAVES

APPELLATION GRAVES CONTROLÉE

Dr Jean DUBOURDIEU
1977 PROPRIÉTAIRE A ILLATS (GIRONDE)
73 cl

MIS EN BOUTEILLE AU CHATEAU
WHITE TABLE WINE   PRODUCT OF FRANCE

France

A mass of wines made from Chardonnay can be called medium-bodied. At the lighter end of the scale, you could include Pouilly-Fuissé of a ripe, more solid year, e.g. 1978. (At the other end of the category would come a group of Chardonnays from California which are relatively full and round, but not the huge, oaked examples with their almost palate-shattering impact.)

Chablis *premier cru* wines and most *grand cru* wines fall into this category. Perhaps some years ago one would have considered *grand cru* Chablis among the fuller dry whites, since most of them spent some time in wood, but now nearly all Chablis is matured in vat, with a consequently fresher taste. Top Chablis has a lovely flavour, if not chilled into submission, and all but aged *grand cru* Chablis of a great, ripe, somewhat atypical year such as 1971, could be termed medium-bodied dry white.

Moving down into the Côte d'Or, and specifically into the Côte de Beaune where the great white Burgundies are made, white Beaune, Meursault (but not the richest *premiers crus* from grand years), Chassagne-Montrachet, and lesser-known beauties such as Auxey-Duresses, St-Aubin and St-Romain are the wines to go for if you like medium-bodied whites. In the Côte Chalonnaise, too, there is great scope for lovers of balanced Chardonnay, especially among bottles of Rully and Montagny.

Going on from Chardonnay to Riesling, Alsace is where medium body combines with dry fruit character. Some Alsatians describe the smell of mature Riesling as resembling 'petrol', but this should not put you off – it is superb! Riesling from the single sites in Alsace and from good years gives bottles of real worth. A classic example is that most distinguished wine from a single site, the Clos Ste Hune Riesling from Trimbach. This really needs bottle age (6 to 8 years if you have the patience) to show its great length of flavour and intriguing bouquet. Look out also for growers' own indications of special selections, e.g. Réserve Spéciale, Réserve Personnelle, Réserve Exceptionnelle, or just Sélection.

Other medium-bodied dry white wines include those from the northern Rhône, Hermitage and Crozes-Hermitage, made without wood-ageing and bottled relatively young; the grapes used (Marsanne and Roussanne) and the soil provide the body. There is also some medium-bodied dry white Graves, usually from individual châteaux.

USA
In California, medium-bodied Chardonnays are likely to be only moderately oaked; not having spent too long in barrel, they are not massive wines. Consequently, their balance is often one of the most attractive things about them. Wineries such as Edna Valley, Hanzell, Firestone, Jekel, Matanzas Creek, Quail Ridge, Round Hill, Spring Mountain, Stony Hill, Rutherford Hill, Trefethen, Ventana, Zaca Mesa and Z-D make this type of Chardonnay; these are often the most elegant examples of this grape variety in California. The straight Robert Mondavi Chardonnay fits in here, but not the Reserve, which is bigger in every sense of the word.

Italy
Medium-bodied dry white wines are likely to come from the centre or south of the country, rather than the north, where the wines tend to be lighter. Orvieto, with its round, warm taste, is a good example of a white wine of medium body made mainly from the Trebbiano grape. Avoid the *abboccato* if it is a dry wine you want, and look out for the word *secco* on the label. Frascati, the wine of the Romans, made from Malvasia and Trebbiano, is another excellent

wine for pasta with seafood, or a *salade niçoise*; near-by Marino may be a touch lighter, but will be even less expensive, if only found locally. Farther south, in Campania, try those white wines touched with a hint of Greece (for the grapes which make them are of Greek origin), Greco di Tufo and Fiano di Avellino, both made in a thoroughly modern way by the firm of Mastroberardino. In Tuscany, look for the rather esoteric, but quite delicious, Montecarlo, a small DOC near Lucca, which has real dimensions of taste and fragrance.

Spain and Portugal
Rioja is now providing a good source of medium-bodied dry white wine, especially when firms with modern equipment are responsible for the wines. These tend to be the large, relatively recent concerns such as Marqués de Cáceres and Olarra, rather than smaller, older firms still espousing old traditions of later bottling and wood-ageing. In Portuguese Dão, look out for white Grão Vasco as very good value and full of flavour.

Central Europe
The Chardonnays from **Bulgaria,** mainly from the temperate eastern coastal region, are excellent value, with firm varietal character.

SUGGESTED TASTINGS

Taste one of the fresher white Rhônes, such as Paul Jaboulet Ainé's Hermitage Blanc Le Chevalier de Stérimberg or their Crozes-Hermitage La Mule Blanche against a fresh white Rioja.

Try an Orvieto or Frascati against a white Dão.

Compare a *premier cru* Chablis with an Auxey-Duresses or a white Beaune (the latter will probably be a touch more earthy) to show variations between wines from the different areas of Burgundy.

Put up a Meursault against a medium-weight Chardonnay from California – try Carneros Creek, Jordan or Round Hill.

FULL-BODIED DRY WHITES

It is usually at this point of vinous description that the comments start to get frivolous. What exactly is meant by full-bodied? It sounds tempting, but . . . the anti-wine snobs have a field day.

But anyone who has ever drunk a really full-bodied, full-textured, full-flavoured wine of any type knows what it means. It means a massive taste in the mouth, a feeling of weight and volume; it usually means that a wine has 'fat' – the French call it *gras*. It is often a marriage of enormous grape flavour, ripeness and harmony with oak. The taste of the wine lingers on the palate.

Many people may not have experienced this rich taste and all-enveloping sensation because, for a combination of reasons, this type of wine is often rather expensive. Picking prime grapes at optimum condition, often from the best sites and from the ideal soil, and then maturing the wine in wood and handling it with infinite care cannot possibly be cheap. But it *is* worth splashing out occasionally and treating yourself and a few interested friends to such a wine when the mood is right, with plenty of time to savour it in all its aspects, and when the food will set off the wine to perfection.

When to drink these wines

Rich-tasting, yet dry, full-bodied white wines demand perfect, simple food as a foil. Nothing should interrupt maximum flavours rolling in over the tongue; the wine should be allowed to speak for itself. Beautifully cooked, sea-fresh sole and plaice are heavenly twins to rich Chardonnay, especially when the fish is cooked *al dente*, like pasta – overcooking ruins the flavour and texture. Buttery haddock is another choice, and lobster and crab, whether cold or hot, can take the most full-flavoured wines. These wines can stand up to lobster with a rich sauce but, to accompany great wines, the freshest of creatures is best, simply boiled and served with butter. Fresh salmon adores top Chardonnay. Aristocratic white Graves likes all these fish and shellfish, but perhaps goes better with cold salmon, rather than hot. Don't be too pedantic about it – just grateful for the opportunity to try out the theory.

USA

This is the category of the whopping Chardonnays of California. Sometimes they are criticized and people wonder if they are subtle or elegant (they are not!) but they are great, sensuous experiences, full of rich fruit and flavour, and many have real class as well. Wineries such as Chalone, Freemark Abbey, Grgich Hills, Chateau Montelena, Mount Eden (also under the MEV label), Mayacamas and the Robert Mondavi Reserves are very fine indeed. Chateau St Jean makes a battery of superb wines from different vineyards, wines which demand time in bottle. Acacia has weighed in with rich, fruity wines. Time in oak, and even types of oak, will vary, but what you are promised with these fat and chewy Chardonnays is real quality. You don't need to drink much of them – a single glassful is as good as a whole bottle.

France

Chardonnays do not come so huge in the Côte de Beaune as in California, even in the very fine years, but bottle-aged Corton-Charlemagne is a wonderfully complex taste, with immense after-flavours lingering on the palate. The Meursault *premiers crus*, such as Perrières, Charmes and Genevrières, and the Montrachet 'family' of wines from the village of Puligny, are more 'Californian'. Yet while the great distinguished character of the Burgundian wines steals up on you, with the Californian, it almost hits you in the face.

In Bordeaux, only the greatest white Graves have this flavour and depth – and then only after bottle-ageing. But Laville Haut-Brion and Domaine de Chevalier are amazing wines of intense taste and length on the palate.

The king of the *vins jaunes*, Château Chalon, might seem an odd choice for this category, but this Jura rarity is worth finding. It is a non-fortified wine that tastes like austere Sherry, with a flavour imparted by the *flor* grown on its surface during the six years spent in cask. The dryness is tempered by a somewhat earthy, honey-like taste, all of which adds up to a drinking experience for the curious. Château Chalon is not an individual property, but an AC.

Australia

The great white Graves have an affinity with some of the finest white wines of Australia – the whites made from the Sémillon grape variety in the Hunter Valley. The Graves wines are a mixture of Sémillon and Sauvignon, but there is no doubt that the Sémillon, more famous for its vital role in Sauternes/Barsac wines, can make superb dry, full-flavoured white wines in the right place. In the Hunter Valley, where the Sémillon is often confusingly called the Hunter Riesling, the wines can appear fresh and enticing when young, but if the consumer can resist drinking them at this stage, they make fascinating, deep-flavoured bottles at anything from 5 to 20 years of age. The Rothbury Estate, Tulloch and Tyrrell are formidable exponents of the art. Chardonnays, too, from the Hunter Valley can be remarkable for flavour and strength of fruit. Don't miss 'em.

SUGGESTED TASTINGS

The obvious comparisons are between Californian Chardonnays of this category and Côte de Beaune white Burgundies, but it only becomes interesting if the white Burgundy is older than the Californian Chardonnay and from a rich, ripe year. Otherwise the differences can be jarring, or unfairly detrimental to one or the other, depending on personal preferences. Include a Hunter Valley Chardonnay for good measure. 🍷

Set a top white Graves against a Hunter Sémillon – but the same rules apply as for Chardonnay, and the Bordeaux wine should be older than the Australian bottle. 🍷

Château Chalon should be tried quite on its own as an aperitif with a few walnuts, since the finish of the wine is said to resemble their taste. You could find an aged Fino, or true Amontillado, to sample alongside it, of course, if you like an intellectual exercise.

FRUITY WHITES WITH A TOUCH OF SWEETNESS

This category of wines is immensely popular because of its charm and great drinkability, with or without food. These wines can be among the most delicate, flowery and enticing in the whole wine-drinking spectrum. They are easy on the palate and on the pocket, and please connoisseur and beginner alike.

It is difficult to define 'slightly sweet'. It means, really, with a hint of sweetness, but, as always, detecting the exact amount is an impossible task, because the degree of acidity has an enormous effect on whether residual sugar is evident or not. With low acidity, even the slightest amount of sweetness can seem quite marked. In a wine of relatively high acidity, on the other hand, the residual sugar is often barely detectable, and is anyway welcomed to counterbalance the acidity.

Although no one would want more bureaucratic labelling restrictions, there is a good case for labels to indicate the residual sugar in a wine. Naturally, this does not give a definite view of exactly how the wine will taste, since the degree of acidity can alter the relative sweetness on the palate, but it would give a good basic idea of the style of wine. And this kind of information would be most helpful when planning a meal and choosing the dishes to go with the wine.

When to drink these wines

Wines with a touch of sweetness are perfect without food, served as aperitifs or 'anytime' wines. They are soft and easily digestible, sometimes more so than a bone-dry wine if it has too much acidity. And sipping cool Johannisberg Riesling from California, or Chenin Blanc from France, South Africa or California, can be a wonderful way to while away a day, especially since many of these wines are fairly low in alcohol, which makes them ideal for drinking in hot weather and avoids causing head-aches.

Something like a German *Kabinett* can be wonderful with the new *salades composées* which have come in on a wave of *nouvelle cuisine* from France and which may be based on anything from shellfish and crustaceans to *foie gras*.

GRAPE VARIETIES

WÄLSCHRIESLING
This grape makes soft, easy-to-drink wines suitable for young drinking. The variety is not a Riesling at all, but is thought to be French in origin. Grown throughout Central Europe, it is known as Laski Riesling in Yugoslavia, Olasz-rizling in Hungary, Wälschriesling in Austria and Riesling Italico in north-east Italy.

MÜLLER-THURGAU
This produces soft, fruity wines which are easy to drink and temptingly flowery, but it does not age as well as the Rhine Riesling. A crossing of two *vinifera* varieties, developed by Dr Müller from Thurgau in Switzerland, it is not known for sure whether this is a Riesling/ Silvaner cross or a Riesling/Riesling cross. It is the most extensively planted variety in Germany, and it is also found in Austria and in New Zealand – where the wine is labelled interchangeably Müller-Thurgau/Riesling Sylvaner.

CHENIN
The soft, slightly sweet white wines made with Chenin Blanc become very honeyed and rich in ripe years; an underlying acidity is nearly always present in French Chenin wines, and causes them to develop well in bottle.

In France the grape variety is to be found in the Loire Valley, in Touraine and Anjou, where it makes Vouvray and sweet Coteaux-du-Layon, Quarts de Chaume and Bonnezeaux. When dry and with good acidity – especially in the Loire Valley – Chenin makes a suitable base wine for turning into sparkling wine or *vin mousseux*.

In California and South Africa, where it is often known as the Steen, the style is softer, usually off-dry and made for young drinking.

Germany

It is no surprise that Germany is the greatest exponent of the art of making fruity white wines with a touch of sweetness. This comes about as a result of the country's climate, its intelligently thought-out wine-making techniques, and the grape varieties the Germans have elected to encourage. In fact in Germany fruity acidity is the most prized asset of a wine, and there is no doubt that some residual sugar throws this into relief.

The wines which most easily fulfil these requirements are the large number called QbA wines, or quality wine from a specified region. Happily for the wine-drinker, this also happens to be the type of wine produced in the greatest quantity in Germany, often amounting to over 70 per cent of the total crop. German regions which traditionally produce a high proportion of QbA wines are Baden, Württemberg and Franconia.

The first of the QmP, or quality wines with distinction, is *Kabinett*, which also falls very nicely into this category of fruity, slightly sweet wines.

Certainly, the most distinguished wines, whether QbA or QmP, will be made of Riesling, for if there is one characteristic which sets Riesling apart, it is this noble grape's ability to give a wine a really fine bouquet. However, other grape varieties, such as Müller-Thurgau, also provide delicious wines.

Other European countries

Austria has a wealth of wines where the touch of sweetness makes them easy on the palate. Some of them will be brands, such as Blue Danube (with a neck label saying Medium Dry, which is an apt description for this type of wine), and the ever-popular Schluck. The grape varieties are likely to be Grüner Veltliner, Müller-Thurgau or Wälschriesling.

Over the border in **Italy**, there is some Riesling Italico, made from the grape of the same name, which is bottled with a trace of residual sugar. Often these wines are simply sold as *vino da tavola*, and are reasonable in price and excellent for parties.

The Wälschriesling is one of the key grape varieties for making fruity white wines with a touch of sweetness. Nowhere is the art better

demonstrated than in **Yugoslavia**, where the grape is called the Laski Riesling. It is not, in fact, a Riesling at all, but the drinker who likes the soft, easy style of the wines will not worry about that. There are well-known brands, such as Cloberg, as well as a considerable amount of wine sold under the name of Ljutomer Riesling. The Ljutomer hills are in the Drava region of Slovenia, where the large cooperatives are geared to exporting in bulk.

Hungary, too, has its wines from what is here called Olaszrizling. Some of the most reasonable and easy to drink come from Balaton, on the north shore of the great lake. The volcanic district of Badacsony produces more pungent, fuller-flavoured white wines, sometimes a bit richer than others in this category. Wonderfully individual grape varieties appear on the labels here, of which Szürkebarát (Grey Friar) and Kéknyelü (Blue Stalk) are the prime examples. Similar wines are made in nearby Balatonfüred-Csopak from Wälschriesling, Sylvaner, Müller-Thurgau and Furmint.

Many **English** wines have a touch of sweetness induced by the judicious addition of sweet reserve, on the German principle of adding *Süssreserve* to counteract acidity. Most will be labelled Medium Dry.

Spain and Portugal
In Spain, a few white Riojas have some sweetness. Probably the most popular is Diamante from Bodegas Franco Españolas, which could go into the Medium Sweet category were it not for its dryish finish. In the Penedès, the firm of Torres produces San Valentín and Viña Esmeralda (with Semi-Dry written on the label) which has both Gewürztraminer and Muscat d'Alsace in it, and so could be termed an aromatic as well as a slightly sweet wine.

Some Portuguese Vinho Verde wines sold on the export markets have a touch of sweetness. Gatão is the most flowery of them and a very nice balance is achieved.

France
In France, wines with a touch of sweetness include some Vouvrays from Touraine in the Loire Valley; they may have Medium Dry on the label, which is a helpful indication, since Vouvray can vary from dry to rather luscious in the best, ripest years. Other wines from the same grape, the Chenin Blanc, but made in neighbouring Anjou, can also have a touch of sweetness: Anjou Blanc, Savennières and less common *appellations* such as Coteaux de l'Aubance.

The problem is knowing how much or how little sweetness the wines have before drawing the cork, since the Chenin is a grape which can make wines ranging from completely dry and rather acid to sweet and luscious. All depends on the character of the year; so to get just a touch of sweetness, go for a good but not a great year. Whatever the sweetness, the wines need some bottle age to taste smoother, and the sweetest need years in bottle to show at their finest.

Some wines labelled Bordeaux Blanc, Medium Dry, also fall into this category.

wines of varying degrees of sweetness, but the off-dry style is very popular in California. Wente make an off-dry Blanc de Blancs which is a blend of Chenin Blanc and Ugni Blanc. It is usually easier to know exactly how sweet your Chenin is going to be here than in the Loire Valley, because back labels giving additional information of this kind are more common than in Europe. Chenin Blanc adapts itself well to soft wines with low alcohol, as does the Johannisberg Riesling, and both of these wines are made really well by the San Martin Winery in Santa Clara, which pioneered this style in the USA.

It should be remembered that most white 'jug' or carafe wines in America are off-dry, with some residual sugar, in order to appeal to a wide range of consumers, some of whom may not expect a bone-dry wine. A very fragrant brand in normal bottle size is Paul Masson's Emerald.

USA

Johannisberg Riesling goes through all the shades of sweetness in California, as anywhere else. Although all those wines having about 1.5 per cent residual sugar could be termed Moderately Sweet, remember that in California the wines will be soft and may appear sweeter than, say, a Riesling *Kabinett* from the Mosel-Saar-Ruwer of Germany, since the acidity will be lower.

Chateau St Jean makes wines of every degree of sweetness, but perhaps their Johannisberg Riesling (often known as JR in California) which they term Early Harvest best corresponds to this category of wine. Chateau St Jean also always indicates the exact vineyard from which the grapes came. Joseph Phelps, Stag's Leap Wine Cellars and Kenwood Vineyard are other makers of this type of wine.

The Gray Riesling is not a Riesling, but makes pleasant off-dry wines, usually of under one per cent residual sugar; Wente Bros make a good example.

Again, the Chenin Blanc shows itself as almost chameleon-like in its ability to make

The rest of the world

South Africa abounds in slightly sweet fruity white wines, which are ideally suited to the hot climate and outdoor life calling for good quaffing wines rather than complicated tastes which demand concentration.

The Chenin Blanc, or Steen as it is often called in South Africa, nearly always has a touch of residual sugar, which makes the wine soft and tempting. The fragrant, fruity Chenin

Blanc from KWV has an off-dry, honeyed flavour, and makes a superb aperitif. Nederburg's Fonternel tastes sweeter, with good fruit-acid content and is slightly aromatic. The Grünberger Stein, sold in a *bocksbeutel* type of bottle as found in Franconia, is a delicate, refreshing wine with a tang to it, produced at the Bergkelder mainly from the Chenin Blanc.

The white wines from the Twee Jonge Gezellen estate are very well known, from the TJ 39 Grand Prix to the Rieslings. The estate of Simonsig in the Stellenbosch area produces formidably good Weisser Riesling, which is the German Riesling – this is a wine of lovely scent and balance and a great deal of class. Fleur du Cap is a reliable brand, and although their Riesling is South African rather than German in style, nevertheless it will be fruity and fresh.

Australia, too, has a wide choice of white wines with a touch of fruity sweetness. The finest are those made from the Rhine Riesling, which is especially classy from the Barossa Valley of South Australia. There is a German touch about the wine-making here, and the wines are technically excellent and have great charm. As in every place where the Rhine Riesling is grown, the wines here can range from dry to late-picked and much sweeter, depending on vineyard site and conditions, but often the most commercial and competitively priced wines are those which are just off-dry. Many wines are labelled with the grape variety responsible for them (as well as with informative vinification details), while others rely on a brand name.

In **New Zealand**, many of the Riesling Sylvaner or Müller-Thurgau wines have a touch of sweetness induced by the addition of some sweet reserve – local terminology is 'back-blending'. As in Germany, this serves to highlight the fruity-acidity character and gives good varietal flavour.

SUGGESTED TASTINGS

Try a Chenin Blanc, or Steen, from South Africa (the KWV wine would be good) against a Vouvray from the Loire Valley.

Taste a *Kabinett* from the Mosel-Saar-Ruwer and a *Kabinett* from the Rhein-gau. The difference will probably be a more marked steely character in the Mosel version. For a valid comparison, the grape variety should be the same for both wines.

Match Wälschrieslings from Austria, Yugoslavia and Hungary.

Do a three-way tasting, with something like Petaluma Rhine Riesling from Clare in the northern part of South Australia; a Johannisberg Riesling from the Napa, made by Joseph Phelps (one of the more 'German-style' wines), and a *Kabinett* from a top German estate.

Put a Rhine Riesling from the Barossa in Australia against a Johannisberg Riesling (the same variety under a different name) from California.

Compare a Müller-Thurgau QbA wine from Germany with a Medium Dry English wine, if possible from the same grape variety.

MEDIUM-SWEET TO SWEET WHITES

These wines are definitely more luscious than the preceding group, with more ripeness of fruit noticeable on the palate and a richer nose. Again, the actual sweet sensation will be tempered by the amount of acidity in the wine. When the acidity is low, the taste is more luscious, but when there is good balancing acidity, a lovely projection of fruit and harmony occurs.

When to drink these wines

Medium-sweet to sweet white wines with a strong balancing acidity are suitable for aperitifs and can even be served in unusual combinations such as with smoked fish – a *Spätlese* from the Mosel is superb with smoked haddock mousse, for example. Wines with less acidity and more luscious character go better with fruit or fruity puddings – the Hungarian, Austrian and South African sweet wines are examples. Try Orvieto Abboccato with ripe melon.

Germany

The marriage of grape ripeness and underlying acidity is seen here at its most distinguished. It is the *Spätlese* category of wines that best fits this taste description, although *Spätlesen* vary with the type of year. One from a light year could even go into the previous section, something like a Mosel from 1979 for example, but one from a fuller, bigger year such as 1976 would fall happily into this category. Even an *Auslese* wine from a lighter year, and perhaps from the Saar or Ruwer where the wines are less full, would fall into the medium-sweet to sweet category.

Spätlesen need a few years in bottle for their balance to become evident and for their richness to open out. The late-harvested grapes are picked with a higher sugar content than *Kabinett* wines. There are differences between the regions, and a *Spätlese* from the Rheingau will probably have a higher sugar reading than those from other districts. Much depends on the vineyard site being perfectly placed to benefit from maximum sun.

Auslesen, too, may seem quite light when young, but as the wine ages in bottle, their richness comes through. The sheer class of the Riesling will produce much more distinguished *Spätlese* and *Auslese* wines than other varieties (remember that you can always pick out the grape variety in the lengthy descriptions on a German label), since the

---

GRAPE VARIETY

RHINE RIESLING

One of the classiest white grape varieties in the world, Rhine Riesling wines can be slightly sweet, medium-sweet or very sweet, and are sometimes touched by noble rot (*Edelfäule* in German). A wonderful balancing acidity means that Rhine Riesling wine is never mawkish. It reaches its apogee in the best sites of the Mosel-Saar-Ruwer, Rheingau, Rheinhessen and Rheinpfalz regions of Germany. It is also excellent in Alsace, where it is usually dry. In California, where it is called Johannisberg Riesling (and sometimes White Riesling), it usually makes flowery, off-dry wines but occasionally produces magnificent, rich wines that rival the best from Germany. Australia's Rhine Rieslings, too, show great style, and range from the good everyday to the really superb. In northeast Italy, the grape variety is known as the Riesling Renano and can make excellent wines in the style of Alsace – especially in Alto Adige.

Riesling combines fruit and acidity better than any other grape. Sometimes you will see more recently developed grape varieties such as Optima and Kanzler on the labels of these sweeter German wines; they do not have the balancing acidity, although they have the sugar content. The Kerner is more like Riesling in flavour and bouquet. The Müller-Thurgau is deliciously soft, but lacks the sheer 'breed' and classy nose and taste of Riesling.

Firestone, Joseph Phelps, Zaca Mesa, Buehler, Franciscan and Hacienda all produce wines of this type, and they show real ripeness, coming from grapes kissed by the sun, with balancing acidity. That acidity, however, will never be so evident as in a Mosel wine, for instance.

The noble rot that is often in these wines can be detected on the nose. It is not, however, as evident as in the sweeter dessert wines of the next category.

Central Europe

Gumpoldskirchner, a heady medium-sweet white wine from the Baden district of Lower **Austria**, is well known on export markets. The Eastern Burgenland also produces a quantity of sweet wines, but these are not the type to keep in bottle, and require young drinking.

In **Hungary** some Tokay Szamorodni will fall into this category of sweetness, depending on the nature of the year. Tokay Aszú of three *puttonyos* gives a sweet wine, but a Tokay with more measures of *aszú* paste will move into the very sweet category. The Mátra region produces the scented, strong Debröi Hárslevelü, which is worth hunting down.

USA

Californian Johannisberg Rieslings of about 2-3 per cent residual sugar could simply be called sweet, whereas at over 4 per cent they could be described as sweet to very sweet and come into our next category.

Wineries such as Chateau St Jean,

Other European countries

Italy does not nowadays abound in sweet white wine. In the past, sweet Frascati and Orvieto were very common, but now only the Orvieto Abboccato has survived to any extent on the export markets. Sometimes it is called Amabile, and could be a touch sweeter than the Abboccato, but the choice of term may be a marketing decision rather than an attempt to make a subtle difference. Orvieto Abboccato has a lovely, round, somewhat almondy sweetness, and often more regional character than Orvieto Secco.

Sweet wines are also not as common in **Spain** as they were, as tastes 'go drier'. Extrísimo Bach from the Penedès could go into this category, and might even creep into the next.

In **France,** Bordeaux starts to come into its own with sweet white wines. Whereas Sauternes and Barsac fall into the very sweet category, there is a small group of 'satellite' areas around these two internationally known names which produce medium-sweet to sweet wines. They also have the added advantage of being more reasonable in price. If you like sweet white Bordeaux, go for names like Premières Côtes de Bordeaux, Cérons and Côtes de Bordeaux St Macaire. These wines

have the soft sweetness of Sauternes and Barsac, but less richness and body. The more classy *appellations* of Ste Croix du Mont and Loupiac are really the stepping-stone between sweet and very sweet wines. At their best, they are up among the good Sauternes and Barsac; in lighter years they are merely sweet wines.

Chenin in the Loire Valley weighs in with semi-sweet Vouvrays and Coteaux-du-Layon from Anjou.

The rest of the world
The Chenin grape can also be sweet in **South Africa**. A delicious example is the KWV Golden Vintage, with its fragrant bouquet, its sweetish, honey-like after-taste and excellent balancing acidity.

In **Australia**, Rhine Rieslings of a late-picked style from the Barossa Valley are definitely sweet, but some of those labelled *Auslese* are so full and deep-flavoured that they should be termed very sweet. Orlando-Gramp make a Green Ribbon late-picked Rhine Riesling which is always delicious.

PREMIERES
COTES DE BORDEAUX
Appellation Contrôlée

SUGGESTED TASTINGS

Taste a Chenin from Coteaux-du-Layon in the Loire Valley against a South African late-harvest Chenin or Steen.

Put a rich Riesling Spätlese from a hottish year in Germany against a Johannisberg Riesling from California, but see that the German wine has more years in bottle than its Californian counterpart.

Compare a Debröi Hárslevelü from Hungary with a Gumpoldskirchner or *Auslese* from the Austrian Burgenland.

It is difficult to match the sweet white wines of Bordeaux against those of other regions, since grape varieties are so different; it is often more instructive to compare the different mini-areas within Bordeaux itself with one another. But if you want to do an international comparison, a Premières Côtes de Bordeaux or a Cérons should have the same weight as a sweet Spanish white.

VERY SWEET/DESSERT WHITES

Many people consider such wines among the great luxuries of the world. Even a few drops of these luscious liquids can revive and intoxicate. Fables have been written about them and stories spun around them. They are the essence of what the grape can give when taken to its ripest level, and the heady, honeyed aromas and flavours often defy even the most experienced manipulator of wine vocabulary.

One of the problems is that these wines, through their sheer sugar levels, are so delicious when young that many people succumb to the temptation to drink them too early. Great sweet dessert wines nearly always become even finer when given some time in bottle. However, at what stage these wines reach their best is entirely subjective, and there are drinkers who prefer relative youth and fruit in their very sweet wines, while others bide their time to experience all the great complexities of flavour that enhance the sweetness. The only recommendation is to try as many wines as possible at different stages of their respective lives and to note your preferences.

The word 'inevitable' has to come in when one talks about the high cost of great sweet white wines, for these wonders of Nature (and man, for he has a hand in the wine-making) are not economical to produce. These wines are made from grapes picked late in the season when they are really ripe. Since there is then far less juice in the fruit, especially if noble rot is also present, the yield is considerably reduced. Grapes are largely composed of water, and as they become ripe – even overripe – the water evaporates and the sugar intensifies. Moreover, a great risk is involved in leaving grapes on the vine in order for them to attain this ripeness, especially in a country as far north as Germany, where the weather can break at any time.

'Noble rot' is what sets many of these wines apart from the merely sweet; in German, it is called *Edelfäule*, in French *pourriture noble*; its Latin name is *Botrytis cinerea*. It is a mould which attacks the skins of the grapes in autumn when there is a combination of warmth and some humidity. If it penetrates the skins of healthy white grapes, it causes the water to evaporate, and increases their sugar content and concentration. This effect is only obtained when the grapes are already ripe – the mould is a disaster on unripe or on red grapes. It looks horrible in the vineyard, but it produces nectar in the bottle.

There is a special flavour and smell to wines made from grapes with noble rot, which adds an intriguing dimension to mere sweetness. In the right conditions, it appears in the Sauternes/Barsac area of Bordeaux, in Germany, in Hungary, in Austria and in California. At first it was thought not to appear in California, and attempts were made to introduce *Botrytis cinerea* by spraying, but in areas where the heat and humidity are right, it does appear naturally and produces extraordinarily good results.

When to drink these wines
As one never needs to drink much of this type of wine at one sitting, one bottle is more than enough for a party of eight, which helps to mitigate the high cost.

These wines are such complete tastes in themselves that often they are best sipped, respectfully, on their own. The immense flavour and ever-opening dimensions of taste do not really need any interference from food. A perfectly ripe pear or peach, or an uncomplicated fruit pudding can be a good accompaniment, but a creamy dessert concoction only detracts from the splendour in the glass. The French suggest foie gras with Sauternes: either a glass of something simple, young and chilled (a minor château, for example), or, for a different taste sensation, a very old venerable wine which could gradually be losing some of its sweetness.

Château d'Arche
GRAND CRU CLASSÉ

Sauternes
1970

APPELLATION SAUTERNES CONTROLÉE   BASTIT SAINT-MARTIN
Propriétaire
MISE EN BOUTEILLES AU CHATEAU

France

In France, the great sweet wines are top properties from Sauternes and Barsac. Nowhere else in the world is the mixture of Sémillon and Sauvignon grapes so judiciously handled to produce great, rich – but not cloying – white wines. *Pourriture noble* adds the final, vital ingredient, and in those years where all combine felicitously, the result is rich scent, depth, and the round luscious taste of grapes that have changed character on the vine. They will also be far more alcoholic than top German or Californian Rhine Rieslings – easily 4 per cent more. Châteaux like Yquem, Suduiraut, Climens and Coutet head the field, and for the perfect marriage of all the component parts, about 15 years should elapse before you open your best bottles from the finest years. A very young Sauternes/Barsac can appear clumsy, but this is nothing other than the fight within the bottle of an array of forceful characteristics awaiting their opportunity to mature and bloom.

In the Loire, the Vouvrays of the ripest years, those which are really *moelleux*, are the ones to keep and savour. In Anjou, Bonnezeaux and Quarts de Chaume have the same honeyed, peachy flavour and the same capacity to age with grace. They will never be so luscious as Sauternes, since the acidity tends to be higher, but drinking them is like eating your way through all the warm fruit in a conservatory.

Germany

In Germany this category of very sweet white wine comes from *Beerenauslese* and *Trockenbeerenauslese* wines. The grapes are individually selected and picked. In the case of *Trockenbeerenauslesen*, as well as being affected by noble rot, the grapes are also dried out on the vine until they look like shrivelled raisins. Naturally, this results in wines of almost liqueur consistency, often amber-coloured. *Auslese* wines sneak into this category only when they are from particularly fine, ripe years, and then only after a period of time in bottle. The great 1971 *Auslesen* from the Mosel, for example, seemed relatively dry and high in acidity when young, but now have a lovely honeyed richness, balancing the firm acidity which 'binds' the whole thing together. *Beerenauslese* and *Trockenbeerenauslese* wines have a berryish quality and are altogether 'thicker' in texture.

The richest sweet white wines tend to come from the top estates in Germany, particularly the Rheingau. This area makes exceptionally luscious wines since, however beautiful, the Mosels have an underlying acidity which makes them a little different, and the rich, sweet Rheinpfalz wines have a slight earthiness, which sets them apart, although they are remarkable wines in their own right.

Austria
Austria has its fair share of the really sweet wines, which are described in German terms. They are significantly cheaper than German or Californian wines, but are not usually in the same class, and are frequently made from grape varieties other than Rhine Riesling. *Ausbruch* wines, often from Rust in the Western Burgenland, bear a resemblance to Tokay; the Eastern Burgenland makes a speciality of very sweet wines too, but these are for young drinking.

Eiswein, or ice wine, has such an enticing name that people almost taste the wine as they read the label. This type of wine is highly prized in Germany and appears only when conditions are right, since it is made from grapes which are frozen at the time of picking, and still frozen when pressed. It is necessarily concentrated, for much of the water in the grapes is held back in the form of ice crystals. '*Eiswein*' is always used with one of the other terms of distinction, e.g. *Auslese*.

Hungary
Tokay, made in the north-eastern corner of **Hungary**, is one of the most fabled dessert wines in the world. When five *puttonyos* of *aszú* are added to the wine, the result is very sweet. In fact, at this level, there is more *aszú* paste than ordinary must in the wine, so the result is amber, fragrant liqueur. Tokay Essencia is the juice of the *aszú* berries which oozes out naturally as a result of the pressure of the grapes above in the small wooden *puttonyos*, or wooden tubs. This is literally essence, but the name 'Essence' can now also be applied to *aszú* with a small proportion of real Essence added. It is all ambrosial.

GRAPE VARIETIES

SÉMILLON

Noble rot may flavour the best examples among the superb, luscious sweet white wines made from Sémillon. It is mixed with Sauvignon to make both top sweet Sauternes/Barsac and also – vinified dry – top white Graves. It is especially magnificent in the Hunter Valley of Australia, where it is sometimes called the Hunter Riesling and makes dry but huge, rich and fat wines that age beautifully in bottle.

FURMINT

This makes sweetish to very sweet white wines in Hungary, both around Lake Balaton and at Tokay. It is the most important component in Tokay wine, and it is frequently affected by noble rot, which adds to the unique style of Tokay Aszú. The sweetness of Furmint is never cloying, however, as there is a good balance of acidity in the grape.

USA

The immensely sweet late-harvest Johannisberg Rieslings from California are a great achievement in a wine-making country which has been attempting them for such a short time – the first appeared only in the 1970s. Joseph Phelps and Chateau St Jean perhaps lead the field, but Jekel and Firestone are making fine examples, as well as Lohr, San Martin and Chappellet; there is the occasional really good-value wine from Almadén's Paicines Vineyards. In California, German terminology is not permitted, so one finds labels with rather cumbersome descriptions of wine made from 'Individual Dried Bunch Selected Late Harvest' grapes.

Australia

Australian Barossa Rhine Rieslings can have more body than German *Auslesen* and be very luscious and deep-flavoured – wines like Orlando-Gramp's Gold Ribbon Auslese and Kaiser-Stuhl's Purple Ribbon Auslese.

SUGGESTED TASTINGS

Although the value of California/ Europe blind tastings is open to question, one of the most fascinating comparisons in the entire repertoire is that of botrytized, really luscious Johannisberg Rieslings from a few wineries in California who really know how to handle extremely ripe grapes with the richest Rhine Rieslings from top estates of the Rheingau.

Apart from this top flight of German/ Californian pairings, there is little advantage in setting one luscious wine of a different origin and grape variety against another in comparative tastings. A sweet Tokay will look no better against Quarts de Chaume; Austrian *Trockenbeerenauslesen* can look too sticky and sweet against a top German estate, so keep these beautiful courtesans of wine from meeting.

As sips rather than gulps are in order, tastings of great sweet wines are an excellent idea. When organizing guided tastings and workshops, bear in mind that keen wine drinkers often welcome the chance to try a few top sweet whites, even at the end of a tasting of wines of another type.

FRESH, LIVELY REDS

These are some of the most attractive and tempting wines available on the shelves, and anyone who dislikes them is unlikely to enjoy drinking wine of any kind. In fact, it is doubtful whether many people if they were blindfolded before tasting these wines would instantly recognize the lightest of them as being a red wine at all. There is so much lively fruit and instant appeal in this type of red wine that they can almost be taken for white. They combine the charm of a white wine with the extra body and definition of a red, and thus are much in demand by wine drinkers right across the board.

Another trait shared with white wines is that many of these fresh lively reds are better when drunk slightly cool. They lose all their vivacity if drunk too *chambré* and the cooling brings out the fruit and instant charm in them. They should also be drunk relatively young, as are the majority of white wines. Ageing in bottle does nothing for this type of wine; the fruit only gets tired and no extra dimensions are added by maturity. Some wines which by their weight could almost be described as medium-bodied are in this section as they are best drunk young.

The lack of ageing is one reason why, as a category, these are not expensive wines. The quick turnaround of capital by the wine producer means that he can ask less than if he was maturing a wine for two years in cask before bottling, and then perhaps giving his 'baby' a few months in bottle to settle down or grow up, as the case might be. The wine merchant, also, will look to sell this type of wine very quickly after taking delivery of it, because no one benefits if it languishes in the warehouse or cellar for too long – least of all the wine. In fact, some wines in this category are probably the fastest off the vine and on to your table in the world of wine production.

When to drink these wines

Whatever the food, unless you are drinking white or rosé wine, always go for a light rather than a heavy red in hot weather. Heavy red wines taste horrible when the temperature climbs, but a slightly cool, light, fresh red wine, on the other hand, is often most welcome.

A lively red wine goes with a simple veal escalope or Wiener Schnitzel, a hamburger or a dish of *charcuterie*. But don't forget that light red wines complement firm-fleshed fish very well, especially those pink-toned ones like salmon and salmon trout, making a change from Chardonnay wines. In the Loire, salmon is often accompanied by a light, cool Saumur-Champigny.

GRAPE VARIETY

GAMAY

The Gamay produces light, scented red wines – with an easily recognizable fruity aroma – that are ideal for young drinking. Except when the grape is grown on the granite of the nine Beaujolais *crus*, Gamay wines are almost always very light. Apart from in the Beaujolais region, the grape variety is grown in other parts of France such as the Loire and the Massif Central.

The Gamay Beaujolais of California is not what it appears to be, but is a clone of Pinot Noir. However, it usually makes better wines than the Napa Gamay variety, which is possibly related to the Gamay of the French Beaujolais.

Mark West Vineyards

Sonoma County
Gamay Beaujolais

Cellared and Bottled by Mark West Vineyards
Forestville. Sonoma County. Calif. Alcohol 12% by Vol.

France

If readers have not by now identified Beaujolais Nouveau as the leader of this type of wine, then they have been missing something. Much criticized, and even more drunk, Beaujolais Nouveau seems to be with us to stay, even though professionals might bewail the fact that the more wine goes to Nouveau, the less there is to sell during the rest of the year. In years when the yield is only average, this problem becomes acute; certainly a good deal of wine which might have made even nicer bottles later in the year is sacrificed to Nouveau.

The Gamay grape is eminently suitable to making wine for very young drinking, especially when it is grown in the Beaujolais area of France. When it is destined for Beaujolais Primeur, or Beaujolais Nouveau (the two terms are now interchangeable), it has to be vinified very carefully to ensure that it is stable in the bottle. The great fruitiness comes both from the nature of the Gamay grape itself and from the carbonic maceration method of fermenting the wine.

Beaujolais Nouveau is sold from the middle of November onwards (sometimes the date is delayed by a week, if the vintage is unusually late) and should be drunk over the next few months, to enjoy its maximum youthful bounce. Everyone has tales of finding forgotten bottles of Nouveau a year or two after its birth which prove to be good drinking, but to play safe, all should be

consumed by the spring after the vintage.

When your Beaujolais is labelled just that, and nothing else, drink it within the year. Beaujolais Villages, from a set of villages in the north of the region, is good, on average, for a year or two longer. The Beaujolais *crus*, those nine villages with famous names, such as Fleurie, Côte de Brouilly, Juliénas and St Amour taste better after a year than six months, and last well for from two to four years, depending on the character of the vintage. The most robust of the *crus*, Morgon and Moulin-à-Vent, become quite solid when in bottle for two years or so, and go into the next category, medium-bodied red wines. It is another curious trait of these Beaujolais *crus* that after some years they cease to have the ultra-fruity taste of Gamay, and more resemble wines from the southern Côte d'Or (Santenay, etc) with an almost Pinot Noir smell and flavour.

Wherever you see the name Gamay on a label in France – and there are a number of regional wines made from this grape variety, particularly in the Loire and the Massif Central – you know that the wine should be drunk young and on the cool side.

The Loire Valley, chiefly known for its white and rosé wines, also produces some of the lighter, most enchanting red wines of France. It is the Cabernet Franc which is almost entirely responsible for making the two best wines, Bourgueil and Chinon, in Touraine. Chinon is usually a touch lighter than Bourgueil, and both are full of vivid fruit and very 'more-ish'. The Cabernet Franc is strongly scented and has less tannin than the Cabernet Sauvignon; therefore, wines made from it require less ageing. Saumur-Champigny is another red from the Cabernet Franc – drink it even younger than Chinon and Bourgueil to get it at its best.

In the centre of France, in Sancerre, the Pinot Noir makes rare red wines which only seem to work well when it is a ripe year – otherwise the wines are pale and a touch acidic. In the south-west of France, there are some Merlot/Cabernet blends which are often fruity and for young drinking, without the body of illustrious *appellations,* but giving excellent value. Côtes du Marmandais, a VDQS in the Lot-et-Garonne, is an example and Bergerac from the lighter years is much better young.

The south of France is a happy hunting ground for lovers of zestful red wines for drinking young. Coteaux-d'Aix-en-Provence, and to a lesser extent Côtes de Provence, produce wines of great charm, with the traditional southern grape varieties such as Grenache slightly aided by an admixture of Cabernet. In the Languedoc, many of the wines are medium-bodied but large, modern concerns like the Domaines Viticoles des Salins du Midi are producing lovely light red wines, from vines planted in the sand, under the Listel label.

Italy

The Cabernet Franc grape fulfils the same role in north-eastern Italy as it does in the Loire. If anything, the Italian versions are even more full of sappy fruit than their French cousins. They do sit astride the frontier between light red and medium-bodied red, but the fact that they are nice when drunk cellar-cool and young, and simply brimming over with young fruit character, makes them fall very naturally into the 'lively' set. The DOCs of Friuli-Venezia Giulia are the natural home of this type of Cabernet, but some Cabernets from Trentino have a claim to fame and they can be softer and less assertive than the Friuli ones. Young Sangiovese from Emilia-Romagna is both light and cheap, never better than in carafes in the splendid local restaurants.

Young Novello, or Nouveau, wines have never caught on as they have in the Beaujolais, largely because the grape varieties seem not to be as suitable as the bouncy Gamay. Although Tuscan firms sometimes market these precocious youngsters, the most successful example of the genre is probably the Primaticcio Vino Novello del Piemonte, made from Dolcetto grapes by the firm of Franco-Fiorina.

Bardolino and Valpolicella from the Veneto are also delicious and lively when drunk young; Valpolicella Superiore has more body, but for all that it is not intended for ageing.

USA

The obvious candidates from California for this section come from the Gamay, but this is not quite as simple as it first sounds. There is the Gamay, or Napa Gamay, probably only a distant relation of the Gamay in Beaujolais itself. This makes a light, soft wine, which can be in Nouveau style and made by carbonic maceration, or soft and fruity and labelled Gamay Beaujolais, or firmer and called Gamay or Napa Gamay. There is, in addition, the Gamay Beaujolais grape, now identified as a distant cousin of Pinot Noir; the wine from it can also be called Gamay Beaujolais. You will probably get a better drink if the label states categorically that the wine is made from the Gamay Beaujolais grape.

Jug wines in California will sometimes be light and soft; at other times they will be a little bigger, but many of the mass-distributed brands will have a touch of sugar to make them supple enough for all tastes.

The rest of the world

Many countries noted for their red wines produce almost none that are light enough to fall within this category. The hotter climates of Australia, South Africa, South America and even of Spain and Portugal almost inevitably make reds that are fuller-bodied. On the other hand, it is no accident that the lightest reds of all are made in **Germany**, at the northernmost limits of the wine-making latitudes. However, Assmanshausen has a local appeal, and is not found on the shelves of the world.

Central Europe

Switzerland has a collection of light reds which drink well when young. Dôle, made from Pinot Noir and Gamay, is the most famous name. It could be called medium-bodied, but the light finish often puts it more naturally among the lighter reds. Pinot Noir (called Klevner or Blauburgunder in German-speaking Switzerland) is sometimes made with a touch of sweetness, which the Swiss and Germans like, but which can surprise a 'drier' palate. But they are soft wines which slip down.

Red wines, of course, are somewhat eclipsed in **Austria** by the ubiquitous whites, but when they appear they are light and gulpable. Vöslau, south of Vienna, specializes in red wines, whether made from the Blauer Portugieser or the St Laurent, which is quite a pungently scented grape variety. Western Burgenland produces Blaufränkisch (Gamay) and Blauburgunder (Pinot Noir); don't be tardy about drinking either, as youth is part of their charm.

Many of **Yugoslavia's** reds are quite forceful in character, but in Kosovo near the borders with Albania and Macedonia the grape varieties are mainly the classic French ones, Cabernet Franc, Gamay, Merlot and Pinot Noir. Although not the lightest wines of this category, they are for young drinking. Plavina from Dalmatia is light and dry.

MEDIUM-BODIED REDS

If we did not have a huge array of medium-bodied red wines throughout the world, most of our meals would not taste nearly so good. These are the wines which enhance almost any main dish, and many people in continents as far apart as South America and South Africa drink nothing else. Good, fruity red wine of some body and smooth taste goes with just about everything, including fish, is digestible and well-balanced and does not fatigue the palate or brain.

Many medium-bodied red wines are produced on quite a large scale, so the price is usually in the medium bracket too. A few are more highly priced, because of the special care needed to make them or because they are from small, specialized areas long known for their quality wines.

Some wines which would not at first sight appear to be medium-bodied make this group by dint of their vintage. A lighter vintage, sometimes, but not always, with a bigger yield, produces a wine with medium rather than full body. Examples are Bordeaux in 1973 (large vintage) and 1977 (light vintage) which fall into the medium-bodied category, while Bordeaux from the 1975 and 1978 vintages are bigger wines altogether. In Burgundy, 1973 and 1977 could be taken as similar examples, while 1976 and 1978 are of quite a different nature, with 1976 really heavy.

But to this qualification must be added something more – a full-blooded ramification. In areas like Burgundy and Bordeaux, where vintages are more important than in some other areas of the world but where the soil and drainage of vineyard plots are absolutely vital to the final quality of the wine, the *type* of wine, or its place in the hierarchy, also very much decides what category it falls into within this book.

While a *petit château* in Bordeaux from 1975 would fall into the medium-bodied section, a top Bourgeois or Classified Growth from the same vintage would be termed full-bodied.

Whereas a Savigny-Lès-Beaune in Burgundy from the 1978 vintage would fall into the medium-bodied group, a *grand* or *premier cru* wine from the Côte de Nuits (say, a Gevrey-Chambertin Clos St Jacques) from the same vintage would undoubtedly go into the full-bodied section. Conversely, a Clos-Vougeot from a light year like 1977 comes into this group, but the same wine from the 1976 or 1978 vintages most certainly would not. A top Bordeaux Classified or Bourgeois Growth in the Médoc from a 'soft' vintage like 1976 (low in acidity) would fall quite happily into this group of wines, whereas the same wine in the 1975 or 1978 vintages would go straight into the full-bodied range.

In California, differences do occur between Cabernet Sauvignon vintages, but not to such a marked degree as in Europe. However, the same winery may produce, in different years, wines which are softer and more 'luscious' than others which are harder, more tannic, and pack more punch and power. (And wineries do change their vinification methods in keeping with the flexible Californian approach to wine-making, which can also alter the style of some wines from year to year, usually towards more refined reds.)

All this ties in with the keeping time of red wine. Medium-bodied wine of the type in this section only needs medium keeping for it to be at its best: sometimes it is ready to drink within two to three years of its birth. More normally many of these wines will be soft, mature and fruity at about five to eight years, and occasionally the biggest among them, or the most definite-tasting, could need 10 years or more. Additionally, time in bottle can make a wine more soft and accessible and take it out of the full-bodied category and into this one. For example, a lesser *premier cru* from Gevrey-Chambertin, at 12 years of age and from a medium-bodied year, could fall into this category with logical precision, whereas at five years of age its whole character might have been more forceful.

As always, *when* you drink a wine, whether with youthful power or with the mellowness of age, is purely a matter of personal choice and preference, but this example shows that some wines can go from one category to another according to their age.

This illustrates that a wine's taste cannot be defined in a precise profile which will remain constant for all time. Wines change and develop, and one of the fascinations for the wine-drinker is watching their evolution in bottle.

It is no accident that a very high proportion of wines in this medium-bodied category are Cabernet or Cabernet-dominated, wherever they come from. The characteristics of the Cabernet Sauvignon, sometimes blended with a proportion of Cabernet Franc and Merlot, tend to make medium-bodied wines. Whereas Cabernet Franc on its own makes delicious, scented lighter-bodied red wines, Cabernet Sauvignon makes wines of more power. The most powerful of the latter will fall into the full-bodied category, either because of the climate or by virtue of the particularly fine vineyard sites on which the grapes are grown.

When to drink these wines

No reasonably flavoured dish will not go with this type of red wine. Many people would feel that if they had to survive on one kind of wine for the rest of their lives, this would be it. It is made for meat and cheese, and all but the most delicate flavoured fish can be eaten with a red wine which is not too robust: try it with cod or swordfish steaks. Drink these wines at room temperature, unless you live in a hot-house, when they would be nicer cellar-cool.

France

Cabernet wines in France of this weight are largely concentrated in the south-west of the country, most notably in the Bordeaux area. Merlot is usually present in the wines, too. Most red Bordeaux wines fall into this category, except top Bourgeois or Classified Growths of bigger years. Perhaps straight Bordeaux Rouge or one of the wines from the 'satellite' areas outside St Emilion, in a light year, would sit on the borderline between light- and medium-bodied, but it would certainly be safe to say that the whole wonderful range of *petits châteaux* wines are medium-bodied, and some of the best value in the world for lovers of a glass of red wine with their meal.

GRAPE VARIETIES

MERLOT

This red grape variety produces wines of great drinkability, often slightly luscious in taste and varying from young and soft (in north-east Italy) to deep-flavoured and big (in California). Merlot is a component part of the wines of the Médoc and Graves in Bordeaux, and a vital part of the wines of St Emilion and Pomerol in the same area. It is found all over south-west France. Both California and Bordeaux blend it with Cabernet. It makes most appealing wines for young drinking in north-east Italy.

CABERNET FRANC

This grape variety makes particularly scented wines of great fruit and charm, but without the staying power of Cabernet Sauvignon wines. It is blended with Cabernet Sauvignon and Merlot for the fine red wines of Bordeaux, especially in St Emilion and Pomerol. Cabernet Franc makes charming red wines in Touraine and Anjou in the Loire Valley.

The areas of Bourg and Blaye are happy hunting grounds for this type of wine, and still very reasonable in price for what you get. In areas like St Estèphe, you will get something beefier, in St Emilion something softer partly because there is more Merlot in the blend here. An area like Listrac has a pronounced 'Clarety' taste with underlying firmness, while Graves has a scent and finesse all of its own. All these wines should be drunk relatively young, for *petits châteaux* are not designed to live long.

When the wine is of a grander pedigree, a Bourgeois or Classified Growth, it will have a greater intensity of flavour and of bouquet and a longer finish.

One of the great attributes of red Bordeaux is that you will rarely, if ever, tire of it. The subtle nuances of flavour and differences of taste between districts and between the châteaux themselves, even at a modest level, are endlessly fascinating. One of the tests is a journey to a wine-making region: on your return you usually wish to drink a totally different wine. After a trip to Bordeaux, you find you are always ready for more.

An excellent wine of the Pyrenees, Madiran, is now happily seen in specialist shops outside its area, in France and abroad. This does contain some Cabernet of both types, but the grape variety which gives it its special character is the Tannat. This should be preserved, since no one would want a preponderance of Cabernet the world over, and regional flavours, like local dialects,

should be encouraged. These regional flavours, allied to soil, can, of course, show themselves through the Cabernet characteristics, but if there are good, healthy, local grapes, it is important that they remain in the blend to give the wine individuality.

Cahors is another wine of the south-west, largely made from the Malbec, or Côt, grape (in St Emilion it is called the Pressac, so this is a variety which can be confusing to follow). Cahors used to be very dark in years past, then it became much lighter and rather poor, but now the region has had a renaissance and there are some beautiful wines to be found.

Bandol, in Provence, is a small but very 'serious' *appellation,* making wines of definite character and even a slightly chewy taste. Here, the Mourvèdre grape is more important than the ubiquitous Grenache and Cinsault, which spread their tentacles all over the south of France. These wines have to spend 18 months in cask before being sold, and this helps to give them their structure, which is balanced by fruity richness and an interesting range of tastes.

The Rhône Valley gives us above all Côtes du Rhône which is the staple red AC wine of many Frenchmen, and one of the most reasonable quality wines to be found throughout the country. There are different types of Côtes du Rhône wine, and some of the lightest, made by the carbonic maceration method, could almost be described as having the weight of a Beaujolais and therefore do not come into this category at all. But most Côtes du Rhône wines have more body and more firmness; they have a distinct touch of the sun. Côtes du Rhône Villages wines are usually a bit fuller in taste, and villages like Cairanne and Vacqueyras have an identity of their own.

Lirac, just to the north of Tavel, makes superb red wines, still most reasonably priced for their quality. With such a famous neighbour making rosé, the growers of Lirac decided to concentrate on red, and there is a clutch of *domaines* making some of the best wines of the southern Rhône Valley.

Over in Languedoc-Roussillon, robust Côtes du Roussillon Villages, St Chinian, Minervois, Corbières and Fitou all come into the medium-bodied category. They have no capacity to age, and are at their warming best at one to three years old. Most Corsican red wines which are bottled, as opposed to shipped in bulk to fortify weaker brethren, are about this weight, but have a slightly spicy, *maquis*-influenced taste about them.

Beaujolais is not a candidate for medium-bodied red wines, except for the two most powerful *crus*, Moulin-à-Vent and Morgon which, with a few years in bottle, have a mouth-enveloping character about them. They also at this stage often seem to resemble Pinot Noir rather than the Gamay from which they are made.

The real Pinot Noir wines of France, those from the Côte d'Or and Côte Chalonnaise in Burgundy, fall partly into this category, but into the fuller group when from the grandest origins and in good years. However, some wines from south of Beaune fall into the medium-bodied group more often than not – *appellations* such as Santenay, Chassagne-Montrachet and Volnay – while

Savigny-Lès-Beaune and Pernand-Vergelesses north of Beaune are of similar weight. Except for a top *premier cru* like Volnay's Caillerets in a really ripe year, these wines should not have great power (it would be suspicious if they did), but they should have great scent, delicious taste and a fragrant, long-lasting flavour.

Red wines with the *appellations* of Côte de Beaune Villages, Hautes-Côtes de Beaune and Hautes-Côtes de Nuits are of medium body and can be good value for Burgundy. Wines from the Côtes de Nuits fall into this category when they are from light vintages or from years when there has been a high yield, which inevitably gives red wines of less concentration and power. Then, even big, fat wines like Clos Vougeot or sturdy wines like Nuits St Georges metamorphose into more elegant, refined beings.

The Côte Chalonnaise produces wines which are pre-eminently medium-bodied. The red wines of Rully, Givry and Mercurey are very good buys for those who love the pure taste of Pinot Noir but find the prices on the high side on the Côte d'Or. Mercurey is the most robust of the three *appellations*, but even in a big year, it will not have the ageing capacity in bottle, or staying power, of a wine from the Côte de Nuits. A good deal of Bourgogne Passetoutgrain, that blend of Gamay and Pinot Noir, also comes from the Côte Chalonnaise, and this just makes it into the band of the medium-bodied.

has an enormous amount of red wine of balance and fruit allied to good structure. Obviously, the structure is more evident in a Chianti Classico, especially a Riserva, than in a straight young Chianti intended for youthful drinking, but the weight of the wines across the board is thoroughly drinkable and easy on the palate. Vino Nobile di Montepulciano can be a more powerful wine, but it will not usually have more intrinsic weight than Chianti Classico.

In Umbria, another manifestation of Sangiovese is the dependable Rubesco di Torgiano; the Riserva, more difficult to find, is a very fine wine indeed.

Most Cabernet wines from the north-east tend to be fairly light, in weight if not in flavour, but the Cabernets from Alto Adige can be much more full and fat, and many age to perfection. The Venegazzù, from near Treviso in the Veneto, is a magnificent example of a balanced, elegant Cabernet/Merlot wine, and the Riserva is most distinguished.

Most of the wines of north-west Italy are too big and forceful to come into this category, but Carema, a top-quality wine from the Nebbiolo grape but grown in the high Aosta Valley, is a refined example of medium weight but marked flavour.

In the Veneto, the fullest Valpolicella, that of Valpantena, could fall into this category, and the wonderfully rich and flavourful Campo Fiorin from the house of Masi most certainly does.

Italy

Italy abounds in fine-flavoured red wines of medium body. They can be found in the north, in the centre and in the south of the country, and even in the island of Sicily. Until recently no one could say that Sicilian red wines were anything other than powerful and full of heat, but changed viticultural and vinification practices have given us world brands such as Corvo di Salaparuta and the Conte Tasca d'Almerita's Regaleali.

Tuscany, with its Sangiovese red grape,

immediately to almost all wine drinkers.

In the Penedès, Bosch-Guell make good *clarete fino* and Torres produce a range of wines in this category, amongst them Coronas, a very lusty mouthful, and Viña Magdala, with a high proportion of Pinot Noir. But the overriding taste in most Torres wines is of wood-ageing, which *aficionados* simply lap up. Do not forget the extremely good younger wines of the Bodega Ribera Duero in Penafiel, in Valladolid.

Spain

Spain has a wealth of medium-bodied red wines, most of them coming from the Rioja. All the wines are stamped with a vaguely vanilla smell and taste, purporting to come from the wood-ageing (although in newer *bodegas* there are more vats than barrels, and even in the traditional houses, the barrels are often so old that they could no longer be imparting a flavour to the wine). However the traditional houses tend to make fuller wines than the more modern *bodegas*. They are very smooth-tasting wines and appeal

GRAPE VARIETIES

PINOT NOIR
The taste of the wines made around the world from the Pinot Noir grape varies immensely. In Burgundy, where it is at its best, it produces finely flavoured red wines, with an inimitable smell that some people term 'farmyard', and great fruity length on the palate. In California, few of the many styles have much connection with Burgundy; most are wood-aged and quite alcoholic, although some are now more elegant.

A few remarkable Pinot Noir wines have emerged in Australia, but the makers think they can be better still. Yugoslavia and north-east Italy (where the grape is called Pinot Nero) make some pleasant wines. Pinot Noir is also a component in most Champagnes.

SANGIOVESE
This is the most widely planted red grape variety in Italy, appearing predominantly in Tuscany and Umbria. Sangiovese has the ability to make wines that are delicious when young (as in straightforward Chianti and in Emilia-Romagna), as well as wines that are more solid when made from vines grown on better sites and after suitable maturation in barrel and bottle (e.g. Chianti Classico and Vino Nobile di Montepulciano).

BALKAN VINE

CABERNET - SAUVIGNON

Product of Bulgaria   70cl
— from the Suhindol District   e

Central Europe

The Cabernet Sauvignon appears throughout Central Europe, for these countries realize that it is a thoroughly exportable taste, whereas some of their more indigenous varieties have a flavour not readily appreciated by outsiders. **Bulgaria** has perhaps succeeded the best, but the wines are not suitable for ageing. **Romania** has made giant strides very quickly with this grape variety. Egri Bikavér, or Bull's Blood, is made from a range of grape varieties and may be shipped in bulk from **Hungary** and bottled on arrival in the importing country.

South America

South America really comes into its own with medium-bodied, highly drinkable red wines, having failed to enter the lists with many white wines which are acceptable to the export markets. **Chile** leads the field for making wines of real breed and finesse, among which one would single out the Reservado of Concha y Toro and the Cousiño Macul Antiguas Reservas. Viña Linderos has astonishingly good Cabernet Sauvignon, and the grape also makes good wines in the hands of two other firms, San Pedro and Viña Undurraga.

USA

Many Cabernet Sauvignon wines from individual Californian wineries (boutique wineries is a term still used by some) are too massive to fall into this category. However, the large companies seem to be making a speciality of finely balanced, but fully varietal flavoured wines, none more so than Taylor California Cellars' Cabernet Sauvignon. This shows remarkable value and remarkable blending skill, using grapes from different areas within the Golden State.

Some of the large companies, such as Christian Brothers, have both vintage-dated and non-vintage Cabernet Sauvignon, of which the latter will probably be more medium-bodied and the former fuller and more forceful. Parducci in Mendocino and Pedroncelli in Sonoma make wines of balance, with fruit more important than wood-ageing. Mirassou make good examples of the grape. Sonoma firms often make slightly softer Cabernet Sauvignon wines than Napa, wines which possess elegance as well as great fruit – Dry Creek and Clos du Bois are examples. Trefethen in the Napa concentrates on fruit rather than pure power – the non-vintage Eshcol Red has a touch of vanilla, and the straight Cabernet Sauvignon has great balance.

Years can play a part in the body of the wine, and some 1977s are not as massive as, say, 1974s among Cabernet Sauvignons; Firestone Vineyard 1977 from Santa Ynez is very fruity and soft, and Rutherford Hill 1977 from Napa is beautifully luscious rather than purely tannic. Of course, tannin should soften with some bottle age, but the danger is that when the tannin is too massive, the time it needs to soften is also the time the wine takes to 'dry out', i.e. lose its fruity attractions.

Pinot Noir in California is a strange animal, almost always very unlike Burgundy and not quite like anything else at present – styles vary with the years and with whatever the wine-makers change in their vinification techniques at this largely experimental stage. Firestone make a good mouthful of a wine, if a bit tannic for the variety, but both Joseph Phelps and Trefethen make a much more 'Burgundian' style of wine, more delicate and really delicious. However, the most

devastating example so far must be Kalin Cellars, using grapes from Sonoma, which have produced a Pinot Noir of such supreme breed that it surely heralds a new wave of great wines. In a blind tasting it would be difficult to distinguish this from a top Burgundy.

South Africa

South Africa is virtually afloat with splendid medium-bodied red wines, most of them Cabernet or Cabernet based, priced with great restraint. Start with excellent value wines, such as Nederburg Baronne (mixed grape varieties) or the KWV Cabernet Sauvignon, sold when they are ready to drink. Then go on to the KWV Roodeberg, mixed grape varieties and lots of juicy fruit on the palate, and the Backsberg Estate Cabernet Sauvignon, which combines structure, elegance and balance.

None of these wines falls into the trap of too high alcohol, and at around 12 per cent they are the kind of bottles which one finishes without any trouble at all.

The rest of the world

Cabernet Sauvignon wines from **New Zealand** are medium-bodied, a far lighter genre than their Australian cousins, as befits totally different climates. **Lebanese** Cabernet wines have more weight, and something faintly spicy and exotic on the nose, in spite of their French grape varieties – the fragrance of the bazaar has left its mark.

SUGGESTED TASTINGS

The possibilities for comparative tastings are immense, both between regions and between countries. A truly cosmopolitan tasting can be organized on the basis of the various manifestations of Cabernet Sauvignon alone.

Try an inter-district tasting within Bordeaux, putting a Fronsac (mostly Cabernet Franc) against the Médoc wines of Listrac or Moulis, more dominated by Cabernet Sauvignon.

Put a Médoc and a Graves against a St Emilion or Pomerol (the last two with more Merlot). Stay with the same year – or years of a similar type of vintage – for the comparison to be valid: a big, ripe year (e.g. 1971, 1976 or 1979) in St Emilion, or particularly Pomerol, would tend to eclipse a wine from a lighter year in the Médoc, such as a 1973. Pomerols have the most enveloping taste of all, and from good years many can go into the full-bodied category. Similar-standard châteaux would also make the tasting more relevant. Remember that St Emilion and Pomerol usually show well sooner than Médoc in the top echelon of properties.

Put a good-quality château wine from the Médoc – a Bourgeois Growth or a well-proven *petit château*, against a Cabernet Sauvignon wine from South Africa and one from South America.

You could throw in a Rioja for good measure, but its oaky, vanilla character will probably stand out so that people will recognize it even at a blind tasting.

Do a tasting from south-west France, with a Madiran, a Cahors and a top wine from the Dordogne – the little *appellation* of Pécharmant (basically Cabernet and Merlot): the Château de Tiregand there is excellent.

Have a Rhône/Provence tasting, with a Lirac, a Bandol and a Vacqueyras.

Compare *appellations* within the Côte de Beaune: a Volnay against a Chassagne-Montrachet against a Savigny-Lès-Beaune, or a Monthelie against a Pernand-Vergelesses. Compare either at village/*commune* level, or at *premier cru* level: it would be unfair to mix the categories.

There is little point in comparing Pinot Noir wines around the world, as they are so different. Among the Californian examples, (and apart from Kalin Cellars), Trefethen, and perhaps Joseph Phelps, are nearest the Côte de Beaune.

However, do an inter-Californian Pinot Noir tasting, with the slightly floral Acacia against a firmer, well-rounded, solid Mount Eden plus the Monterey wineries of Jekel and Ventana and Santa Ynez Valley's Zaca Mesa.

The only European Pinot Noir which would go with these would be Torres' Viña Magdala, as the influence of barrel-ageing is evident in all the wines.

Pinot Nero wines from north-east Italy are much lighter, but compare examples from Alto Adige, Trentino and Collio in the Friuli.

With the Cabernet Sauvignon grape, set South Africa versus South America versus California. The latter should not be one of the whopping styles, so pick a Taylor California Cellars, a Christian Brothers or a fruity-impact Parducci from Mendocino.

With the Sangiovese grape, it is better to compare and contrast Chianti properties rather than to taste against a totally different grape variety.

Venegazzù could be matched with a well-balanced Médoc or even a St Emilion.

Take a Central European Cabernet Sauvignon (from Bulgaria or Romania) and compare it against one from New Zealand (for fun) and something simple from Bordeaux: Bordeaux Rouge or a *petit château*.

FULL, ASSERTIVE REDS

This section is really devoted to those red wines made with grape varieties which have a particularly assertive, individual taste; it is divided according to grape variety rather than country by country.

These are not wines intended for the faint-hearted, or for people who prefer wines to form a background for their food. Such rugged individualists will absolutely demand your attention when you are drinking them, and will come right out and challenge the food rather than just complement it.

This is not to say that assertive red wines do not 'go' with food – they make some of the most exciting taste combinations. But you can use your herbs and flavourings with less reticence than usual when cooking a meal to go with these grape varieties. They are preeminently winter wines, superb in cold weather, even if they are often produced in areas with a much more 'southern' climate. They are the sun's gift to the beleaguered souls of the north, and we should cut down the fuel bills and invest in crates of these wines instead. Central heating can warm the body, but these wines bring *joie de vivre* as well!

Many of these red wines will be strong in alcohol, but not excessively so, save in the case of late-harvest Zinfandels from California. Forceful taste and rugged individuality in a wine do not necessarily depend on a high alcohol content, but the very fact that they are made in hot and sunny parts of the world means that one is talking about wines of between 13 and 14 per cent alcohol; exceptions are many of the wines from South Africa, which seem to keep nearer 12 per cent.

But such is the fruity intensity and depth of flavour of this group of wines, that the alcohol is superbly balanced and never overpowering. If a wine has richness, high glycerine and is redolent of varietal fruit, the alcohol only serves as a backbone – one could say that it is part of the natural structure or scaffolding, holding it all up and contributing to the overall body.

The good thing about these wines is that, in spite of their individual character, they are not rarities, hiding behind a screen of unavailability in order to boost prices. They are freely available, and often the grape varieties responsible for them are some of the most widely planted in a whole viticultural area. The Zinfandel is among the most planted red grape varieties in California, the Barbera flourishes all over Italy and is also a thoroughly successful export to the Californian vineyards, while the Syrah/Shiraz dominates the northern Rhône valley and is the staple red grape variety of Australia.

When to drink these wines
These are wines to drink when snow or winter rain is falling outside, and there is a warming dish on the table. Well-flavoured stews and casseroles, game like venison and wild boar, are all ideal accompaniments for these exciting, strapping red wines.

Port-like or late-harvest Zinfandels from California are too assertive to drink throughout a meal, and are best with a mature, well-flavoured cheese. One exception which you can drink with meals with the utmost pleasure is The Monterey Vineyard 'December Harvest' Zinfandel, a remarkable and fascinating wine at around 14 per cent alcohol.

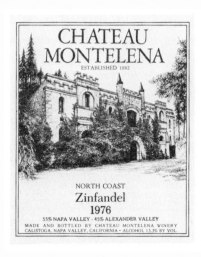

CHATEAU MONTELENA
ESTABLISHED 1882

NORTH COAST
Zinfandel
1976
55% NAPA VALLEY · 45% ALEXANDER VALLEY
MADE AND BOTTLED BY CHATEAU MONTELENA WINERY
CALISTOGA, NAPA VALLEY, CALIFORNIA · ALCOHOL 13.3% BY VOL.

Zinfandel

This must be the most exotic grape variety name of the lot. Zingy, zestful 'Zin', as CALIFORNIANS sometimes affectionately refer to it, is regarded as the natural property of the Golden State. Its origins have been much researched, but without turning up anything concrete. The most likely suggestion is that it came originally from southern Italy, where it was the Primitivo of places like Puglia. Tasters sometimes see a vague resemblance, a certain spiciness, a propensity to move into the higher alcohol stratosphere, but this may become auto-suggestion once the idea is implanted.

Whatever its origins, Zinfandel is a super grape variety. It is reminiscent of the reaction of many outsiders to New York City – at first they hate it, then they learn to love it as an exciting addition to life. When at its most concentrated and powerful, the spiciness of Zinfandel is overlaid with a certain berryish quality, which some go so far as to identify as blackberry.

The Zinfandel is an extraordinarily adaptable grape variety, growing well in almost every area of California and making wines from rosé right through to Port-type. Amador County is famous for its big, robust Zinfandels, and San Luis Obispo and Lodi follow in the same style. But Sonoma, Napa, Mendocino, Monterey and Santa Clara all have Zinfandels of note.

The sensational wines are the Port-like or late-harvest examples, hovering around 15-16 per cent alcohol. If you wish to see what these are all about, try Monteviña (Amador County, Shenandoah Valley), Monterey Peninsula (Amador County, Sweet Late Harvest) or Ridge Vineyards (San Luis Obispo County, Paso Robles, Late Harvest).

Big-bodied, high-alcohol Zinfandels are made by Clos du Val in Napa, Lytton Springs in Sonoma, and by Ridge Vineyards (Amador County, Fiddletown, Esola Vineyards, and Santa Cruz, Monte Bello).

The problem, and this is a typically Californian problem, is that the wineries often make a whole clutch of wines; so you must look at both the front and the back labels for the details indicating alcohol strength, picking dates (late-harvest or not) and sugar content (both residual and at time of harvesting), to be sure of the style of wine you are getting.

For instance, Burgess Cellars in Napa make Zinfandels you can drink within two to three years of their making, as well as the odd one which needs ten years in bottle. Fetzer make anything from a 15 per cent whopper from the Scharffenberger Vineyard, to one of the fruitiest and easiest to drink on the market. Ridge always make a whole posse of wines, with the vineyard and component part details clearly marked. An example is their 1979 from Paso Robles, soft and spicy, but the late-harvest 1978 from the same vineyard has a

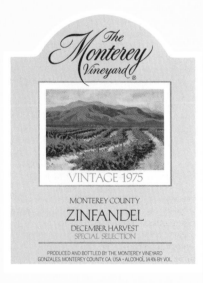

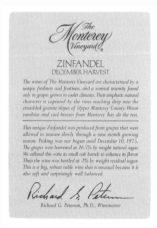

resounding 16.3 per cent alcohol. Grgich Hills could make a fruity wine for young drinking one year, and one which has to be aged in another, both from the Alexander Valley.

Lighter, fruitier wines are made by Chateau Montelena in Napa, as well as by large firms such as Beringer and Paul Masson. Joseph Phelps Zinfandels can go high in alcohol but the wines are lovely and luscious. Foppiano and Round Hill do not make styles to knock you out either. These are probably the wines which will be most appreciated by newcomers to the grape variety.

Zinfandel is not grown anywhere else in the world, so California enjoys all the advantages of a monopoly.

Syrah/Shiraz

This grape variety really sits astride both the New World and the Old, with its roots firmly entrenched in the Rhône Valley, particularly in the Hermitage area of the northern Rhône, as well as in Australia and in South Africa. The true Syrah is also beginning to appear in California, and should not be confused with the Petite Sirah, which has quite different parentage, even if the Rhône origins are the same.

The Shiraz made in AUSTRALIA seems to be considerably more assertive in its sheer force of character than the product of its cousins in the northern Rhône. (In France, the grape produces wines of great depth and marvellous flavour, entirely suitable for ageing in bottle, but the varietal impact is less than that of the

wine as a whole, so it fits better into the next category – powerful reds, maturing with age.)

Shiraz can be very forceful indeed, perhaps especially from areas like Clare in South Australia or in north-east Victoria. These are very robust wines, big, full-blooded reds of a type not seen elsewhere very often. They are perhaps even bigger when they are not matured in small casks, and a smoother taste, still with great depth, is achieved when small, Bordeaux-sized barrels are used.

The classic wine of this genre is Penfolds Grange Hermitage, which does have a small undisclosed amount of Cabernet Sauvignon in it to aid balance. No one knows the exact origin of the grapes which make this wine, but it is a mixture from the Adelaide area in South Australia and Coonawarra. Penfolds have other top wines, such as St Henri, and also wines labelled with Bin numbers, in the Australian fashion.

The Hunter Valley in New South Wales and Coonawarra produce intensely flavoured red wines from the Shiraz – perhaps the wines have more acid and tannin from Coonawarra, but the comparisons are for those well versed in the styles.

Shiraz is often used to blend with Cabernet Sauvignon, since it gives body and backbone to the latter variety. The Hunter Valley has many firms making fine Shiraz or part-Shiraz wines, among which are Brokenwood (Cabernet Sauvignon blended with Shiraz from Coonawarra) – wine of wonderful value, Drayton's Bellevue, Tulloch's Private Bin Hermitage, and a succession of Vat Numbers, such as 5, 9, 11 and 12, to denote the excellent Shiraz wines of Tyrrell. These need time in bottle to show their great earthy richness. The Rothbury Estate produces both Shiraz and Cabernet Sauvignon – try the Individual Paddock Hermitage.

It could be said that the Shiraz is at its most elegant in Coonawarra, although some people would not apply this particular adjective to the variety, devotees though they may be. Redman have a 'Claret' made from Shiraz – the name is regrettable but the wine is not – and Wynns follow the same labelling principle, with no bad effects on the wine. In the Southern Vales, the firm of Thomas Hardy make Nottage Hill Claret from Shiraz, which is hearty wine; look out also for their special cuvée, Eileen Hardy red, often made from Shiraz, but sometimes from Cabernet Sauvignon.

Pinotage

SOUTH AFRICA feels very proprietary about the Pinotage, rather as the Californians feel about the Zinfandel. It is a crossing of Pinot Noir and Hermitage: most confusingly, the Hermitage is not the Shiraz/Syrah in South Africa, but the softer Cinsaut.

The taste of Pinotage is rather hard to fix in terms of vocabulary and there are two schools of thought on the wines it makes, one maintaining that it should be drunk young, the other insisting that it is better with some bottle age, when it takes on richness and a mellow roundness. The initial grape aroma fades with age, and some people prefer the fruit and freshness of youth. This is understandable when the wine is deliberately made to be drunk young, but those Pinotage wines with a high proportion of tannin and acid do need time to soften.

An example of a Pinotage which thrives on a youthful taste is that from the KWV, with its fruity nose, nice balance and raspberry jam finish. The Meerendal Pinotage has a very deep colour, and a strongly scented, almost floral nose, but finishes on the palate as a very big mouthful with both tannin and fruit – it is not a good idea to have one without the other in wines which keep, and this wine is good after six to seven years.

There is also another 'curiosity' grape,

produced in the Malmesbury area of South Africa, but this is much more unusual than the Pinotage. Allesverloren Estate already has a reputation for Port-type wines, but they now make full-bodied red wines, one of which is from the Tinta Barocca, a grape variety of Portuguese origin. This has a nice scented nose, but the taste is big and tannic, with vanilla overtones – real winter wine.

GRAPE VARIETIES

ZINFANDEL

Zinfandel produces wines (named after the grape variety) which have a somewhat spicy – even peppery – taste, sometimes berryish. It has a distinctly exotic feel to it, especially to Europeans. Zinfandel can be made into medium-bodied, fruity wines for young drinking; alternatively, it can make huge, heavy, almost Port-like red wines, strong in alcohol and very heady. The grape variety is only found in California. It is now thought to be derived from the Primitivo of Southern Italy.

BARBERA

The Barbera can make both fruity, assertive wines for young drinking and more serious wood-aged wines. Much grown in Piedmont, as well as other parts of Italy, it has transported most successfully to California. The wines are named after the grape variety.

PINOTAGE

Unlike any other grape, Pinotage makes wines with a highly individual aroma and taste. They can be drunk young and fruity, or can take some bottle ageing when they are more tannic. Pinotage is a crossing of Pinot Noir and Hermitage (Cinsaut); it is found on a large scale in South Africa and to a small extent in New Zealand. The wines are called after the grape variety.

SYRAH/SHIRAZ

Syrah makes big, dark wines of depth, tannin and fruit in the northern Rhône (Hermitage, Côte Rôtie). In Australia, it is known as Shiraz or Hermitage, and the wines are even more robust, assertive – and perhaps more earthy. Shiraz is also grown in South Africa, and the true Syrah is beginning to appear in California.

SUGGESTED TASTINGS

Californian Zinfandels can be compared only with one another. Try wines from different areas (at least eight areas within the Golden State produce good Zinfandels to choose from), but match the wines for weight, i.e. look at the alcohol content on the label. There is no point in tasting a 15-16 per cent whopper against a more suave example of 12-13 per cent.

Taste a Barbera d'Alba from Italy against a Sebastiani Barbera from California – e.g. the Proprietor's Reserve.

There is no point in comparing Pinotage with anything else, so stay with the grape variety in South Africa and look at different styles. Alternatively, compare South African with New Zealand.

Shiraz is a law unto itself in Australia, good for inter-regional tastings of, say, Hunter Valley and Coonawarra. Compare an Australian Shiraz with a northern Rhône wine of a very good vintage; the latter type of wine is not so 'varietal' in character and is described in the next section of this book.

Barbera

In ITALY Barbera makes its most forceful statement in Piedmont, where much of it is drunk young. It usually has a very vivid colour and a marked fruity taste, projected by a high acidity. Barbera d'Alba probably has the most body, but try Barbera d'Asti and del Monferrato too.

In CALIFORNIA, no one makes better Barbera than the Sebastiani family firm who, loyal to the country or their origins, make splendid, bold and robust Barbera. Don't miss it.

Kadarka

This might seem esoteric, but this is *the* red grape variety of HUNGARY, especially of the Great Plain, where it makes dark, strongly flavoured red wine with an almost spicy, peppery finish. More good Kadarka is made in Szekszárd in Transdanubia, and the grape certainly accounts for more than half of the mixture in Bull's Blood. The Kadarka also appears in BULGARIA.

Mavrud

This grape is native to BULGARIA, and many people consider that it makes their best red wines. It certainly produces dark, tannic wines, distinctively Balkan in flavour. The best Mavrud is made south of the Balkan Mountains in the Maritsa basin.

Other assertive wines

Other wines round the world that could be said to have an assertive character are the wonderful red **Taurasi** of ITALY's Campania. The Greek-origin Aglianico grape gives it an individual character, full of body, but it is also a wine of breed which ages well.

Basilicata, a poor region of Italy in every other way, has the splendid red wine, **Aglianico del Vulture**, again made from the Aglianico grape. If you want a few years of ageing, you should buy the Vecchio or the Riserva, and then the wine can show great complexity of flavour and dimensions of taste.

Dão might not seem at first sight a candidate for this section, since it is not made from one assertive grape, but a mixture of PORTUGUESE varieties. However, the taste of red Dão is inimitable and the bouquet clearly recognizable. The red Dãos always have high glycerine and a rich, almost vegetal bouquet – if there is any wine that has a texture, this is it, thick and velvety. The newly demarcated area of the Bairrada is also making red wines of marked character.

POWERFUL REDS, MATURING WITH AGE

Regardless of how often they are drunk, these wines are more discussed and more written about than any others. Their development in bottle is a ceaseless source of interest to the wine drinker, and identifying them from memory is one of his sports.

Normally these wines are powerful in body and structure, but sometimes the word is more applicable to the strength and persistence of their flavour. They all seem full on the palate, with a huge array of tastes and a feeling of weight and volume. Their pronounced bouquet becomes more complex and multi-dimensional with age in bottle.

Since these wines are built to last, many of these attributes, particularly the bouquet, are not evident in extreme youth. If they were, the wines' staying power would be in doubt, for they are not designed to show at their best at only 4-5 years old. If they did, they would probably no longer be great wines at 10 years old, let alone when they are 20 or 30.

Obviously, for a wine to have this capacity to age and to improve as it matures, the pedigree must be absolutely right. This means not only that the origin of the wine and its place in a recognized hierarchy must be impeccable, but that the wine itself must be made with immense skill.

Particularly in Europe, a wine with this potential to age may be what the professionals call 'closed' in its early years. The nose can be 'dumb' and the taste rather overlaid with tannin, but experienced wine-tasters are able to judge whether the other ingredients, such as good fruit and balanced acidity, are there too.

Wines of this type, which generally should not be opened for many years, cannot be cheap; but as always with wines of intense flavour, a little goes a long way, and a glass or two will suffice. Invest in these wines when you can, appreciate them with friends of like mind, and savour them to the full.

When to drink these wines
Aristocratic wines of great flavour need simple food made with beautiful ingredients. Leave the complicated dishes for another time, and let the food be a foil to the wine. Succulent roast beef or delicious roast spring lamb cannot be bettered. Pheasant, partridge and grouse are also excellent, both hot and cold, and plain roast chicken goes with top wines, whether red or white.

English cheeses, such as Cheddar, Gloucester and Cheshire, need the biggest wines – Hermitage, the biggest Californian Cabernet Sauvignons, Châteauneuf-du-Pape, Barbaresco or Barolo.

GRAPE VARIETIES

CABERNET SAUVIGNON
One of the greatest red grape varieties, Cabernet Sauvignon makes wines full of fruit, tannin and flavour, with excellent acidity balance – all the prerequisites for ageing. Mixed with Cabernet Franc and Merlot, it produces magnificent, long-lived wines in Bordeaux.

It is majestic in California and Australia, and fine in South Africa and in pockets of Italy. Whatever the soil and climate, the unique bouquet is always recognizable.

NEBBIOLO
This grape produces long-lived wines of high tannin, deep colour and an intense, almost tarry flavour. As the wine matures, it takes on an orange tinge and the taste softens and mellows. This is the great grape variety of north-western Italy, responsible for such wines as Barolo, Barbaresco, Gattinara and Ghemme.

It is also known as the Spanna.

France

This category is where Bordeaux comes into its own. The greatest growths of the area, the *crus classés*, provide both intellectual and sensual stimulation. A newcomer to wine drinking should never start with these wines – they are difficult to appreciate. Begin with something simpler, work upwards, and the final reward will be the greater.

If you invest in a small collection of top Bordeaux wines, you will be able to monitor their progress and learn at exactly what point you find them at their most attractive – a much cheaper way than to try out expensive wines in restaurants.

Domaine de Chevalier (these two in the Graves), and Ausone, Cheval Blanc, Figeac, Belair, Pétrus, La Conseillante and Trotanoy (in St Emilion and Pomerol).

Most of the other *crus classés*, as well as some of the best *crus bourgeois*, are also fine-flavoured candidates for keeping.

Burgundy's top wines are as exciting and intoxicating as those from Bordeaux, and arguably even more splendid because there are fewer of them. Unfortunately, fine Burgundy does not have as wide a distribution as fine Bordeaux, primarily because the area is much smaller.

The *crus classés* of the Médoc (St Estèphe, Pauillac, St Julien and Margaux), Graves, St Emilion and Pomerol are the ones to mature and watch. Choose good to great vintages, and drink the good before the great since, if you drink in chronological order, you may miss the best time for each wine.

Obviously, the Premiers Crus Classés (Châteaux Latour, Lafite, Mouton-Rothschild, and Margaux in the Médoc and Haut-Brion in the Graves) are always candidates for keeping, for a longer or shorter time, according to the nature of the vintage. To these great works of wine can be added châteaux like Léoville-Las-Cases, Ducru-Beaucaillou, Palmer, Pichon-Lalande, Cos d'Estournel, La Mission Haut-Brion and

In Burgundy, the estate or *négociant* responsible for the wine is more important than its exact place in the hierarchy. Better to have a *premier cru* from a talented winemaker than the grandest of *grands crus* from a mediocre source.

Provided you are sure of your winemaker than the grandest of *grands crus* from a their superior sites and lower yields, which make those wines destined for the most lengthy keeping in bottle. With the exception of red Corton, these are to be found in the Côte de Nuits. The *grands crus* of Gevrey-Chambertin, Chambolle-Musigny, Morey-St-Denis, Vosne-Romanée and Flagey-Echézeaux are capable of superb development in bottle, as is some Clos Vougeot. *Premiers crus* are almost as long-lived, especially Clos St Jacques and Les Varoilles from Gevrey-Chambertin, and the top wines of Nuits St Georges, such as Les Saint-Georges, Les Vaucrains, Les Porrets and Les Pruliers.

What should one be looking for in these magnificent wines? As a rough guide, Chambertin and Chambertin-Clos de Bèze should be majestic, beautifully constructed, generous and perfectly balanced. Latricières-Chambertin should be elegance itself, married to absolute length on the palate. The Clos de la Roche is probably the biggest *grand cru* of Morey-St-Denis, while the Clos St-Denis marries charm with backbone. Le

Musigny should have exquisite finesse hiding the firm note behind, while Bonnes Mares should have great flavour and structure. Clos Vougeot at its best is fat and glossy. The greatest wines of Flagey-Echézeaux and Vosne-Romanée are opulent, almost exotic, with a *goût de terroir* behind them. And Nuits St Georges *premiers crus* have a wonderful earthy splendour about them, an almost irony taste.

In the Côte de Beaune, Corton is the obvious candidate for this category. Any wine with Corton on the label is a *grand cru*, so this includes Louis Latour's Clos de la Vigne-au-Saint, as well as Corton-Pougets, Corton Clos du Roi, and the slightly earlier maturing Corton-Bressandes. In Beaune, the *premiers crus* of Teurons and even more, Marconnets, are keepers, as well as Bouchard Père's Beaune Grèves Vigne de l'Enfant Jésus. Chanson's Beaune Clos des Fèves, Louis Latour's Les Vignes Franches, Louis Jadot's Clos-des-Ursules and Joseph Drouhin's Clos des Mouches, also improve with bottle age.

Premiers crus which are right up with *grands crus* are Pommard Les Epenots and Les Rugiens, together with Volnay Les Caillerets and even Santenots in ripe years. Pommard Clos des Epeneaux of the Comte Armand is an enclave within Les Epenots (Burgundian spelling is confusing) and this is one of the longest-living wines on the Côte de Beaune.

Down in the Rhône, the possibilities for ageing wines to greatness are considerable. Hermitage and Côte Rôtie are the two outstanding *appellations* in the northern Rhône, but the best Crozes-Hermitage and Cornas also need maturing in bottle. When young, these wines are deep purple and have a peppery, tannic taste, but they mature to a kind of vegetal splendour which is magnificent.

In the southern Rhône, Châteauneuf-du-Pape is the wine to age. When young, it has tannin and a delightful cherry taste about it, less peppery than the pure Syrah Hermitage of the north. Châteauneuf-du-Pape, from a good estate, which makes wines intended for ageing, gets rich and fuller-flavoured with 10-15 years in bottle. Gigondas from a good source also ages well.

Italy

Piedmont is the area from which the great aged Barolos and Barbarescos come. How long they last seems to depend on how long they have spent in barrel – some of the longer-wood-aged wines seem to need less time in bottle, since they have already done their softening in cask.

The young Nebbiolo grape is somewhat astringent, and wood-ageing is certainly necessary, but there is controversy as to how much. Once Barolo or Barbaresco has spent a considerable time in barrel, it tends to become 'dried out', with the fruit submerged for ever.

When buying Barolo, remember that there are big differences between vintages, as in Bordeaux, so do not pay high prices for inferior vintages. Top producers, all with individual styles, are Bruno Giacosa, Ratti, Ceretto, Conterno, Oddero, Prunotto and Pio Cesare. Some of the larger firms make slightly lighter wines – an example is Fontanafredda – which some people find easier to appreciate than the 'whoppers'. However, something like an aged Annunziata wine from Ratti, or a selection from Franco-Fiorina, is a great experience.

Barbaresco is slightly softer than Barolo and may be easier to appreciate. The undoubted king of Barbaresco is the family firm of Gaja, with two magnificent special site wines, Sorì San Lorenzo and Sorì Tildin. But any Barbaresco from Gaja, Franco-

Fiorina, Ceretto, Pio Cesare, Giacosa, Prunotto or the Castello di Neive is remarkable.

Still in Piedmont, Gattinara, as made by Dessilani, is worthy of ageing, and the great Spanna wines of Vallana should never be missed. Ghemme from Brugo is a top wine; but Lessona from Sella is now lighter, though still delicious.

In Trentino, the distinctive Teroldego needs ageing, especially when from Zeni or the Barone de Cles, whose Teroldego Maso Scari is one of the greatest red wines of Italy. Castel San Michele, made from Cabernet and Merlot, needs, perhaps, more ageing than the other good French-style wines made here: Fedrigotti's Foianeghe and Cabernet San Leonardo. While in the Veneto, the great Recioto della Valpolicella Amarone wines, immensely rich and opulent, need moderate ageing in bottle.

In Tuscany the Bordeaux-flavoured Sassicaia needs 10 years or more to develop fully. This is Cabernet Sauvignon at its most majestic, and although not as refined as Antinori's Tignanello, which mixes the native Sangiovese grape with some Cabernet Sauvignon, it seems to need longer in bottle to soften. Brunello di Montalcino, made in traditional style, is fabled for its capacity to age. Only a few Chianti Classico Riservas of excellent years need great ageing, e.g. remarkable old wines from the Badia a Coltibuono.

Spain

Only the biggest, richest Riojas of good vintage need extensive ageing, but there are 20- and even 30-year-old wonders.

In the Penedès, Torres blend local grape varieties with classic French varieties (as Antinori does in Tuscany) and the Gran Coronas and Black Label fall back on Cabernet Sauvignon, together with both cask and bottle-ageing. The wines are deep, intense and impact-making: true Reservas.

With Vega Sicilia, from near Valladolid, the estate matures the wine and none is sold under 10 years old; Valbuena is sold younger, and perhaps has a more accessible taste. Protos, from Bodega Ribera Duero, ages superbly.

USA

The Cabernet Sauvignon in California undoubtedly makes some of this grape variety's most astonishing wines. When one discusses ageing potential, even the winemakers are reluctant to commit themselves. So much has changed, in both grape varieties and techniques, since the older Californian wines were made that there is really very little with which to compare current wines. Whereas in Bordeaux there are examples of wines going back to the last century, which help form judgements of younger wines, in California one has to rely entirely on assessing a wine's intrinsic quality in order to guess at its longevity in bottle. Some wines made in the early 1970s appeared somewhat unbalanced and too massive to age well, but latterly truly great, harmonious Cabernet Sauvignons have emerged, and seem sure to make distinguished old wines.

The benefits of 100 per cent varietal Cabernet Sauvignons have been questioned, and a small proportion of Merlot is occasionally added to the blend.

Although on the massive side, the 1974s were considered some of the greatest Cabernet Sauvignons. Heitz Martha's Vineyard 1974 is a most exciting wine, and the Mirassou Harvest Selection has great density and a blackcurrant nose reminiscent of Mouton-Rothschild. 1975 seems to combine power with breed, best shown in

the superbly balanced Robert Mondavi Reserve or the wine of Chateau Montelena. Mount Veeder 1975 is soft and minty. Mayacamas 1976 is ripe and soft with a slight mintiness; while the 1976 Heitz Bella Oaks Vineyard is luscious wine. Among 1977s Zaca Mesa has lovely fruit intensity; Mondavi has a classic wine, and Ridge York Creek, excellent scent and breed.

The 1978 Cabernet Sauvignons are looking in the top rank, none more so than that from Stag's Leap Wine Cellars and the formidable Jekel Special Reserve from Monterey. However, Robert Mondavi has made another classic-style wine; Joseph Phelps' wine has great ripeness and beauty;

Trefethen's is extremely fruity, and Mount Veeder comes up with the scent of mint and intriguing attraction.

Some wineries make Merlot wines, which may have some Cabernet Sauvignon in them. Stag's Leap Wine Cellars and Sterling make big, glossy wines which age.

Some people would argue that Californian Pinot Noir should go into this category, but perhaps its ageing potential has not yet been sufficiently proved.

California has made truly amazing progress in wine-making in the last 15 years, but with recent vintages like 1978, one realizes that there is even more to come in the future.

SUGGESTED TASTINGS

Although interregional comparisons are perhaps preferable, the obvious international comparison is between Californian Cabernet Sauvignons and top red Bordeaux. Match wines with similar grape-variety proportions, e.g. Latour or Mouton-Rothschild rather than top St Emilion or Pomerol. You may find different development processes and lifespans: a young top Bordeaux is more 'closed' than a top Californian Cabernet Sauvignon, which is always 'showy' from the start, even if it has the qualities to age. 🍷

A Cabernet/Merlot or straight Cabernet wine from Italy may be a more valid comparison with Bordeaux; the climates are less far apart.

Alternatively, put a top Torres Coronas wine against a Sassicaia, or even Tignanello. 🍷

Put Barolo against Barbaresco: many locals cannot detect any difference. 🍷

One top Burgundy is really best compared to another: try to pick out the *appellations* of top estate or *domaine* wines. Staying with *premiers crus*, put a Beaune, a Volnay and a Pommard together; or, in the Côte de Nuits, match *grands crus* from Gevrey-Chambertin, Morey-St-Denis and Vosne-Romanée. 🍷

Try to distinguish a southern Rhône wine from a northern Rhône one.

ROSÉ WINES

Rosé, or pink, wine is much denigrated by wine snobs who relegate it to the ranks of a 'fun wine', reserved for people who cannot decide whether to drink red or white.

In fact, a rosé should be chosen with as much forethought as any other wine. A rosé is *not* a rosé is not a rosé. The variety is immense, and about the only generalizations to make are that all – light or heavy, bone-dry or sweet – should be drunk cold, and young.

Most rosés get their colour from a limited period of contact between the skins of red grapes and fermenting wine. Lower-quality rosés can be made by blending red and white wines.

France

Rosé d'Anjou from the Loire is one of France's most important wine exports, and one of the wines found on most supermarket shelves. Some people scoff at this soft, fragrant, slightly sweet wine, but many begin their wine drinking with it, and stay faithful to the end. It is the European equivalent of the jug or carafe rosé of California, with its residual sugar on the palate and its come-hither bouquet.

Cabernet d'Anjou, made mostly from Cabernet Franc, has more character and fruity interest. Rosé de la Loire is always dry. At Sancerre, rosé wines made from Pinot Noir can be a bit hollow in less-than-ripe years. Pinot Noir also makes a Rosé de Marsannay, a fragrant, dry wine of character from this village in the Côte de Nuits.

The famous Tavel rosé and that of Lirac, both in the southern Rhône, tend to be on the alcoholic side: the vineyards at Tavel are covered in large flat stones which absorb and radiate the heat from the sun, and the grapes get very ripe from the constant warmth; so if you drink several glasses, don't get up from the table in a hurry. These wines have a lovely, very definite taste – drink them young. In spite of misguided advice that Tavel tastes better with bottle age, don't keep it, for it does not.

In the Arbois region of the Jura, rosé or *gris* wines can be nice drunk on the spot. *Cendré* is another name applied to the pale and dry rosés of the Jura.

Dry rosés, close in style to each other, come from the Côtes-de-Provence and Coteaux-d'Aix-en-Provence. A wine from

When to drink these wines

Chilled rosé is the ideal wine to drink in hot weather, with dishes which in colder weather would call for a red wine. Côtes-de-Provence rosé, in the bottle with the hourglass figure, is *the* wine of sun and sand.

Dry rosé is immensely adaptable – it goes dreamily with all Mediterranean-type food, including fish soups and stews, hors d'oeuvres and pasta. It can even cope with strong, garlicky Provençal dishes such as *aioli* and *tapénade*. Robust Tavel will go with kebabs or lamb cooked with herbs.

Lovers of sweet rosé will probably enjoy it with everything.

the *négociant* Pradel is always safe: indeed, all these wines are generally made to a good commercial standard. Bandol rosé is also good, though the red is better. In Languedoc excellent rosé wines are produced from vines grown in the sand – Listel Gris de Gris 'Salmon Rosé wine' is most palatable.

Italy

Italy's rosé wines are nearly all from the south. This is no accident, for in the hot weather which prevails for about half the year, no one wants to drink heavy reds. *Rosato* is the order of the day. In Puglia, you

LAGREIN ROSATO DEL TRENTINO

DENOMINAZIONE D'ORIGINE CONTROLLATA

V.Q.P.R.D.

Deriva dalla vinificazione Kretzer del vitigno omonimo effettuata direttamente dal produttore all'origine. Si consiglia di berlo giovane e fresco ad una temperatura di 8° – 10° cent. ca. Ottimo quale aperitivo, con antipasti e in riunioni conviviali. D'estate ghiacciato disseta.

Questa bottiglia contiene 0/5l ℮ ed il contenuto alcolico è di 12% vol.

IMBOTTIGLIATO ALL'ORIGINE DALLA CANTINA SOC. COOP. MEZZOCORONA - S.C.R.L. – TN

ITALIA

Spain and Portugal

The *rosado* wines of Spain are mostly brands, but that from the Marqués de Riscal in Rioja is the most interesting. In Penedès, Torres make De Casta, which is everything a crisp, fruity *rosado* should be. Don't miss the *rosado* of the Señorio de Sarria, in Navarra.

In Portugal, the big brand names of Mateus and Lancers are slightly sparkling carbonated rosé wines, with a touch of sweetness. Lagosta is another brand name, perhaps marginally more interesting, but the sugar levels of all these wines do vary with the markets on which they are sold, and they tend to be sweeter when exported.

North Africa

Dry rosé, sometimes called *gris*, is a good bet, excellent with couscous. In **Morocco,** try Gris de Boulaouane or Les Trois Domaines.

USA

The jug or carafe rosé wines in California are a touch sweet. Rosés are made from grape varieties such as Cabernet Sauvignon or even Pinot Noir, when there is too much red wine about; Grenache here makes pleasant, fruity rosé, with some sweetness. Dry rosé from Zinfandel is a very interesting wine, but the undoubted king has to be the rare Grignolino rosé. As made by Heitz in the Napa, it is a terrific drink.

must try Copertino, made near Lecce. It is the only rosé wine which ages – if you can resist it when young. There is also excellent Castel del Monte (look for the Rivera label) and San Severo. From Calabria, right down in the toe, come Savuto and Cirò, which can be a touch more alcoholic than some of the Puglia wines made by large companies.

At the opposite end of Italy, in the Alto Adige, don't miss Lagrein Rosato (Lagrein Kretzer in German), which is probably the most intriguing rosé produced from any grape. Bardolino Chiaretto, from the shores of Lake Garda, is pink and worth drinking.

GRAPE VARIETY

GRENACHE
Used for both red and rosé wines, the Grenache produces wines of good alcohol, usually with a scented nose. It is the dominant variety of southern France, playing an important part in making the wines of Châteauneuf-du-Pape, Tavel, Lirac, Côtes du Rhône and Provence, as well as being found all over Languedoc-Roussillon.

The principal type of Grenache is the same as the Spanish Garnacha of Rioja and Penedès.

In California, wine made from the Grenache is particularly scented and is better made into rosé than into red wine. Most is grown in the San Joaquin Valley, some in Mendocino.

SUGGESTED TASTINGS

Compare three wines which may be the best rosés in the world: Lagrein Rosato and Copertino from Italy with Grignolino rosé from the Napa. Your problem will be assembling them all.

In France, compare the southern rosés: a Tavel or Lirac, a Côtes-de-Provence or Coteaux-d'Aix-en-Provence, and a Bandol.

Compare a Rosé d'Anjou with a Californian jug rosé: the former may have a little more underlying acidity.

Try Bourgogne Rosé de Marsannay against that other rosé made from Pinot Noir, Sancerre.

SPARKLING WINES

Why celebrate with Champagne? Why choose sparkling wines for weddings, anniversaries, birthdays, for special parties as well as for launching ships?

The very sight of the froth on the surface of the wine and the fine bubbles swirling up the centre generates a lively, happy feeling; the delicious tingle on the palate stimulates the appetite, making Champagne, and sparkling wines in general, ideal as aperitifs.

The invigorating sensation of the bubbles in the wine gives every drinker a 'lift', raising the spirits and seeming to do genuine good. It works wonders at the end of a tiring day, and is even better offered as a complete surprise.

It is regrettable that so many people associate the start of a festivity with the 'pop' of the cork shooting out of the bottle, closely followed by a fountain of froth – for this is emphatically not the way sparkling wine should be opened. That violent explosion results in the loss of too many of those precious bubbles.

When to drink sparkling wines

As an aperitif, drink the lighter sparkling wines or a Blanc de Blancs Champagne. Some non-vintage Champagnes are fuller in style than others: pick the 'bigger' Champagnes, like Roederer and Krug, to drink with a meal. A Californian Blanc de Noirs can be drunk both before and with a meal. Rosé Champagne is delicious with light food, for example a cold buffet. (A member of a famous Champagne house once suggested that to accompany rosé Champagne, the whole meal should be pink: lobster, fresh salmon, and strawberries. What better combination?)

The French sometimes offer Champagne at the end of a meal – during or after the dessert. However, *brut* tastes too dry and hard at this stage, and *rich* Champagne is preferable; its taste is not as cloying as it sounds, but is simply rounder, fuller and softer than *brut* – and it is ideal to drink while eating sweeter things, such as *petits fours*.

People are often snobbish about Asti Spumante and other sparkling wines made from the sweet Muscat or Moscato grape. But very chilled Asti is quite delicious with some ripe fresh fruit, or served alone in a tingling glass, mid-morning on a summer's day. It is low in alcohol, too.

Germans like to drink Sekt quite late in the evening, as the conversation gets animated. Spaniards open a bottle of *cava* at family gatherings – and there are a good many family gatherings in Spain.

GRAPE VARIETY

PINOT BLANC

Pinot Blanc is often a constituent of sparkling wine. In the USA it is used in sparkling wines and in Californian 'champagnes'. As Pinot Bianco, it is grown in north-eastern Italy for both delicious still white wine and some of the best dry sparkling wines.

It is grown increasingly in Alsace, where it makes an attractive, slightly fruity wine. The variety is known as Klevner or as Weissburgunder in Germany, and is also found in Austria, Hungary and Chile.

In the past, this white grape variety has often been confused with the Chardonnay, but the latter is no longer grouped with the Pinot family.

Wine-making

The word 'blend' in the context of a top sparkling wine is far from being a pejorative term. Champagne itself is usually a blend of black Pinot Noir and Pinot Meunier grapes with white Chardonnay, except in the case of a Blanc de Blancs Champagne, where the brew is all Chardonnay. In California, the combination might be Pinot Noir, Chardonnay and Pinot Blanc. In a non-vintage wine, the contents of the bottle are also a blend of years, and always there is a blend of wines from different sites. This contributes greatly to the interest and complexity of the taste.

There are two principal methods by which the bubbles are introduced into sparkling wine: by induced secondary fermentation or by addition of CO_2.

Méthode champenoise In this 'Champagne method' the normal alcoholic fermentation of the still wine is succeeded by a secondary fermentation which is induced in the bottle; the resulting natural CO_2 is trapped in the form of bubbles, only to be released when the cork is eased off. This is the best way of making sparkling wine, but it is a slow and costly process since each bottle has to be handled many times, culminating in the *dégorgement*, or the removal of the sediment, caused by the secondary fermentation. This used to be done everywhere by hand, with the picturesque shaking down of the sediment to the neck of the bottle by experienced *remueurs*, but mechanical frames are now widely used. All Champagne from France is made in this way (hence the name), as well as many other French sparkling wines: Bourgogne Mousseux, Crémant de Bourgogne, Crémant d'Alsace, Crémant de Loire, Saumur, Anjou and Vouvray Mousseux from the Loire; St Péray from the Rhône and some sparkling wine made in Savoie, such as Seyssel Mousseux.

In Spain the great houses of Catalonia produce their *cava* wines by this method; many of Italy's top sparkling wines are made by *metodo champenois*; California, too makes its best sparkling wines in this way.

The Charmat method (also called autoclave, *cuve close*, or tank method) of introducing the bubble into the wine is an alternative which is nearly as good (and in exceptional instances quite as good) as the *méthode champenoise*. It is particularly successful in Germany for the production of much of the better-quality Sekt, and in many good Italian sparkling wines. Here the second fermentation takes place in vat rather than in bottle, and the resultant sparkling wine is subsequently bottled under pressure.

Transvasage is a method mid-way between the previous two, whereby the sparkle develops in the bottle, but the contents are then transferred under pressure into a vat for the final stage of the preparation.

Carbonation is an inferior way of providing sparkle by adding CO_2 'artificially' – the gas does not develop naturally through a secondary fermentation. The bubble never seems as well 'married' to the wine when this happens, and some drinkers find that this leaves uncomfortable after-effects and causes indigestion.

Sparkling wine, perhaps more than any other kind, illustrates the old maxim 'you get what you pay for'. Cheap sparkling wine produces a feeling that is far from effervescent: if the base wine is of poor quality, green, or unripe, no amount of bubble will disguise that fact.

France

Champagne It is the region – la Champagne – which gives its name to the sparkling drink – le Champagne. Each Champagne house has an individual style, shown most clearly in its *brut* non-vintage wines. These styles vary in weight: lighter Champagne is exemplified by Piper-Heidsieck and Laurent Perrier; fuller Champagne by Roederer and Krug. A Blanc de Blancs is lighter than the more usual black-white blend or Blanc de Noirs: Le Mesnil is a marvellous Blanc de Blancs, from the Union des Propriétaires-Récoltants at Le Mesnil-sur-Oger. *Crémant* (literally 'creaming') Champagnes have less pressure in the bottle: about four atmospheres compared with five to six for standard Champagne. Three Champagnes are bone dry: Brut Sauvage from Piper-Heidsieck, Ultra Brut from Laurent Perrier, and Brut Intégral from Besserat de Bellefon.

The Champagne houses also make vintage wines, from a single year; some make a *de luxe cuvée,* which is a blend considered to be superior, whether vintage or non-vintage; and a rosé Champagne.

If one had to distinguish between Champagne and some of the other very good sparkling wines made around the world, it would perhaps be the bouquet and persistence of taste on the palate that held the key to the difference. The smell of true Champagne is like no other, and unbelievably tempting. If you don't find this irresistible, try one of the many other good alternatives. Besides, when the mood is frivolous and the guests are numerous, a good alternative to Champagne is the sensible choice.

Other sparkling wines Excellent Bourgogne Mousseux and Crémant de Bourgogne come from the firm of André Delorme. The sparkling wines of Saumur and Anjou are well made by Ackerman-Laurance, Gratien-Meyer, Bouvet-Ladubay, Veuve Amiot and Langlois-Château. Sparkling Vouvray is first rate from Marc Brédif, Aimé Boucher and Monmousseau; the latter is also responsible for delicious Crémant de Loire. Dopff au Moulin are well known for Crémant d'Alsace.

'Regional' sparkling wines, which are found more in France itself than on the export market, are Blanquette-de-Limoux, made in the Languedoc by the Champagne method, and Clairette-de-Die from the Rhône. The latter is made by the Champagne method when *brut,* and otherwise by an old process call the *méthode dioise* – which involves bottle fermentation – when slightly sweet and more Muscat-flavoured. Neither should be missed.

Veuve du Vernay is an example of a non-AC sparkling wine made in France, where only wines made by the *méthode champenoise* merit an *appellation contrôlée* designation.

Champagne houses
These are the main houses with a reputation for high quality:
Ayala; Besserat de Bellefon; Bollinger; Deutz; Canard-Duchêne; Giesler; Gosset; George Goulet; Alfred Gratien; Heidsieck Dry Monopole; Charles Heidsieck; Piper-Heidsieck; Krug; Lanson; Abel Lepître; Mercier; Moët & Chandon; Mumm; Joseph Perrier; Laurent Perrier, Perrier-Jouët; Philipponat; Pol Roger; Pommery & Greno; Louis Roederer; A. Rothschild; Ruinart; Salon; Taittinger; Trouillard; de Venoge; Veuve Clicquot.

Storing sparkling wine

Champagne (the only sparkling wine that is worth while laying down) is the most difficult of all wines to store. It is extremely sensitive to heat, to fluctuating temperatures, and also to light. In perfect cellar conditions allow both non-vintage and vintage Champagnes to improve for a few years in bottle. Otherwise, don't take the risk.

Magnums are the ideal size for laying down vintage Champagne. The magnum is the largest bottle in which the wine is actually made. For the larger sizes of bottle, from Jeroboam upwards, the secondary fermentation takes place in normal bottles and the Champagne is disgorged into the giants when required.

Half bottles are risky if not drunk quite young: more halves than bottles go flat. They also cost more than just half the price of a full-sized bottle. It is better to open a full bottle and protect the contents with a pressure top if the Champagne is not all consumed at one sitting.

Spain

The area of Penedès, near Barcelona, is the home of Spanish sparkling wine. It is an old-established industry here, and very fine *méthode champenoise* wines (often known as *cava* wines) are made from quite different grapes – the Parellada, Xarel-lo and Macabeo. Although the wines are made with infinite care and attention to detail, which results in high-class sparkle, these grape varieties ensure that the taste is more 'earthy' than that of Champagne. Reliable names are Codorníu, Freixenet, Segura Viudas and Monistrol.

Italy

The range of sparkling wines in Italy is vast: given that the Italians are among the foremost consumers of Champagne, they clearly like the bubble. All Italian sparkling wine is called *spumante*, whether it be sweet or dry, Champagne or Charmat method. '*Metodo champenois*' on the label indicates that the wine had its second fermentation in bottle. Top *brut* wines made by this method include Riccadonna President, Cinzano Brut, Ferrari Brut, Contratto Brut and Cesarini Sforza. Amongst Charmat method *brut* wines, Baccarat, Gancia Pinot di Pinot and Venegazzù Prosecco are good value. Pinot grapes are used for the best dry wines, often with a small proportion of other grapes added. Prosecco is the name of a grape and of a sparkling wine made in north-east Italy: it can be either slightly sweet or dry. Prosecco sparklers with some sweetness include Cantina Colli del Soligo and Col Sandago, both from the Conegliano DOC. Asti Spumante and Moscato Spumante are always sweet and grapy, tasting of the pungent Muscat. Asti Spumante is always very good from Contratto, Martini & Rossi, Fontanafredda, Gancia and Cinzano.

Germany

Most German sparkling wine is bought by brand name or by grape variety, rather than geographical origin. The sparkle in *Sekt* or *Qualitätsschaumwein* (quality sparkling wine) must have been introduced by secondary fermentation in bottle or in tank; sparkling wine that meets less rigorous technical standards is known as *Schaumwein*.

The best Sekt wines come from the Riesling and Elbling grapes, but there are other, more pungent styles of Sekt. Deinhard's Lila is very fine, and shows off the finesse of the Riesling grape. Henkell Trocken is another reliable name, as are Kupferberg, Matheus Müller and Sohnlein.

USA

In California, the two finest sparkling wines come from Domaine Chandon, owned by Moët & Chandon, and Schramsberg. Both make their wine by the *méthode champenoise*. Domaine Chandon never call their wine 'Champagne' in deference to the English-French ruling which decided that only the wine from the Champagne district of France was entitled to the name. Many American wineries use the word indiscriminately. Both Domaine Chandon and Schramsberg make several *cuvées* or types of Champagne, including a Blanc de Noirs predominantly from Pinot Noir, which results in a pinkish wine.

Other Californian sparkling wine houses are Kornell and Korbel, but most of the big wineries produce sparkling wines to complete their range of still wines. Two New York State firms – Gold Seal and Great Western – produce sparkling wines. Europeans might well find that they taste faintly of apples.

Semi-sparkling wines

A category of wine mid-way between true sparkling wines and perfectly still wines is characterized by a slight prickliness on the tongue and a lively, refreshing taste. Such wine is described as *pétillant* in French, *spritzig* in German and *frizzante* in Italian.

Such *pétillance* is caused by residual carbon dioxide in the wine, which gives a lovely freshness. The prickliness of these wines, with their pleasant CO_2, should not be confused with the fizziness of Portuguese rosés and German Perlwein, which are artificially carbonated.

SUGGESTED TASTINGS

Try tasting a group of Pinot/Chardonnay sparkling wines to see regional differences. Compare a Crémant de Bourgogne, a non-vintage Champagne Brut from France, Domaine Chandon from California and Spumante *metodo champenois* (e.g. Ferrari or Cesarini Sforza) from Italy.

Alternatively, put up a top Spanish sparkler (e.g. Codorníu or Freixenet) against a Korbel or a Kornell from California. Both types have distinctive tastes and plenty of flavour, rather than refined subtlety.

Finally, put a top German Sekt against a sparkling wine from Saumur: the grape varieties are different, but the wines are comparable in weight – both are light.

FORTIFIED WINES

These wines are so named because at some stage during their vinification they are 'fortified' by the addition of either brandy or rectified alcohol. This has the effect of stopping the fermentation before all the sugar has been converted into alcohol, so most are sweet – and hence often regarded as synonymous with 'dessert wines'. They are usually between 16 and 20 per cent alcohol.

An exception is Sherry, which is always fermented to complete dryness and fortified later; any sweetening wine is also added at a subsequent stage.

The most celebrated fortified wines of the world are Sherry and Port, both of which have many imitators. Others are Madeira, Marsala, Málaga and the sweet fortified wines made from Muscat.

drink, a wine of great distinction and class and an example of some of the most skilful blending in the world. (Like Port and Champagne, Sherry is an example of high-class blended wine.) But often blends made to suit a commercial need, however successful the brand, are disappointing to those who know what fine Sherry is all about.

What kind of Sherry to drink when
Always buy the best you can afford, and search out the less widely distributed, fine-quality Sherries. This may mean going to specialists, or importers to find out sources of supply.

Serve Fino chilled, and don't keep it too long opened – after 3-4 days it loses its freshness, but in the refrigerator it will keep well for a week. Serve Amontillado, Oloroso and sweet Sherries at room temperature. These keep a little longer, though the aerating action of decanting them will hasten oxidation.

Serve Sherry in wineglasses, especially ISO tasting glasses rather than in the customary Sherry glasses, which are often too small.

Sherry is very seasonal – Fino is lovely when the weather is hot, and Amontillado and Oloroso when there is a nip in the air. Sweet Sherries are perfect with fruit or nuts.

Store Sherry bottles upright (an exception to the rule for wine bottles), since the spirit in the blend can damage the cork – but also affords the wine adequate protection against oxidation.

SHERRY

If there is one drink that the English man or woman will have in the cupboard, it will be Sherry, although this taste is not so extensively shared by Americans. Sherry comes from the Jerez area of southern Spain – hence the derivation of the name; wines of similar nature from anywhere else, however good, can only be called Sherry-type wines. The best Sherry still certainly comes from Jerez but, unfortunately, some of the cheaper brands are the result of 'buying down to a price' and a good Sherry-type wine from South Africa, for example, may well be better.

Really good Sherry is an unforgettable

Wine-making

The climate, terrain and historical skills of Jerez combine to make one of the great fortified wines of the world. The best vineyards are on fine calcareous soil, called *albariza*, because of its extreme whiteness, which captures and stores the spring rain to feed the vines during the arid summer months. Less good soils are the darker *barro* and *arena*, which has some sand. The topography consists of vine-covered, gentle slopes: however, soil and not site rules where vines are planted within the permitted area.

Before the white Palomino grapes are pressed, a small amount of gypsum, or *yeso*, is sprinkled on them. This effectively increases the tartaric acid content of the must, often necessary in a hot climate.

Following fermentation, the wine in cask or butt is not 'topped up' to avoid oxidation, as in other parts of the world, but air is allowed to reach it. This enables the special film of yeast cells, known as *flor*, almost unique to Sherry, to form on the surface of some casks a few months after fermentation. The covering prevents the wine from becoming vinegary and also imparts a special flavour and character to it.

Classification

The wine is classified at intervals during maturation. Each butt has a character of its own and nothing can alter the style it chooses to follow at the outset. But after the first classification, the best light wines (those with the most *flor*) are only slightly fortified by an addition of alcohol, while the lesser wines (with less style and *flor*, and slightly coarser) are fortified to between 17 and 18 per cent alcohol, which kills off what *flor* there is. Thereafter the wines with *flor* are called *fino*, and those without, *oloroso*.

As the wine develops, the fine wines with *flor*, called *palma* and *palma cortada*, can be divided into lighter or fuller styles – later, the lighter ones will be *finos* and the fuller styles will be 'real' *amontillado* (as opposed to sweetened commercial blends which call themselves Amontillado).

A medium category, *palo cortado*, is an intriguing, delicately flavoured wine, more full-bodied than *fino* and without *flor*.

Sherry is naturally completely dry; sweet styles are made by adding sweetening wine.

Fino Sherry is the light style, excellent for drinking fresh and cool. True Amontillado

Sherry is aged Fino, when the wine gains weight of bouquet and a slightly nutty flavour – genuine Amontillado is not sweet, although nearly all commercial Amontillados are sweetened to become 'Medium'. True Amontillado will not be cheap, as there is ageing involved. Palo Cortado is a category of its own, combining characteristics of a light Oloroso and a true Amontillado, but it is rare. Oloroso is fuller, rich in flavour, but dry in finish.

The *solera* system is the one process in Sherry-making that both attracts and mystifies the consumer. Given the way that each butt of Sherry develops in its own fashion, some sort of equalizing is necessary to produce a consistent type of wine. Wines of identical nature are put into the same *solera*. It is a special feature of Sherry that if, say, a third of the wine is taken from a butt and it is then filled with a younger wine of similar nature,

the new wine will take on the character of the older wine. Consequently, a style can be perpetuated by a regular system of *soleras*, scaled down in age so that the wines enter the system when quite young, and emerge in a mature style which is ready to be sold.

Only the most expensive dry Sherries come direct from the *solera*, however. Cheap Sherries have as their base a mature *solera* wine, and may then be blended with a very young wine indeed. The more expensive the Sherry, the more mature *solera* base wine will be in the blend. Sometimes, with a very fine old Sherry, such is the concentration that only a little is needed to add class and distinction to the blend.

Sweetening wine is now mostly made from the Palomino grape, and the principle is the same as for Port – alcohol stops the fermentation before all the sweetness has been fermented out. When Moscatel sweetening wine is used, the grapy smell of the variety is often detectable on the 'nose', which detracts from true Jerez character. Most Sherries are slightly fortified once more before being exported, which is why a Fino will be several per cent lighter in alcohol when drunk in Andalusia than when drunk in Britain or America.

Manzanilla is produced in the cooler coastal region of Sanlúcar de Barrameda. It goes straight into a *solera* system, always with *flor*, and goes up the scale rather more rapidly than a Fino Sherry. The lightest wine is Manzanilla Fina, delicate and with a salty tang; when it ages it becomes, first, Manzanilla Pasada, and then Manzanilla Amontillada. There is even a Manzanilla in Oloroso style, with no *flor*, but a marked character. Manzanilla is a subtle change from Sherry and well worth looking out for.

GRAPE VARIETIES

The dominating Sherry grape is the **Palomino Fino**, which can make dry or sweet Sherries. There is now very little **Pedro Ximénez**, but the **Moscatel** survives for making sweet wines.

SOME RECOMMENDED SHERRIES

MANZANILLA Solear Manzanilla Pasada (Barbadillo); La Lidia (Garvey); Manzanilla Pasada Piedra (Gonzalez Byass); Manzanilla (Harveys); La Guita (Ramiro Perez Marin); Manzanilla (Don Zoilo)
VERY DRY FINO Duke of Wellington Fino (Bodegas Internationales); Carta Blanca (Blazquez); Fino (Croft); Tres Palmas (De la Riva); Palma (Diez-Merito); La Ina (Domecq); San Patricio (Garvey); Tio Pepe and Elegante (Gonzalez Byass); Bristol Fino and Luncheon Dry (Harveys); Dry Lustau (Lustau); Fino Quinta (Osborne); Tio Mateo (Palomino & Vergara); Apitiv (Sandeman); Fino Campero (de Soto); Inocente (Valdespino); Fino Oliver (Wisdom & Warter); Fino (Don Zoilo)
OLD FINO Fino Imperial (Diez-Merito)
VERY DRY AMONTILLADO Amontillado Extra Tonel, Amontillado Viejisimo Reserva, Guadalupe (De la Riva); Tio Guillermo (Garvey); El Duque (Gonzalez Byass); Fine Old Amontillado (Harveys); Tio Diego (Valdespino)
AMONTILLADO Finest old Amontillado (Cuvillo); Botaina (Domecq); Amontillado del Duque (Gonzalez Byass); Reina Victoria (Harveys); Los Cisnes (O'Neale); Royal Esmeralda (Sandeman); Royal Palace (Wisdom & Warter); Amontillado (Don Zoilo)
VERY DRY OLOROSO Oloroso Seco (Barbadillo); Cartujo (Bobadilla); Rio Viejo (Domecq); Alfonso, Apostoles (Gonzalez Byass); Dry Lustau (Lustau); Viejo Oloroso 1830 (De la Riva)
PALO CORTADO Capuchino (Blazquez); Palo Cortado (Cuvillo); Solera Palo Cortada (De la Riva); Palo Cortado (Harveys); Palo Cortado (Lustau); De Luxe Sherry (sweetened) (Sandeman); Dos Cortados (Williams & Humbert)
OLOROSO Fabuloso (Cuvillo); Oloroso Extra Tonel 1806 (De la Riva); Victoria Regina (Diez-Merito); Flor de Jerez (Garvey); Matusalém (Gonzalez Byass); Royal Corrigidor and Imperial Corrigidor (Sandeman); Solera 1804 (Valdespino); Walnut Brown (Williams & Humbert); Oloroso (Don Zoilo)
RICH DESSERT OLOROSO A Winter's Tale, As You Like It (Williams & Humbert)
CREAM SHERRY Sanlucar Cream (Barbadillo); Nectar Cream (Gonzalez Byass); Casilda Cream (O'Neale); Armada Cream (Sandeman); Choice Cream of the Century (Wisdom & Warter)
SWEET BROWN SHERRY Old East India (Williams & Humbert)

MADEIRA

Madeira is very much a wine of our days, in spite of its place in history. While it holds the distinction of being the longest-living wine (people who have recently tasted Madeira from the eighteenth century attest to its good state), most of it is made for far quicker consumption!

Madeira always has excellent acidity to balance the sweetness, and this imparts an element of austerity and dryness to the finish of even the sweetest wines. It is this 'battle of the tastes' which is so intriguing.

Wine-making

The mountainous island of Madeira lies in the Atlantic, to the west of the Moroccan coast, and belongs to Portugal. The naturally temperate climate and the volcanic nature of the soil contribute to the ease with which everything grows here; the only problem can be rain at vintage time.

Like Port, Madeira was originally an unfortified wine. When the wine was exported, the heat and movement of a long sea voyage was found to improve its taste. So, the wine was then deliberately sent on 'the round voyage'. When this became too expensive a procedure, a system was devised to simulate, on shore, the effects of a long, hot sea voyage.

This process in the vinification of Madeira wine is called *estufagem*, and it no doubt contributes to the longevity of the wine – although the volcanic soil and careful preparation are other factors. After fermentation, the wine is heated by one of two methods. In the first (the hot vat system), it is put into vat and heated by means of hot water circulating through stainless-steel coils at the base of the vat, causing the hot wine to rise and circulate. The wine is also 'roused' by a propellor or compressed air. The heating process must last for a minimum of 90 days, and the heat must not go above 50°C. The top-quality wines, on the other hand, are treated by a more gentle process. They are heated for longer and to a lower temperature, by keeping in casks in a hot store. Some Shippers finish off their hot-vat wines with a period in the hot store. The top-quality wines are also fortified before the heating process, but the wines of normal quality are fortified afterwards, since the loss of alcohol during the process would otherwise be too costly.

There are two ways of sweetening the rich Madeiras. This can be done by arresting the

fermentation when there is still residual sugar (the Port principle) or by fermenting the wine until it is quite dry, and then adding very sweet must. The first method probably produces the finer wine in the long run, but in a straightforward Madeira which is intended for relatively young drinking, it is not important.

After the *estufagem*, the wine is rested for over a year, after being fortified with alcohol rectified to 99.6 per cent (not with brandy as

---

GRAPE VARIETIES

The first vines on the island were the famous **Malmsey**, followed by **Bual**, **Verdelho** and **Sercial**. The names of these grape varieties are now applied to the styles of Madeira wine: Malmsey is the sweetest then Bual and Verdelho in descending sweetness, and finally Sercial, which is dry. A small proportion of these grape varieties is still grown, but there is much more **Negra Mole**, which could originally have been the French Pinot Noir. The wine it produces is called Tinta, or 'Tent'. In the past, famous wines were made from the **Terrantez** and the **Bastardo** grapes, but these now appear only in wine auction sales.

in Port). The final fortification before shipment will give Madeiras an alcohol content of 18 per cent. Madeira is not shipped before its fifth year; selected wines for Vintage and Solera Reserves are put into cask for more maturation.

Unfortunately, dated Soleras are almost a thing of the past. The character of the wine of the original vintage date was kept by judicious additions of similar wine which 'blended' in. Straight Vintage Madeira is rare, but obtainable. Malmsey and Bual are the two types of Madeira most suitable for laying down; if it is rich and strong, Verdelho, too, is suitable.

Types of Madeira

Sercial is the driest Madeira, wonderful as an aperitif. It is also the palest in colour. Tinta is often blended into it to soften the initial harsh taste. The bouquet is slightly 'nutty' and with age its dryness becomes more mellow.
Verdelho is a golden colour, which darkens with age. It has style and medium body, finishing dry.
Bual is darker, very fruity and full-bodied. It could be described as Medium Rich, and is not as heavy as Malmsey or Port, with great mellowness of flavour.
Malmsey is the darkest Madeira, with a very fragrant nose and great, luscious flavour. Over the years, it will become a bit drier and very complex.
Tinta, or **'Tent'** wine, is now used for blending or sweetening, but old Madeira bottles can bear this name.
Rainwater is a blend, which describes a wine which is pale golden, soft and easy to drink, with a touch of sweetness.

Old Madeira has a particular 'bottle stink' when first uncorked, so it requires decanting. A Madeira 20 years old could take decanting six hours before drinking.

Occasionally, a Madeira house will bring out a special wine to mark a centenary or other anniversary. These are usually splendid wines. Two examples, on the market recently, are Duo Centenary Celebration 1745/1945 Bual and Special Reserve Very Old Bual Royal Wedding, both from Cossart Gordon.

Some recommended Madeira houses

Cossart Gordon & Co; Rutherford & Miles; Leacock & Co; Blandy Brothers; T.T. da Camara Lomelino; Henriques & Henriques; H.M. Borges; Vinhos Barbeito

PORT

Port was the creation of the British, and the finest Ports are still to be found in British cellars; happily, however, other nations are discovering its undoubted merits. Some countries do import in greater quantities than Britain, but this is mostly Port of rather cheap, young Ruby quality, for aperitif drinking. To the British palate, Port is hardly best placed before a meal, when its sweetness and alcoholic strength combine to cut the appetite. It is preferred at the end of a meal, when there is the time and inclination to digest, and to appreciate its incomparable flavour.

As with Sherry, true Port may come only from one area; but its style is imitated with varying success in other parts of the world, e.g. Australia and South Africa. Californian examples to note are Ficklin's Tinta Port and Paul Masson's Rare Souzao Port.

Wine-making

Port comes from the region in the north of Portugal which stretches along the Douro river from about 100 kilometres east of Oporto to the Spanish border. The finest area is that of the Upper Corgo with its centre at Pinhão. It is steep and wild, with the vines grown on terraces blasted out of the hard, schistous soil which is most suitable for Port.

All aspects of both the land, such as altitude, slope, aspect and soil, and of the grape variety, including the age of the vines, the method of

Types of Port

Wood Port is, essentially, matured in wood; Vintage Port is matured for the greater part in bottle.

Wood Port is of three main types: Ruby, Tawny and White. Young Ruby Port is the cheapest because there is less financing and stocking involved in its production. White Port can be sweet or dry, but is best when bone dry and tangy. Cheap Tawny Port is a mixture of Ruby and White Port, and there is really little difference between it and Ruby. 'Real' Tawny, however, is aged Wood Port, which becomes tawny-coloured as the years go by; with age, it also acquires a slightly drier, more austere taste which is fascinating. Along with the quite different Vintage, this is the greatest Port taste. Some old Tawny Ports have an indication of age on them, such as 10, 15, 20, 30 or over 40 years. At about 20 years old they have a real nutty flavour, whereas those at 40 years old have great concentration, but can sometimes be a bit too 'dried out'.

A further category of Ruby Port is Vintage Reserve or Vintage Character, which is of very high quality and matured longer than Ruby. These wines are made for people who like a full, fruity taste and a Port which is easy to serve. As Wood Ports, they throw their deposit in cask and need no decanting. All Wood Port is ready for drinking when sold.

Vintage Port is quite a different thing. It occurs only when a year is 'declared', which is when a Shipper thinks that particular vintage is outstanding. Sometimes not all Shippers declare the same year, but this is natural in an area as varied as the Douro. The properties from which a Shipper usually takes his Vintage-quality Ports may be in a sub-region particularly favoured one year. He must not take too great a quantity away from his lots of maturing Wood Ports, and what he declares must be balanced with demand. But Vintage Port, by definition, is always an exceptionally good wine. It is bottled in its second or third year and thereafter matures in bottle.

Some shipping houses own exceptionally fine and large *quintas*, and so you get single-*quinta* Vintage Ports, often in years 'in between' the Vintage Ports of the owning houses. Late-Bottled Vintage Port is bottled between the fourth and the sixth years of its life. As it is matured in wood for longer than Vintage Port, it does not have a deposit, but it

training and the yield, are graded, and a points system is used to classify the properties.

A mass of grape varieties, all of Portuguese origin, is permitted in Port production. Different types suit different soils, and this can change from valley to valley.

Some of the old, picturesque vinification, with men treading the grapes, still exists on small properties, or *quintas*, but most Port is now made with modern machinery. As much colour as possible is extracted from the grapes, since a deep colour is desirable in Port.

At the stage during fermentation when the must contains 4-6 per cent natural alcohol, it is put into a vat and fortified with brandy, thereby raising the alcohol content and arresting the fermentation when there is still residual sugar – which is why Port is both sweet and high in alcohol.

In the spring after the vintage, the Port is brought down to the large airy sheds, or lodges, in Vila Nova de Gaia, Oporto.

The Port houses are the lynch-pin of the trade. The wine is made by big farmers and cooperatives, as well as by the Shippers, but it is the latter group which is known on the export markets. They each have their 'house style', and develop brands whose consistency they maintain year in and year out. As there is no Sherry-like *solera* system in the production of Port, perpetuating a distinctive character requires tasting and blending. Evaluation puts the different Ports into 'lots' from which the shipping 'marks' will be made up.

also lacks the colour, body and enormous character of Vintage Port. However, LBV wines are excellent in their own right, as long as they are not confused with true Vintage.

Crusted Port is not seen very often now. It does not come from a single year but is a blend that is ready to drink when comparatively young; however, since it is bottled young, it throws a deposit and should be decanted.

Tasting Port
Vintage Port provides a challenging game for the wine world, in which you guess which year and which house are responsible for the wine in the glass. Each declared year has a distinctive character of its own, and each Port house has its own style, which is possible to recognize once you know it. For instance, Taylor and Fonseca have a 'classic' style, quite hard and austere when young and very deep-coloured. Warre and Cockburn are most distinguished, often with a wonderful nose. Quinta do Noval has a wonderful fruity taste to it. Croft has great fullness and fruit, and Offley is very scented. Graham is attractive and luscious, seemingly a touch sweeter than the others. But there is no 'bad' Vintage Port: it must be one of the safest of all wines to buy.

All the Port houses do a whole range of Ports. The finest will always be expensive. You do not get a magnificent 20-year-old Tawny such as Sandeman's Imperial without paying for the quality and the ageing. Other favourites are Cockburn's Director's Reserve, an excellent Tawny, Warre's Nimrod and the Noval 20-year-old.

Among Late-Bottled Port, Graham and Noval are particularly good. Taylor make superb Late-Bottled Vintage Reserve – this is always with a date. Fonseca's Bin 27 Vintage Character has something of the classic, austere style of the Vintage of this house. Cockburn's Special Reserve is another Vintage Character of quality, a bit softer than the Bin 27.

Some leading Port houses
A.A. Calem & F. Lda; Cockburn Smithes & Co Ltd; Croft & Co Ltd; Delaforce Sons & Co; Dow & Co; A.A. Ferreira; Fonseca; W.J. Graham & Co; Guimaraens Vinhos SARL; Kopke; Mackenzie; Morgan; Offley; Quarles Harris; Quinta do Noval Vinhos SARL; Rebello Valente (Robertsons); Sandeman; Smith Woodhouse; Taylor; Tuke Holdsworth; Warre & Co.

Other fortified wines
Fortified wines made from the Muscat grape are perhaps the most voluptuous-tasting in the world. The glorious grapy aroma is followed by full, luscious fruit on the palate. They are fruit and wine at the same time. The shades of colour and sheer, vibrant warmth deserve labels by Rubens or Titian.

Muscat-de-Beaumes-de-Venise from the French Rhône Valley has one of the most beautiful wine names. The wine can vary from amber to spun gold, but it should always be drunk young and slightly chilled to appreciate the fruity Muscat at its most appealing.

Moscatel de Setúbal, made in Portugal, south of Lisbon, is a truly fascinating fortified wine. Here, barrel-ageing is a feature of the wine production. As the wine matures, it softens and becomes richer, darkening with the decades and taking on whole new flavours far removed from fruity Muscat grapiness.

Great Liqueur Muscats are one of the half-hidden treasures of Australia, especially as made by Morris, Bailey and Chambers, all in north-east Victoria. In South Africa, the best Muscat dessert wines come from Worcester.

Málaga, from southern Spain, varies from dry to very sweet. The most interesting wines, e.g. Solera Scholtz 1885, combine a luscious character with an intriguing dry finish.

Marsala, made in Sicily from a variety of grapes, ranges in style from dry to sweet, long-aged to less-aged: young Marsala is sweeter.

PART TWO: THE WINE PRODUCERS

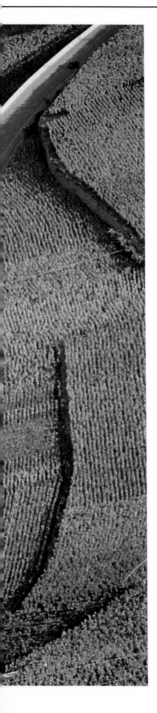

Just like people, wines reflect their background and origins. To understand the wine in your glass thoroughly, it helps to know where it comes from, how it was made, whether the sun shone on its harvest and what traditions influenced it – its pedigree.

To enjoy a wine, you don't *need* to know whether it was made in an ultra-modern winery or in a hut in the hills. But any mnemonic for an elusive taste-memory which helps you rediscover a taste that pleased (and to avoid one that did not) must be valuable. It helps wine orientation world-wide to associate the Cabernet grape flavour with Bordeaux in the south-west of France. It is useful to know whether a country's wine laws fulfil a taste standard or simply guarantee the place of origin and conformity with wine-making and bottling regulations. Remembering where a wine comes from (and the part various harvest conditions play in its making) explains, for example, how there come to be Vouvrays of varying sweetness.

Country-by-country, wine-making practice is examined. Which wines are made by traditional methods, which by new; which are attuned to esoteric local tastes, and which may be made sweeter or stronger for particular export markets. Which wines are popular and which are neglected. Which wines to seek out on business or vacation trips, because they will not reach the wine shops back home. Which wines are best with local food and sunshine, and which are better suited to a formal dinner on return.

By looking at systems of quality control, at changing wine-making methods and fashions, this section provides signposts to understanding the taste. By not only challenging – but explaining – misconceptions (wine from Spain is party plonk; Burgundy is heavier than Bordeaux; hot-country wines are unsubtle), these pages give the map references and compass bearings for a voyage through the world of wine.

France is treated in greatest depth, since the variety and traditions make it a touchstone for wine-makers the world over.

FRANCE

F OR BETTER or worse, France provides a yardstick for fine wines all over the world. It generally lives up to this reputation by producing very fine wines indeed; but it has sometimes exploited its success, with wines that rely on their origin rather than on their quality.

Nevertheless, both wine-makers and wine drinkers continue to look to France for inspiration. Innovative producers in countries relatively new to wine-making still set their standards by comparing their wines with those produced in France.

Diversity as well as quality has helped to create this dominant position in international wine-making. Most types of wine can be made, from dry red, dry white and sweet white wines, sparkling wine *(vin mousseux)* to fortified wines *(vins de liqueur* or *vins doux naturels)*.

Although tradition still plays a large part in French wine-making, over the last 20 years an appreciation of the advantages of technology has grown, and new methods are being adopted everywhere. Along with oak barrels and cultivated yeasts, this knowledge also is exported to wine-makers world-wide.

France can be divided into wine-making chunks: Bordeaux in the south-west; the Loire extending into central France from the west; Burgundy, the Rhône, Savoy and the Jura in the east; Alsace and Champagne in the north-east; and Provence, Languedoc and Roussillon in the south. Very few areas have no vines at all (Normandy is an example), but some areas are far more densely covered with them than others.

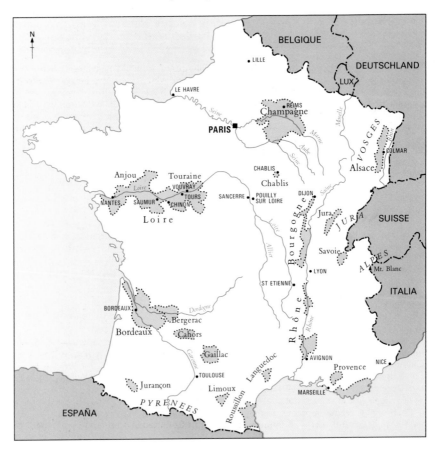

HOW FRANCE DEFINES QUALITY

AC	The best wine in France is nearly always *Appellation Contrôlée*, which means that it comes from the area designated on the label. It will also have been subjected to rules governing the grape	varieties permitted, the amount of wine that can be made from the given vineyard, the alcohol level, and the viticultural and vinification processes. Most AC wines are now tasted before they are passed and can acquire the status.
VDQS	*Vins Délimités de Qualité Supérieure* (VDQS) have rules resembling those for AC but less	strict on such aspects as yield and zones of production. The wines must be tasted and passed before they can become VDQS.
Vin de table	*Vin de table* is the wine often referred to as *'vin ordinaire'*. Within this category come *vins de pays*,	which have a regional origin, whereas *vin de table* bears only the designation of the country (or countries) from which it comes.

FRENCH GRAPE VARIETIES

THE GRAPE variety, on the whole, denotes the type of wine made in an area. The red wines of western France are dominated by both Cabernet Sauvignon and Cabernet Franc, with Merlot as boon companion. Cabernet Sauvignon, which ages well, predominates in the Médoc region of Bordeaux, where it is mixed with a smaller proportion of Merlot and Cabernet Franc; the roles are reversed across the Gironde in St Emilion and Pomerol, where the larger proportion of Merlot makes wines that are drinkable earlier but also mature well.

These three grape varieties are found all over south-west France, and the Cabernets have also travelled to the Loire for wines such as Chinon and Bourgueil.

The red wines of eastern France are dominated by Pinot Noir, the grape variety of the Côte d'Or and Côte Chalonnaise in Burgundy, and an ingredient in Champagne. The red wines of northern Rhône are made from Syrah, while the southern Rhône and the whole of the South of France is under the influence of Grenache, with Syrah and Cinsault making some contribution. Though Pinot Noir has less tannin than Cabernet, the top Burgundies can age well; the sturdy Syrah needs time to smooth out.

Chardonnay reigns supreme among the white wines of the east – Burgundy and Champagne – while Sauvignon dominates the white wines of western France. The west is also the home of Sémillon, a component of Sauternes and Barsac; of Muscadet, which makes the wine of the same name; and of Chenin Blanc of Touraine and Anjou on the Loire. Chardonnay grown on the best sites likes time in bottle to develop. When Sauvignon and Sémillon are combined to produce top-quality Sauternes/Barsac, the marriage needs time to settle after bottling; but Sauvignon alone, made into light, dry wines should be drunk young – as should Muscadet.

Alsace has a separate system, with a whole range of grape varieties which give their names to the wines made: Riesling, Gewürztraminer, Pinot Gris, Muscat and Sylvaner.

Of course, some grape varieties travel more than others. The red Gamay, entirely responsible for the Beaujolais family of wines (light, fruity and for young drinking), also crops up in the Loire and in small local wines in the centre of France. Cabernet has been making inroads into the vineyards of southern France, where it is used to add distinction to the wines produced from the southern mixtures of grapes. Then there are rarities such as Viognier, which makes the white Condrieu of northern Rhône.

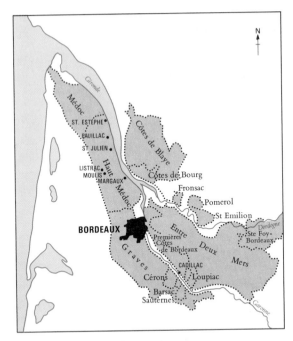

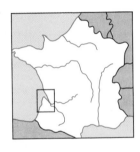

Bordeaux is famous for both the quality of its wines and its sheer size. In an average year, about 2,000,000 hl of AC red wine are produced, and about 1,000,000 hl of white. Bordeaux also produces just under 2,000,000 hl of red and white *vin de table*. There are no VDQS or *vins de pays*. The very breadth of choice can look daunting, but Bordeaux has a wine to suit most tastes and pockets.

BORDEAUX

Bordeaux can mean the dizzy heights of fine wine, or good-value, everyday drinking. The amount and variety of its wines are staggering: one could never stir from the region and drink well. It is not for nothing that other countries try to ape the Bordeaux wine style.

The Bordeaux wine-making region is divided by the great Gironde, which begins at the confluence of two rivers, the Garonne and the Dordogne. The Médoc lies on the left bank of the Gironde, while St Emilion and Pomerol are on the right bank. In fact, the vineyards of St Emilion, Pomerol and Fronsac are really around the Dordogne, while Blaye and Bourg are truly on the right bank of the Gironde. South of the town of Bordeaux lie the areas of Graves, Sauternes and Barsac, and, for sweet white wine, Cérons.

Between the Dordogne and Garonne lie the quantity-producing Entre-Deux-Mers and Premières Côtes de Bordeaux, both excellent sources of supply for good everyday red and white wines – some of the best value in France. Two small areas produce sweet white wines, Ste-Croix-du-Mont and Loupiac.

The Médoc is divided into four main *appellations:* from north to south, St Estèphe, Pauillac, St Julien and Margaux. Other areas in Haut Médoc are Listrac and Moulis. Wine bearing a label with any of these names will be red: dry white wine from this area is called Bordeaux or Bordeaux Supérieur.

St Emilion and Pomerol produce no white wines; Sauternes and Barsac are always sweet and white. Graves can be red or white: the latter is now mostly dry, but there is some medium-sweet. Entre-Deux-Mers is, nowadays, dry and white. Fronsac is red. Wines from Bourg and Blaye can be red or white, but the more often encountered reds are better.

Good basic Bordeaux Rouge and Bordeaux Blanc can come from anywhere in the area, but are less likely to come from, say, the Médoc than the Premières Côtes de Bordeaux. These are the wines the French themselves tend to drink.

THE GRAPES OF BORDEAUX

Why are such good wines produced in Bordeaux? The climate is temperate, influenced by the near-by Atlantic Ocean. Severe frost is rare (1956 was exceptionally bad), but rain at flowering time can affect the year's crop. A long, slow ripening period is necessary for the production of fine wines, and a warm, sunny September is essential for a good vintage.

Red Bordeaux, which the British often call 'Claret', is almost entirely made from Cabernet Sauvignon, Cabernet Franc and Merlot grapes, with a small amount of Malbec and Petit Verdot. White Bordeaux is made from Sauvignon, Sémillon and Muscadelle.

Usually, red Bordeaux is made from all three principal grape varieties, with only the proportions varying. The grapes are predominantly Cabernet Sauvignon in the Médoc, and predominantly Merlot and Cabernet Franc in St Emilion and Pomerol. Cabernet Sauvignon makes wines that are suitable for long ageing, so larger amounts of Merlot and Cabernet Franc tend to be used in modest wines intended for young drinking, rather than in those for laying down and keeping.

Inexpensive dry white Bordeaux is often made from the Sauvignon grape, perhaps with a little Muscadelle. Good-quality dry white Graves is made of Sauvignon and Sémillon blended. The same grape varieties are used for good Sauternes and Barsac, but the grapes are picked later so that they have more sugar, and should be affected by the fungus called *pourriture noble (Botrytis cinerea)* which gives a special, luscious taste and smell to the wine and only appears when the autumns are warm and humid. The harvest of these grapes can last until November, whereas the harvest for dry white wines and red wines usually runs from mid-September into October.

The only Graves in the 1855 Classification, Château Haut-Brion makes wines of great breed and delicacy. The vineyards lie in the *commune* of Pessac.

Wine-making

Wine-making in Bordeaux is traditional. Fine red wines and the best sweet white wines are matured in oak barrels (called *barriques*) which contain 225 litres. Dry white Sauvignon-based wines and the simpler red wines do not go into oak barrels but are stored in stainless steel or lined concrete vats until bottling. Bottling occurs when the wine is ready: 20-21 months after the harvest for a fine red wine, a year earlier for a lighter, more simple red wine, and in the New Year after the vintage for a fresh dry white wine. Wine kept in vat, protected by a covering of inert gas or carbon dioxide, does not oxidize or age rapidly, and therefore can be kept more or less in suspension until it is convenient to bottle it. Wine kept in barrel develops much more quickly, through the reaction of the oak on the wine and through oxidation, and so the correct bottling time must be judged much more exactly.

Vintages do vary in Bordeaux, as the distribution of sun and rain is different every year. The same amount of rain might fall in two separate years, but the wines made would be totally different because, for example, one year the rain fell at good intervals throughout the summer but was interspersed with hot, dry weather, whereas another year it fell in those last vital days before the harvest, and again during the harvest, thereby diluting the quality of the wine and causing the degree of sugar in the grapes to fall.

Choosing your Bordeaux

The top châteaux bottle their own wine, but many small properties (*petits châteaux*) sell their wine in bulk to *négociants* who bottle it for them. There are some cooperatives, which are more important in areas making pleasant, everyday wines than in AC areas.

The best wines in Bordeaux, coming from the best sites, are the most suitable for ageing. The Classified Growths provide (at a price) the finest of them; the *crus bourgeois* the next best. These are the wines that develop and improve with time – that are suitable for 'laying down'. If you buy them, have patience; in the meanwhile, there is a wealth of *petits châteaux* to enjoy.

When choosing wine, if you know one château name, but not another, take the wine from the better year. Wine from a not very good year will be more pleasant young than old and tired.

A Bordeaux Supérieur is not intrinsically better than Bordeaux, it just has half a per cent more alcohol.

Bordeaux négociants to trust

Barton & Guestier ● Calvet ● Castel Frères & Cie ● D. Cordier ● Cruse & Fils Frères ● CVBG (Maison Dourthe) ● A. Delor & Cie ● Dulong Frères & Fils ● Louis Eschenauer ● R. Joanne & Cie ● J. Lebègue & Cie ● Alexis Lichine & Cie ● Gilbey de Loudenne ● A. de Luze & Fils ● Borie Manoux ● Les Fils de Marcel Quancard ● De Rivoyre & Diprovin/Dubroca ● Schroder & Schyler & Cie ● Maison Sichel ● Sté Distribution des Vins Fins

What 'Château' means

The term 'château' riddles the wine gazetteer of Bordeaux with a bewildering suggestion of grandeur. In fact, the name is grander than the reality: there are comparatively few magnificent castles, and a château denotes a winemaking property; the actual residence of the owner/wine-maker is often modest. The *chais* or cellars can be more imposing, yet even this is a misnomer: because of the high water table, most cellars are above ground in the winemaking regions of Bordeaux.

A further psychological hurdle when coming to terms with Bordeaux is the seemingly rigid hierarchy in which some of the wines are placed. With hundreds of châteaux within each area, how is the drinker to know which is which and whether some really are better than others? Yes, some are better than others, by virtue of their privileged site, which should lead to wines of superior intrinsic merit: provided, of course, that the owner/wine-maker has quality in view.

1855 CLASSIFICATION OF THE MÉDOC

In 1855 a group of Bordeaux properties was classified according to the prices their wines had been fetching, and the châteaux (Growths) were put into five categories. All the Growths were in the Médoc, save one from Graves. Today there would be some shuffling of the pack, but the listing stands the test of time remarkably well, although some châteaux have disappeared, and the considerable price gap between First Growths and the rest is not always justified.

The *crus bourgeois*, or Bourgeois Growths, are the step just below the Classified Growths. In 1978 these properties were reassessed and divided into *grands bourgeois* (with 18 *crus exceptionnels*) and Bourgeois Growths, and the list will probably be reviewed periodically.

FIRST GROWTHS

Lafite-Rothschild (*Pauillac*) ● Margaux (*Margaux*) ● Latour (*Pauillac*)
Haut-Brion (Pessac, *Graves*)

SECOND GROWTHS

Mouton-Rothschild: decreed a First Growth in 1973 (*Pauillac*) ● Rausan-Ségla (*Margaux*)
Rauzan-Gassies (*Margaux*) ● Léoville-Las-Cases (*St Julien*) ● Léoville-Poyferré (*St Julien*)
Léoville-Barton (*St Julien*) ● Durfort-Vivens (*Margaux*) ● Gruaud-Larose (*St Julien*)
Lascombes (*Margaux*) ● Brane-Cantenac (*Cantenac-Margaux*)
Pichon-Longueville-Baron (*Pauillac*) ● Pichon-Lalande (*Pauillac*)
Ducru-Beaucaillou (*St Julien*) ● Cos d'Estournel (*St Estèphe*) ● Montrose (*St Estèphe*)

THIRD GROWTHS

Kirwan (*Cantenac-Margaux*) ● d'Issan (*Cantenac-Margaux*) ● Lagrange (*St Julien*)
Langoa-Barton (*St Julien*) ● Giscours (*Labarde-Margaux*)
Malescot-St-Exupéry (*Margaux*) ● Boyd-Cantenac (*Cantenac-Margaux*)
Cantenac-Brown (*Cantenac-Margaux*) ● Palmer (*Cantenac-Margaux*)
La Lagune (*Ludon-Haut-Médoc*) ● Desmirail (*Margaux*) ● Calon-Ségur (*St Estèphe*)
Ferrière (*Margaux*) ● Marquis d'Alesme-Becker (*Margaux*)

FOURTH GROWTHS

St-Pierre (*St Julien*) ● Talbot (*St Julien*) ● Branaire (*St Julien*)
Duhart-Milon-Rothschild (*Pauillac*) ● Pouget (*Cantenac-Margaux*)
La Tour-Carnet (*St Laurent-Haut-Médoc*) ● Lafon-Rochet (*St Estèphe*)
Beychevelle (*St Julien*) ● Prieuré-Lichine (*Cantenac-Margaux*)
Marquis-de-Terme (*Margaux*)

FIFTH GROWTHS

Pontet-Canet (*Pauillac*) ● Batailley (*Pauillac*) ● Grand-Puy-Lacoste (*Pauillac*)
Grand-Puy-Ducasse (*Pauillac*) ● Haut-Batailley (*Pauillac*) ● Lynch-Bages (*Pauillac*)
Lynch-Moussas (*Pauillac*) ● Dauzac (*Labarde-Margaux*)
Mouton-Baronne-Philippe: formerly known as Mouton Baron Philippe (*Pauillac*)
du Tertre (*Arsac-Margaux*) ● Haut-Bages-Libéral (*Pauillac*) ● Pédesclaux (*Pauillac*)
Belgrave (*St Laurent-Haut-Médoc*) ● de Camensac (*St Laurent-Haut-Médoc*)
Cos Labory (*St Estèphe*) ● Clerc-Milon-Rothschild (*Pauillac*) ● Croizet-Bages (*Pauillac*)
Cantemerle (*Macau-Haut-Médoc*)

BURGUNDY (BOURGOGNE)

'Burgundy' describes such disparate wines as Chablis, Nuits St Georges and Beaujolais. Sixty kilometres from Dijon to Chagny provide some of the best red wines in the world. The 'heart' of Burgundy is the Côte d'Or, or 'golden slope', which encompasses the Côte de Nuits in the north, between Dijon and Nuits St Georges, and the Côte de Beaune in the south. South of Chagny is the Côte Chalonnaise, rapidly becoming better known for its good-value Burgundies. Farther south appears the Mâconnais, particularly noted for its white wines, and these vineyards merge into the Beaujolais, famed for its attractive, easy-to-drink red wines. Chablis is an isolated area, roughly equidistant between Paris and Dijon.

Burgundy lies at the northerly limit for making fine red wine, and this shows in the differences between vintages, always more marked for red wines than for whites. With ripening a problem, the best sites are on slopes facing east or south. The soil is of a very complicated and varied nature, but red vines tend to be planted where marl predominates, and white vines where there is more limestone in the mix.

Chablis suffers from the most bitter weather conditions. Late frost is a constant danger here, but risks have been reduced on the best slopes by spraying systems installed during the 1970s. Water sprayed on to the vines freezes and forms a protective layer, preventing frost doing serious damage.

The continental climate is more marked in the Côte de Nuits than in other areas, but dry cold in winter, warm summers and good early autumns are what is expected in Burgundy. As everywhere in France, a warm, sunny September is essential for the grapes to ripen fully, and in Burgundy a good September has often saved a vintage after a mediocre summer. The Côte d'Or and Côte Chalonnaise can suffer from localized hail – the vines in one village can be badly hit, while the neighbouring village (and *appellation*) can escape entirely.

Vineyards at Monthelie on the Côte de Beaune. The wines of this *appellation* are faster-maturing than those of its better-known neighbour Volnay, but represent very good value. The Château de Monthelie is the best site.

Vineyards and growers

Burgundy is often called the greatest wine democracy by virtue of the way its vineyards are divided. There are few big estate holdings in Burgundy (a number of Beaune *négociant*, or merchant, houses are the exception), and for the most part the area is split into little parcels of vineyard, owned by a myriad of small growers.

Most of these *viticulteurs* are good at growing grapes, but less able at *élevage* or 'bringing up' a wine and bottling it; top estates are notable exceptions. Check the label to ensure someone good has done the *élevage*, especially when buying an Hospices de Beaune wine, or one from the Hospices de Nuits auction sales.

The word *clos* means that the vineyard is an enclosed one. There are no big châteaux in Burgundy, only growers' houses with cellars underneath.

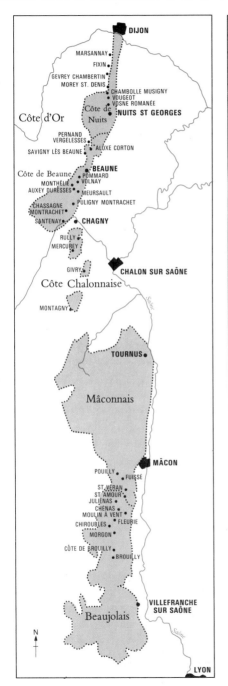

Map labels:
DIJON
MARSANNAY
FIXIN
GEVREY CHAMBERTIN
MOREY ST. DENIS
CHAMBOLLE MUSIGNY
VOUGEOT
VOSNE ROMANÉE
Côte d'Or
Côte de Nuits
NUITS ST GEORGES
PERNAND VERGELESSES
SAVIGNY LÈS BEAUNE
ALOXE CORTON
BEAUNE
Côte de Beaune
POMMARD
MONTHÉLIÉ
VOLNAY
AUXEY DURESSES
MEURSAULT
CHASSAGNE MONTRACHET
PULIGNY MONTRACHET
SANTENAY
CHAGNY
RULLY
MERCUREY
GIVRY
CHALON SUR SAÔNE
Côte Chalonnaise
MONTAGNY
TOURNUS
Mâconnais
MÂCON
POUILLY
FUISSÉ
ST. VÉRAN
ST AMOUR
JULIÉNAS
CHÉNAS
MOULIN À VENT
CHIROUBLES
FLEURIE
MORGON
CÔTE DE BROUILLY
BROUILLY
VILLEFRANCHE SUR SAÔNE
Beaujolais
N
LYON

THE GRAPES OF BURGUNDY

The red grape variety of the Côte d'Or and Côte Chalonnaise is Pinot Noir; Beaujolais is made from Gamay. Neither variety does so well anywhere else in the world: Pinot Noir does not make wines of such finesse when planted in a hotter climate, and Gamay particularly likes the granite-based soil of the northern Beaujolais, where the best Beaujolais Villages and the nine *crus*, or Growths, are produced. These are Fleurie, Moulin-à-Vent, Juliénas, Morgon, St-Amour, Chiroubles, Chénas, Côte de Brouilly and Brouilly.

The main white grape of Burgundy is the Chardonnay, which is responsible for the great white wines of the Côte de Beaune (all the wines of the Montrachet family, Meursault, white Corton), Chablis, and the white wines of the Mâconnais (Mâcon Blanc, Pouilly-Fuissé, Pouilly-Vinzelles, etc). The wines of the Côte de Beaune are the richest in flavour and texture and the most long-lasting. Chablis can make wines for drinking within a few years, but the *grands crus* need keeping longer. Drink the white wines of the Mâconnais young.

The other white grape variety of Burgundy is the Aligoté, which is grown in limited quantity, mostly on the Côte Chalonnaise. It can be most refreshing when the year has had plenty of sun, but if the grapes are not ripe enough, the wine made from the Aligoté can be rather green and acid.

Although Burgundy stretches for many kilometres from north to south, it is never wide, with the Côte d'Or at the narrowest point. Total production is only about one-third that of Bordeaux. In a prolific year, some 2,000,000 hl of wine are produced – perhaps half being Beaujolais. Only about 300,000 hl come from the Cote d'Or, a factor in the wines' high prices.

Apart from a VDQS wine made from Sauvignon in the Yonne (the same *département* as Chablis), no VDQS or *vins de pays* are produced in Burgundy.

91

Wine-making

Wine-making is essentially traditional in Burgundy, with the red wines and the best whites all being matured in oak casks or barrels of about 228 litres. Good red wines usually receive about 1½ years in cask before bottling, the whites a bit less. In Chablis and the Mâconnais, the white wines are often kept in vats of stainless steel or lined concrete instead of casks in order to give the wines freshness, rather than body. But the great white wines of the Côte de Beaune are even fermented in oak barrels (often new oak) to give extra 'backbone' to a wine that is not meant to be drunk for some years after its birth.

Much is talked about the Burgundies of today not comparing well with those of former times. Certainly there is great diversity of quality in Burgundy, a natural result of a vineyard area made up of hundreds of small growers, but the best of today's wines are much better than most Burgundy drunk in France and abroad by our forefathers. As the area is small, there was formerly considerable blending from outside the region, and wines were made to look much 'bigger' than they originally were – Pinot Noir does not, naturally, make heavy, purple-coloured wine. Some of the best sites, especially on the Côte de Nuits, can certainly produce wines of great depth of taste and flavour, but

CHAPTALIZATION
Chaptalization is an aspect of Burgundian wine-making that is often misunderstood. It is, quite simply, the addition of sugar to the unfermented juice to increase the potential alcoholic level. The sugar is converted into alcohol during the fermentation process and the wine made is, of course, dry. Chaptalization takes place only when the must has already attained the minimum alcohol levels required by the AC laws. A wine intended for keeping needs a fairly high alcohol level (12-13 per cent) to withstand the maturation process, and when chaptalization is carefully done, the effect is beneficial. This is not a process restricted to Burgundy (it happens in Bordeaux, for instance) but Burgundy seems to come in for more criticism than other areas.

some *appellations* in Burgundy produce fairly light-coloured wines, of fragrance and delicacy – Savigny-Lès-Beaune and Pernand-Vergelesses, for instance.

The wines are completely dry everywhere in Burgundy. *Grands crus* are the top wines made in the best sites. Then come *premiers crus,* and then the village or *commune* wines, i.e. straight Volnay or Nuits St Georges.

Négociants

Much of the Burgundy trade is handled by the *négociant* houses. Many of them have existed for a century or more, and they are centred on Beaune and, to a lesser extent, Nuits St Georges. They buy in wine from growers and mature, bottle and market it. As a result, they are often called *négociant-éleveurs.*

Which are better, *négociant* or grower wines? The answer is that there are good and bad wines within both groups. On the whole, the *négociants* who also own vineyards tend to be the most reputable.

Burgundy is not an area of cooperatives, the exceptions being found in the Mâconnais, where their

production is often taken up almost *in toto* by the *négociant* houses, and in the Beaujolais.

Some *négociants* might be criticized because their wines lack definition between the *appellations;* in other words, a standard 'house style' overrides the nuances of soil and site.

Négociants who own vineyards
Louis Latour ● Joseph Drouhin ●
Bouchard Père & Fils ● Chanson ●
Louis Jadot
Other reputable négociants
Bouchard Aîné ● Champy ● Clerget ●
Delaunay ● Faively ● Leroy ●
Maufoux/Marcel Amance ● Moillard ●
Remoissenet ● Ropiteau ● Thévenin

PRODUCERS TO TRUST IN BURGUNDY

CÔTE DE NUITS

Bouchard Père et Fils
Domaine Camus
Chicotot
Domaine Clair-Daü
Michel et Georges Clerget
Pierre Damoy
Delaunay (for Hautes-
   Côtes de Nuits)
Joseph Drouhin
Drouhin-Laroze
Domaine Dujac
René Engel
Faiveley
Domaine Pierre Gelin
Domaine Henri Gouges
Domaine Machard
   de Gramot
Gros
Hudelot (for Hautes-Côtes
   de Nuits)
Henri Lamarche
Louis Latour
Domaine Marion
Charles Noëllat
Domaine Jacques Prieur
Henri Rebourseau
Louis Rémy
Domaine de la Romanée-
   Conti
Domaine Roumier
Domaine Armand
   Rousseau
Tortochot
Trapet
Domaine des Varoilles
Domaine Comte Georges
   de Vogüé

CÔTE DE BEAUNE

Robert et Michel Ampeau
Domaine du Marquis
   d'Angerville
Comte Armand
Bachelet-Ramonet
Basancenot-Mathouillet
Henri Boillot
Bonneau de Martray
Bouchard Père et Fils
Chandon de Briailles
Chanson

Domaine de Courcel
Darviot
Delaunay
   (Savigny selections)
Joseph Drouhin
Dubreuil-Fontaine
René Fleurot
J.P. Gauffroy
Michel Gaunoux
Louis Glantenay
Machard de Gramont
Domaine de la Guyonnière
Louis Jadot
Joliot (for Hautes-Côtes
   de Beaune)
Domaine Comtes Lafon
Marquis de Laguiche
Louis Latour
Launay
Leflaive
Domaine du Duc de
   Magenta
Château de la Maltroye
Domaine Joseph Matrot
Maufoux
Prince de Mérode
Domaine du Château de
   Meursault
Bernard Michelot
Jean et René Monnier
Domaine de Montille
Domaine Albert Morey
Albert Morot
Domaine Parent
Domaine de la Pousse d'Or
G. Prieur
Domaine Jacques Prieur
Ramonet-Prudhon
Rapet
Ropiteau
Guy Roulot
Bernard Roy
Etienne Sauzet
Daniel Sénard
de Suremain
Domaine Baron Thénard
Roland Thévenin
Tollot-Beaut
Voarick

CÔTE CHALONNAISE

Cave Coopérative de Buxy
Chanzy
Jean Coulon
Delorme (Domaine
   de la Renarde)
Domaine de la Folie
Michel Juillot
Louis Latour
Monassier
de Suremain
Domaine Baron Thénard
Voarick

MÂCONNAIS

Dépagneux
Joseph Drouhin
Georges Duboeuf
   (Mâcon- Prissé)
Louis Latour
   (Mâcon-Lugny)
Piat (Mâcon-Viré)
Domaine Jean Thévenet

BEAUJOLAIS

Dépagneux
Duboeuf
L'Eventail de Vignerons
Ferraud
Gobet
Loron
Piat
Louis Tête
Trenel

CHABLIS

Bacheroy-Josselin
La Chablisienne
Dauvissat
Jean Durup
William Fèvre
Lamblin
Long-Depaquit
Louis Michel
Moreau
Albert Pic/Regnard/
   Michel Remon
Raveneau
Servin
Testut
Vocoret

RHÔNE

Rhône wines provide some of the best value in France. Basic Côtes du Rhône is one of the staple AC wines for the Frenchman. Since the area produces about 1,500,000 hl annually, it is wise not to buy the very cheapest and worth paying a little more.

Viticulturally, the Rhône is divided into the north (the Rhône Septentrional) and the south (the Rhône Méridional). They differ in climate, topography and grape-variety distribution. The north has the steep-sided slopes of the Rhône river, the hard granite of the Massif Central. The south has more rolling, flatter countryside, sometimes covered with huge stones (at Châteauneuf-du-Pape and Tavel, particularly). It also has the more scorching sun and the assiduous attentions of the mistral which blows down the Rhône valley.

In the steep vineyards of the north, particularly Hermitage, Côte Rôtie, Condrieu, St-Joseph and Cornas, where the vines can only be planted on terraces, production is far less than in the abundant south, where vines often roll as far as the eye can see and mechanical harvesting comes into its own.

Wine-making

Some Châteauneuf-du-Pape wines, still made in a 'traditional' way with long fermentation and time in cask, need maturing in bottle, but others are now made lighter. Gigondas is the next most 'weighty' wine, but the others are pleasant when young. Some Côtes du Rhône red wines are particularly light and fruity, with a tempting bouquet – reminiscent of young Beaujolais; these are made by the carbonic maceration process, and are for young drinking.

Northern Rhône

The northern Rhône has a group of well-known négociants, who are often important vineyard owners at the same time. The most famous 'name' of the northern Rhône is the family firm of Paul Jaboulet Aîné, who also have the Jaboulet-Isnard label. Their red wines are big and meant for keeping; their whites are made in a modern way, bottled young and destined for drinking soon after buying. The reds are the undoubted 'kings' of the region, with the La Chapelle Hermitage, Domaine de Thalabert in Crozes-Hermitage and Les Jumelles in Côte Rôtie leading the field. You will never be disappointed by a Paul Jaboulet wine.

Other important names are Chapoutier and Delas; the latter particularly good value for St-Joseph. Vidal Fleury makes superb Côte Rôtie, as does the firm of Guigal.

Even relatively small growers are now exporting their wines:
Côte Rôtie: Jasmin, Champet, Gérin.
Hermitage: Chave, Revol.
Crozes-Hermitage: Roure, Fayolle.
Cornas: Clape, de Barjac.
Condrieu: Vernay, Château du Rozay (Multier).
St-Joseph: Coursodon, Grippat.
The cooperative at Tain has wines of variable quality, but the best *cuvées* are good.

Southern Rhône

The southern Rhône has many co-operatives – a natural development in an area producing a huge amount of wine. There are also important estates, particularly in Châteauneuf-du-Pape, which is where you will be spending your big money. The big houses, or *négociants*, buy their wines most carefully, and the Jaboulet Les Cèdres is superb. Top *domaines* include: Château Rayas (very expensive), Domaine de Mont Redon, Domaine de Beaucastel, Chante Cigale, Clos de l'Oratoire des Papes, Château La Nerte, Château des Fines Roches, Château Fortia, Domaine du Vieux Télégraphe, Clos du Mont-Olivet. Domaine de Beaurenard, Domaine de la Solitude and Domaine de Nalys make lighter wines, nice for drinking after 3-5 years, while the others should taste at their most interesting at 5-10 years old, sometimes more.

Tavel Rosé, probably the most famous dry rosé in the world, should be drunk young, when it is pink and not tawny in colour. The cooperative is good here, as are properties such as Genestière, Aqueria, Forcadière and Trinquevedel.

Lirac makes thoroughly gulpable, robust red wines, as well as white and rosé. Among good *domaines* are Castel-Oualou, La Tour-de-Lirac, Rousseau, and Château de Ségriès, Devoy, Château St-Roch, and Les Garrigues. Philippe Testut is making excellent Lirac and, as he is also a grower in Chablis and so knowledgeable in white wine vinification, his white wine in Lirac is exceptional for the region. Many of these producers also have Côtes du Rhône wine. Côtes du Rhône Villages comes from specified villages such as Cairanne, Chusclan, Laudun, Vacqueyras, Vinsobres, Rasteau, Valréas, Visan, and Beaumes-de-Venise. Most of these villages have good cooperatives, which are happy hunting grounds for both the holidaymaker and consumers whose wine is imported.

Gigondas is a wonderful substitute for Châteauneuf-du-Pape when there is less patience (for keeping the wine) and less money in the pocket. The wines from St Gayan, Montmirail, St Cosmé, Raspail and Roger Combe are excellent.

Two good fortified wines, which can be drunk, slightly chilled, before or after a meal are made here. Rasteau is least known, and can be drunk with some cask age, but the delicious Muscat-de-Beaumes-de-Venise, now often seen outside France, should be drunk young to catch the full Muscat flavour. It is one of the few wines which really complements Christmas Pudding.

Coteaux du Tricastin is a wine region extensively planted during the 1970s.

In Côte Rôtie (the 'roasted' slope), in the northern Rhône, the Syrah is planted on steep hillsides. Groups of vines are trained up individual stakes to form pyramids.

Good *domaines* are Grangeneuve, and La Tour d'Elyssas. Further reasonably priced red wine can be had from the Côtes du Ventoux, where two good *domaines* are Les Anges and St Sauveur. Côtes du Lubéron is a VDQS, and the light red and white wines are pleasant.

THE GRAPES OF THE RHÔNE

Grape varieties are a very simple matter in the northern Rhône, where the red wines are all made from the Syrah grape, giving deep-coloured, tannic wines which last well. Côte Rôtie is one of the few red wines (Chianti is another) that has a small admixture of white grapes – in this case, the fragrant Viognier. The Viognier is grown nowhere else in the world and is responsible for the intriguing dry white wine of Condrieu and the rare Château Grillet. White Hermitage and Crozes-Hermitage are made from Marsanne and Roussanne.

St-Joseph is an *appellation* that is both red and white: the red wines can give real value, with something of the peppery taste of Hermitage across the river, but without its power and need to be matured.

Châteauneuf-du-Pape, Gigondas and Côtes du Rhône red wines from the south are dominated by the Grenache grape variety, which makes full wines, rich in flavour and warmth. But Châteauneuf-du-Pape also permits other grapes in its make-up – Syrah, Cinsault, Mourvèdre, and some white varieties.

THE LOIRE

Some of the most reliable drinking in France comes from the Loire valley and one of its specialities is dry white wine, which is gaining popularity everywhere. Apart from the crisp whites, there are fresh, fruity red wines which do not need ageing, and the ubiquitous rosés that are many people's introduction to wine. There are also a few great sweet white wines.

There are big differences between vintages, especially of quantity: spring frosts and poor flowering can take their toll throughout the region.

The viticultural Loire stretches from the west around Nantes, into Anjou, then Touraine, and finally to Pouilly and Sancerre. The terrain varies, but not dramatically; the vineyards are nearly always on relatively flat land, with the exception of the slopes of Pouilly and Sancerre, and some gentle slopes near Bonnezeaux in Anjou.

Climatically, the Atlantic influence is the strongest in the Muscadet area near Nantes, but it is still temperate farther inland, although winters can be cold. The areas round the River Layon in Anjou are particularly sheltered, as are parts of Vouvray, creating the conditions for making the sweeter white wines in which these areas specialize.

Soil is very mixed along the river, but generally the lighter wine comes from the chalky soil and heavier wine from the schist where the heat is better stored.

Muscadet

This is one of the most useful dry white wines of the world – perfect at any time, but especially lovely with seafood. The wine is named after its grape variety. Most Muscadet is from the Sèvre-et-Maine district, but you also see Muscadet des Coteaux de la Loire, and Muscadet just on its own.

Much is now made in a modern way, with vats often taking over from wooden barrels. The emphasis should always be on freshness, with the wine becoming good to drink in the spring after the vintage and lasting for a few years. *Mis en bouteille sur lie* on the label means that the

wine has been bottled directly off its lees which gives an extra fruity flavour and occasionally a touch of a 'prickle' to it. Good individual *domaines* are Château de la Galissonnière (adjacent properties are Château de la Jannière and Château de la Maisdonnière). Château de la Casse-michère, Domaine des Quatre Routes, Château du Cléray, Métaireu, Drouet and Guéry are all good names.

Gros Plant is a VDQS dry white wine produced in the Muscadet area. Buy it only after tasting or when it is a ripe vintage, otherwise it can be horribly acid.

Anjou-Saumur

The grape varieties change completely here. The dry white wines and the more rare sweet ones are made from the Chenin Blanc, which can be acid in very unripe years, or when too young, but after a year or two it rounds up and becomes much gentler on the palate. With enough sun, and occasionally *pourriture noble*, rare sweet *'moelleux'* wines can be made.

The red and better rosé (Cabernet d'Anjou) wines are made from the Cabernet Franc, but other grape varieties such as Groslot, Gamay and the Côt (Malbec) are used in the production of Rosé d'Anjou. Rosé d'Anjou will have a bit of sweetness, but can be pleasant when chilled. Rosé de la Loire is dry. But all these wines should have a pinkish, rather than a tawny, hue to them if they are to taste fresh. Basic red and white wines are called Anjou or Saumur and some are *pétillant*. Red Saumur-Champigny is usually delicious, with a fresh, 'sappy' taste of Cabernet. The wines from M. Filliatreau at Chaintres and the Château de Chaintres are both very good. But two big cooperatives are also recommended for all the Anjou-Saumur *appellations*, the cellars of the Vignerons de Saumur at St-Cyr-en-Bourg and Les Caves de la Loire at Brissac.

Saumur is also famous for sparkling wine, and the big houses of Gratien-Meyer, Ackerman-Laurance, Bouvet-Ladubay, Veuve Amiot and Langlois-Château are all good.

The specialities of Anjou-Aaumur are the wines of the Coteaux-du-Layon, which encompasses the other *appellations* of Bonnezeaux and Quarts de Chaume. Here the white Chenin wines are full, sometimes medium-dry, especially when young, but becoming softer and often richer as they age. In very hot years, the wines are superb examples of honey-sweet wine, and they keep for decades. The wines of Jean Baumard, Châteaux de Fesles, Bellerive, Bellevue and Guimonière are well known.

Savennières is a classy *appellation* in Anjou, famous for its dry white wines of La Roche aux Moines and La Coulée de Serrant. In ripe years they become quite rich, but in other years, and when young, they can have a steely edge to them, matched with finesse. The Château de la Bizolière, Château de Chamboureau, Château de la Roche aux Moines of Madame Joly and the Château d'Epiré are all highly prized.

Touraine

All types of wine, from the reds of Chinon and Bourgueil, to the white Vouvrays and Montlouis, and on to Sauvignon and Gamay de Touraine are made here.

Chinon, Bourgueil and St Nicolas-de-Bourgueil are red wines of real worth, usually at their best at about 4-6 years, and occasionally older. But relatively youthful fruit is one of the charms in these *appellations*. Well-known properties include, in Chinon, the Clos de l'Echo and those of the Raffault family. Two reputable Loire *négociants*, Aimé Boucher and Langlois-Château, produce excellent examples of both Chinon and Bourgueil. *Domaines* in Bourgueil and St Nicolas include the Clos de la Contrie, La Hurolaie, the Clos de l'Abbaye, and the wines of Paul Maître and Lamé-Delille-Boucard.

Vouvray can be dry, medium-dry or sweet, depending on the weather and the site. In a year with good weather, really ripe wines might be made from grapes grown in one or two sheltered spots, while the rest of the wine will be drier. The degrees of sweetness are described as *sec, demi-sec,* and *moelleux.*

One of the most famous names in Vouvray is that of Marc Brédif; some rare 50-year-old wines from here are still in good condition and taste fascinating. Other highly recommended names are M. Gaston Huet of the Haut-Lieu, M.

Foreau's Clos Naudin, M. Allias at the Petit Mont, M. Audebert with Coteau Chatrie, Prince Poniatowski at Le Clos Baudoin and the Château Moncontour.

Montlouis faces Vouvray across the Loire; similar, but never as luscious as top Vouvray, it is usually a touch lighter and more acid. Dardeau and Berger make good wines here. While visiting the Loire châteaux drink Chenin whites from Azay-le-Rideau and Amboise.

Gamay de Touraine and Sauvignon de Touraine are often cooperative wines and can be good value, but drink them young. Good Gamay comes from the banks of the River Cher, and Sauvignon from around Oisly-Thésée.

Pouilly Fumé and Sancerre are usually twinned, as they are produced so near one another and taste remarkably alike. Both from the Sauvignon grape, they are crisp, fairly pungent on the bouquet and well-defined in taste. Both should be drunk young, especially Sancerre – a Pouilly Fumé can be good at 3-4 years, although it is often drunk younger. People often call these wines flinty or steely – they smell of blackcurrant leaves. Pouilly-sur-Loire is another, much softer, unaromatic white wine made from the Chasselas grape. Ladoucette is the big name at Pouilly, and makes high-standard wines. Other good producers of Pouilly Blanc Fumé are Maurice Bailly, Serge Dagueneau, Michel Redde, Blanchet and Blondelet.

Sancerre has chalky hills and little villages, famed for their wine and goat cheeses. Good makers are Vacheron, Vatan, Gitton, Laporte, and Henri Brochard. The cooperatives at Pouilly and Sancerre make good wine.

Slightly cheaper but comparable Sauvignon wines come from nearby *appellations* of Menetou-Salon, Quincy and Reuilly, and these can be rewarding. Way south of here, there is the VDQS of St Pourçain-sur-Sioule making red and rosé from Gamay and light, dry white.

In the unlikely area of Poitou can be found the excellent VDQS wines of the Haut-Poitou, which are all made at the cooperative at Neuville-de-Poitou. The white Sauvignon is the best-known wine, in the style of Sancerre, but much more reasonably priced.

ALSACE

This highly individual region, now part of France, belongs more accurately to the people of Alsace themselves. The wines made in Alsace are probably the most consistent of all those of France: they are labelled with their grape variety.

The climate is continental, with hard winters and warm summers, but the vineyards of Alsace are protected by the Vosges mountains: the rain falls on their western slopes, making Alsace one of the driest regions of France. Frost is the biggest danger: in late spring it can seriously affect quantity. The plain of Alsace gives way to the vine-covered sub-Vosges hills running east-west.

An enormous multiplicity of soil types allows the ideal site to be chosen for each grape variety. Some (Tokay or Pinot Gris, and Pinot Blanc) are hardier than others, while the late-ripening Riesling must have a protected position. Almost all of the wines of Alsace are white.

The wine-growing area falls in the two *départements* of Bas-Rhin and Haut-Rhin. The most famous and most picturesque wine villages are those of Haut-Rhin, concentrated to the west of Colmar.

Wine-making

Wine-making is both traditional, using casks, and modern, using stainless steel vats. Big houses usually have a mixture of the two; smaller growers on the whole stick to wood. The sizes of casks differ widely, since there are often only small quantities of certain grape varieties and all have to be kept separate.

There are a number of historical site names where the slopes are particularly favoured, and it is now felt that it might be useful to name them on the label. A top echelon of *grands crus* is proposed – based on certain proven vineyards, not on a superior natural sugar strength.

All Alsace wines are bottled within the region of production. The 'big names' of the *producteurs-négociants* predominate on the export market (e.g. Hugel, who export 80 per cent of their wines, and Trimbach, 65 per cent). *Propriétaires-viticulteurs* and cooperatives are more important on the French market.

Names to trust in Alsace

Hugel (Riquewihr) International name with a well-deserved reputation for quality. Basic wine: Couronne d'Alsace or Flambeau d'Alsace. Top wines designated Réserve Exceptionnelle or Réserve Personnelle.

A big house like Hugel can take full advantage of special weather conditions in great *vendange tardive* years (1971, 1976): some top *cuvées* last for decades.

Trimbach (Ribeaupierre) is another international name. Wines of great elegance and austerity that appeal to purists. Top wines: Gewürztraminer Cuvée des Seigneurs de Ribeaupierre and Riesling Cuvée Frédéric Emile; also Clos Ste Hune. With 5-10 years of bottle age, depending on the year's character, this Riesling from a small, sheltered vineyard above Hunawihr, has a complex bouquet and a glorious, long taste.

Léon Beyer (Eguisheim) Makes fine *vendange tardive* wines. Top wine: Gewürztraminer Cuvée des Comtes d'Eguisheim.

Dopff & Irion (Riquewihr) Try their Gewürztraminer Les Sorcières and Muscat Les Amandiers; the rare Gewürztraminer Domaine du Château de Riquewihr is superb. Also Riesling Les Murailles.

Dopff au Moulin (Riquewihr) Excellent Gewürztraminer from the site of Eichberg.

Willm (Barr) Another excellent single-site Gewürztraminer: the Clos Gaensbroennel Grande Réserve Exceptionnelle.

Louis Gisselbrecht (Dambach-La-Ville) High-standard wines, remarkably good value.

Willy Gisselbrecht (Dambach-La-Ville) Really good wines.

Zind-Humbrecht (Wintzenheim) Unique style: some bottle age smooths out initial acidity in certain wines. Wines from the Rangen (Thann), Hengst (Wintzenheim) and Brand (Turckheim) are distinguished.

Schlumberger (Guebwiller) Unique style, big and earthy. Gewürztraminer and Riesling from Kitterlé slope; Gewürztraminer Cuvée Christine Schlumberger great in ripe years.

Renée Schmidt, Kuehn, Michel Laugel, Heim, Gustave Lorentz, Kuentz-Bas, Boeckel, Bott, Jux, Klipfel, Uller, Preiss-Henny, Preiss-Zimmer, Louis Sipp, Ziegler and Sparr are other really reputable houses.

Wiederhirn (Riquewihr) epitomizes the fine small grower, doing all the work himself with his son.

CHAMPAGNE

Champagne is a land of gently rolling chalky hills about 140 kilometres north-east of Paris. The Marne carves its way through the centre of the region, which has three principal sub-divisions: the Montagne de Reims, south-east of Reims, with famous Champagne villages such as Verzenay, Verzy, Mailly Beaumont-sur-Vesle, and Bouzy; the Vallée de la Marne with Dizy, Champillon, Ay, Avenay, Cumières and Hautvillers; and the Côte des Blancs south of Epernay with Cramant, Avize, Oger, Le Mesnil and Vertus. More isolated, to the south-east lies the Aube, where Champagne may also be produced. Most of the Champagne houses are in Reims, Epernay and Ay.

Cramant sometimes appears on a label as an individual village name. The most confusing, but rare, wine is Crémant de Cramant: a *crémant* Champagne from the village of Cramant on the Côte des Blancs.

Since 'still Champagne' sounds like a contradiction in terms, non-sparkling wine from this area is now called Coteaux Champenois. It can be red or rosé, but most of it is white and made from the Chardonnay grape. The wine

THE GRAPES OF CHAMPAGNE

The Montagne de Reims is famous for its Pinot Noir grapes, which give body and backbone to the Champagne blend. The Vallée de la Marne is also planted with Pinot Noir as well as Pinot Meunier, and the wines made here can be round and ripe. The Côte des Blancs, not surprisingly, is devoted to Chardonnay, which gives elegance and finesse to the blend. Wine from here which is not blended with Pinot Noir wine is called Blanc de Blancs.

is drier and has less body than white Burgundy (also made from Chardonnay). It is fresh and pleasant, but the price may seem high for the taste.

The still red wines are made from the Pinot Noir, mostly in the Montagne de Reims area. Again, when compared with red Burgundy, they lack intensity of flavour. Bouzy is the most famous name for red wine from the Champagne area; others are Ay, Ambonnay, Dizy, Cumières, Verzenay and Rilly.

Cobwebs of nylon netting protect the vines of Champagne from the birds. Grapes must be in prime condition and any damaged or diseased ones are still sometimes snipped out of the bunches.

SOUTH-WEST FRANCE

The wines of **Bergerac, Côtes-du-Buzet** and **Côtes du Marmandais** bear a family resemblance to the wines of Bordeaux, especially those from the right bank, such as Bourg, Blaye and the surrounding areas of St Emilion. The dominant red grape varieties are now the two Cabernets, Merlot and some Malbec; the whites are of Sauvignon (increasingly so, if dry), Sémillon and Muscadelle. These are wines to enjoy relatively young. **Pécharmant** is an *appellation* near Bergerac which can produce really good reds, and **Monbazillac** and **Côtes de Saussignac** make sweet white wine. Montravel can produce some good dry white wines.

Cooperatives at Monbazillac, the delightfully named Cocumont for Côtes du Marmandais and at Buzet (the Cuvée Napoléon is the best wine) are reliable. Single-property wines can sometimes be very good: in the Bergerac area, Château de la Jaubertie, Château Court-les-Mûts, Château de Panisseau, Château Fayolle; Château de Tiregand for Pécharmant. South of Bergerac, the **Côtes de Duras** makes roughly similar wines – drink the dry white Sauvignons when very young. The cooperative is a good source.

Red **Cahors** wines are predominantly made of the Malbec grape variety and are good, medium-bodied, with a normal bottle age of 3-6 years. The most important producer is the cooperative Les Côtes d'Olt at Parnac – look out for the vintage Cahors Comte André de Monpezat. Good *domaines* include the Château de Cayrou, Clos de Gamot, Clos Triguedina, Domaine de Pailhas, Domaine de Meriguet, Domaine du Cèdre and Château de Haute-Serre.

North of Toulouse there is a new *appellation*, the **Côtes du Frontonnais**, and here is a chance to taste a little-known red grape variety, the Négrette, which is mixed with a little Cabernet and Syrah. The cooperative at Villaudric is a good source of supply, and good *domaines* include the Château Bellevue-la-Forêt, and the Domaine de la Colombière.

Gaillac, which is almost next door, is now making some of the best dry, fresh, cheap white wines in France. Co-operatives abound here and are reliable. The Sec Perlé is a dry white wine with a slight 'prickle' on the tongue, and the red wines are predominantly Gamay and light. All drink well in the year after their vintage. Some of the best *vin de pays* in France is made here – the Côtes du Tarn, which is made well at the Cave de Cunac.

Madiran provides another chance to see an unusual red grape variety – this time, the Tannat, which is mixed with some Cabernet. The wine has character and very good flavour, and is good at between 4-10 years of age. The co-operative of Vic-Bilh produces the excellent Madiran Rôt du Roy, as well as *appellation* Béarn wines and the rare Pacherenc sweet wine – the dry version is more usual. Good *domaine* wines are Château de Peyros, Domaine la Place, Domaine Barréjat, Domaine Lalanne and Domaine Labranche-Laffont.

Jurançon is a name to conjure with, famous for rare *moelleux*, or sweet, wines, but better known nowadays for dry white wines. All have an intriguing taste, as the grape varieties are entirely local, with the Gros and Petit Manseng to the fore. The cooperative of Gan Jurançon exports, but also try the wines of the Cru Lamouroux, and the Clos Cancaillaū for the *moelleux* wines, with the Clos Uroulat and the Clos de la Vierge from the Cave Brana for Jurançon *sec*.

PROVENCE

Known for its dry rosés, Provence is now making some delectable red wines from basically the same grape varieties as those found in the southern Rhône, but often with some Cabernet Sauvignon in the mixture.

Côtes-de-Provence is the AC wine, but often the VDQS **Coteaux-d'Aix-en-Provence** can be finer. You should not miss Château Vignelaure (now rather expensive), the delicious Château de Fonscolombe with its other property, the Domaine de la Crémade, Château La Coste and Château de Beaulieu.

Much Côtes-de-Provence wine comes from big companies, such as Pradel. Brands in which to have confidence are

Rouge Estandon, Mistral and Bouquet de Provence Réserve. While in St Tropez, the tourist might like to call in on the excellent cooperative Les Maîtres-Vignerons de la Presqu'île de St Tropez. Castel-Roubine, Domaine des Féraud, Château Ste Roseline and Château de Selle are all recommended.

Bellet, Palette and **Cassis** are three *appellations* which have somewhat inflated prices because of their small size.

Bandol is more evident outside its area (near Toulon), and the red wines give a really good mouthful. Good *domaines* are Domaine Tempier, Château des Vannières, Moulin des Costes, Mas de la Rouvière, Domaine du Val d'Arenc, La Laidière, and the cooperative, Moulin de la Roque.

LANGUEDOC-ROUSSILLON

The Midi covers the whole of the South of France down to the Spanish border. A huge amount of awful wine is made here, from the wrong grape varieties, in the wrong way. The wines are often impossible to sell as themselves, and have either to be blended with some good, strong southern Italian wine or distilled into industrial alcohol.

But amidst the quantity, there is some quality. Large companies have taken an interest in the area, applied scientific methods to the wine-making, and provide some really worthwhile wines at low prices. The vast majority of the wines are red, and should be drunk within a few years of their appearance, but there are now a few fresh, dry whites.

The following companies inspire confidence: Sicarex-Méditerranée and Domaine Viticole des Salins du Midi (Listel); Francevin; Chantovent; Demolombe; Vignerons Catalans; SICA du Val d'Orbieu; Nicolas. Sometimes these companies market single-estate wines.

Appellations are **Corbières, Côtes du Roussillon, Côtes-du-Roussillon-Villages,** and **Fitou** – Faugères and St Chinian imminently so; VDQS wines are Costières du Gard, St Saturnin and Minervois, which are by no means less good. The *vin du pays* called Vin du Sable du Golfe de Lyon is excellent value.

CORSICA

Corsica is an enchanted, scented, sometimes wild island. Somehow, the scent of the maquis gets into the wines. All *appellation* wines are called **Vin de Corse,** with seven regional names: Patrimonio; Coteaux d'Ajaccio; Sartène; Calvi (Balagne); Coteaux du Cap Corse; Figari; and Porto Vecchio. Individual *domaines* are usually a good bet.

SAVOIE

Savoie is skiing wine, usually drunk after a hard day on the slopes of the French Alps. Vin de Savoie can be red, white or rosé, sometimes with the name of the village where the wine is made printed immediately afterwards on the label. **Abymes** and **Apremont** are two good examples. White **Seyssel, Crépy** and **Roussette-de-Savoie** are also popular.

The whites are never full but can be pleasant and dry. The reds are mostly made from Gamay or Pinot Noir and are light in weight and colour. Wines from nearby Bugey ar similar, and some white wines can have a slight 'prickle'.

JURA

The most famous wine of the Jura is the Sherry-like Vin jaune. It is rather an acquired taste, but has intriguing flavours imparted by the Savagnin grape variety, the long ageing in cask and the development of *flor*, the yeast cells which develop in Fino sherries from Jerez. **Château-Chalon** is the famous *appellation* for Vin jaune.

Vin de paille is a dessert wine of the area, made from grapes whih have been dried on straw mats or hung up to dry to increase the sugar content. You will also come across red, rosé and white wines, all on the slight side, and even *gris* wines— which are not grey, but rosé.

Arbois wines come in all three colours, although the prettily named L'Etoile is an *appellation* only for white and 'yellow' wine. Henri Maire is a huge firm in the Jura, which also has *domaine* wines.

THE APPEAL of German wine lies in its freshness and its fruit. Even in its simplest forms, it is a pleasant drink to accompany food or to be enjoyed by itself. With a growing export market, the pleasures of German wine are accessible in every sense.

The Rhine and its tributaries form the link between the 11 vine-growing regions of West Germany. Sometimes the connection is slender, for some of the vineyards seem to prefer the shelter of a secluded wood to the added warmth so often found beside a river or lake. Every successful vineyard enjoys a good micro-climate, to ripen the grapes even in indifferent summers. By harvest time in late autumn, the sugar in the grapes will be sufficient to provide the body expected of a light wine; and the crisp, refreshing style will come from the tartaric acid allowed to remain by the slow ripening process: thus the balance in German wine. The flavour will depend on the soil of the vineyard and on the variety of grape.

In 1979, 92,013 ha of vineyards were in production, almost 90 per cent planted with white wine varieties. The vineyards stretch from the Swiss border in the south to Bonn in the north. Through Schloss Johannisberg in the Rheingau region runs the 50th degree of latitude, on its way to Land's End in the extreme south-west of England and to Winnipeg in Canada.

In the northern vineyard areas, the best sites are usually found not higher than 160 metres above sea level. In the warmer south vines can be planted

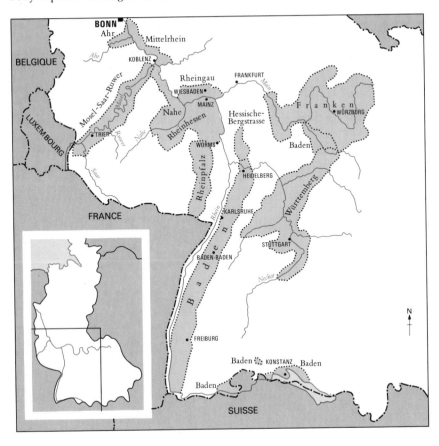

farther up the slopes. Over half the vineyards lie on sloping ground; the best are found on inclines of 30 per cent or more, facing south-south-east to south-west.

The region of Baden, lying parallel to the Alsatian vineyards across the Rhine in France, has, on average, 313 hours more sunshine between spring and autumn than Koblenz, in the Mittelrhein region farther north. Wines from the warmer south have less acidity than those from the Rheingau, the Nahe or the Mosel-Saar-Ruwer but it is these, with their balance of fruit and acidity, which have established an international reputation for German wines.

There are 11 *Anbaugebiete*, specified regions for vine growing, only five of which produce wine well known outside Germany. These are sub-divided into *Bereiche* (districts), and further into vine-growing communities, towns and villages, *Grosslagen* (collective vineyard sites), and *Einzellagen* (individual vineyard sites). A *Grosslage* consists of a number of *Einzellagen*, which must, by law, be at least 5 ha in size. Wine from

The attractive village of Zell on the lower Mosel is famous in Germany for its sprightly and fruity Schwarze Katz (Black Cat) wine.

any one *Grosslage* will be of potentially the same style and quality, for it is this that has dictated the establishment and lay-out of the collective sites.

GERMAN GRAPE VARIETIES

VITICULTURAL research institutes in Germany have put much successful effort into improving the quality of the existing vine varieties, and have developed new crossings within the family of the European vine, *Vitis vinifera*. As a result, the yield per hectare of grape juice is high, which helps to compensate for the expense of maintaining what are, sometimes, extremely steep vineyards. New crossings are judged by their performance in the vineyard, and, of course, by the quality of their grapes. The choice of vine available to a grower is controlled by law, and may vary from region to region. The two vines that were grown most widely in the 92,013 ha of German vineyards in 1979 were:

Müller-Thurgau (24,528 ha). Undemanding as to site, but likes a richer soil than the Riesling. Can yield up to 200 hl/ha, but more usually 100 to 150 hl/ha. Ripens early,

often in mid-September in the south. The wine is pleasant, soft, and develops quickly. The backbone of many commercial blends.

Riesling (18,269 ha). One of the great vines of the world, not to be confused with the Wälschriesling of Eastern Europe, which produces a sound, but far less distinguished wine. Yields from 70 to 110 hl/ha. Frost-resistant in winter, and ripens its crop as late as November. Probably at its most delicate on the Mosel and Nahe rivers.

In the last 30 years some 45 per cent of the viticultural area has undergone *Flurbereinigung*. This means the reconstruction of vineyards so that they can be worked more efficiently and economically, and the re-allocation of parcels of land among their owners with the aim of forming larger, more viable units. Since 1950, the yield per hectare has, on average, doubled, and this has helped to stabilize German wine prices.

MOSEL-SAAR-RUWER

Well over half of the 11,801 ha under vine in 1979 were planted in Riesling vines; Müller-Thurgau occupied a further quarter of the area, while Elbling formed a significant proportion of the remainder.

This is a region of exceptionally steep vineyards closely following the winding River Mosel, and mainly found where the slopes face south. The slaty, but technically varied, soil remains in position even on slopes as severe as 60-70 per cent. However, many steep vineyards have been abandoned in recent years as high labour and maintenance costs have made them uneconomic. In the best-situated sites, the Riesling produces wonderfully fruity wines of subtlety and elegance.

On more fertile soils, or in parts of the vineyard where the Riesling would not ripen easily, attractive, softer wines are made from the Müller-Thurgau grape. On the steep slopes, the vines are trained up posts, rather than along wires. They are often grown ungrafted on their European root-stocks, for the phylloxera vine louse does not flourish in Mosel slate.

There are many fine, long-established wine-making estates on the Mosel, particularly in the villages of Wehlen, Graach, Bernkastel, Piesport and Brauneberg. The ancient city of Trier has a number of well-known estate houses, covering vineyards on the two tributaries of the Mosel, the Saar and the Ruwer. Several district co-operatives also exist, with a central cellar at Bernkastel-Kues.

Most of the wines from this region are sold in the slender green 70 or 75 cl bottle that complements their elegance and freshness. They are light in alcohol, but rich in minerals. In years of little sunshine, the Bereich Saar-Ruwer, near Trier, produces wines which are crisp but neutral-flavoured, and which make excellent sparkling wine. The cheapest Mosel wine should be drunk when it is still young, but the fine Riesling wines need time if they are to offer more than agreeable fruit and acidity.

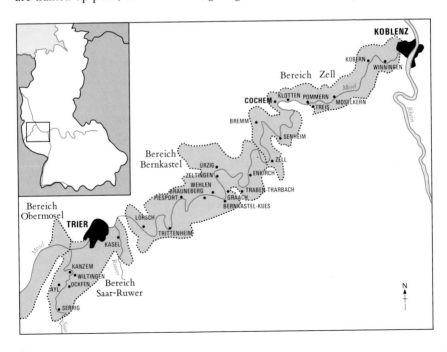

How Germany Defines Quality

As a member of the EEC, Germany places its wine under two main headings: table wine and quality wine. At harvest time, the must weight (of which sugar is the heaviest constituent) is measured in degrees Oechsle. The sugar content is seen as a good guide to the standard of the harvest. By law, the different officially recognized qualities of wine require musts of certain minimum weights, depending on vine variety and region. All the vineyards may produce both table wine and quality wine; there are no separate areas set aside exclusively for quality-wine production, as under the French *Appellation Contrôlée* system.

QbA	A quality wine from a specified region is known in German	as a *Qualitätswein eines Bestimmten Anbaugebietes*, or QbA for short.
QmP	There is a further, very important subdivision of German quality wine, bearing the description	*Qualitätswein mit Prädikat*, 'quality wine with distinction', usually referred to as QmP. (See also under 'Harvest' p110.).
DTW	These letters after a wine's name mean *Deutscher Tafelwein*, which	must be made from German-grown grapes and conform to strict standards.

The right to call a German wine by a quality-wine name, no matter how distinguished its pedigree, is given only after it has passed an examination by an official control centre, and received a control number to prove it *(Amtliche Prüfungsnummer)*. Samples of wine to be tested are sent in triplicate to one of nine centres, depending on their region of origin. Two samples will be retained by the control authorities for at least two years for reference. An official chemical analysis, a history, and details of certain treatments given to the wine accompany the samples. The system is not perfect, but it is a serious attempt to prevent unsound or incorrectly produced wine from reaching the market.

Recommended vine-growers (Mosel-Saar-Ruwer)

Weingut Forstmeister Geltz Erben (Saarburg)
Egon Müller (Scharzhof bei Wiltingen)
Staatsminister a.d. Otto van Volxem (Wiltingen)
Maximilian von Othegraven (Kanzem)
Weingut Edmund Reverchon (Konz-Filzen)
Weingut von Hövel (Konz-Oberemmel)
Reichsgraf von Kesselstatt (Trier)
Verwaltung der Bischöflichen Weingüter (Trier)
Güterverwaltung Vereinigte Hospitien (Trier)
Verwaltung der Staatlichen Weinbaudomänen (Trier)
Stiftung Staatliches Friedrich-Wilhelm-Gymnasium (Trier)
Weingut Thiergarten Georg Fritz von Nell (Trier)
Karthäuserhof Eitelsbach (Trier-Eitelsbach)
C. von Schubert'sche Gutsverwaltung (Grünhaus-Mertesdorf)

Weingut Milz (Trittenheim)
Johann Haart (Piesport)
Weingut Weller-Lehnert (Piesport)
Weingut Hauth-Kerpen (Wehlen)
Weingut SA Prüm Erben (Bernkastel-Wehlen)
Deinhard'sche Gutsverwaltung (Bernkastel-Kues)
Weingut Wwe. Dr H Thanisch (Bernkastel-Kues)
Stephanus Hermann Freiherr von Schorlemer (Bernkastel-Kues)
Weingut Dr Pauly-Bergweiler (Bernkastel-Kues)
Weingut T. Lauerburg (Bernkastel)
Weingut St Johannishof (Bernkastel)
Weingut Ehses-Berres (Zeltingen)
Nicolay'sche Weingutsverwaltung, CH Berres Erben (Ürzig)
Schneider'sche Weingüterverwaltung (Zell-Merl)

RHEINGAU

Of the 2,793 ha under vine in 1979, about three-quarters were planted with Riesling vines.

One of the driest regions of Central Europe, the Rheingau extends from the touristic Rhine Gorge near Assmannshausen, following the Rhine upstream in an easterly direction to Wiesbaden and its final outpost at Hochheim. For the most part, the vineyards lie on gently sloping or level terrain, protected by hills and ancient woods to the north. Terracing has almost disappeared from many of the vineyards and small tractors can be used to work them. They may be easily visited by road on the clearly signposted Rheingauer Riesling Route, or by well-defined footpaths.

The wine from Rheingau villages such as Rüdesheim, Geisenheim, Johannisberg, Winkel, Oestrich and Erbach, to name but a few, is exported widely, and especially to the main overseas markets for German wine – Britain and the USA. The largest State-owned cellar in Germany (196 ha) is found at Eltville in the Rheingau. Like most of the principal Rheingau estates, its vineyards are not concentrated around any one village, but are found in good

Terracing has now virtually disappeared from the hillsides of Rüdesheim. In such open country, the grapes attain full ripeness.

sites throughout the region. There are also many long-established estates of aristocratic or ecclesiastical foundation.

The classic Rheingau wine is made from the Riesling grape, and is renowned for its balance of flavour.

Recommended vine-growers (Rheingau)
Weingut Dr Heinrich Nagler (Rüdesheim)
Landgräflich Hessisches Weingut
 (Johannisberg)
Furst von Metternich-Winneberg'sches
 Domane Rentamt Schloss Johannisberg
 (Johannisberg)
G.H. von Mumm'sches Weingut
 (Johannisberg)
Schloss Vollrads (Winkel)
Weingut Fritz Allendorf (Oestrich)
Domaneweingut Schloss Schönborn
 (Hattenheim)
Schloss Reinhartshausen (Erbach)
Schloss Groenesteyn Weingut des
 Reichsfreiherren von Ritter zu
 Groenesteyn (Kiedrich)
Schloss Eltz Gräflich Eltz'sche
 Guterverwaltung (Eltville)
Verwaltung der Staatsweingüter Eltville
 (Eltville)
Freiherrlich Langwerth von Simmern'sches
 Rentamt (Eltville)
Weingut Königin Victoria Berg (Hochheim)

RHEINHESSEN

The area under vine in 1979 amounted to 21,864 ha, in which the principal vine varieties were the Silvaner, Müller-Thurgau and Scheurebe. Viticulture shares the rolling terrain of the region with other types of fruit crop and arable farming. About half the viticultural area is planted in vines less than 10 years old and many new crossings are found.

Towns such as Nackenheim (famous in the wine trade for its capsule factory), Nierstein, Oppenheim and Dienheim, south of Mainz, produce absolutely top-quality wines, softer than those of the Rheingau. In the hinterland of the region originates much of the sound, inexpensive but unexciting wine that finds its way on to the market under brand names, or as Liebfraumilch, or simply under the district names of Bereich Nierstein, Bingen or the lesser-known Wonnegau.

Of the great number of small growers in the Rheinhessen, few bottle their entire crop themselves, and much of the region's grape harvest is both handled and bottled by the well-equipped and efficient cooperative cellars, the first of which was formed in 1897 at Gau-Bickelheim.

Recommended vine-growers (Rheinhessen)

Weingut Villa Sachsen (Bingen)
Weingut Franz Karl Schmitt (Nierstein)
Weingut Adolf Schmitt'sches Weingut (Nierstein)
Weingut Geschwister Schuch (Nierstein)
Weingut Louis Guntrum (Nierstein)
Weingut Winzermeister Heinrich Seip (Nierstein)
Weingut J. u H.A. Strub (Nierstein)
Weingut Bürgermeister Anton Balbach Erben (Nierstein)
Weingut Heinrich Seebrich (Nierstein)
Weingut Carl Sittmann (Oppenheim)
Weingut Rappenhof Dr Reinhard Muth (Alsheim)
Brenner'sches Weingut (Bechtheim)
Weingut H. Stallmann (Ülversheim)

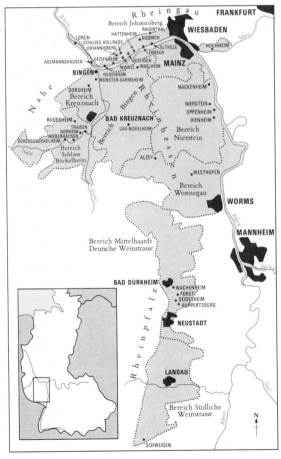

RHEINPFALZ (PALATINATE)

Of the 21,576 ha under vine in 1979, Müller-Thurgau was the most widely planted variety, followed by Silvaner and Riesling.

The region has a gentle climate, where figs and citrus fruits ripen and *Spätlese* (late-picked) wines can often be made from the best sites. The southern part of the region in the Bereich Südliche Weinstrasse normally has one of the highest yields per hectare in West Germany. A high proportion of Riesling is planted on top-quality estates in the villages of Wachenheim, Forst, Deidesheim and Ruppertsberg in the Bereich Mittelhaardt Deutsche Weinstrasse.

The modern Rheinpfalz wine combines the fresh style that pleases the consumer with a background flavour deriving from a heavy soil. As in the Rheinhessen, many new vine varieties are established in the Rheinpfalz. Their often scented bouquet and pronounced flavour seem appropriate to wines from these regions, whereas in the Rheingau or Mosel-Saar-Ruwer, for instance, a more neutral flavour is expected. *Kabinett* (See 'The Harvest and QmP') and *Spätlese* estate-bottled wines from the Rheinpfalz offer particularly good value for money, and cost less than those from the smaller Rheingau region.

Recommended vine-growers (Rheinpfalz)
Weingut Schlossgut Janson (Bockenheim)
Weingut Köhler-Ruprecht (Kallstadt)
Weingut Pfeffingen (Bad Dürkheim)
Weingut K. Fitz-Ritter (Bad Dürkheim)
Stumpf-Fitz'sches Weingut Annaberg
    (Bad Dürkheim)
Weingut Karl Schaefer (Bad Dürkheim)
Weingut Dr Bürklin-Wolf (Wachenheim)
Eugen Spindler, Weingut Lindenhof (Forst)
Weingut Reichsrat von Buhl (Deidesheim)
Gutsverwaltung Deinhard (Deidesheim)
Weingut Geheimer Rat Dr v Bassermann-
    Jordan (Diedesheim)
Weingut Hahnhof (Deidesheim)
Weingut Schlossgut Janson (Bockenheim)

GERMAN WINE LAWS

EEC regulations and German wine law lay down what procedures and preservatives may be used in wine-making – with extreme care being shown for the health of the consumer. As an attractive freshness is expected of all German white wines nowadays, the prevention of oxidation is a major preoccupation in its vinification and storage. The decorative, but expensive to maintain, wooden cask is rapidly giving way to the inert vat. The majority of German wines up to *Spätlese* or even *Auslese* quality are sweetened shortly before bottling with grape juice containing not more than one degree of alcohol *(Süssreserve)*. There are regulations concerning the origin and quality category of *Süssreserve* to be used with the various styles of German wine: e.g. a *Süssreserve* of QbA quality may not be added to a wine of *Kabinett* quality. The residual unfermented sugar in German wine, combined with a relatively low alcohol content, means that sterile bottling must be carried out so no yeast is found in the bottle after filling.

NAHE

Müller-Thurgau vines occupied almost a third of the 4,518 ha under vine in 1979; other principal varieties grown were Riesling and Silvaner.

The Nahe is a somewhat diffuse region, in which vineyards are found in isolation from each other wherever a favourable site is available. About a quarter of the vineyards lie on slopes of over 20 per cent, but terracing to retain soil is now rare. Between the major town of the area, Bad Kreuznach, and the village of Schlossböckelheim, there are massive rhyolite porphyry rocks, fragments of which provide a particular background flavour to distinguished Riesling wines from the villages of Traisen and Norheim. Probably the best-known wines of the region are made at Niederhausen where the State Cellars set extremely high standards in wine-making. The finest Riesling wines of the Nahe are comparable to those of the Rheingau, if lighter in style, but the number of top-quality sites and estates in the Rheingau is far greater.

Recommended vine-growers (Nahe)
Verwaltung der Staatlichen
    Weinbaudomänen Niederhausen-
    Schlossböckelheim (Oberhausen)
Weingut Jakob Schneider (Niederhausen)
Weingut Hans Crusius (Traisen)
Reichsgräflich von Plettenberg'sche
    Verwaltung (Bad Kreuznach)
Rudolf Anheuser'sche Weingutsverwaltung
    (Bad Kreuznach)
Weingut August Anheuser (Bad Kreuznach)
Staatsweingut Weinbaulehranstalt
    Bad Kreuznach (Bad Kreuznach)
Weingut Gutleuthof, Carl Andres
    (Bad Kreuznach)
Weingut Erbhof Tesch (Langenlonsheim)

Other specified regions
Of the remaining six specified regions, **Franken (Franconia)**, bordering the River Main, is probably the best known outside Germany. Its wines, sold in the flagon-shaped *Bocksbeutel*, have a positive, earthy character, but the region suffers from a severe continental climate which has been particularly un-cooperative in recent years. As a result, Franconian wine is often over-priced compared to wine from other regions of Germany. The wines of **Württemberg,** farther south, are mainly drunk within the region, with such enthusiasm that there is little left for outsiders. The region of **Baden,** most of whose vine-yards run between the Black Forest and the Rhine, delivers 85 per cent of its crop to the *Winzergenossenschaften* or Cooperative Cellars. They make wine with care, and market it with skill, promoting the name of Baden, rather than those of narrower geographical descriptions. The remaining regions for wine-making of the **Ahr, Mittelrhein** and **Hessische Bergstrasse** are all worth a visit, for their scenery is often romantic and nearly always pretty. In a good year, the last two can produce Riesling wine of a quality that makes it difficult to understand why it is not more widely known.

The eleven German vine-growing regions can produce either quality wines or table wines. The relationship of the quality-wine regional names to those reserved for table wines is shown in this chart.

Quality wine (QbA and QmP) Specified regions	Table wines (DTW) Regions	Sub-regions
Ahr		
Hessische Bergstrasse		
Mittelrhein	Rhein	
Nahe	und	Rhein
Rheingau	Mosel	
Rheinhessen		
Rheinpfalz		
Mosel-Saar-Ruwer		Mosel
Franken	Main	
Württemberg	Neckar	
Baden	Oberrhein	Römertor
		Burgengau

WHEN TO DRINK GERMAN WINES

Non-vintage simple quality wine can be drunk at the time of retail purchase. In general terms, other German wines are likely to be ready for drinking at the following intervals of time after the harvest. The particular characteristics of a vintage can lengthen or shorten the necessary period of maturation in bottle. The finest vintages, such as 1971 or 1976, will always take longer to develop. The individuality and complexity of German wine make it a rewarding subject for study – and fun to drink.

Wine		Drink after
Simple quality wine (vintage)	non Riesling	1 year
	Riesling	2 years
Kabinett	non Riesling	1-2 years
	Riesling	2-3 years
Spätlese		3-4 years
Auslese		6 years
Beerenauslese		8 years
Trockenbeerenauslese		8 years
Eiswein		8 years

THE HARVEST AND QmP

German grapes are usually gathered as and when they ripen, so the pickers may well visit the same spot several times before the entire crop is safely harvested. Once the date for the start of the harvest has been officially announced, each grower, when planning his picking programme, has to consider the relationship of sugar to acidity in his grapes, their general condition, and likely weather during the coming weeks. Fine weather can increase the must weight by one degree Oechsle per day, but rain can dilute the sugar content of overripe grapes to a similar extent. The following types of harvest are possible:

Vorlese
An early gathering of grapes before the main harvest, allowed when adverse weather conditions indicate that the crop would be lost due to excessive rot, damage from hail storms, etc.

Hauptlese
The general harvest, taking place between the *Vorlese* and the *Spätlese*.

Spätlese
The late-season harvesting of ripe grapes with an enhanced sugar content.

Auslese
The harvesting of grape bunches, specially selected for their advanced state of ripeness.

Beerenauslese
The harvesting of overripe top-quality grapes, in which the juice is highly concentrated through the action of noble rot or *Botrytis cinerea*, known in German as *Edelfäule*.

Trockenbeerenauslese
The harvesting of grapes attacked by noble rot, and dried on the vine; only possible in the greatest vintages.

Eiswein
To harvest an *Eiswein*, a temperature of at least −6°C is necessary, so that the grapes can be pressed with much of the water content frozen. A good *Eiswein*

The grapes are harvested by hand in the south-facing vineyards of Bacharach in the Mittelrhein. The steepness of these slopes defies the introduction of the more economical mechanized pickers which are now brought in wherever the terrain allows.

must will have a high sugar and acid content which gives the wine its style.

The descriptive distinctions *Spätlese, Auslese, Beerenauslese, Trockenbeerenauslese,* form part of the name of the wine that will later appear on the label. All fall into the QmP category, as will a *Kabinett* wine. This may be gathered at any stage during the harvest, but will have been produced from grapes with certain minimum must weights, greater than those needed for QbA, dependent on vine variety and region. As with all quality wines of distinction (QmP), no sugar will have been added to it to increase the alcohol content. Such enrichment is not allowed for German QmP wines, which depend on the total balance of their constituents, rather than a high alcohol content, for their character and style.

BUYING HINTS

As a result of the laws of inheritance, most of the German vineyards have many different owners. The average size of holding is 1.05 ha, even smaller in some regions; therefore, many small owners sell either their grapes, their must or their wine in bulk to larger concerns to form part of big blends. This means that the consumer can expect to find cheaper wines originating from large suppliers, and fine and more expensive wines from individual estates, though some shippers manage to fill both roles. Of the non-estate-bottled wines the most expensive may not always be the best, but the very cheapest will almost certainly be the worst, and offer the poorest value for money. In recent years, the real cost of German wines has increased relatively little, even on export markets.

The best-known style of German wine, Liebfraumilch, has become debased as a name in recent years by the flooding of the market with much poor wine. According to German law, a Liebfraumilch should be a quality wine from the Rheingau, Nahe, Rheinhessen or Rheinpfalz regions. You can expect to find it in stores where the standard of the other products on sale is also good.

The consumer must be on his guard against wines which appear to be German in origin, but in fact are the result of blending German wine or *Süssreserve* with wine from another country of the EEC — usually Italy. Such wines are often given a deceptively Germanic presentation in a German bottle, and only reveal their origin after an informed examination of the label. (See below: 'How the name is built up'.)

Since the early 1970s, Germany has been producing an increasing amount of *trocken*, or truly dry wine, with very little residual sugar. The worst may seem harsh and hollow; the best improve in bottle, having probably been enriched (i.e. received an addition of sugar) to increase their alcohol content, and will, therefore, fall into the simple QbA category. The wines from Franken, Rheinhessen, Rheinpfalz and Baden lend themselves well to presentation in this form.

The fragmentation of the German wine trade makes it difficult to advise what wines to buy at any given moment. It is probably useful to remember that those companies which are the most closely associated with German wine have the most to lose by shipping a poor product. Therefore, wines from Deinhard, Hallgarten, Langenbach, St Ursula Weinkellerei, Sichel and Siegel have a history and tradition behind them upon which the shipper's reputation depends.

HOW THE NAME IS BUILT UP

German wine names often seem formidable, to the point of incomprehensibility, but taken slowly they offer much useful information. The table shows how the different components in a name are built up.

The most basic wine shows the least detailed information on the label. The 1979 Oestricher Lenchen QbA – simple quality wine from the site of Lenchen near the village of Oestrich (with the suffix -er added, as in New Yorker) – has no mention of grape variety and no distinctive character derived from special harvesting conditions. This is a good, but certainly not a great wine, but the same vineyard in the same year could also produce the magnificent 1979 Oestricher Lenchen Riesling Auslese Eiswein QmP, and other wines with special attributes.

Vintage	Village name	Vineyard name	Grape variety	Quality category
1979	Oestrich	Lenchen	—	QbA
1979	Oestrich	Lenchen	Riesling	QbA
1979	Oestrich	Lenchen	Riesling	*Auslese* QmP
1979	Oestrich	Lenchen	Riesling	*Auslese Eiswein* QmP

ITALY

ITALY HAS THE greatest variety of wines of any country. This is hardly surprising in a nation with so much regional diversity. Just as human temperament, dialect, topography, food and architecture change radically from region to region, Italy's wines change identity and emphasis throughout the country.

It is probably the most rewarding country of all for the wine-loving traveller, because the regional wines are good, widely available and cheap. In other countries the choice often lies between famous, expensive names; rather neutral, nationally distributed brands, and not very pleasant local wines. In Italy it is nearly always safe to order the local wines, in bottle or carafe. Vastly increased export sales have not diminished the Italians' own enthusiasm for their product, and they expect and get interesting wine at all levels, from

PROVINCES

1	Valle d'Aosta	11	Marche
2	Piemonte	12	Lazio
3	Lombardia	13	Abruzzo
4	Trentino-Alto Adige	14	Molise
5	Veneto	15	Campania
6	Friuli-Venezia Giulia	16	Puglia
7	Liguria	17	Basilicata
8	Emilia-Romagna	18	Calabria
9	Toscana	19	Sicilia
10	Umbria	20	Sardegna

GRAPE VARIETIES
Bold Type red grapes
Italic Type white grapes

the most expensive to the almost derisively cheap. Those who do not believe this have probably had the misfortune to experience only the worst examples of exported Italian wines, and never the luck to meander through the country itself, sampling its wares in fine restaurants, country *trattorie* and homes. In months of travelling, one need not meet a bad wine. Fortunately for those of us who do not have the leisure for such an experience, many of these wines are now beginning to make their way abroad.

Italy is one of the world's largest wine-producers, making approximately 70,000,000 hl in an average year and 80,000,000 hl in a really generous one. These figures are proof of the good organization and husbandry of the Italian wine-producer, for much of the country is too mountainous for vine-growing. However, the Italians take advantage of every suitable slope, and much of the gently rolling countryside is covered with vines. The plains can produce good wine too.

Naturally, the areas where the real quantity is produced are not the most mountainous; the Veneto and Emilia-Romagna in the north, and Sicily and Puglia in the south. Equally to be expected, a great deal of this wine, especially from the two southern regions, disappears anonymously into blends, both in Italy and abroad, but this does not exclude fine wines from being made in their own right. Generally speaking, the better wines of the south are both less seen and less acclaimed abroad than those of the north, although they are much appreciated in their region of production. The Italian hardly ever drinks wines produced outside his immediate area, for within it he has a wide choice of type and quality.

ITALIAN GRAPE VARIETIES

LIKE FRANCE, Italy can be divided into rough areas producing different types of wine. The dynamic north-eastern provinces are strongly influenced by both French and German grape varieties, and hence their wines readily attract an admiring audience abroad. The reds include Cabernet Sauvignon and Cabernet Franc, Merlot and Pinot Noir (here known as Pinot Nero). Among the whites are Rhine Riesling (Riesling Renano) and Italico Riesling – of which more anon; Pinot Gris or Ruländer (here called Pinot Grigio); Gewürztraminer (Traminer Aromatico); Pinot Blanc (Pinot Bianco), Silvaner and Sauvignon. Both red and white wines are characterized, in general, by a youthful fruitiness and charm rather than by lengthy wood-ageing; but certain noble Cabernets from Trentino-Alto Adige are superb and will keep. Local grape varieties, such as Lagrein and Teroldego, should not be ignored.

In the north-west are long-lasting wood-aged red wines of tannin and substance, such as Barolo, Barbaresco, Gattinara, Carema and Ghemme. Nebbiolo, unique to the region,

and Barbera are the grapes most often used.

Emilia-Romagna produces good quaffing wine; the reds include Lambrusco and Sangiovese, while the whites are mostly made from Trebbiano. These last two varieties are the most widespread nationally, appearing in most regions. In central Italy – Tuscany and Umbria – Sangiovese reigns supreme, and is largely responsible for Chianti, Brunello di Montalcino and Vino Nobile de Montepulciano. White wines are made from Trebbiano, Malvasia and sometimes Vernaccia; on the Adriatic, Verdicchio makes a dry white.

In Latium, Malvasia and Trebbiano make the now dry and fresh Frascati. Farther south, some of the originally Greek grape varieties help to give an intriguing regional taste to Aglianico del Vulture, Taurasi, Greco di Tufo and Fiano. Montepulciano makes a wonderful red in Abruzzo, and the increasingly well-made white and rosé wines of the south are good buys.

In Puglia a fine red and rosé, Copertino, is made from Negro Amaro. A vast quantity of high-alcohol blending wine is made here and in Sicily and shipped all over Europe.

PIEDMONT (PIEMONTE)

Piedmont, in the north-west, is the area for grand red wines, often aged long in wood and ideal for drinking with meat and game. The name of the red grape variety producing the most famous wines, Nebbiolo, comes from the Italian word for the fog which makes its autumnal appearance in the green, rolling hills. Piedmont is prone to storms; consequently there are marked differences between vintages.

Much Barolo is still traditionally made with long fermentations and ageing in wood. The wines have an almost tarry nose and very dry, tannic taste, but also great flavour, especially when given plenty of decanting time. Barolo has to age for three years, two of them in chestnut or oak casks. These are much larger than the Bordeaux-sized barrels, so the wood influences the wine less. Barolo Riserva is aged for four years; Riserva Speciale for more than five. Barbaresco, made from the same grape, is softer and fruitier, and has a year less of ageing in each category.

Large companies like Fontanafredda perhaps make their wines more acceptable in taste to the foreign market, but more traditional tastes are produced by houses such as Ratti, with his marvellous Abbazia dell'Annunziata, and by Conterno, Giacosa, Ceretto, Oddero, Prunotto and the excellent Franco Fiorina. Many of these also make the best Barbarescos, as does Angelo Gaja.

Barbera, the commonest grape variety in Piedmont, can be made into fresh, robust wine for young drinking, but the Barberas of Asti, Alba and Monferrato are aged and have real character.

Another sometimes slightly fizzy red wine with a very vivid taste and purple colour is Dolcetto. The Dolcetto d'Alba of Franco Fiorina is recommended. Grignolino and Freisa, two further red varieties, are unfortunately becoming rather scarce.

In the north, towards Aosta, the great Carema is a red wine made from Nebbiolo, but less tough and tarry than Barolo. Luigi Ferrando makes the best Carema, and the unusual red Donnaz.

Much fine red wine is made in the Novara hills, mainly from Nebbiolo. The most famous names are Gattinara, Ghemme, Boca, Sizzano, Fara and Lessona, but the non-DOC Spanna (the local name for Nebbiolo) is also excellent, especially made by the Vallana family. Rich with glycerine and fruit, these wines often taste better for less wood-ageing than some of the DOCs. Luigi Dessilani and Brugo produce good Gattinara and other DOCs.

White wines are few and far between, and are thus expensive; they are generally dry. Gavi, or Cortese di Gavi, made from the Cortese grape, is the most famous; drink it young. Other wines are Arneis, Favorita and Erbaluce (the Erbaluce Passito is sweet); Fontanafredda make the good Vino Fiore and the super Pinot.

Wine snobs may scorn Asti Spumante as sweet and sticky but, ice-cold, this sparkling wine can be a treat. Fontanafredda and the big vermouth houses make the best.

The vast size of the casks in which the Barolo of Fontanafredda is matured means that the ratio of wood to wine is relatively low, and the tannic influence of the wood not excessively drying.

HOW ITALY DEFINES QUALITY

DOC Italian wines flooded on to the markets abroad after the wine laws had been established in the early 1960s. The system of Denominazione di Origine Controllata, or DOC, was roughly based on the French Appellation Contrôlée system, with some modifications, and currently applies to some 200 wines. As with the AC system, the DOC cannot guarantee quality, but it goes some way towards establishing conditions conducive to it in both vineyard and winery. Place of origin, grape variety or varieties (often with the proportion specified, unlike France), yield, alcohol level and viticultural and vinification processes are laid down, and inspections made. Specifications can be precise, detailing the material in which the wine has to be aged, and the duration of the ageing. The alcohol level of Italian wines may be raised by the addition of concentrated must, rather than by chaptalization.

The Veneto produces most DOC wine, Tuscany only a little less; the greatest proportion of DOC wine to total output is made in Trentino-Alto Adige.

Vino da tavola Certain very good Italian wines are not DOC, but *vino da tavola*. Some of these are among Italy's best, but do not come into the DOC category for a variety of reasons, among them a non-authorized choice of grape varieties, a lack of wood-ageing before bottling (because the makers are – rightly – convinced that this does not suit their particular wine) and the use of vineyards which fall outside the designated area. Most *vino da tavola* is, however, straightforward wine for young drinking.

DOCG Also, unlike France, Italy has a category superior to DOC: the DOCG (G stands for *garantita*), which is as yet neither fully operational nor visible on labels. It will involve even tighter controls.

LOMBARDY

In Lombardy, the ingredients are all there, but sometimes the wines are not sufficiently well made to be great. Perhaps 'could do better' is most true of the red wines made in northern Lombardy from Nebbiolo (called here Chiavennasca). The Valtellina reds are made in high terrain, and names like Sassella, Inferno and Grumello are the best known. Recommended producers are Rainoldi, Tona, Negri, Bettini and Pellizzatti. Sfursat is a particularly fine red, benefiting from grapes which are semi-dried, so producing generous wines, full and high in glycerine; those of Negri and Tona are excellent.

A good white wine, Lugana, is made at the southern end of Lake Garda. It is a stylish dry wine, delicious with the small salmon trout caught in the lake.

The western shores produce both red and rosé Riviera del Garda Bresciano, which is good value drunk young.

Between Lake Garda and Bergamo, Franciacorta sparkling wines are produced by the Champagne method; red Franciacorta is also a good buy locally. Near Pavia the wines of Oltrepò Pavese are numerous but easy to identify: the name of the grape variety is on the label. Reds are Bonarda, Pinot Nero, Barbera or just Oltrepò Pavese, and whites are Cortese, Pinot Grigio, Riesling and Moscato (always grapy and sweet). Riesling here can mean the Riesling Renano, which is more German-tasting, or the Riesling Italico – not a true Riesling grape, but giving a soft, easy-to-drink white wine. Now white Müller-Thurgau and Chardonnay are also appearing. Recently both the reds and whites have improved; there are many fine estates, as well as the cooperatives.

TRENTINO-ALTO ADIGE

Trentino is Italian-speaking and Alto Adige (or Südtirol) German-speaking. As a result, much of the wine of Alto Adige and Trentino is exported to German-speaking countries and, increasingly, to Britain and the USA. In Alto Adige, or Südtirol, the apparently complicated nomenclature of the wines is made easier by remembering that the name of the grape variety usually appears on the label. Two exceptions are light red Lago di Caldaro or Kalterersee and the more robust Santa Maddalena or St Magdalener.

The two overall DOCs are Alto Adige and Terlano (Terlaner in German). The whites are Moscato Giallo, Pinot Bianco (Weissburgunder), Pinot Grigio (Ruländer), Riesling Italico (Wälschriesling), Riesling Renano, Müller-Thurgau, Sylvaner, Sauvignon, Traminer Aromatico (Gewürztraminer – both languages usually appear on the label). The reds are Cabernet, Lagrein Rosato and Scuro (Lagrein Kretzer and Dunkel), the red Malvasia, Merlot, Moscato Rosa, Pinot Nero (Blauburgunder) and Schiava.

Except the Lagrein, these varieties are common to other countries. Either rosé or dark red, Lagrein is a beautifully flavoured wine, which urban encroachment is making scarce.

Gewürztraminer in Alto Adige is elegant and refined; the Riesling Renano wines have great style, and last well. The Cabernets are some of the finest outside Bordeaux, harmonious and rich in fruit. Pinot Nero tends to be lighter than Burgundy, fruity and soft.

Wine-making is of a high standard in Alto Adige. Some of the most splendid wines come from Hofstätter, Schloss Kehlburg, Muri-Gries, Schloss Rametz, Abbazia Novacella, Schloss Schwanburg, Kettmeir, Brigl, Lun and some good cooperatives.

Farther south, the overall DOC of Trentino covers the red Cabernet, Merlot, Lagrein, the local Marzemino and the Pinot Nero; also the white Pinot, Riesling and Traminer Aromatico as well as the two dessert wines Moscato and Vin Santo. Marzemino is

fresh and zingy, a thirst-quenching red wine. Casteller is a light red, made from Schiava, Lambrusco and Merlot, but the real gem is Teroldego Rotaliano. A rich wine of great class, it is made from the Teroldego grape in the area around Mezzocorona, Mezzolombardo and San Michele all'Adige. One of Italy's greatest red wines is the Teroldego Maso Scari made by Barone de Cles.

The wine school at San Michele makes the excellent Cabernet and Merlot blend, Castel San Michele. Conte Fedrigotti's Cabernet/Merlot mix, with the unpronounceable name of Foianeghe, is very fine. (These grape variety mixes are not DOC.) Excellent Cabernet also comes from Marchese Gonzaga (San Leonardo) and Endrizzi.

The Trentino's good cooperatives often market their wines through Càvit; look for Cabernet/Merlot 4 Vicariati. Other reputable firms are Girelli and Lagariavini.

VENETO

The Veneto brims over with wine, much of it exported. The best-known DOCs, Soave, Valpolicella and Bardolino, encompass the good, the bad and the beautiful. Some Soave wines are too neutral, but those from Masi, Pieropan and Bertani have a good regional taste, while Bolla maintains its standards. The principal grape is the Garganega, with a proportion of Trebbiano.

Two white wines which make good alternatives to world-renowned Soave are Gambellara and Bianco di Custoza.

Drink the light red Bardolino, from the eastern shores of Lake Garda, young and cool. Like Valpolicella, it is made of local grapes such as Corvina, Rondinella and Molinara. Valpolicella made north of Verona is slightly fuller, but still best when young. The categories of wine common to Valpolicella, Soave and Bardelino are *Superiore*, meaning the wine has a year of ageing (less for Soave) and more alcohol, and *Classico*, from the original production zone.

A Valpolicella of body and high in alcohol is Recioto Amarone, made from sugar-rich dried grapes; with a few years in bottle, it is a great wine. Fine Amarone is made by Masi, Bertani and Bolla. Masi also have Campo Fiorin, a red wine of great scent and flavour, made on the lees of the Recioto, which gives a second fermentation. Other good producers of Valpolicella are Allegrini, Tedeschi, Quinterelli, Villa Girardi and Guerrin.

The basin of the Piave river is well known for Merlot, Cabernet, Tocai and Verduzzo grapes; the latter is a local variety making dry white wines. Tocai di Lison is a dry white with a *goût de terroir*; the company of Santa Margherita make a really good example. The area of Conegliano is famous for its sparkling Prosecco wines.

Merlot and Cabernet di Pramaggiore are red wines from those grape varieties produced north of Lison, where they do well on the flat land.

A clutch of red and white wines under the Breganze DOC, north of Vicenza, are fruity and tempting for young drinking. Near by, Montello-Colli Asolani has good red Merlot; an excellent estate, the Villa Loredan Gasparini, whose Venegazzù Riserva, made of Cabernet Sauvignon, Cabernet Franc and Merlot, is non-DOC but famous. There is also Venegazzù Cabernet and a good Pinot Grigio white wine. An unusual local red grape variety, Raboso, makes tannic, robust wines.

FRIULI-VENEZIA GIULIA

This hilly area is fertile and beautiful, and the climate mild, although hail can sometimes be a localized problem.

The Collio area west of Gorizia is probably the best DOC. The wines bear the names of the grape varieties: for the whites, Riesling Italico, Tocai, Malvasia, which is dry and unusually delicious, Pinot Bianco, Pinot Grigio, Sauvignon and Traminer; for the reds, Merlot, Cabernet Franc and Pinot Nero. The wines have great freshness and appealing fruitiness, and do not have to be kept to be enjoyed. Some of the best producers are Conti Attems, Schiopetto, Princic, Conte Formentini, the Fellugas, Villa Russiz, and Gradnik.

Tocai is the most widely produced white wine. Some Pinot Grigio wines have a desirable pinkish tinge when contact with the skins gives extra fragrance and flavour.

Colli Orientali del Friuli, in Udine province, is another DOC: for white grape varieties Tocai, Verduzzo, Ribolla, Pinot Bianco, Pinot Grigio, Sauvignon, Riesling Renano and Picolit, a rare dessert wine, perhaps overpriced for the taste, and for reds Merlot, Cabernet, Pinot Nero and the native Refosco, which makes dry, tannic reds capable of ageing. Good producers are Bernarda Rocca near Ipplis, Conti di Maniago, Collavini and Attimis.

Grave del Friuli, is another overall DOC, with red Merlot (the most popular wine), Cabernet and Refosco, and white Tocai, Pinot Bianco, Pinot Grigio and Verduzzo. Look for the wines of Duca Badoglio, Pighin and Plozner. Isonzo, Aquileia and Latisana are DOCs seldom seen elsewhere.

EMILIA-ROMAGNA

The staple wines of this fertile area in the Po Valley are red Sangiovese di Romagna and white Trebbiano di Romagna, always cheap, fruity and ready to be drunk young. Albana di Romagna is another white named after its grape variety, and available dry *(secco)* or semi-sweet *(amabile)*.

However, this area is known as the great producer of Lambrusco. The sweet, slightly sparkling exported variety is non-DOC, but if this is not to your taste, the dry, naturally bubbly Lambruscos of Emilia-Romagna are quite delicious. Every local restaurant serves this low-alcohol *frizzante* (frothing) wine with the plentiful, solid food of the area; trust the proprietor, even if he suggests a non-DOC Lambrusco. The two best DOC wines are probably Lambrusco Grasparossa di Castelvetro and Lambrusco di Sorbara.

In America, Lambrusco is sold by giant concerns, e.g. Riunite, Giacobazzi and Cella. In Italy, try Agostinelli's version, or those of Contessa Matilde, Chiarli and Cavicchioli.

TUSCANY (TOSCANA)

Many people's first glass of Italian wine is Tuscan: a bottle of Chianti in a restaurant often starts a love affair with Italian wines. Discovery should not stop with Chianti, but don't drink one and think you have tried them all – there are as many Chiantis as Bordeaux wines.

The original production zone, Chianti Classico, is in high, hilly country between Florence and Siena. Surrounding this kernel, other beautiful hills produce excellent wine: Colli Senesi, Colli Aretini, Colline Pisane, Colli Fiorentini, Montalbano and Rufina.

Chianti used to be grown in a rather haphazard manner between olive and fruit trees, but now, especially in Chianti Classico, the rows of vines are carefully laid out, in breathtaking scenery. Some Chianti is still sold in flask, but bottles are now more frequently seen, being far easier to store and keeping the wine in better condition.

All Chianti is red and is made from predominantly Sangiovese grapes with some Canaiolo Nero and a little white Trebbiano and Malvasia. White wine from the area is called Bianco di Toscana, and sometimes Galestro or Bianco della Lega. A marvellous dessert wine, Vin Santo, is aged in casks and described by one proprietor as 'our Sherry'!

Chianti Classico's wild hills produce slightly 'bigger' wines than the other areas. In exceptional years, a Riserva is made with the best, and aged for three years before sale. The wine is kept in large wooden barrels, but producers tend now to bottle after 1½-2 years.

The *governo* system, still used by some estates, adds glycerine and richness to wine intended for ageing. Some grapes are kept apart and dried, and in the winter after the harvest this must is added to the wine, starting a new fermentation in the bulk of the wine, which gains body as a result.

A Consorzio, or consortium, was formed in 1924 to control the quality of Chianti Classico over and above the much more recent DOC, and most estates belong to this association. Called the Gallo Nero, wines approved by the Consorzio show a neck label of a black cockerel. The Chianti Putto Consortium is the largest producers' association in Italy, and its members come from the other six DOC zones; their wines have a cherub, or *putto*, on the neck label.

It would be impossible to list all the estates in Chianti making fine wine. There are large companies also, who make wine based on estates as well as a mass of other lines – Antinori has an excellent array, including Villa Antinori and the splendid non-DOC Tignanello, with some Cabernet Sauvignon added to the traditional grape mixture. Others are Ricasoli (Brolio), Baroncini, Ruffino, Frescobaldi, Spalletti, Bertolli and Melini. Other respected names are Artimino, Bibbiani, Pasolini and Bonacossi.

Historical estates in Chianti Classico make wine to the best modern standards: Castello di Uzzano, Calcinaia, Fonterutoli, Badia a Coltibuono, Volpaia, San Polo in Rosso, Vicchiomaggio, Cacchiano, Lilliano,

Sangiovese is the major grape variety used in making Chianti – including the wine of Castello Vicchiomaggio, at Greve in the heart of the Chianti Classico area, where the Riserva wines age well.

Schiava (Vernatsch) grapes are picked on the steep slopes of the Adige valley above Bolzano to make Lago di Caldaero and Santa Maddalena. These are wines to drink young and charming, not keep.

Montepaldi. Other estates, some small, of the highest standards are Castell'in Villa, Pagliarese, Riecine and Le Pici.

There are other great wines of Tuscany. Brunello di Montalcino has the uncertain fame of being the most expensive DOC in Italy. Made from a type of Sangiovese, it is usually kept in wood for four years (five if Riserva) before being bottled; the most famous producer is the estate of Biondi-Santi. Some of these wines have an astonishing flavour and richness, if opened well before drinking and not until at least 10 years old. Other Brunello wines come from the Fattoria dei Barbi, Poggio Alle Mura, Costanti and Tenuta Il Poggione.

Vino Nobile di Montepulciano is another legendary DOC, made from the Sangiovese grape and the Chianti 'mixture' in hills around Montepulciano. It is sold when aged for at least two years in wood, with three for Riserva, and four for Riserva Speciale. Some of the best examples come from the Poderi Boscarelli, Fattoria di Gracciano, Buonsignori, Fanetti, Riunite di Cavaliere Mario Contucci and Fassati.

Carmignano is a DOC within a DOC, since it is made within the Montalbano Chianti zone. Here the Chianti mixture of grapes has a very small addition of Cabernet, which gives it another dimension. Count Bonacossi's Villa di Capezzana is the best-known wine.

Sassicaia is a non-DOC red wine, made in the Maremma region of Tuscany. Made almost entirely from Cabernet Sauvignon grapes, it is a classic in the 'French' sense, worthy of ageing and with great depth of flavour. It would be a pity if all Italian wines tasted like French wines, but this is intrinsically a very fine wine.

The most common Tuscan white wine is probably Vernaccia di San Gimignano. Light and dry, the best examples come from Guicciardini Strozzi, Cantine Baroncini, Fattoria di Pietrafitta and Serristori.

Montecarlo Bianco is an intriguing DOC near Lucca, made from a fascinating array of white grapes: Trebbiano, Pinot Grigio, Sémillon, Sauvignon, Pinot Bianco, Vermentino and Roussanne. It is dry but full, and really interesting when well made, e.g. by the Fattorie del Buonamico and di Montecarlo (Mazzini Franca). Don't keep it more than a year or two, and try their marvellous red wines too. Bianco Vergine Val di Chiana is an up-and-coming dry white wine.

These three versions of the black rooster neck label are for normal Chianti Classico wine, Classico Vecchio (2 years' ageing), and Riserva (3 years' ageing).

UMBRIA

Orvieto used to be rather heavy and traditionally *abboccato*. Now, this white wine is lighter and fresher, and while *abboccato* still exists, the dry white is more favoured. But the round regional flavour of true Orvieto is distinctive, and it would be a pity if it disappeared entirely in favour of crisp anonymity. Orvieto is made mostly of Trebbiano Toscano. Antinori's, Castello della Sala, and Bigi's Vigneto Torricella are wines to be admired. Other good producers are Baroncini, and Conte Vaselli. Ask for Orvieto Classico, from the original vineyards nearest the lovely old town.

Torgiano is a DOC virtually created by one man, Dr Giorgio Lungarotti. His red Rubesco di Torgiano, made almost exactly from the Chianti mixture, is a really reliable wine, in some years very good indeed. The Riserva is the top quality, and Torre di Giano is the white.

The hills around lake Trasimeno produce good red and white wine, both from the La Fiorita estate of Lamborghini (he of the cars), and from the cooperative.

LATIUM (LAZIO)

Much of the wine of Latium is consumed in Rome, but luckily a good amount of Frascati makes its way on to the export market. Frascati used to be rather 'southern', oxidized and heavy, but now it, too, has 'gone modern' and become fresh and delicious. The best-known producer, Fontana Candida, is utterly reliable, and wines from the co-operative of Marino Gotto d'Oro, De Sanctis, San Matteo, Mennuni and the Colli di Catone should also be tried. The grapes used are Malvasia and Trebbiano, which is also the mixture for another dry white DOC, Marino. An excellent example comes from the Marino cooperative, and it is cheaper than Frascati. The other dry white of Rome is Colli Albani, also to be drunk young and fresh. Est! Est!! Est!!! di Montefiascone, from near Lake Bolsena, is an overrated white wine. The dry version now travels abroad, and Bigi produce a fresh example. Mazziotti make the prestige Est Est Est, this time without the exclamation marks usually found on the label.

The red wines of Latium, usually served in open carafes in Roman restaurants, can be very good – fruity, vivid and suitable for young drinking.

THE MARCHES (MARCHE)

The Marches comprise a slice of Adriatic coast as well as hill towns around which lie the vineyards. The most famous wine is the dry white Verdicchio dei Castelli di Jesi, made basically from the Verdicchio grape. Often the amphora-shaped bottle attracts people to try Verdicchio, and if the wine is from the largest producer, Fazi Battaglia, with its lovely, almost nutty flavour, it is not disappointing. There are also good cooperatives and large firms like Umani Ronchi, Garofoli and Tombolini, which uphold the reputation of the DOC. Bad Verdicchio is rare.

Rosso Piceno is the widely produced DOC red, made from Sangiovese and Montepulciano, while Rosso Conero is a largely Montepulciano wine, and more robust. Garofoli make a superb example. Vernaccia di Serrapetrona is sparkling red, sometimes sweet; sparkling Verdicchio is also to be found.

THE ABRUZZO

The most famous wine is the splendid red Montepulciano d'Abruzzo, one of the best-value reds in Italy, perhaps because the relative inaccessibility of the hard, mountain territory has saved it from over-exposure. The grape variety, Montepulciano, has a robust, individual character. It is essentially bottle-aged rather than wood-aged wine and develops great bouquet and flavour after a few years. Casal Thaulero is a co-operative with an international reputation. Don't miss their cherry-coloured Cerasuolo, but drink it younger than the red. Trebbiano d'Abruzzo is the white wine of the region: drink it young.

SOUTHERN ITALY AND THE ISLANDS

Campania

Many of the grape varieties used in Campania are Greek in origin. The taste they give may take a while to appreciate, but the adjustment is rewarding. The Greco di Tufo makes the DOC white wine of the same name, and the Fiano, Fiano di Avellino. When made by Mastroberardino, both wines have an interesting if somewhat earthy flavour and are excellent with food.

The Aglianico grape (the name comes from *hellenico*) makes Taurasi, the fine, full-bodied red wine, not sold until it is three years old. Again Mastroberardino is the name to know. They also make the best white Lachryma Christi del Vesuvio, which ranges from dry to quite sweet. Cilento, red, *rosato* and white, is the best of the many non-DOC wines.

Apulia (Puglia)

Well-planned irrigation has changed this region dramatically in the last 20 years, and from this arid land now spring lush fruit, olives and vines. Certainly the vast quantities of wine have improved. Blending wine is still made on a massive scale, but much wine is now far lighter in alcohol, and is delicious drinking in its own right, although sadly not a great deal of this quality is shipped abroad.

Copertino is the most impressive DOC, especially from Barone Fabio Bacile di Castiglione, based on the Negro Amaro; both red and *rosato* age magnificently.

Good Salento wines of all kinds are made by the winery of Leone De Castris. Very good white wines (sometimes sparkling) are made at the villages of Locorotondo and lovely Martina Franca. The DOC of Castel del Monte covers all colours of wine and maintains a high standard, especially from the Rivera winery. The rosato is a pleasant surprise for those who find dry rosé dull. San Severo, another DOC covering all colours, is good value from del Sordo. Rich dessert wines are Aleatico, Moscato and Primitivo.

Basilicata

The great wine of this poor, backward region is the fine red Aglianico del Vulture. Aged Aglianico wines, when labelled Vecchio or Riserva are 'serious' wines of great style and body. Top producers are D'Angelo, Martino, Paternoster and Napolitano. There is also a sweet sparkling Aglianico.

Calabria

The finest Calabrian wine is Cirò, which comes in all three colours, with the red the most prestigious. Ippolito, Librandi and Cantina Enotria make good examples. Pollino is a red to be drunk younger, and the cooperative, Vini del Pollino, makes good wine; Savuto red or rosé is usually dependable.

Sicily (Sicilia)

Sicily's reputation abroad now rests firmly on a few well-distributed, well-made brands, rather than on dessert Marsala. The well-vinified, light table wines have improved immeasurably, and they are now easily obtainable everywhere.

It is picturesque to buy a wine with the DOC of Etna (it comes in all three colours), but Corvo Duca di Salaparuta is probably the best-known Sicilian wine. Their red and white wines are reliable and pleasant. The estate of Conte Tasca d'Almerita makes non-DOC Regaleali red, rosé and white wines of good standard in export quantities. Sicily also has Moscato, often sweet and sparkling, sometimes fortified *(liquoroso)*.

Sardinia

The same switch from heavy to light wines has taken place here, due largely to the dynamism of the firm of Sella e Mosca. Their light dry white Torbato and Vermentino are excellent and good value, and their red Cannonau is highly drinkable. It is good, too, from the cooperative of Marmilla, who also make Monica di Sardegna, a lovely fruity red.

Dry white Nuragus can also be good when young. Vernaccia di Oristano is a good Sherry-like aperitif. The many dessert wines are perhaps more appreciated in colder weather than in summer.

SPAIN AND PORTUGAL

It is surprising that the table wines of the Iberian Peninsula, produced as they are on the same land mass, are so different. There are few similar grape varieties, and tasting the wines side by side, the drinker will find few similar tastes, except where vineyard areas are contiguous, such as Galicia and the Minho, and the Douro (Portugal) and the Duero (Spain).

Each country has its famous fortified wine – Sherry in Spain and Port in Portugal.

SPAIN

SPANISH WINES have at last come out of their anonymity on the export markets. When bulk shipments were more popular, the wine disappeared into brands, with no indication of the region whence it came. Although high-strength wine still props up weaker cousins on the export markets, the emphasis is now on selling wine in bottle, with a clearly defined region of origin.

At the same time Spanish viticulture and vinification methods have been improving. With the largest area of land under vine in Europe, Spain usually produces only about half the annual output of France and Italy. Even allowing for the fact that much of Spain is far from fertile, the low yields were largely attributable to lack of good husbandry. Old, unsuitable grape varieties soldiered on, and no one sprayed against rot if conditions were humid. The country and socio-economic structure are not suited to intensive vine farming on the grand scale and Spain has, wisely, decided to work towards quality.

Good-quality wine is much easier to achieve in the cooler northern regions than in the hot, dry central plateau, or in the arid south. The areas prized most highly for their wines, the Rioja and the Penedès, are in the north; it is with these wines that most progress has been made on the export market.

Vines are grown as individual bushes in Rioja, and picking usually takes place in mid-October.

RIOJA

This is the name best known to drinkers of Spanish wine outside Spain, and it represents some of the best value in medium-priced wines to be found. The great potential of the area was seen by many large companies and conglomerates, and much outside investment has gone into Rioja. The traditional houses now compete alongside companies which were not there a decade ago. There has been extensive planting and patchy and scattered vineyards have been developed into modern, workable units.

The Rioja is divided into three areas: Rioja Alta, Rioja Alavesa and Rioja Baja. The first two make the better wines. The hotter, drier Rioja Baja makes heavier wine, not so good on its own, but often useful to add body in a blend with the others. The better areas are on either side of the Ebro, and the soil is influenced by the alluvial deposits of the river, as well as containing calcareous clay. The Rioja Alavesa is all calcareous clay, which confers a certain finesse on the wines.

The climate is temperate, which means that rain can fall at unfortunate times – at flowering and during ripening. However, provided rot is controlled by spraying, vintages are more even than in Bordeaux and Burgundy, and vintage years are consequently of less significance here than in more northerly regions.

Wine-making

Vinification processes vary with the *bodega*. The most modern have advanced equipment, and little wood is to be seen. The traditional houses have nothing but wood, with oak fermentation vats and barrels for maturing the wine. The oak reputedly bestows a 'vanilla' flavour on the reds, although a slight dryness in the taste results from too-lengthy maturation in small casks. The time has now been shortened, often to 18 months, and the emphasis is on maturation in bottle, which produces fresher, more fruity wine.

Even white Riojas used to be aged in wood for long periods, which gave them a heavy, oxidized flavour; newer examples are fresh and exciting, with little or no

Horizontal presses in use at the large modern winery of Bodegas Olarra in the Rioja Alta, where fine, fruity, deep-coloured wines are made.

wood ageing, although a hint of wood makes them more interesting.

The labelling and description of Riojas may be vague. *Clarete* Rioja was always supposed to be lighter red than *tinto*, but the difference is often now minimal, and varies from *bodega* to *bodega*.

If a vintage year is given, it is probably only the year that predominates in the blend. However, a *Reserva* will probably be more accurately described as vintage, and will come from a very good year. '3°*año*' or '5°*año*' means that the wine was bottled in the third or fifth year after the harvest. A wine which is *crianza* must be two years old, and one of those years must have been spent in a Bordeaux-sized small oak barrel. If one really wants to age Rioja, it is better to go for a Rioja Alta.

GRAPES OF RIOJA

Rioja Alavesa uses Tempranillo, an indigenous red variety, with a small amount of white Viura and sometimes some Garnacho Tinto (related to the French Grenache). The Rioja Alta uses Tempranillo with Graciano and Mazuelo, and perhaps a little Garnacho. The Rioja Baja is made almost entirely from Garnacho Tinto. White Riojas are made from Viura and Malvasia, with a little Garnacho Blanco.

HOW SPAIN DEFINES QUALITY

The better wine-producing regions of Spain are defined and given a *Denominación de Origen*. Each of the 24 regions has a *Consejo Regulador* which controls the way the vine is grown and the wine made, along the lines of the French AC and the Italian DOC systems. As in these two countries, the *denominación* is not an absolute guarantee of quality, but the measures should lead towards better quality, and they ensure that the wine comes from the region stated. The vintages are not, however, as tightly controlled in Spain as elsewhere. It is a pity, also, that irrigation is not permitted: its use in California and South America shows that it can augment an inadequate rainfall without resulting in overcropping.

Wine producers

The *bodegas* usually own vineyards but also buy in grapes. Examples of splendid and really traditional *bodegas* are Marqués de Murrieta and Muga. Huge new enterprises are Sociedad General de Vinos (Domecq), Olarra and Lan. Marqués de Caceres is owned by a man who also has châteaux in Bordeaux, and the wine is elegant and more 'French'. Bodegas Riojanas with Monte Real, La Rioja Alta with Viña Ardanza, Bodegas Alavesas with Solar de Samaniego, López de Heredia with Tondonia, and Marqués de Riscal are all fine examples.

Whites vary in style between the rich oak and fruit of Tondonia, a mid-way wine like Medieval (almost like a white Burgundy on the nose) and the smooth, less 'regional' Marqués de Caceres.

Logroño in the Rioja Alta is the trade capital, but Haro is also important.

Principal Rioja wine producers

LA RIOJA ALTA
AGE, Bodegas Unidas, SA, Azpilicueta, Cruz Garcia & Entrena (Fuenmayor, Navarrete)
Bodegas Berberana, SA (Cenicero)
Bodegas Beronia (Ollauri)
Bodegas Bilbainas, SA (Haro)
Bodegas Campo Viejo (Logroño)
Bodegas Carlos Serres, Hijo (Haro)
Bodegas Castillo de Cuzcurrita (Rio Tirón)
Bodegas Cooperativas Santa Maria la Real (Nájera)
Bodegas Corral (Navarrete)
Bodegas Delicia (Ollauri)
Bodegas Federico Paternina, Vinos Riojas, SA (Ollauri, Haro)
Bodegas Francisco Viguera (Haro)
Bodegas Franco Españolas (Logroño)
Bodegas Gómez Cruzado, SA (Haro)
Bodegas Lafuente, SA (Fuenmayor)

Bodegas Lagunilla, SA (Cenicero)
Bodegas Lan (Fuenmayor)
Bodegas La Rioja Alta, SA (Haro)
Bodegas López Agos (Fuenmayor)
Bodegas Olarra (Logroño)
Bodegas Marqués de Caceres (Cenicero)
Bodegas Marqués de Murrieta (Logroño)
Bodegas Martinez Lacuesta Hermanos, Ltda (Haro)
Bodegas Montecillo, SA (Fuenmayor)
Bodegas Muga (Haro)
Bodegas Ramón Bilbao (Haro)
Bodegas Rioja Santiago, SA (Haro)
Bodegas Riojanas, SA (Cenicero)
Bodegas R. López de Heredia, Viña Tondonia (Haro)
Bodegas Velazquez, SA (Cenicero)
Bodegas Vista Alegre, SA (Haro)
Compañia Vinicola del Norte de España, SA (Haro)

LA RIOJA ALAVESA
Bodegas Alavesas, SA (Laguardia)
Bodegas Cantabria, SA (Laguardia)
Bodegas Cooperativa Vinícola de Labastida (Labastida)
Bodegas Faustino Martínez (Oyon)
Bodegas Real Divisa (Abalos)
Bodegas Riojas Cía, SRO (Laguardia)
Bodegas Palacio (Laguardia)
Bodegas Viña Salceda (Elciego)
Rioja Alavesa SMS
Sociedad General de Vinos, SA (Elciegò)
Vinos de los Herederos del Marqués de Riscal, SA (Elciego)

LA RIOJA BAJA
Bodegas Gurpegui (San Adrián)
Bodegas Latorre y Lapuerta (Alfaro)
Bodegas Muerza, SA (San Adrián)
Bodegas Palacios, Vino Rioja, SA (Alfaro)
Bodegas Rivero (Arnedo)
Savin, SA (Adenueva de Ebro)

THE PENEDÈS

Catalan firms have been making wine here, just south of Barcelona, for centuries and thoroughly deserve the world-wide success that has come to them. They are chiefly known for the name of Torres and for their high-quality sparkling wine.

Wine producers
The methods at Torres are modern French rather than traditional, and ageing in wood has been dramatically cut, especially for white wines. Top red wines are the Black Label and the Gran Coronas, both with a high proportion of Cabernet Sauvignon and retaining the flavour of wood ageing, and a Pinot Noir, formerly called Santa Digna but now designated Viña Magdala. Whites include the Gran Viña Sol Green Label, which has about 30 per cent Sauvignon and is aged in wood, and the Gran Viña

Sol, which has about the same proportion of Chardonnay. Another tempting white wine is the Esmeralda, which is made from Gewürztraminer and Muscat d'Alsace and is naturally aromatic. Tres Torres is really good-value red, while Gran Sangredetoro has more bottle age.

Masía Bach (owned by the huge sparkling-wine company, Codorníu), Marqués de Monistrol (owned by Martini & Rossi), Bosch-Guell and Freixenet, who make still wines alongside the sparklers, are good firms. Masía Bach Seco is to be recommended as well as Marqués de Monistrol Blanc de Blancs. Two sweet white wines are Torres's San Valentin and Masía Bach's Extrísimo.

Other wine-making areas
Alella, to the north of Barcelona, also specializes in sweetish white wine, the Legitimo Marfil Blanco. There is also a dry version.

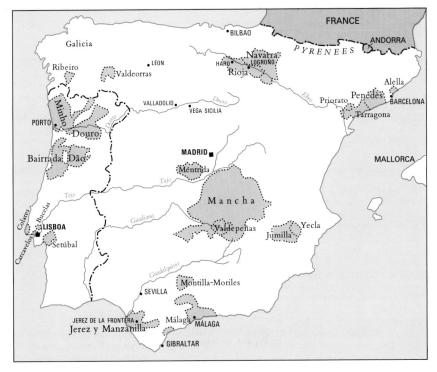

Tarragona used to be far better known but its heavy wines are more suitable for blending than for drinking 'neat' in these days of more lightweight wines. **Priorato** lies within Tarragona, but again makes heavy red wines.

NORTHERN SPAIN

Wines from **Navarra** are not yet widely distributed outside Spain, although they are very honourable, in the genre of Rioja. The best wines come from the Vinícola Navarra in Pamplona, and the Señorío de Sarría. Rosé wines are a speciality here.

Valladolid is famous for the rare and expensive red wine, Vega Sicilia. It does have complexity, but the long ageing in wood can impart an element of volatile acidity (the first step to vinegar, though that is a long way off) which detracts from the overall impression. The Valbuena is not aged for so long in wood, and so can be more accessible.

Through this area runs the River Duero, which becomes the Douro of Port fame when it crosses the border into Portugal. One wine produced here represents really good value for money: Protos, from the Bodega Ribera Duero at Peñafiel, has real depth of flavour.

Galicia, in the far north-west, is much influenced by the Atlantic, with resultant rain and mild weather. As a consequence, the wines are light and can be acidic in much the same way as the wines of the neighbouring Minho in Portugal. Much of the wine has a slight 'prickle' to it, again resembling Portuguese Vinho Verde. The reds are very dry and acidic to most tastes outside the region – they only taste less so if accompanying rich, oily food. A white Albariño is usually the best bet.

León lies to the south-east of Galicia, and its full-bodied reds can be good value. Rueda is a rather Sherry-like drink. A consortium of local growers called Valdeobispo is now exporting, and some large importing companies are making their own selections, which are good at the cheap end of the market. The Coyanza range from Bodegas Vinos de León can be recommended.

GRAPES OF THE PENEDÈS

Again, the climate is temperate, with adequate rainfall, and the soil is basically limestone. The Baja Penedès near the coast provides the big red wines made from Spanish grape varieties such as Cariñena, Garnacha, Tempranillo and Samsó. The black Monastrell is also used. The Medio Penedès specializes in producing a vast quantity of white base wine from the Xarel-lo and Macabeo grapes for the sparkling-wine industry. The Alto Penedès, the highest zone and, therefore, suitable for white grape production, specializes in the Parellada grape. But the wines that have made the news are those produced from grape varieties imported from France and Germany by the firm of Torres. These include Pinot Noir and Cabernet Sauvignon for red wines, and Gewürztraminer, Chardonnay and Riesling for whites. Clearly, this gives the wines less 'regional character' but it also makes them more delicious.

CENTRAL SPAIN

In **Valdepenas** and **La Mancha,** literature combines with wine production on a grand scale. This great plateau provides wine for carafe drinking, wine for blending, and spirit for making Spanish brandy. The wine is for young drinking, uncomplicated and pleasing, often sold by supermarkets in the export markets. There has been a big improvement here, for the reds used to be slightly baked and the whites yellow and oxidized. Valdepeñas today is usually a good buy.

The **Levante** runs along the Mediterranean coast, and includes two wine areas whose product is appearing outside Spain, Yecla and Jumilla. The big firm of Savin produces some amazingly cheap, good red Jumilla. Some of the red wines here were traditionally alcoholic and heavy; now a percentage of white wine is added to them, with improved results. The cooperative La Purisma (a promising name) at Yecla is also a good source of supply.

THE SOUTH

Montilla-Moriles is a demarcated area named after two towns south of Córdoba, and its wines are similar to Sherry. The soil is the very chalky Albero, which makes the finest Sherries. The grape variety is the Pedro Ximénez; whereas in Jerez this is used for making sweet wines, here the wines are fermented until they are dry, and then sweetened as required, so that the resulting wine may be either dry, medium or sweet.

Picturesque large earthenware *tinajas*, which resemble amphorae, are used for the fermentation, whereas all Sherry is vinified in wood. Montilla is matured in oak butts in a *solera* (see Sherry) and rarely fortified. The vocabulary is the same as in Jerez, with Fino, Ámontillado, Palo Cortado and Oloroso. The Fino is the best: nice and tangy and not too strong. This is often a better buy than a *cheap* Fino from Jerez, although the best of these do have the edge.

A delicious example of a Montilla Fino is the J.R. of Bodegas Montulia. At 14.9 per cent alcohol, you can drink considerably more of this than of most Sherries, which are exported at a higher alcohol level, and it has the topaz colour and tangy freshness of a perfect apéritif or hors-d'oeuvre wine. Albero is another well-known name. As with Sherry, some Amontillado wines are commercially sweetened, whereas others are the 'real thing' and are aged, even more nutty versions of the Fino.

Málaga should regain the popularity of its past if all the wines are of the interest and entrancing flavour of the Solera Scholtz 1885. This is much stronger than most Montilla, usually around 18 per cent, but has an exotic nose and a lovely, lingering flavour, rich and yet ending quite dry – a real battle of sensations takes place inside one's mouth. Try sipping this with walnuts. There are very sweet Málagas, real dessert wines, and these often have an unmistakable Muscatel taste about them. Try them *seco*, yet rich.

PORTUGAL

APART FROM internationally distributed brands of sweetish rosé, Portugal has found it difficult to impose her finer table wines on the consciousness of the world. This is a pity, since the wines are still sold at remarkably reasonable prices for the quality, particularly the red and white wines from the Dão.

THE DÃO

Make straight for this area, in a wine shop or on holiday, for real value. The consumer still does not seem to be charged for financing wines that have some age to them, and the flavour, character and richness of the red wines win converts every time a bottle is opened.

The Dão is a rocky, high plateau in the

The steeply terraced granitic slopes of the Douro vineyards are famed for Port, but also produce good table wines.

centre of Portugal, with Viseu its main town. The area is vast, but you won't see many vineyards if you visit it – they are isolated and scattered, mostly at altitudes of 200-500 metres. The grape varieties are Portuguese and help impart the truly regional flavour to the wines – red Dão is made of the Tourigo, Tinto Pinheira and the Alvarelhão, and whites from the Arinto and the Dona Branca.

Wine-making has become much more modern and less individually 'peasant', but the red wines still tend to have quite a long fermentation and maceration on the skins, which helps to give them the glycerine for which they are known. Red Dão must be aged in wood for at least two years, but as the casks hold thousands of litres, rather than hundreds (as in Bordeaux and Burgundy), the influence of wood is not obvious and the time spent in cask is of less importance. The far smaller amount of white Dão which is made sometimes suffers from too long in wood, but the better brands are now avoiding this and the results are much fresher, without sacrificing an extremely pleasant regional character. They are also good value for money.

The Dão is dominated by cooperatives, from which the large firms buy their wine. Most of the firms even take their selections out of the area, to Oporto or Lisbon, for blending and maturing, but J. M. Fonseca and the Vinicola do Vale do Dão have facilities for this within the region. The only private estate exporting wine is that of the Conde de Santar.

The red wines are not as hard and astringent as they used to be, largely because the bigger firms are well aware that the export markets like their wines to be more mellow, and blend judiciously to achieve this end. A Dão red at 6-10 years is usually a splendid glass of wine, whereas the whites should be half that age. The best reds will be labelled *reserva* or *garrafeira*.

Best wines
Grão Vasco from the Vinicola do Vale do Dão
Terras Altas from J.M. da Fonseca
Reservas from Caves Velhas ● Reservas from Caves Aliança ● Conde de Santar, under the Carvalho, Ribeiro & Ferreira label

THE MINHO

This Atlantic-influenced area in the north-west of Portugal is synonymous with the production of Vinho Verde; it borders on Galicia in Spain and reaches down to south of Oporto. The soil is hard granite, and the vegetation lush, due to the heavy rainfall. Some vines are trained high on pergolas; some are still trained up trees; while the most modern vineyards train high along wires. Often other crops are grown underneath the vines, and many say this is enriching for the soil. There are six sub-regions within the Minho, but wines from these are nearly always blended to produce a harmonious result. The only area whose name is sometimes seen on labels is Monção.

Both red and white wines are produced but nearly all the Vinho Verde seen on export markets is white. This is because the high acidity of the reds is more a local taste than one appreciated internationally, but it goes very well with the rather oily food in the region.

Wine-making
There is often a slight *pétillance*, or prickle, to a Vinho Verde, and this is given to the wine by a small addition of carbon dioxide before bottling. Again, this is an area of cooperatives, and the wine is made on the grand scale in huge vats. The emphasis is on freshness and light flavour, and the wines should always be drunk young, beginning the year after the harvest.

Many of the white Vinhos Verdes exported are slightly sweetened for popular taste, but this is no bad thing, provided it is not exaggerated, since the sweetness brings out the fruit and bouquet. But they are certainly not sweet wines, rather, soft and flowery.

Best wines
Aveleda (this can be found in both a dry and a slightly sweeter style)
Gatão (flowery and soft) ● Aliança (dry)
Palácio de Brejoeira (an Alvarinho from Monção and quite the best Vinho Verde)
Cépa Velha ● Vercoope, with the Verdegar and Felgueiras labels
● Casalinho ● Quinta de São Claudio

GRAPES OF THE MINHO

Vinho Verde does not sound very appetizing – green wine implies acidity. But the term is used to describe fresh, young wines. The white grapes used are the Azal Branco, the Loureiro and the Trajadura, with a small amount of the famous Alvarinho grape which gives especially good wine – Alvarinho from the Monção is the best Vinho Verde.

Other demarcated areas

Around Lisbon, there are four demarcated areas that were more important historically than they are now. **Carcavelos** and **Colares** are two areas that are virtually disappearing through urban development. The red wines of Colares are famous because the vines are grown on sand dunes and, therefore, were never attacked by the *phylloxera* blight so did not have to be grafted on to American root stocks. If you ever come across a Colares, it should have some years of age to it to be pleasant drinking. Carcavelos is a fortified dessert wine, and only one property now produces it – you will see it only in Lisbon or Estoril. **Bucelas** is a light, dry white wine, which needs a few years of bottle age to soften the acidity. The Caves Velhas produce a good example, as does João Camiles Alves. **Moscatel de Setúbal** is a famous dessert wine, made south of Lisbon, now enjoying a small revival.

In the same area, the firm of J.M. da Fonseca also make the excellent red wine, Periquita. It is not a demarcated wine, but none the worse for that. The wine is called after the original vineyard in which it was made, and is gutsy and full-bodied. Look out for Camarate, a lighter wine made by the same company, which is introducing a few French grapes, such as Cabernet Sauvignon and Merlot.

The **Bairrada,** the coastal region to the south of Oporto, has only recently been demarcated, but produces a vast amount of wine, much of it very good. Caves Aliança and Caves do Barroção do some good bottlings. Often a red wine will just be labelled *garrafeira*, but it will be a full-bodied red with some oak-cask ageing. The Bairrada also produces good

sparkling wine made by the Champagne method, and a lot of rosé.

Undemarcated areas

The **Upper Douro Valley** is demarcated only for Port, and good table wines are a comparatively recent innovation here. Look out for Vila Real Clarete from Sogrape and Evel from the Real Companhia Vinicola do Norte de Portugal, as well as Quinta do Corval. Barca Velha is a bit esoteric, resembling Spain's Vega Sicilia.

The **Ribatejo,** north-west of Lisbon, produces a vast amount of everyday wine. The best wine is the Serradayres, which is a brand name. It is an elegant red, produced by the reliable firm of Carvalho, Ribeiro & Ferreira, which also makes a pleasant white Serradayres and wines simply labelled *garrafeira*, with a vintage often 20 years old.

The **Alentejo** produces nothing of note, except the red wines from Borba and the tongue-twisting Reguengos de Monsaraz. The **Algarve** is more for holidays than serious wine-making; but there are some pleasant whites from Lagoa.

HOW PORTUGAL DEFINES QUALITY

Portugal's Denominação de Origem system was established in 1756 to protect the reputation of the Port trade. It has been extended to cover the growth, production and quality of table wines in Minho (for Vinhos Verdes), Dão, Moscatel de Setúbal, Bucelas, Colares and Carcavelos as well as Madeira and Douro (for Port); the Bairrada is now also included.

The *selo de origem* – the paper band fixed over the cork and under the capsule, shows a wine has met set standards of production and been passed by a taster.

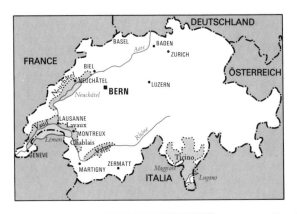

Despite its small size and mountainous nature, there are 12,141 ha under vine in Switzerland, producing wines similar to those of the surrounding countries.

SWITZERLAND

The most striking feature of Switzerland, seen from any angle, is its contours: and the variety of its vineyards reflects this. At one extreme the terraces rising above the Zermatt railway and the valleys south of Visp are the highest in Europe (nearly 1,200 metres); at the other, vineyards draw warmth and radiation from the calm water of the lakes of Geneva and Neuchâtel. Another contrast is found between the different viticultural traditions obtaining in the different cantons, depending on whether their origins are French, Italian or German. Switzerland's most-exported wines, and arguably the country's best, come from the French-speaking provinces in the west of the country.

Valais

The name derives from the valley of the upper Rhône. Vineyards line the north wall, fed by water conducted from the snowfields above. The Valais produces both red and white wines. The latter predominate, as they do throughout Switzerland. The most important of them is the Fendant, made from the grape of the same name (the local synonym for Chasselas), which gives a soft style of wine with a pleasant flavour. Fendant is best drunk young and fresh, since it tends to oxidize early and lose its charm. The best red wine of the Valais is Dôle, produced from a blend of Pinot Noir and Gamay. A good Dôle is a deep, generous wine; Dôle of lesser quality is known as Goron. Other good wines from the Valais are Johannisberger, produced from Riesling and Sylvaner, and Malvoisie, a rich dessert wine.

Vaud

At Martigny, the Rhône turns northwards towards Lake Geneva passing the Château of Aigle on its way. Vineyards line the eastern valley walls, the district here being Chablais and the wine mainly Fendant (known in Vaud as Dorin). North of Montreux, rising in steep terraces from the lake shore, lie the vineyards of Lavaux. The predominant grape is again the Chasselas; red wine of the Dôle type is known as Salvagnin. The best white wines of Lavaux come from Dézaley, just east of Lausanne. Beyond Lausanne, vineyards interspersed with meadows and orchards follow the lake shore to Geneva and beyond. Befitting the gentler landscape of 'La Côte', the wines are lighter and less distinguished than the mountain wines: the main grapes are Gamay and Chasselas.

Neuchâtel

The vineyards of Neuchâtel lie with the hills of the Jura at their back, and the lakes of Neuchâtel itself and Bienn (the Bieler See) at their front. Red and white wines are equally respectable: the best red (from Pinot Noir) comes from the village of Cortaillod, while the whites may be still, *pétillant* or fully sparkling. All are made from Chasselas, and bottling *sur lie* is common.

Other wine-making areas

North of a line from Basel to Zurich, in German-speaking Switzerland, lie scattered vineyards producing respectable but unspectacular white wines, mainly from Müller-Thurgau and Ruländer. A few red wines on the Baden pattern are made from Blauburgunder (Pinot Noir), known also as Klevner.

The Italian-speaking Ticino is one of Switzerland's most attractive provinces, with a large part of Lakes Maggiore and Lugano within its borders. Its wines are mainly robust reds in the tradition of Lombardy, the best of them made from Merlot. They may taste harsh to the visitor on first acquaintance, but they match the local cuisine to perfection.

LUXEMBURG

The vineyards of the Grand Duchy stretch for some 40 kilometres along the western banks of the Mosel, from Remich in the south to Wasserbillig in the north, and up the valley of the Sur on the eastern border. The best sites are found upstream from Grevenmacher towards the French frontier. All the vineyards face east, sheltered from the wind by wooded hills, though frost is a yearly menace.

Luxemburg wines are unmistakably 'Mosels' though with more than a hint of Alsace in their perfumed bouquets and dryness of finish. They are exclusively white, light in alcohol and characterized by a cutting fruit acidity. The predominant grapes grown are Elbling and the Müller-Thurgau (often called Rivaner, i.e. Riesling x Sylvaner), which produces the most distinctive Luxemburg wines even though occasionally outshone by the pure Rieslings. Other varieties are Traminer, Auxerrois, Pinot Blanc and Pinot Gris (Ruländer).

The majority of the wines are produced by cooperatives, with the government viticultural station at Remich maintaining close supervision of quality. The best are granted *Appellation Contrôlée* or *Appellation Complète,* with the *Marque Nationale* as the ultimate accolade.

Snow on the steep, terraced slopes of the Vaud protects the vines from frost damage.

AUSTRIA

The Austrian vineyards fall into four distinct geographical zones, concentrated at the eastern end of the country, where the Alpine peaks and ski-slopes give way to the great plains of central Europe.

Lower Austria (Nieder-Osterreich)

This is the most prolific of the regions and includes eight separate districts within its borders. The most spectacular and renowned of these is the **Wachau,** where the Danube emerges from an imposing gorge and terraced vineyards line the steep slopes. This is Rhein Riesling country, and the wines have a finesse, firmness and length of flavour which sets them apart from the wines of the flatlands. Around **Krems** and **Langenlois,** the valley walls recede to form a low escarpment of loess, into which generations of wine-growers have carved a labyrinth of cellars. North and east of the Wachau, towards the 'dead' frontier with Czechoslovakia, vineyards of the rolling plateau-land form the extensive zones of **Retz** and **Falkenstein-Matzen.** East and west of Vienna is the district of **Traismauer-Carnuntum,** its most noteworthy feature being the imposing Chorherrenstift (Abbey) of Klosterneuburg, where are situated the Government Wine Testing Station and a renowned viticultural school. South of the capital, on the slopes of the Vienna Woods, lie the two remaining districts, **Vöslau,** famous for its red wines, and **Gumpoldskirchen,** producing white wines, full-flavoured and rich in extract.

Burgenland

This region in the south-east of Austria, embracing the shallow Neusiedler See, was Hungarian until the reshaping of frontiers after World War I, and both geography and climate have much in common with Hungary. The landscape is flat and sandy, the climate hot and dry in summer, cold in winter. Frost is a relatively infrequent spring visitor, *Botrytis* a common summer one, and all conditions are favourable to the making of sweet dessert wines of *Auslese* quality and above. East of the Neusiedler See,

GRAPE VARIETIES

Eighty per cent of Austrian wines are white. Contrary to common belief, they differ from German wines, the Austrians preferring drier everyday wines: this is seen particularly in those made from the Grüner Veltliner, a grape unique to Austria and providing some 40 per cent of the white wine total. Its characteristics are a lemony acidity and background austerity, delicious combined with the freshness of the new *Heurige*. After Grüner Veltliner comes a bewildering abundance of grape varieties: Wälschriesling, Müller-Thurgau, Weissburgunder (Pinot Blanc), Rhein Riesling, Traminer, Ruländer (Pinot Gris), and Muskat Ottonel among them. Some districts, e.g. Gumpoldskirchen, grow local specialities, in this case, the Zierfandler and Rotgipfler.

Austrian red wines are not well known abroad, though the best of them, e.g. the St Laurent Ausstich of Klosterneuburg, are excellent. Centres of production are Vöslau, south of Vienna, and Pottelsdorf in Burgenland. Deep-coloured, rich in flavour and often in extract, the softness of Austrian reds in the mouth is nicely balanced by a refreshing hint of bitterness on the finish. Main grape varieties are Blauburgunder (Pinot Noir) Blauer Portugieser, Blaufränkischer, St Laurent and Zweigelt.

The luscious dessert wines of the Burgenland, their sugar measured in degrees Klosterneuburger Mostwaage vie in richness and elegance with the finest German Prädikatsweine, whose terminology they share. They offer excellent value for money.

Labelling of Austrian wines conforms broadly to the German pattern, with the name of the village preceding that of the vineyard, grape variety, quality grade and vintage. The term *Ried* means a defined site within a larger vineyard.

squeezed between the reedy shore of the lake and the border with Hungary, lies a small enclave known as the 'Seewinkel', where the grapes attain a ripeness unusual even by the standards of this exceptionally warm and dry region.

Styria (Steiermark)
South and east of Graz lie vineyards interspersed in a patchwork of undulating hills and woodland. Few Styrian wines reach export markets, as production is largely in the hands of small growers, and mainly local.

Vienna (Wien)
Vineyards abound in the western suburbs of Vienna, lining the lower slopes of the Wienerwald, or Vienna Woods, in an arc from Grinzing, Nussdorf and Sievering in the north to Perchtoldsdorf in the south. Under a decree of Maria Theresa (1780) each Viennese grower is permitted to sell his new wines for consumption 'on' or 'off' the premises until the vintage is exhausted, when the green bush, signifying that he has wines on sale, is removed. The new wine is known as *Heurige*, green, bitingly fresh and acidic, and often prickling with carbon dioxide from fermentation: the *Heurigen*, cellars-cum-wine-gardens where it is drunk, provide the visitor with the essence of gaiety, for which Vienna is renowned.

HUNGARY

Hungary (Magyarorszag) produces a broad spectrum of wines from the everyday, such as the Olaszrizling and commercial Bull's Blood to the classic Tokay, one of the world's great dessert wines. Exports are controlled by the State monopoly, Monimpex. The vineyards are in four main regions.

Some of the native grape varieties grown in these districts have colourful descriptive names. These are all white varieties: Szürkebarát (Grey Friar), Kéknyelü (Blue Stalk), Ezerjó (A Thousand Boons), Mézesfehér (Honey-white) and Juhfark (Lamb's Tail).

The Great Plain
Half the country's production comes from this vast sandy expanse, where the emphasis is primarily on quantity. The red wines are mainly from the Kadarka grape, which gives a peppery flavour and finish, and the whites from Olaszrizling (Wälschriesling). Kecskemét and Szeged are centres of production.

The Small Plain
In the far north-west, near the Neusiedler See, lie the vineyards of Sopron.
Soproni Kékfrankos is a soft, fruity red,
often slightly sweet, made from Gamay.

Transdanubia
West of the Danube, vineyards
producing good-quality white wines
line the northern shore of Lake Balaton.
Production centres are Badacsony,
Balatonfüred and Csopak; Balatoni is
the generic term for the wines of the
region. Somló, a little to the north,
produces good white wines in dry or
dessert styles; Mount Somló, like
Mount Badacsony, is an extinct volcano.
Mór, known for its Móri Ezerjó, a full-
flavoured dry white, lies to the west of
Budapest. Villány-Siklós and Szekszárd,
near the Yugoslav border, produce
excellent red wines from Nagybur-
gundi (Pinot Noir) and Kadarka.

The Northern Massif
From Budapest to the Russian border
runs a line of hills known at their
western end as the Mátra, in the centre
as the Bükk, and in the east as the
Hegyalja. The best wine of the Mátra is
Debröi Hárslevelü, a sweet, alcoholic

Excellent white wines are produced on the fertile
volcanic soil of Badacsony, which basks in a mild
and sunny micro-climate.

white. On the southern slopes of the
Bükk lies Eger, renowned for its red
Kadarka and white Leányka (Young
Girl) but, above all, for Egri Bikavér, the
Bull's Blood of legend, made from a
blend of Kadarka, Pinot Noir, Merlot
and sometimes other varieties.

Where the river Bodrog leaves the
hills, lies the district of Tokaj-Hegyalja,
home of Tokay. This unique, amber-
coloured dessert wine is made from
Furmint, Hárslevelü (Lime Leaf) and
Yellow Muskat grapes; the volcanic soil
leavened with a topsoil of lava and
loess gives it its unique quality. Its
relative sweetness depends upon how
many *puttonyos* (wooden measures,
each containing 35 litres) of *aszú*, a paste
made from over-ripe grapes, are added
to the must during a long, slow fermentation. Most blends contain either three,
four or five *puttonyos*, the last being the
sweetest. Traditional Tokay is called
Tokay Aszú; Tokay Furmint and Tokay
Szamorodni are lighter table wines,
which may be either sweet or dry. The
finest of all is Tokay Essencia, always
rare and a former elixir of kings.

YUGOSLAVIA

Yugoslavia (Jugoslavija) is a meeting place of Western with Eastern Europe, of the Alpine countries with the Balkans, of Catholic with Orthodox and Muslim, of Latin script with Cyrillic. Its wines are correspondingly diverse, and fascinating in consequence: they come from all six of the republics.

Serbia (Srbija)

The Yugoslav heartland, centred on Belgrade, includes two autonomous provinces, Vojvodina and Kosmet. The first lies north of the capital: its most famous district is Fruška Gora, a long ridge overlooking the Danube to the west of Petrovaradin and Sremski Karlovci (Carlowitz in Habsburg times), planted mainly in white grape varieties such as Laski Riesling (Wälschriesling), Traminer, Sauvignon and Smederevka.

To the east lie the Yugoslav Banat and Subotica, making white wines mainly from Wälschriesling, and attractive, fruity reds from the native Prokupac and Hungarian Kadarka. A pleasant dry rosé, known as Ruzica, is also made.

Kosmet, bordering Albania and Macedonia in southern Serbia, makes excellent red wines, increasingly from Cabernet Franc, Merlot, Pinot Noir and Gamay. Good Cabernet wines are also made farther north, in the areas of Župa and Venčac-Oplenac.

Other Serbian areas of note are Krajina and Timok, on the border with Romania and Bulgaria, where good Gamay wines are to be found. Although made from the same grape, they are dark and strong, quite unlike Beaujolais.

The Sava region of Slovenia produces white, red and rosé wines. Whites are Laski Riesling and Sylvaner; the dry rosé is Cviček, and the reds are largely Austrian in type.

Slovenia (Slovenija)

Austrian influence is clearly seen in the fresh, acidic white wines which are the speciality of this former Austrian province. The best of them are made in the far north, in the **Drava** area around and between the Drava and Mura rivers. Grape varieties are mainly of the Germanic type, with Laski (also known as Grasevina) and Renski (Rhine) Riesling at their head, followed by Sauvignon, Sylvaner, Gewürztraminer, Beli Burgundec (Pinot Blanc) and Ruländer. Šipon is a local variety producing an austere, dry white. Famous vineyard zones are Ljutomer, Ormož, Ptuj, Haloze and Radgona (the home of Tiger Milk); Maribor is the main town. Jeruzalem and Svetinje are site-names within the Ljutomer region; the beauty of the first of these so captivated Crusaders on their way to the Holy Land that many settled there. The natural acidity of the Slovene wines endows them with exceptional keeping qualities.

The **Sava** region of southern Slovenia produces Cviček, a refreshingly dry rosé. Farther to the west, vineyards stretch from Istria to the Italian border on the Isonzo, the wines here being made in the Italian way. The reds are made from Cabernet, Merlot and Refosco (the wine is known as 'Kraški Teran'); the whites include a Rebula from Brda, golden, dry and heady.

The South

The republics of **Bosnia-Herzegovina** and **Montenegro** each produce a single wine of note. In the former, the wine is Žilavka, a pungent, alcoholic dry white of complex flavour; the best comes from Mostar. Vranac is an inky, powerful red from Montenegro with a faint resemblance to Châteauneuf-du-Pape.

Macedonia and **Kosovo** are best known for red wines. Plantings of Cabernet, Merlot, Pinot Noir and Gamay are on the increase: local grape varieties produce Vranac and Kratosija.

Croatia (Hrvatska)

Inland Croatia links Slovenia to Fruška Gora, but its wines lack the distinction of either. They are mainly white, with Laski Riesling and Beli Burgundec predominant. The wines of the Adriatic coast, from Istria in the north to Dalmatia in the south, are rather more individual and impressive. The following is a short selection:

Teran Robust red from Istria, similar to Italian Refosco
Malvasia Rich dessert wine, also from Istria
Plavina and Babic Light dry reds from Dalmatia
Maraština Dry white, best drunk young, from Dalmatia
Opol Dalmatian rosé
Plavac Full-bodied, soft red
Postup and Dingač Deep-coloured, sweet red wines of high alcoholic degree from Pelješac, in Dalmatia
Prosek Luscious dessert wine from Dalmatia
Pošip Full-flavoured white from Korčula
Grk, Bogdanuša and Vugava Heady, golden whites from the islands

Wine-makers

Wine production is controlled by a dozen or so cooperative groupings, in which the State takes a close but indirect interest. Some of the more important are Slovenija Vino and Vinag in Slovenia, Navip in Serbia, Istravino in Istria and Tikves and Makedonija Vino in Macedonia.

CZECHOSLOVAKIA

Wine production in Czechoslovakia (Ceskoslovensko) is controlled by the State, which is made up of three provinces: Bohemia, Moravia and Slovakia. Wine is made in all of them, though the country is associated more with Pilsener lager. Perhaps this is because so little Czech wine is exported: demand exceeds supply on the domestic market, and most of the red wine consumed there is imported from elsewhere in Europe.

The most prolific of the provinces is **Slovakia,** whose vineyards stretch from Znojmo in the west, past Bratislava on the Danube to a south-eastern outpost which claims to make the original 'Tokay' sweet dessert wine.

The best Czech wines are white, and made from German and Austrian grape varieties such as Müller-Thurgau, Vlassky Ryzling (Wälschriesling), Rhine Riesling, Ruländer, Muskat Sylvaner (Sauvignon) and Weissburgunder (Pinot Blanc). Most of them are dry, with an aromatic bouquet and pronounced natural acidity. Red wines are made from Blauburgunder (Pinot Noir), Blauer Portugieser and St Laurent: Mělnik, north of Prague, is a centre of red wine production.

ROMANIA

Romanian geography is dominated by the Carpathian mountains which, to the west and north-west, enclose the high sandy plateau of Transylvania and the Banat (the eastern end of the Hungarian plain). They also shelter the eastern plains of Wallachia and Moldavia, inland from the Black Sea. Wine production, which is substantial and still growing, is divided between the State, local cooperatives and private growers. There are three main vineyard areas:

West of the Carpathians
Red and white wines are made around Arad and Timișoara on the Banat, the red from Cabernet, Merlot and Cadarca, and the white from the principal Romanian variety, the Fetească. Farther east, on the Tirnave excellent aromatic whites are made from Wälschriesling, Muskat Sylvaner (Sauvignon) and Traminer grapes; Perla is one successful brand made from a blend of these varieties and commonly exported.

South of the Carpathians
Sadova and Segarcea produce good red wines from Cabernet and Pinot Noir; in Drăgășani, and farther east in Argeș and Pitești, aromatic whites are produced from Muskat Ottonel, Muskat Sylvaner (Sauvignon) and Tămîioasa, a local variety of Muscat. The Dealul Mare vineyard, lying on the south-east slopes of the Carpathian massif, produces Romania's richest red wines from Cabernet, Merlot and Pinot Noir. Valea Călugărească, the Valley of the Monks, is an experimental state-run vineyard making some good reds.

East of the Carpathians
A fine dessert wine in the style of Tokay comes from Cotnari in Moldavia. Focșani is known for both red and white wines, particularly the red Bâbeascâ Neagrâ from Nicorești. The Dobrudja, a limestone plateau between the Danube and the Black Sea, produces excellent red and white wines from classic western European grape varieties, and a rather heavy and sweet Muscat dessert wine called Murfatlar.

Romanian table wines occasionally err on the side of sweetness and heaviness, but quality is improving fast.

BULGARIA

Bulgaria (Bâlgarija) is divided by the Balkan mountains. North of the massif, broad plains run down to the Danube, with vast vineyards scattered around local cooperative wineries; south lie more vineyards, with particular concentrations in the Maritsa valley and behind the Rhodope massif around Melnik.

Broadly speaking, Bulgaria's red wines are made in the west of the country, on the stonier soils of the uplands, and white wines on the sandier plains to the east, inland from the Black Sea. The better Bulgarian reds are made from Cabernet Sauvignon (with at best a slightly brittle finesse reminiscent of the Médoc), and local varieties such as Mavrud (dark and tannic), Gamza (pleasant but neutral) and Pami (light and fruity). Whites are made from Wälschriesling, Chardonnay (some of which are excellent), Misket (Muscat, usually dry), Rcatsitelli (reminiscent of Chasselas, and attractive when fresh), and Dimiat (pleasant, if neutral). Bulgaria has enjoyed a special rapport with Germany, and many of her export brands, controlled by the State monopoly Vinimpex, have German-sounding names, e.g. Rosenthaler Riesling. Hemus is a sweet Misket from Karlovo.

Some of the best Bulgarian wines are sold under the brand Euxinograd; varietal wines are qualified by regional names, e.g. Mavrud from Asenovgrad, Cabernet from Sukhindol, Pavlikeni or Tolbukhin.

THE EASTERN MEDITERRANEAN

GREECE

Virgil commented of Greece that 'it would be easier to count the grains of sand than the varieties of vines', and it is impossible in a few paragraphs to do more than list the more notable wines. Other than Retsina, Mavrodaphne and such leading brands as Demestica, few of them are yet seen abroad.

The main production areas are:

The Peloponnese
Accounting for a third of production, its wines are Mavrodaphne, a deep red dessert wine (*mavro* means black), Muscat of Patras (rich, scented and golden), Mantinia (dry white) and Nemea, a powerful red, at its best one of Greece's finest wines.

Central Greece
(Attica, Boeotia and Euboea) This is the centre of production for Retsina, since the Alep pine flourishes here. Dry whites and Kokkineli, a generic term for rosé, are also produced.

Northern Greece
(Thessaly, Macedonia and Thrace) The mountainous district west of Thessaloniki produces a dark, astringent red, Naoussa, comparable to the better wines of Piedmont. Amynteon, and Rapsani from Mount Olympus, are other powerful reds of a rather more astringent character.

Western Greece
(Epirus and the Ionian islands) Cephalonia, like Patras, makes good Mavrodaphne and Muscat, and the Robola is a full, complex, dry white wine. Zitsa is a fresh, pleasant semi-sparkling white from Epirus. Verdea is a lesser, but agreeable, white from Zante.

The Aegean
The peninsulas and islands of the Aegean produce a legion of different wines of which the most notable are:
Malvasia An amber coloured dessert wine (the original 'malmsey')
Cretan wines Predominantly red, powerful, full-bodied and tannic

Muscat of Samos Luscious and scented, reputed to be the finest Muscat in the world
Santorin/Vinsanto Dry or sweet, strongly alcoholic white wines produced on Thera, an extinct volcano
Lindos Pleasant dry white from Rhodes
Chalkidiki and Mount Athos wines An up-and-coming area, with enlightened investment from the Carras family, producing rich reds

Among wine-makers, Metaxas, Achaia Clauss and Andrew Cambas are old, established firms; Courtakis and Calligas are modern and progressive. Two companies, Tsantalis and Boutaris, dominate the north. Carras is a lone pioneer of varietal wines.

CYPRUS

Of the eastern Mediterranean countries, Cyprus has deservedly the leading reputation as an exporter. The vineyards lie on the southern slopes of the Troodos mountains, which enjoy cooler temperatures and higher rainfall than the plains of the north-east.

Three grape varieties are grown almost exclusively: Mavron (a red variety), Xynisteri (white) and Muscat d'Alexandrie. Cyprus's leading export is Sherry-type wine, which was traditionally less alcoholic than true Sherry from Jerez. The trend now is towards higher-strength wines, and production is moving increasingly towards the Spanish pattern. *Flor* is encouraged in the making of *fino*-style wines, and the wines mature in traditional *soleras*. Cyprus 'Sherry' comes in all styles from dry to very sweet; the sweet wines have a marked Muscat character and orange colour. Cyprus's most distinguished wine is Commanderia, made from sun-dried grapes, rich in natural sugars. It is a deep red, sweet dessert wine, fortified up to 25 per cent alcohol.

Pleasant table wines are also made on Cyprus, the best of which are powerful reds such as the Othello brand; white wine brands are Aphrodite and Arsinoë. Rosé, as in Greece, is known as Kokkineli. Leading producers are Keo, Sodap and Etko/Haggipavlu.

TURKEY

The wine industry is at an early stage of development, though the State has intervened to the extent of dividing the country into nine administrative zones for viticultural purposes. The most important are:

Thrace/Marmara
The most productive zone, including vineyards on both sides of the Bosphorus. Wines are generally sold under the generic term Trakya (Thrace). Tekirdag is a sweet white.

The Aegean
The western seaboard and hinterland, home of the 'Sultaniye' (Sultana) which is grown for the table. The best wines are Muscats (labelled as Misket or Bornóva Misket), natural or fortified.

Central and eastern Anatolia
White wine vineyards lie north, south and east of Ankara. The better areas for red wines lie farther east. Grape varieties are mainly native and obscure. The best wine of the area is Buzbag, a dark, powerful red from near Elâzig.

South-eastern Turkey
Good red and white wines are made from local varieties around Gaziantep.

Classic European grape varieties such as Chardonnay, Riesling, Cabernet Sauvignon, Pinot Noir and Gamay are gaining a foothold, particularly in Thrace/Marmara and along the Aegean, but production is still limited. The State monopoly accounts for most exports. Private exporters include Aral, Kavaklidere, Doluca and Kutman.

LEBANON

The main vineyards of Lebanon lie in the Bekaa valley, cradled between Mount Lebanon and the Syrian border. White wine vineyards, with grapes such as Chardonnay, Ugni Blanc and Chasselas lie higher up on the valley walls, with the red wine vineyards, crossing the valley floor, planted with Cabernet Sauvignon, Carignan and Cinsault, among other varieties.

Three producers are worthy of note: the most energetic of these is Caves Musar, led by Serge Hochar, whose red Château Musar is a wine of complexity and fascination. Pierre Brun is reputed for his Domaine des Tourelles; the third is the Jesuit cellar of Ksara in the northern Bekaa valley.

ISRAEL

Modern Israeli wine-making dates only from the late nineteenth century when Baron Edmond de Rothschild founded the great cooperative wineries of Richon-le-Zion, south of Tel Aviv, and Zichron-Jacob, in the shadow of Mount Carmel, which today account for nearly three-quarters of production.

There are three main vineyard zones. The most important stretches from Mount Carmel to the south of Tel Aviv, embracing the plain of Sharon and the hills inland towards Jerusalem; the others are the northern shore of Lake Tiberias (the Sea of Galilee), and oasis-type vineyards around Beersheba.

Israeli wines fall into two main categories: traditional light table wines, and sweet dessert types. Prevailing grape varieties are Carignan, Grenache and Alicante among the reds, which are vinified to produce either dry or sweet wines, and Sémillon, Clairette and Muscat d'Alexandrie among the whites.

Israeli wines are marketed in the USA and the UK by the Carmel Wine company, a subsidiary of the Société Coopérative Vigneronne des Grandes Caves (embracing Richon-le-Zion and Zichron-Jacob), all exported wines being certified as kosher.

Some of the most popular styles are:
White Carmel Hock, Château de la Montagne, Sauvignon Blanc, Sémillon
Red Adom Atic, Cabernet Sauvignon, Carignan
Red and/or white Avdat (dry), Château Rishon (sweet)
Dessert-type Carmel Topaz, Partom, Muscatel, Almog
Sparkling The President's Sparkling Wine

NORTH-WEST AFRICA AND OTHER REGIONS

The emphasis in the vine-growing regions of North-west Africa has always been on the production of wines in bulk for blending, particularly with the thin reds of the French Midi, but quality has improved notably in recent years. The best wines are red, generally dark and powerful, and there are also some pleasant dry rosés. All are prone to oxidation, and should be drunk young.

ALGERIA

The most important of the three countries, and the largest in vineyard area, is Algeria. The vineyards lie in the north of the country, within 100 kilometres of the Mediterranean. They are divided into three main regions: **Oran**, with 70 per cent of production, **Alger**, 25 per cent and **Constantine**, 5 per cent.

The best wines come from the hill zones of the hinterland, which rise to 1,200 metres on the slopes of the Atlas; the more commonplace wines come from the baking coastal plain. Soil composition varies from calcareous gravel, overlaying limestone and marl in the hills, to clay and sand on the plains. The whites tend to be over-alcoholic and heavy, and are not recommended. Grape varieties for making red and rosé wines include Carignan, Cinsault, Alicante-Bouschet and Grenache. The best red wines comes from the following areas:

Oran Coteaux de Mascara, Mascara, Haut Dahra, Coteaux de Tlemcen, Monts du Tessalah.

Alger Medea, Côtes du Zaccar

MOROCCO

The best Moroccan vineyards are of recent planting and lie on the northern slopes of the Middle Atlas around Meknès and Fès. Other vineyard zones are Dar bel Amri, Roumi and Sidi Larbi on the northern coastal plains around the capital Rabat; Boulaouane to the south of Casablanca; Marrakech and a small area around Oujda in the far north-east of the country.

Morocco makes agreeable dry rosés from Grenache, not unlike the *gris* of the Midi and ideal for drinking in hot weather with a dish of couscous, but its speciality is supple, powerful reds based, for quality, on Carignan, Cinsault and Grenache, with Alicante providing quantity. Private companies are encouraged within the wine regime: a leading company is Meknès Vins SA, whose Guerrouane, Les Trois Domaines, and Beni M'Tir are among the best Moroccan reds. Official quality grades reflect French tradition, the top grade wines being awarded an *Appellation d'Origine Garantie*.

TUNISIA

The main areas of production lie in a crescent in the north of the country, from Bizerta in the west, inland from Carthage and Tunis, to the eastern seaboard around Sousse and Hammamet. Cap Bon is famous for its Muscat wines.

At the end of the last century the wine-making industry in Tunisia was regenerated by French settlers, and today the grape varieties used are almost entirely French. The principal grapes for red wines are Alicante-Bouschet, Carignan and Cinsault, with Clairette, Ugni Blanc, and Sauvignon and Sémillon for the whites.

Wine production is largely controlled by the State through the UCCVT (Union des Caves Coopératives du Vin de Tunisie). The better wines marketed by this organization include Coteaux de Carthage, Tyna and Haut Mornag among the reds; and Sidi Rais (rosé) and Muscat Sec de Kelibia (white). Other good names are Coteaux de Khanguet, Tebourba, St Cyprien and Sidi Tabet.

MALTA

Grapes grown on Malta are principally for the table, though agreeable wines are made by some 10,000 minor private growers around Rabat and Siggiewi on Malta itself. The only producer of international note is the Marsovin Company, with interesting Cabernet Sauvignon.

EGYPT

Egypt made wine under the Pharaohs, and Cleopatra served *vinum mereoticum* to Julius Caesar, but it was only Greek settlers who kept the tradition alive into the twentieth century. The work was then taken up by a pioneer called Nestor Gianaclis, whose company today markets the best-known Egyptian wines, produced from vineyards west of the Nile delta between Alexandria and El Alamein. Grape varieties are Chasselas, Pinot Blanc, Pinot Noir, Gamay and Muscat Hamburg. Notable red wines are Gianaclis's Abyard, Ahmar and Omar Khayyam; whites are Reine Cléopâtre, Cru des Ptolemées and Clos Mariout. There is a slightly resinated taste to some Egyptian wines, a legacy of Greek influence.

ENGLAND

Producing wine in England is an uphill struggle. Only every few years is there a vintage worthy of the name, and it needs altruism or a second source of income for the wine-maker to persevere. But, luckily for the domestic consumer, there are those who do, and some of the results are delicious.

English wines are essentially white, since it is almost impossible for red grapes to ripen sufficiently to give wines of adequate colour in the climate of the British Isles. Spring frosts and bad autumns are other dangers, and to have a chance of making wine in England the siting of a vineyard in a place which has a good micro-climate is essential. Netting to protect vines against depradation by birds is also essential.

Grape varieties tend to be those developed in Germany for northern climates, and many of them are crossings. Some of those most commonly found are Müller-Thurgau, Reichensteiner, Magdalen Rivaner, Madeleine Angevine, Huxelrebe and Schönburger, the later a particularly aromatic variety which can be very attractive. Müller-Thurgau and Madeleine Angevine are the varieties most frequently planted, together with a hybrid, Seyval Blanc.

The wines almost always have a flowery, attractive nose and great charm. They are light and lack what wine-tasters call a 'long finish', but are none the less most pleasing. Many have a touch of sweetness to balance the acidity; this is achieved by the addition of Sweet Reserve (unfermented grape juice), akin to the German *Süssreserve*.

Nearly all the vineyards are in the south-east in Kent and Sussex, in the south-west or in East Anglia.

Recommended vineyards include:
Lamberhurst Priory (the largest vineyard, and very professionally managed), Tunbridge Wells, Kent
Adgestone Isle of Wight
Elmham Park Dereham, Norfolk
Wootton Shepton Mallet, Somerset
Kelsale Saxmundham, Suffolk
Pilton Manor Shepton Mallet, Somerset
Felstar Felsted, Essex
Biddenden Ashford, Kent
Pulham Pulham Market, Diss, Norfolk
Cavendish Manor Sudbury, Suffolk
Tenterden Vineyards Small Hythe, Kent
Carr Taylor Westfield, Hastings, Sussex
Hambledon Hampshire
Three Choirs Newent, Gloucestershire

RUSSIA

Wine is produced in six of the Soviet republics, and their combined output places the USSR third in the world as a wine producer, after Italy and France. Both table and dessert wines are heavy and sweet, and few of them reach the West. Moldavia, in the far west adjoining Romania, produces the most 'European' wines: fresh dry whites from Fetească, and reds from Cabernet, Merlot and local varieties. The Southern Crimea is a centre of dessert wine production, as are the republics of Armenia and Azerbaijan. Georgia, the Crimea and the Russian republic are noted for their sparkling wines, generally labelled Champanski; they tend to be heavy and sweet. Beyond the Caspian Sea are vast new vineyards devoted mainly to table grapes and raisins.

CALIFORNIA

THE LAST TWO decades have seen an explosive development in Californian wine production. Nowhere has progress and change been more exciting than in the Golden State, and the wines rank amongst the best produced anywhere. The Old World has come to respect the New, and although California has learned much from the traditional wine-growing areas of the world, the exchange of knowledge has been two-way. The University of California at Davis has spearheaded research into vine-growing and wine-making techniques, and much more is now known about what happens in the vineyards and cellars than ever before.

This seems incredible when one thinks that 20 years ago half of California's production was devoted to fortified wines in both dessert and apéritif styles. But tastes have been changing; by 1973, more than half California's production was made up of light, often dry, table wines. Tastes have also been veering towards dry white wine, rather than red, and this has caused problems in California, where red wine, particularly Cabernet Sauvignon, was expected to be the wine of the future. These wines certainly have their place, but the switch to drinking white wine rather than spirits as an apéritif has made the demand a consideration for wine-makers in California.

The enterprising Californians have got round this difficulty, first by making white wines from black grapes and then by grafting white wine varieties on to red vine roots. Of course, this is easier to achieve in a hot, fertile area; nevertheless it shows the local wine industry's flexibility and technical expertise: two reasons for its undoubted success.

California now produces a huge amount of wine to cater for every taste. Twice as much Cabernet Sauvignon is grown in California as in the Médoc region of Bordeaux, and three times as much white Chardonnay as in the Côte d'Or of Burgundy. Wineries (the word covers both the wine firms and the premises in which they make their wine) vary from the largest in the world, Gallo, to small, independent enterprises set up by enthusiasts determined to make better wine than their neighbours. This element of competition has had an undoubted effect on improving standards, and the Californian wine industry is peppered with those who have left other, prospering careers to enter it.

There are three main reasons for this phenomenal burst of energy in the vineyard and cellar. First, the market existed to encourage fine wine production: no wine industry can ever flourish without an appreciative audience waiting to be satisfied. Secondly, the capital needed for setting up wineries, which are expensive, and for research, was available. And thirdly, there was an abundance of clement weather conducive to fine wine-making.

Climate is the most important factor on the Californian wine scene. In Europe, it is unusual to worry about an excess of sun: the reverse is more likely to be true. But much of California can become too hot for fine wine production. Ideal conditions often exist where breezes from the Pacific Ocean exert a cooling influence. These breezes can only reach the vineyards through breaks in the mountains that form a barrier between the ocean and the interior, and areas with micro-climates enjoying this

The University of California at Davis has devised a rough classification of viticultural California into climatic zones, using sun-heat summation during the growing season. A 'degree day' is a period of 24 hours during which the average temperature exceeds 50°F by one degree; for instance, an average temperature of 60°F in 24 hours equals 10 degree days.

Region	Number of degree days
I	less than 2,500
II	2,501–3,000
III	3,001–3,500
IV	3,501–4,000
V	4,001 or more

cooling influence make desirable sites.

The ocean does not only induce cooling breezes – it also brings in fog and mist, which are elements of the climate of vineyards in the coastal region, if not in the Central Valley. In the Monterey Valley, the wind blows regularly in the afternoon.

The coastal counties, generally, fall into Regions I-III, while farther inland the Central Valley falls into Regions IV and V. The latter are more suited to producing stronger, dessert wines or basic blended table wine, while Regions I-III specialize in fine-quality table wine. Many successful commercial blends are made by a judicious mixture of coastal region and Central Valley (San Joaquin) wines.

However, it is impossible to say 'one viticultural region, one climate,' e.g. Napa Valley varies from Region I to Region III, while the Santa Ynez Valley in Santa Barbara County embraces Regions II and III – with the latter farther inland.

One of the greatest of the Californian wineries, Chateau St Jean vinifies grapes from several different sources, but now has over 40 hectares of vineyards around the house and winery planted with white grape varieties.

In Europe, climates tend to become colder as you travel north, but in California, specific conditions exist in each area. For instance, in the Napa Valley, it is much hotter in Calistoga than in Yountville farther south, and cooler still in Carneros, yet farther south towards San Francisco. However, in the Monterey Valley, more northerly Salinas is much colder than Greenfield. Temecula in southern California, south of Los Angeles, certainly could not make fine wines if it were not for a gap in the mountains which lets the cooling sea-breezes through to the sizzling interior.

The type of wine you wish to make, and, therefore, the grape varieties on which to concentrate, are largely decided by the climate in California. In Europe, the soil is equally important – often more so. Although soil analysis is practised in California, the essential thing is to get the grape variety right for the climate.

The grapes of California

The wines are usually labelled after grape varieties (called varietals), so it is as well to know what wines the grapes can produce. The wine-making picture is far more complex than in Europe, where one area usually specializes in one sort of wine – e.g light, fresh white wines with acidity in the Mosel region of Germany; Cabernet/Merlot wines, which age well, in the Médoc. One winery in any given area in California can make more than half a dozen wines from an array of grape varieties. As from 1983, when a label specifies a grape variety, the wine will have to be made from at least 75 per cent of that variety. Many top wineries have already followed the 100 per cent rule, but this does not necessarily result in better wine, e.g. Cabernet Sauvignon often needs some 'softening' with Merlot.

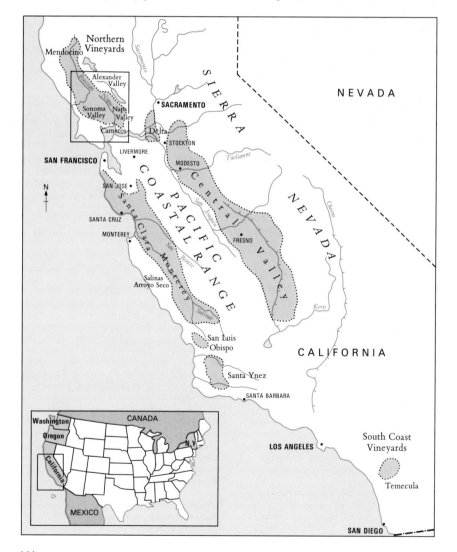

Principal grapes for red wine

Cabernet Sauvignon Planted in the coastal region, it does well in Regions I, II and sometimes III. It can make massive wines – alcoholic and tannic; but softer, more subtle examples are now appearing. Some wine-makers give it less wood-ageing and make a more easily drinkable, gentle wine; other wines demand a wait or are for tasting only. Big wines come from Napa, slightly lesser ones from Sonoma. Monterey's best recent examples have almost lost the earlier 'bell-pepper', capsicum flavour. Good examples are also found in Alexander Valley, Mendocino, San Luis Obispo and Santa Barbara (Santa Ynez and Santa Maria).

Pinot Noir This variety from Burgundy has not been established as successfully as Cabernet Sauvignon from Bordeaux. Many wine-makers mistakenly produced wines that were too 'big', which does not suit this grape. However, some good examples can be found in the cooler Regions I and II in Napa, Sonoma, Carneros, Monterey, San Luis Obispo and Santa Barbara. It seems to be a mistake to age Pinot Noir in new oak, and at the northern end of the Napa Valley, at Calistoga, the heat gives too 'jammy' a taste. But the progress of Californian wines over the 1970s encourages the expectation that a great Pinot Noir will be achieved before long.

Zinfandel Although this grape may have come from southern Italy, its origins seem difficult to trace, and it should be assumed that it is now unique to California. It can make deep, almost Port-like, alcoholic wines of which a glass suffices; or it can be made much lighter, when it is delicious, spicy and quaffable. It is best in Region I and sometimes good in Regions II and III. Sonoma has made some remarkable examples, but Napa, Mendocino, Monterey and Santa Clara have also had big successes. The Amador, San Luis Obispo and Lodi Zinfandels are the rich, alcoholic type. Much depends on how the grape is vinified, regardless of area.

Merlot As in Bordeaux, it is often used to blend with Cabernet Sauvignon. But it can be excellent in its own right – fine examples come from Santa Ynez, Sonoma and Napa.

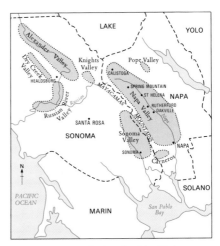

Petite Sirah Not the Syrah of the Rhône, but tannic and robust, often needing ageing and blending with softer grapes. Much is produced in the Central Valley, but Napa, Sonoma and Santa Clara give better results. The real Syrah is also beginning to appear; it has many of the same properties as Petite Sirah, but makes finer wines.

Gamay There is more confusion here. The Napa Gamay may be of Beaujolais origin, and it produces lightish wines in Napa and Monterey. The Gamay Beaujolais is a type of Pinot Noir, and sometimes tastes like it.

Grenache This can make anything from rosé to light red wines and even dessert wines; it is found mostly in San Joaquin.

Carignane Rather a workhorse blending grape, mostly found in San Joaquin.

Barbera Although grown mostly in San Joaquin, this grape produces far better results in Napa, Sonoma and Mendocino.

Ruby Cabernet A grape variety developed in California, and largely grown in San Joaquin.

Grignolino Sparsely grown, this variety can make good wines in Napa and Santa Clara. The rosé is the most intriguing wine.

Tinta Madeira Coming straight from the Douro in Portugal, this makes good Port-type wines in San Joaquin.

Principal grapes for white wine

Chardonnay This was the great success story of the 1970s, and Chardonnays are some of the most highly prized wines of California. They can be made rich, oaky and powerful, especially in Napa and in Alexander Valley, but grand examples also come from Sonoma and Monterey. There is also a lighter, more flowery style of Chardonnay, for younger drinking, which is good value.

Chenin Blanc A widely planted grape, appearing everywhere, both as a varietal and in blends. It often has a touch of sweetness and those who like the Loire Valley's Vouvray will like this.

Johannisberg Riesling (White Riesling) No one would have thought that this grape which makes such splendid wines in the northern wine-making areas of Germany would do so well in sunny California. The most remarkable examples are sweet and luscious, affected by *Botrytis cinerea* or noble rot, and quite stunning from a handful of wineries as far apart as Napa, Sonoma, Alexander Valley, Santa Ynez and Monterey. Usually, Johannisberg Riesling wines have a touch of sweetness, and are fruity and soft.

Sauvignon Blanc (Fumé Blanc) The name varies according to the whim of the winemaker. It makes white wines which rarely resemble Sauvignon wines from France. In California they are fruitier and rounder, less pungent, crisp and 'catty'. Although mostly dry, the wines can be sweet, even botrytized, and sometimes have some wood-ageing. This is a coastal regions grape, good in Napa, Sonoma, Santa Barbara and Livermore.

Sémillon Grown in the Central Valley and coastal regions, this is not yet important, but is good blended with Sauvignon, and can make botrytized dessert wines. One wonders if it could be made as dry and magnificent as in the Hunter Valley of Australia.

Gewürztraminer This is a grape which is becoming steadily more popular. The wines made from it should not be compared with Gewürztraminer from Alsace, often being more flowery, but with less pungency of bouquet. Sometimes the wines have residual sugar and there are examples with *Botrytis*. It

Grapes are picked mechanically in Napa Valley at Trefethen Vineyards, where some very fine Chardonnay, Cabernet Sauvignon and Johannisberg Riesling wines are made.

is exceptional in Sonoma, but there are fine examples nearly everywhere in the coastal zone: Napa, Mendocino, Monterey, San Luis Obispo and Santa Barbara.

French Colombard Widely grown, it makes easily drinkable, flowery white wines at a modest price. It is mostly to be found in the Central Valley, but the best examples come from Sonoma and Mendocino.

Emerald Riesling This crossing of White Riesling and Muscadelle produces wines that are flavoury, with bouquet and a touch of sweetness. Mostly found in San Joaquin.

Gray Riesling Not a Riesling at all, this grape makes pleasant, soft, slightly sweet wines.

Pinot Blanc A coastal grape variety, Pinot Blanc can produce really fine wines in Napa, Sonoma and Monterey. Also an important component of top sparkling wines. If you like Chardonnay, you will like this; the wines can have both fruit and elegance.

Who produces what in California?

The quantity part of the market is dominated by huge companies producing a wide range of wines to a high technical standard. If some are dull to a practised palate, remember that many people are not interested in finding subtle flavours in wines, but prefer to opt for a pleasant taste at a reasonable price. There is also a form of false snobbery which feels that large companies cannot produce good, interesting wines – which they certainly can. Many now produce an excellent top range to satisfy the discerning drinker, and the makers are to be admired in that they often do this in the midst of a huge overall operation. Some of the largest companies are listed below.

Almadén (Santa Clara)
A giant concern belonging to National Distillers and making every type of wine, their well-priced varietals are the best bet, although every type of wine is produced. Another label, Charles Le Franc, has slightly more expensive wines.

Beaulieu (Napa)
Owned by Heublein, Inc, Beaulieu makes an imposing amount of wine. Cabernet Sauvignon is the most famous wine, especially the top *cuvée*, Georges de Latour Private Reserve. But the generics in larger 1.5 litre bottles are also to be recommended.

Beringer Vineyards (Napa)
The wines are sold under both Beringer and Los Hermanos labels, and are utterly reliable for pleasant drinking. Among other good wines, one of the best light Zinfandels on the market comes from this winery.

Christian Brothers (Napa)
A really reliable, huge concern, Christian Brothers is owned by the Catholic teaching order of La Salle, and directed by the ever-modest Brother Timothy. Every type of wine is made, but the varietals are excellent value – all the giant concerns now feel that this is where the future lies, with vintage dating when possible. The vintage-dated wines tend to be bigger than the non-vintage, and can take a few years of ageing, while the non-vintage should be drunk on buying. Among more well-known varietals there is the rare red Pinot St George, while the Pineau de la Loire is the Chenin Blanc, which is white and sweetish.

E. & J. Gallo (Stanislaus)
Virtually a household word in the USA, Gallo is the largest winery in the world and an amazing example of size and logistic efficiency. They make all kinds of wine, from the frivolous to sound varietals. Europeans still wince at the use of names such as Chablis and Hearty Burgundy (a category termed 'generics') on indigenous Californian wines, but they are huge sellers. They are also very drinkable, and it is to be hoped that they will one day stand on their own merits without the 'prop' of borrowed French names. Sales approach 50 million cases annually. People reading this book will probably be more interested in dependable varietals than in the jugs which tend to be soft, with some residual sugar. Do not forget Gallo's Sherry-type wines.

Irrigation is a necessity on the floor of the Napa Valley to provide the vineyards with moisture when rainfall is deficient.

Inglenook Vineyards (Napa/Central Valley)
Owned by Heublein, Inc, this is both an estate and a brand, the latter one of the most important on the US market. In descending order of quality and expense, the ranges are Inglenook Estate, Inglenook Vintage and Inglenook Navalle. Under the Estate label, the Cabernet Sauvignons are big wines, red Charbono is a unique speciality and grape variety, and there is a good range of whites. The Colony label is in the same group.

Charles Krug (Napa)
This giant company makes entirely reliable varietal wines as well as jug wines under the CK label. The red wines can be exceptional, especially the Vintage Selection Cabernets.

Louis M. Martini (Napa)
The reds from this Napa house age very well – look out for the Private Reserve and Special Selection Cabernets, also good Gewürztraminer and slightly *pétillant,* rare Moscato Amabile. Louis Martini always means value and quality.

Paul Masson (Santa Clara)
This firm produces a great quantity of wines, from the attractive carafes of red, white and rosé to the rare Souzao Port, which is a remarkable Port-style wine made from a Portuguese grape of the Douro. A hearteningly high standard of overall quality is achieved, with particular mentions for their fresh, fruity Zinfandel and the Pinnacles Estates selection wines, of which the Gewürztraminer and Fumé Blanc are amazingly good for the price, and also for their delicious Chardonnay and Johannisberg Riesling. These are lightish, elegant wines, not huge, oak-aged blockbusters.

Mirassou (Santa Clara)
A family-owned business with very high standards, this is a name which inspires great confidence. Varietals include excellent Gewürztraminer, Zinfandel and Cabernet Sauvignon, and sometimes their Harvest Selection Cabernet Sauvignon can smell and taste remarkably like a Mouton Rothschild – blackcurranty, with depth and real class.

Robert Mondavi (Napa)
Mondavi combines being a richly merited prestige name in California with being a sizeable concern. The Mondavi family is one of the most dynamic anywhere in the wine world, and they 'made' the Napa. If you can afford them, buy such beauties as their top Cabernet Sauvignons (the Reserve 1975 is one of the best Californian red wines of the decade, if not of Californian history), which all have a deep and classic style. The Pinot Noir is less oaked than it used to be, and white Fumé Blanc, Chardonnay and sweet Johannisberg Riesling are all of real quality. Anything marked Mondavi will give you a treat, and the best wines make one reach for all the superlatives.

The Monterey Vineyard (Monterey)
Owned by Coca Cola, the winery is veering towards whites, with excellent Johannisberg Riesling, but the December Harvest Zinfandel can be very good; this late picking does not happen every year, however. The winery is used for making the Taylor California Cellars wines, blended by that brilliant exponent of the art, Dr Richard Peterson, and here lies some of the best value in the state. Another winery is also under construction for this firm. The varietals Sauvignon Blanc and Cabernet Sauvignon are particularly recommended. The Wine Spectrum is another label covering a range sold on certain markets – the red is excellent value.

Parducci (Mendocino)
Parducci is the king of Mendocino, and a great believer in wines that show their fruit rather than the characteristics of the barrel in which they are kept. You get a lot for your money when you buy Parducci, and all the varietals show real individuality, none more so than the Cabernet Sauvignon and the Chardonnay. White French Colombard is also very good.

Sebastiani (Sonoma)
Their best wines are from Sonoma, and the reds are beefy and robust. Nothing could be better for cold climes than Sebastiani Barbera (happily, the Sebastiani family remain faithful to one of Italy's best grapes); the Zinfandel is a lovely mouthful, too.

Sonoma Vineyards (Sonoma)
Some very well-made wines emerge from this winery, especially Cabernet Sauvignon, Zinfandel, Chardonnay and French Colombard.

Other Californian wineries

No list can be exhaustive, for nowhere do wineries spring up more quickly than in California. Suffice it for someone to get bitten by the wine bug, and another cellar is under construction. It is also unwise to name individual wine-makers, who tend to move on.

MENDOCINO AND LAKE
Cresta Blanca
Edmeades
Fetzer (nice Zinfandel, not too heavy)
Husch
Konocti Cellars
Lower Lake
McDowell Valley (delicious Cabernet Sauvignon, fruity style rather than substantial weight)
Milano
Navarro
Parsons Creek
Tyland

SONOMA
Alexander Valley (superb Chardonnay, suitable for ageing)
Balverne
Bandiera
Buena Vista
Bynum, Davis
Cambiaso
Chateau St Jean (This is one of the best wineries in California. The grape variety is always on the label. Superb Chardonnay from McCrea Vineyard, Wildwood Vineyards, Hunter Farms and Robert Young Vineyards; these are made to last and should be drunk with food – not as an aperitif. Also outstanding Johannisberg Riesling Late Harvest wines, reaching right up to such gems as Belle Terre Vineyard Individual Dried Bunch Selected Late Harvest.

Clos du Bois
Dehlinger
DeLoach
Dry Creek
Field Stone
Fisher
Foppiano
Geyser Peak
Grand Cru
Gundlach-Bundschu
Hacienda
Hanzell (especially for Chardonnay)
Hop Kiln
Horizon
Hultgren-Samperton
Iron Horse (good Chardonnay and Cabernet Sauvignon)
Italian Swiss Colony
Johnson's
Jordan (much-heralded Cabernet Sauvignon)
Kenwood
Kistler
Korbel
La Crema Vinera
Lambert Bridge
Landmark
Lytton Springs
Mark West
Martini & Prati
Matanzas Creek
Mill Creek
Pastori
Pedroncelli (lovely Cabernet Sauvignon)
Preston
Rafanelli
Rege
St Francis
Sausal
Sebastiani
Simi (good wines, getting better and bigger)
Sky
Sotoyame
Souverain
Stemmler
Swan, Joseph
Topolos
Trentadue

Valley of the Moon
Views Land
Vina Vista
Willowside

NAPA
Acacia (heavily oaked Chardonnays)
Alatera
Alta
Buehler
Burgess (massive Cabernet Sauvignon and Zinfandel for ageing, plus distinguished Chardonnays)
Cakebread (good Cabernet and Chardonnay, needing bottle age)
Carneros Creek (big, rich Chardonnay and Pinot Noir, for ageing)
Cassayre-Forni
Caymus (good Cabernet Sauvignon, and look out for second label, Liberty School, which is priced lower)
Chappellet (good winery, particularly fine Merlot)
Chateau Chevalier
Chateau Montelena (splendiferous Chardonnay and Cabernet Sauvignon, worthy of all the superlatives)
Clos du Val (Cabernet and heady Zinfandel: sometimes balance seems to lack in both, but there are vintages when it all comes together)
Conn Creek (very big Chardonnay, Cabernet Sauvignon Zinfandel and White Riesling

Cuvaison (deep, alcoholic wines)
Deer Park
Diamond Creek
Domaine Chandon (top sparkling wines)
Duckhorn
Far Niente
Franciscan
Freemark Abbey (This excellent winery makes quite outstanding Chardonnay, good Cabernet Sauvignon and, in some years, late-harvested Johannisberg Riesling, here called Edelwein, which ranks with the heights of the Rheingau wines.)
Green & Red
Grgich Hills (very high-quality Chardonnay and Johannisberg Riesling)
Heitz (stunning Cabernet Sauvignon – Martha's Vineyard, tasting of mint and eucalyptus, and almost equally exotic Bella Oaks Vineyard. Straight Cabernet Sauvignon is also excellent. Rich Chardonnay, very dry Johannisberg Riesling and scrumptious Grignolino Rosé.)
Hill, William
Keenan, Robert
Kornell, Hanns
Long
Markham
Mayacamas (very good, even minty-flavoured Cabernet Sauvignon from the slopes of Mount Veeder, and waxy, scented Chardonnay)

Other Californian wineries (continued)

Mount Veeder (very good scented, minty Cabernet Sauvignon: compare it with the Mayacamas and consider whether a Mount Veeder regional mountain character is appearing)
Napa Vintners
Napa Wine Cellars
Nichelini
Pannonia
Pecota
Phelps, Joseph (This is one of the greatest wineries in California from the quality angle. The deft hand of German wine-maker Walter Schug produces white wines of finesse, elegance and entrancing fruit, and stylish red wines of real class – not just massive and heavy. Whether it be Sauvignon Blanc, Gewürztraminer, Cabernet Sauvignon or Johannisberg Riesling –in some years there are superlative late-harvest wines which perhaps have the best balance of them all – the result is unerringly memorable.)
Pope Valley
Quail Ridge
Raymond
Ritchie Creek
Round Hill (super Chardonnay)
Rutherford Hill (very good Chardonnay, Merlot and Cabernet)
Rutherford Vintners
St Clement
Sattui
Schramsberg (extremely elegant sparkling wines)
Shafer
Shaw, Charles F.

Silver Oak
Smith-Madrone
Spring Mountain (very high-quality Chardonnay, Sauvignon Blanc, Cabernet Sauvignon and Pinot Noir)
Stag's Leap Wine Cellars (remarkably good Cabernet Sauvignon and a fine array of others)
Stag's Leap Winery
Sterling Vineyards (look out for their Reserve Cabernet Sauvignon and excellent Sauvignon Blanc)
Stonegate
Stony Hill (Chardonnay, White Riesling and dry Gewürztraminer which need a few years of bottle ageing)
Sutter Home
Trefethen (beautifully balanced Chardonnay, very fruity Johannisberg Riesling, very 'Burgundian' Pinot Noir, and fruity Cabernet Sauvignon. Look out for their reasonably priced Eshcol blended Red and White.)
Tulocay
Villa Mount Eden
Vose
Yverdon
Z-D (Chardonnay and Pinot Noir, mixed with American oak)

ALAMEDA, SANTA CLARA AND SANTA CRUZ (The title refers to the counties: remember that Santa Cruz Mountains is a small vine-growing area within Santa Clara County.)
Ahlgren
Bargetto
Bertero

Bruce, David
Carey, Richard
Concannon
Congress Springs
Conrotto
Devlin
Felton-Empire
Fortino
Frick
Gemello
Grover Gulch
Guglielmo
Hecker Pass
Kirigin
Kruse
Lamb, Ronald
La Purisima
Live Oaks
Montclair
Morris, J. W.
Mount Eden (Wines with the Mount Eden label are made from grapes grown on the property, while the MEV label indicates that the grapes were bought in – both are excellent. Superb Chardonnay of intoxicating flavour and richness, and very nice, firm Pinot Noir.)
Novitiate
Oak Barrel
Obester
Page Mill
Parsons, Michael
Pedrizzetti
Pendleton
Rapazzini
Ray, Martin
Richert
Ridge (A prestigious winery making deep powerful Zinfandel and Cabernet Sauvignon of inky colour and massive texture. Definitely classy. 'Natural' methods are followed here: it is probably the only winery in California to use natural, instead of selected, yeasts.)

Rosenblum
Roudon-Smith (very good Chardonnay, and all-round, high quality range; notable Zinfandel)
Rudd, Channing
San Martin (some very good wines indeed at reasonable prices – fruity delicacy and low alcohol are the keys)
Sarah's Vineyard
Sherrill
Silver Mountain
Smothers
Sommelier
Staiger
Stony Ridge
Sunrise
Sycamore Creek
Turgeon & Lohr (particularly good whites)
Veedercrest
Villa Armando
Walker
Weibel
Wente Bros (some of the best value in California, with a remarkable range of whites, as well as reds. Happily, quality is here married with good quantity, as the family firm is large.)
Wine and the People
Woodside

MONTEREY AND SAN BENITO
Calera
Chalone (Unfortunately, this is very small, but the wines are superb: rich, intense Chardonnay, outstanding Pinot Blanc, and beautifully balanced Pinot Noir.)
Cygnet
Durney (small winery to note in Carmel Valley; particularly good Cabernet Sauvignon)
Enz

NEW YORK STATE

Jekel (very quickly made
a richly deserved
reputation for itself,
with excellent
Cabernet Sauvignon,
Chardonnay, fruity
Johannisberg Riesling,
and occasionally
exceptional J.R. Late
Harvest and Pinot
Blanc)
Monterey Peninsula
River Run
Ventana (grows large
amount of grapes for
other wineries, but
own wines very good,
especially the
Chardonnay and
Pinot Blanc)

SAN LUIS OBISPO AND
SANTA BARBARA
Ballard Canyon
Carey Cellars
Estrella River
Firestone (This Santa
Ynez Valley winery is
making wines of very
high standard indeed,
none more so than
Late Harvest and
very luscious Selected
Harvest Johannisberg
Riesling,
Gewürztraminer,
Merlot and Cabernet
Sauvignon. Also good
Chardonnay and Pinot
Noir.)
Hoffman Mountain
Lawrence
La Zaca
Los Alamos
Mastantuono
Pesenti
Ranchita Oaks
Rancho Sisquoc
Sanford & Benedict
Santa Barbara
Santa Ynez Valley
Vega
York Mountain
Zaca Mesa (particularly
good Chardonnay,
Johannisberg Riesling
and Pinot Noir)

SIERRA FOOTHILLS
Here, the county of
Amador is by far the
most important for
vine-growing,
especially for
Zinfandel
Monteviña is the most
important winery, and
makes Zinfandels for
young and more
mature drinking, as
well as other varietals
Santino & Shenandoah
are also good.

SAN JOAQUIN VALLEY
The home of the giant
Gallo, and others such
as Guild, Giumarra,
Ficklin and Papagni.
Ficklin is famous for
Tinta Port, a Port-type
wine.

SOUTHERN CALIFORNIA
Made up of two
districts from a wine-
producing point of
view, Cucamonga has
the Cucamonga
Vineyard Co., and
Temecula has
Callaway, which is a
top-flight winery with
a whole range of
excellent things. The
most unusual wine is
the Late Harvested
Chenin Blanc 'Sweet
Nancy', a honey-like
dessert wine made
with botrytized
grapes, but production
concentrates on dry
white wines from
Chenin Blanc,
Sauvignon Blanc,
Chardonnay and
White Riesling. Also
reds from Cabernet
Sauvignon, Zinfandel
and Petite Sirah. Here,
Sauvignon Blanc has
some residual
sweetness;
Fumé Blanc is dry.

With thirsty New York on its doorstep, the State ranks after California as a wine producer. Two-thirds of the grapes grown are *Vitis labrusca*, the grape variety native to the continent, whose characteristic foxy aroma precludes the making of fine wine. *Labrusca* grapes are usually used for heavily sweetened wines for a certain, usually urban, market. There are also French-American hybrids – crossings of *Vitis vinifera* and American vines; as these crossings become more sophisticated, with increasing 'French' influence in them, the resultant wines improve immensely. However, significant plantings of *Vitis vinifera* in New York State now produce the wines which will probably be of most interest to the reader of this book.

Some of the best East Coast examples of *Vitis vinifera*, or European, vines come from Gold Seal Vineyards, in the Finger Lakes region, now owned by Seagram. Gold Seal is extremely well known for its range of Champagne-method sparkling wines, but now Chardonnay, Johannisberg Riesling and Gewürztraminer are extremely creditable. The cold of winter can be a problem for *vinifera* vines here, but they seem to be surviving well. Gold Seal wines are also sold under the Charles Fournier label.

Heron Hill Vineyards and Vinifera Wine Cellars are at the quality end of the wine-making scene: small and champions of *vinifera* wines. Whites like White Riesling, Chardonnay and Gewürztraminer are the most successful, which is logical in the cold climate – after all, to everyone but German wine drinkers, who pay huge prices for Assmannshausen, that northern country often makes superb whites but disappointing reds.

Other reputable wineries
Benmarl Wine Company, Hudson River Valley (specializes in French American hybrids, but also has Chardonnay) ● Bully Hill, Finger Lakes (specializes in hybrids and *labrusca* wines; Seyval Blanc, both still and sparkling, might be the best buy) ● Taylor

Wine Company, Finger Lakes (the largest winery; famous for Great Western Champagne, it specializes in hybrids and *labrusca*, making blended table wines, many sweet) ● Canandaigua Wine Company (specializes in *labrusca* wines) ● Wagner's Vineyards (superb Chardonnay) ● Widmer's Wine Cellars (*labrusca* and hybrids)

THE PACIFIC NORTH-WEST

Washington

Wine-making is possible in this State beyond the Cascade Mountains, which protect the interior from the rain which falls in areas nearer the Pacific Ocean. In eastern Washington the Yakima Valley is so dry that irrigation is necessary.

Chateau Ste Michelle is the leading producer of wines made from *Vitis vinifera*, and white wines are particularly good. The winery itself is near Seattle, and the must is transported from vineyards 240 km away for vinification. Look out for Chardonnay, Sémillon, Sauvignon Blanc, Chenin Blanc, Johannisberg Riesling, Gewürztraminer and Muscat Canelli, a dessert wine. Ste Michelle also has a small winery at Grand View in the Yakima Valley.

Other wineries in Washington include Associated Vintners, with a very fine Chardonnay, and Preston Wine Cellars.

Oregon

The problem here in some years is too much rain for good wine production. However, the Willamette Valley can produce good wines, and high hopes are held for the Pinot Noir especially. Many small wineries buy in grapes from Washington or Idaho. The main wineries are Eyrie Vineyards, Hillcrest Vineyard, Tualatin Vineyards and Knudsen Erath with a fine Pinot Noir.

Idaho

The only winery here is Chateau Ste Chapelle Vineyards. The long, cool growing season and relatively high acidity favour white wine production, and the Johannisberg Riesling is the most successful grape variety. Ste Chapelle also imports grapes from Washington.

OTHER REGIONS OF THE USA

With the exception of New England, where there are a few small wineries using *vinifera*, virtually all the wineries scattered through the rest of the United States make wines from hybrids, *Vitis labrusca*, or even other fruits.

Since this book is about wine made from *Vitis vinifera*, we will leave them to their efforts and their necessarily local markets. But encouragement should be given to wineries like Wiederkehr in Arkansas, which is experimenting with *Vinifera* varieties such as Johannisberg Riesling.

CANADA

In Ontario, the Niagara peninsula borders New York's Niagara County, and is thus by far the most important vine-growing area in the country. French-American hybrids and some *vinifera* are produced.

On the other side of Canada, British Columbia mostly imports grapes from Washington and California to make wine.

MEXICO

The Mexican drinks beer with his hotly spiced food, followed by brandy. It is thus logical that wine production in Mexico is now dominated by large firms such as Pedro Domecq, Seagram, Martell and Osborne, which initially produced only brandy, but used their capital investment and experience to make wines. Perhaps the best wines come from Baja California. It is difficult to see enormous progress, since for wine-making to be encouraged and quality improved, a ready and receptive market is required.

SOUTH AMERICA

PROBABLY only a few of the more adventurous imbibers in the northern hemisphere are aware of the fact that Latin America produces wine at all, let alone that it can boast of two countries, Argentina and Chile, which rank fifth and tenth respectively in the world league of producers. Brazil and Uruguay, too, have much improved the quality and quantity of their wine.

ARGENTINA

The first vines were planted in the foothills of the Andes by Jesuit missionaries as long ago as 1569. Today the area of viticulture extends from the Tropic of Capricorn in the north to latitude 40° south. There are 350,000 ha under vine; 72 per cent in the province of Mendoza; and the rest in San Juan, Rio Negro and the northern provinces. This relatively small vineyard area nevertheless produces over 25,000,000 hl annually, and the yield per hectare is nearly double that of France.

Apart from the colder Rio Negro province, the vineyards lie in semi-desert at the foot of the Andes mountains, where the annual rainfall never exceeds 250 mm. The secret of Argentina's compact but massive production is a superb irrigation system devised by the early settlers. An intricate network of canals and ditches brings melted snow from the mountain rivers and glaciers to strategically placed reservoirs in the parched land below, and this is now augmented by water from deep boreholes.

There are over 46,000 smallholders in Mendoza and San Juan, and they contract their grapes to privately owned *bodegas* or to state-owned cooperatives.

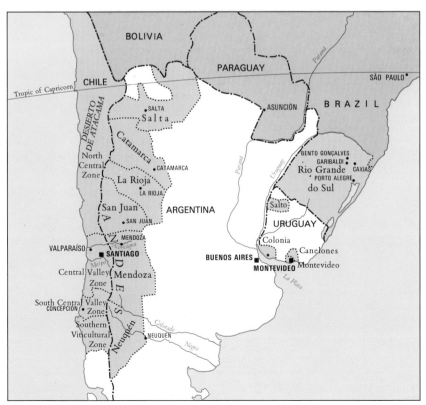

Types of grape

Historically, the most common grape varieties were the rosé Criolla Grande, and its clone, Cereza, but recently there has been a marked swing to white-wine drinking, and also a growing demand for wines of better quality. Fine varietals like Riesling, Chenin Blanc, Chardonnay and Sémillon are beginning to appear alongside the more traditional varieties. Malbec is the predominant black grape, but Cabernet Sauvignon and other European varieties such as Barbera, Tempranillo, Bonarda, Pinot Noir and Merlot are also widely used.

Wines and wine-makers

The quality of Argentine wines continues to improve and at recent fairs and tastings the wines have done well in comparisons with Californian wines such as Cabernet Sauvignon and Chardonnay in particular.

To offset the effects of the hot, dry climate, white wine grapes are now picked early to ensure maximum acidity. By the use of controlled fermentation, pale golden, fresh, almost spicy wines are produced that are worlds apart from the deep-coloured, oxidized and flabby whites of a few years ago.

The reds, too, have improved steadily. Like the better wines from Australia and California, the varietal influence is strong and like all 'hot-country' wines, Argentinian reds have a good, deep colour and plenty of alcohol; but while more supple and less tannic than their Bordeaux counterparts, they do not share the same depth of flavour and length of finish. Argentine wines represent good value for money.

Names to look for in Britain and the USA are the Trapiche and Andean vineyard range of Argentine-bottled wines from the excellent Peñaflor organization. Other good red and white wines come from Lopez; Pascual Toso, who produce an outstanding Cabernet; Bodegas Bianchi; Suter and Norton; Rural; Gargantini, who have an excellent Cabernet Sauvignon under the name Emenencia, and Orfila and Weinert, who are noted for their crisp white wines.

BRAZIL

Until a few years ago, travellers who tried the local wines usually regretted their decision, but times are changing, and the wine industry has taken a more professional approach, following the arrival of big, multi-national firms such as Cinzano, the Heublein Corporation, Martini, Moët & Chandon and National Distillers.

The first vineyards were planted along the steamy coastal strip by early Portuguese colonists, but the climate and soil were not really suitable and today's centre of production is west of Porto Alegre in the cooler mountain regions of the Rio Grande do Sul.

Nearly two-thirds of Brazil's total production of 3,000,000 hl comes from around the towns of Bento Gonçalves, Garibaldi and Caxias, founded by Italian settlers over 100 years ago, although recently National Distillers have

The viticultural skills of experts are gradually overcoming the problems of growing European grape varieties in the humid climate of Brazil's Rio Grande do Sul.

developed a big new vineyard at Sant'ana do Livramento, close to the Uruguayan border.

Types of grape

American hybrid grapes like Isabel and Herbemont do best in the hot, damp conditions, and account for well over half the production. Of the European grape species, the red Cabernet Franc and Barbera do particularly well; Moscato is the predominant white variety.

Wines and wine-makers

Wines made from American hybrids all have a characteristic 'foxy' bouquet and taste. Nevertheless, quality continues to improve and Dreher's Marjollet red wine surprised many people when it was shown at the Bristol World Wine Fair in 1979. Other leading firms are the Cooperativa Vinicola Aurora, and the Companhia Vinicola Rio Grandense.

CHILE

Chile's vineyards are among the oldest in the Americas, but it was not until 1851 that a Basque immigrant, Silvestre Ochagavia, realized that the fertile Central Valley area, close to Santiago, was ideal for the production of quality wine. He sent to Europe for expert viticulturists, and soon French grape varieties replaced Chile's counterpart to the Criolla, the País.

When phylloxera devastated the vineyards of France in the 1870s, it was the Chilean growers who sent back cuttings of ungrafted vines to restock them. Phylloxera has never been able to penetrate the three great natural barriers that protect Chile's vineyards – the Atacama Desert, the Andes, and the cold currents of the Pacific. The vineyards cover 110,000 ha, and are spread over 1,440 kilometres of this long, narrow country. There are three significant production zones: the fertile Central Valley which accounts for more than 52 per cent of the total production of around 5,000,000 hl; the South-Central Valley; the South-Central Unirrigated zone, the source of cheap wine for domestic consumption.

Types of grape

The País grape is widely used for the production of *vino común*, but French influence is still dominant. Red grape varieties in use are Cabernet Sauvignon, Cabernet Franc, Côt and Merlot; the most common whites are Sémillon, Sauvignon, Riesling and Chardonnay.

Wines and wine-makers

Chilean red wines, owing much to the growing conditions and the French mentors, are excellent. White wines are, perhaps, not so good. Chile's wine industry is under-capitalized and poorly equipped compared with those of Argentina and California. There is still too much emphasis on ageing in wood, particularly for the white wines, but modern methods of vinification are being introduced by a new generation of wine-makers.

Probably the most famous Chilean estate is Viña Cousiño Macul, whose Cabernet Sauvignon Antiguas Reservas compares favourably with many a good Bordeaux. Other firms which can be relied upon are Concha y Toro SA – one of Chile's biggest exporters, particularly to the USA; Viña Linderos SA – a small but conscientious maker of good Cabernet; Viña Undurraga SA; Viña Santa Rita SA; Viña Santa Carolina SA, and Viña José Canepa y Cia.

URUGUAY

This relatively small country, with just over three million people, cannot support the type of wine industry one finds in Argentina or Chile; but 19,000 ha are now under vine, mostly in the provinces of Montevideo, Salto, Canelones and Colonia. These produce only about 500,000 hl of wine – a very low yield by South American standards – but the soil and extremely humid climate make growing difficult. Until recently, hybrid American grape varieties were used because they were better suited to the conditions. Now it is possible to find a reasonable home-produced Cabernet Sauvignon, but with much the same earthy taste as in the wine from Brazil's Rio Grande do Sul.

SOUTH AFRICA

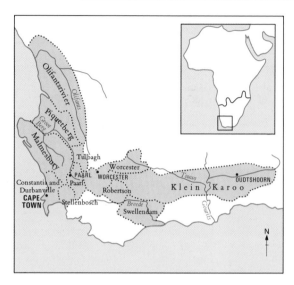

Demarcated areas are Constantia and Durbanville, Paarl, Stellenbosch, Tulbagh and Malmesbury in the coastal region; the hotter, drier Worcester and Robertson; Klein Karoo and the Breede River Valley or Swellendam; and, to the north, Piquetberg and Olifantsrivier. Boberg, which falls within Tulbagh and Paarl, is designated only for fortified or dessert wines. Not shown is the Orange River, 800 km north of Stellenbosch, producing raisins and low-priced table wines.

SOUTH AFRICA has an excellent range of highly drinkable, well-made wines, usually reasonably priced. The Wine and Spirit Board of South Africa controls the quality and origin of wines.

The wine comes from the south-west of Cape Province. Wine-making is largely in the hands of the descendants of Dutch and Huguenot settlers rather than the English, and many of the wine properties are architecturally beautiful, in Cape Dutch style – but equipped with huge plant of the most modern design and run with a scientific approach.

The finest table wines are produced in regions near the sea, where cooling breezes have a beneficial effect. Extreme ripeness in the vineyard can lead to an 'overblown' taste, and so the picking time must be judged correctly.

Constantia and Durbanville
Unfortunately, as Cape Town spreads outwards, many vineyards have disappeared. Groot Constantia, the famous estate in this area, is now government-owned and farmed by the Enological and Viticultural Research Institute at Stellenbosch. Good red and white wines are made, but the historic wine of the 1800s was a Muscat dessert wine. The Meerendal Estate in Durbanville is recommended.

Stellenbosch
Some of the country's greatest wines are made here, particularly the Cabernet Sauvignon reds. The town is a centre for the study of wine, and for vast enterprises. The Stellenbosch Farmers' Wineries are the second largest concern in South Africa, after KWV. Zonnebloem, their top range of wines in most grape varieties, is followed by the somewhat lighter Oude Libertas range. Nederburg wines are within this group, as is the Monis brand.

The Oude Meester group have the Fleur du Cap range, with most grape varieties, as well as Grünberger Stein, a medium-dry, tangy white, produced at the Bergkelder and sold in a *Bocksbeutel*. Gilbey's Distillers and Vintners own Bertrams and the Devonvale Estate, where a good range of reds is made.

Other important estates
Alto ● Audacia ● Blaauklippen ● Bonfoi ● Driesprong/Delheim ● Goede Hoop ● Hazendal ● Jacobsdal ● Kanonkop ● Koopmanskloof ● Meerlust ● Middelvlei ● Montagne ● Mooiplaas ● Muratie ● Neethlingshof ● Overgaauw ● Rustenberg and Schoongezicht (Rustenberg reds are excellent) ● Simonsig (exceptional Weisser Riesling) ● Spier ● Uiterwyk ● Uitkyk ● Verdun ● Vergenoegd (excellent reds)

Paarl

The climate here is hotter than in Stellenbosch, but the cooler mountain slopes are used for varieties such as the Riesling. The huge cellars of the Ko-operatieve Wijnbouwers Vereniging (KWV), or the wine-growers' cooperative, are at Paarl. Their Sherry-type exports are of considerable importance, and the Cape Cavendish range is excellent by any standards, especially the Fino or Dry.

KWV is also highly recommended for such reliable blends as their Chenin Blanc, with its honeyed nose and round flavour, for good Pinotage and for really reliable red Roodeberg, made from mixed grape varieties and always flavoursome and well balanced. Commercial blends at a reasonable price include the Bonne Esperance Red and White.

The firm of Johann Graue in Nederburg (one of the Stellenbosch Wineries) makes some very good wines indeed, both red and white. It is famous for its wine auction and Nederburg Edelkeur wines, luscious sweet wines made from *Botrytis*-affected Chenin Blanc. Nederburg Baronne is a very good red blend, and Fonternel is slightly aromatic and medium-sweet.

Other important estates
Backsberg (particularly good Cabernet Sauvignon) ● Boschendal ● De Zoete Inval ● Fairview ● Landskroon

Other wine-making areas

Some **Tulbagh** vineyards adjoin those of Worcester to the north. The better vineyards are high up on the cooler slopes, and fine white wines are made, especially by the estate of Twee Jongegezellen. Other important estates are Montpellier and Theuniskraal.

Beyond the mountains to the west, **Worcester** has sandy, alluvial soil; yields are high, since irrigation is widespread. Good-quality table wines are made from Chenin Blanc, as well as Sherry-type wine. This is an area of cooperatives.

Again, irrigation is important in **Robertson,** which is also moving away from producing brandy towards making table wine – mostly white, and some of it sweet. Estates include De Wetshof, Mont Blois, Weltevrede and Zandvliet.

GRAPE VARIETIES

In Stellenbosch, white varieties include Chenin Blanc (also called Steen), Clairette Blanche, Riesling and Colombar, with some Palomino, and more Germanic additions such as Kerner, Müller-Thurgau and Sylvaner. In Paarl, white varieties include Chenin Blanc, Sémillon, Palomino, Riesling, Clairette Blanche, and Colombar, with an appealing tang, especially in the Culemborg version.

Chenin Blanc is a good, all-purpose variety here, making soft, fruity yet crisp table wines; some slightly sweet, but more quite dry. It also makes Sherry-type wines. Clairette Blanche is often used in blends. The flowery-nosed Colombar from Robertson is particularly attractive.

The excellent Weisser Riesling is more 'German' in style, and Gewürztraminer and Sauvignon are successful in Tulbagh. In Worcester, Muscat d'Alexandrie produces luscious dessert wine with the typical grapy aroma.

Reds are dominated by Cabernet Sauvignon, Cinsaut and Pinotage, a crossing of Hermitage (Cinsaut) and Pinot Noir unique to South Africa. It makes rich, tannic, sometimes slightly 'jammy' red wine. Cabernet Sauvignon produces fine wines, especially in Stellenbosch, if the alcohol level is controlled; they age well. Cabernet Sauvignon/Merlot blends have, perhaps, the best balance. Cinsaut makes lightish, soft red wines; robust red wines are made from Shiraz (sometimes blended with Cabernet Sauvignon and/or Cinsaut) and Tinta Barocca.

Most of the wine-producing areas of the **Klein Karoo** are around Montagu, and irrigation is necessary. Brandy and dessert wines from Muscadel are made. **Swellendam's** vineyards are largely around Bonnievale, and wine production is similar to that of Robertson.

Other areas tend to concentrate on quantity rather then quality. There are vineyards around **Malmesbury** (note the Allesverloren estate) and **Riebeeck,** and the **Piquetberg** area to the north. **Boberg** falls within Paarl and Tulbagh and is designated for fortified, or dessert wines.

AUSTRALIA AND NEW ZEALAND

AUSTRALIA LIKE California first became a 'wine-drinking' country in the late 1960s. Growing popular demand for inexpensive 'jug' wines which are sold in flagons and casks inspired, in its turn, a market for fine wines.

The vineyards are scattered in every State, although it is the traditional wine-producing States of New South Wales, Victoria and South Australia that account for nearly all the wine made.

NEW SOUTH WALES

The Hunter Valley
Although responsible for only 12 per cent of the State's total 'crush', or harvest, of almost 125,000 tonnes, the Hunter Valley's traditions and quality make it the most important wine-making area. It consists of two main sectors: the older vineyards around Pokolbin and Rothbury, and the Upper Hunter, established as a result of the 1960s wine boom.

The Valley itself is some 2,600,000 ha in area. Grapes grow only on the central lowlands, where the soils are mainly podzolic, fine-textured and lime-free, but there are huge variations, and, para-doxically, one of the best whites comes from the worst type, a mixture of loam and sand on a clay base.

Rain falls on about 80 days a year, with the heaviest falls in summer and a second peak in winter, when hail is a worry. Temperatures are moderate, ranging from a daily average of above 21°C in January, to about 4.4°C in July.

The area escaped phylloxera, but is susceptible to downy mildew, a fungus which causes leaves and berries to wither. Low yields are further reduced by bushfires and depredations by flocks of starlings, and it is only the high quality of the wines which justifies continued viticulture.

The Hunter reputation is founded on dry red and white table wines. Hermitage (or Shiraz) is traditional for the reds and Hunter River Riesling (i.e. Sémillon) for the latter; more recently, Cabernet and Chardonnay have proved successful, although Hunter wine will always be regional before it is varietal.

White wines display a beautiful honeyed vanillan character and are well suited to bottle ageing. The reds are earthy, fragrant, and at their best after about five years in bottle; there are marked differences between vintages.

The most respected names in Hunter wine are: Brokenwood (high-quality red wines), Drayton's Bellevue, Elliotts, Lakes Folly, Lindeman's Ben Ean (Reserve Bin bottlings), McWilliams Mount Pleasant, The Rothbury Estate (Individual Paddock wines), Tulloch (Private Bins) and Tyrrell (excellent Chardonnay and Pinot Noir).

The Murrumbidgee Irrigation Area
Also known as Riverina, this vineyard area is large by Australian standards. Temperatures in summer can be very high, averaging 32°C in February; they fall to 3.8°C in July. The soils vary from heavy clay to light, sandy loam.

A higher proportion of white than red grapes is planted. Sultana and Muscat are used for sweet and fortified wines; White Shiraz (Trebbiano or Ugni Blanc), Sémillon and Riesling variants make table wines. Shiraz, Grenache and some Cabernet are grown for red wines.

Most Murrumbidgee wines are sold by a few very large companies offering 'jug' wines and inexpensive fortified wine, as well as producing spirit for brandy. Recently, however, some among the principal wine-makers – McWilliams at Hanwood, Yenda and Beelbangera, Penfolds, Seppelt, Wynn's and De Bortoli – have shown an interest in growing varietals under controlled irrigation conditions.

Mudgee
Located in the table lands west of Sydney, Mudgee is a small wine region of moderate climate. It lies about 500m above sea level, so the grapes ripen slowly, and the vintage commences about six weeks later than in the Hunter Valley.

The vineyard most renowned for quality is the Huntington Estate, which concentrates on red varietals (wines labelled by their grape types, as in California); Craigmoor makes good table wines and a little fortified wine.

VICTORIA

The southern State of Victoria produced over 95,000 tonnes of wine grapes in 1980, about 18 per cent of the total Australian crush. Apart from the established wine areas, the 1970s saw a proliferation of small wineries. Rising stars include the estates of Mount Mary (exceptional Pinot Noir), Taltarni, Tisdall, Seville (late-harvest Riesling), Yerinberg, and Wantirna (superb Pedro Ximénes and Palomino).

The North-east

The area is roughly triangular, with its base along the Murray River. There is little variation in climate, the main characteristic being the long, hot, dry summers. Most of the 635 mm of rain falls in spring and winter, and frosts are frequent. The vineyards are centred on the King, Ovens and Murray Rivers.

This area is well known for top-quality fortified and dessert wines, as well as reds. The former are sold as Liqueur Muscat and Liqueur Tokay, or under such titles as Madeira and

The Barossa Valley in South Australia is particularly renowned for white wines, some of which are exquisite late-harvest Rhine Rieslings.

Liqueur Tawny Port. The red wines from Shiraz and Cabernet are rich and generous, but recent trends are towards less full-bodied styles. In cooler areas, some successful whites are made from Rhine Riesling, Chardonnay, Muscat and Clare Riesling (Crouchen).

The most impressive winery is that of Brown Bros at Milawa (excellent varietal red and white wines). Other notable wineries include: Campbell's, Bailey (Bundara Hermitage and Cabernet), Chambers (Liqueur Tokay) Gehrigs, Bullers, Morris (Old Liqueur Muscat), Seppelt and G. Smith and Sons.

Goulburn Valley

This region is made famous by the 100-ha estate of Château Tahbilk, which produces only table wines, from Shiraz, Cabernet, Marsanne and Rhine Riesling. It is the red wines that have given Tahbilk its great reputation. New vineyards in the area include Mitchelton (some successful whites and red wines) and Virgin Hills (red wine only).

Great Western

The region is made up of hilly country some 200 kilometres west of Melbourne. Although the volcanic soil is poor, the frosts severe, rainfall insufficient and the yields low, some of Australia's greatest red wines from Shiraz and Cabernet grapes are produced in the region.

Two wineries, Seppelt's Great Western and Best's Concongella produce – among other fortified and table wines – Australia's best-known sparkling wine by the *méthode champenoise*. Nearby Balgownie Vineyard at Ballarat produces high-quality varietal Cabernet and Shiraz wines.

SOUTH AUSTRALIA

The most important wine-producing State grows and makes more than half of Australia's production: 312,485 tonnes in 1980. Many of the country's best vineyards are to be found here.

Adelaide Foot Hills

In and around the spreading State capital of Adelaide are a number of wineries and vineyards which were among the first in the State. Names like Penfolds' Grange Hermitage and St Henri Claret, Petaluma, Normans, Stonyfell and the Seaview Champagne Cellars have an important place in Australian wine history.

Southern Vales

The neighbouring McLaren Vale and Reynella Districts lie to the south of Adelaide. The climate is frost-free and allows good grape-growing. Thomas Hardy, Osborn D'Arenburg, Walter Reynell, Seaview and Wirra-Wirra produce a range of good-quality fortified, table and sparkling wines under both generic and varietal labels.

Barossa Valley

Australia's best-known wine region, which accounts for 10 per cent of the crush, lies to the north-east of Adelaide.

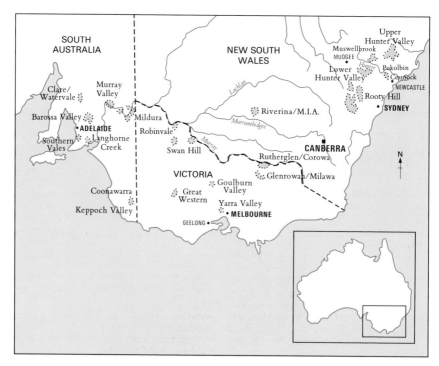

In the valley floor the land is quite arid, and hotter than most European wine regions, with a temperature range between 8° and 20°C. Average annual rainfall is 500 mm. The soils are diverse, ranging from sandy to heavy loams.

Once traditional producers of brandy and fortified wines, the Barossa winemakers have changed to meet the demands of the table-wine market, for which they grow Shiraz, Grenache, Rhine Riesling and Clare Riesling (Crouchen), Cabernet and Mataro.

Many large Australian companies are centred in the Barossa: Kaiser-Stuhl, Penfolds (Kalimna Vineyards), Leo Buring (Private Bin Rhine Riesling), Gramp's Orlando (late-picked white wines), Thomas Hardy (Siegersdorf Vineyards), Seppelt (excellent Port and Sherry styles) and Smith's Yalumba (Signature Series red wines, and Pewsey Vale Riesling).

All are reputable producers making all manner of wines. Generally the reds tend to lack acid and can have a salty character, though modern technique is producing some very fine white wines of Riesling style, especially Orlando and Yalumba.

The Murray Valley

The wine area is situated above the town of Renmark just inside the South Australian border. It is important for its production of 115,000 tonnes of grapes, which end up in bulk wines, both table and fortified, as well as in good-quality spirit for brandy. Many of Australia's largest companies have interests here.

WESTERN AUSTRALIA

The wines from the Swan Valley near Perth are full-flavoured table and fortified wines of hot-climate and fertile-soil character. Houghton/Valencia and Sandalford are the main producers.

Since the end of the 1970s, the main viticultural interest in Western Australia has come from the cooler southern growing areas established at Margaret River, Mount Barker and Frankland River. Here, the planting of quality varietals has met with great success.

NEW ZEALAND

Although the first vines were planted at the beginning of the last century, development in the wine industry was slow. Only with the easing of licensing and consumption laws at the start of the 1970s did wine-making begin to develop seriously, and the potential of and for New Zealand wines has yet to be realized.

Two-thirds of the harvest of 37,000 hl in 1980 was table wine, the rest being dessert wine and some brandy. With the exception of some traditional and new plantings at Nelson and Marlborough at the very top of South Island, the vineyards are mainly concentrated between latitudes 34° and 40° south, compared with Bordeaux, which lies at 44° north. The best-known areas are Hawkes Bay – the largest; the Henderson and Kumeu districts around Auckland; Mangatuna and Te Kauwhata.

The relatively cool, maritime climate favours white grapes, the principal planting being of Riesling Sylvaner (also called Müller-Thurgau). There is some Chardonnay, Gewürztraminer and Chenin Blanc, as well as experimental Rhine Riesling, Pinot Gris and Sauvignon Blanc. Pinot Meunier, Cabernet Sauvignon, Pinot Noir and Pinotage produce the red wines of most interest.

As a relative latecomer to the wine world, New Zealand has been able to take full advantage of the technical developments in wine-making. Mechanization is advanced in both viticulture and wine-making and generally the result is sound, fresh and appealing wines, the whites with a trace of residual sugar, the reds light in body but forward. Considerable government subsidies should encourage their emergence on to the international market.

The best examples of New Zealand wine are those made by Cooks at Te Kauwhata, Montana Wines (the largest winery), Nobilo and Villa Maria. Other producers are Penfolds and McWilliam's Wines, both Australian companies, and Corbans and Glenvale.

Here's how to make the most of the wine in the bottle: identifying it from the lore on the label, deciding whether to open it in advance or immediately before drinking, gaining access to it by means of the least complicated corkscrew, serving it at a comfortable temperature, choosing food that will bring out its best features, even selecting wineglasses that will enhance the pleasure of drinking.

There is advice on caring for bottles in the longer term. To store upright or horizontally? To keep in a cold place or not? How to give your good wines a long and healthy life – but only if they have the pedigree to merit such treatment (and many perfectly drinkable wines do not). In other words, how to get full value for money: not simply by checking the contents and the small print on the bottle label, but by buying early, buying in bulk, or buying jointly with tasting friends. Recognize a restaurant wine list that has been compiled with love and authority. Know when a disappointing wine can be saved, and when it has to be banished from the dining table, but may still work wonders in the kitchen.

These pages not only help you to treat your wine correctly, in the bottle and the glass, in the right place and for the right time, but explain when – and why – there is such a thing as 'right'. Enough has been written about the shoulds and should nots of wine to intimidate the thirstiest enthusiast. We have become used to the debunking of snobbery: aren't wineglasses with stems pretentious? Can you really use an earthenware pitcher as a decanter? Here myths are demystified, but if there is an element in them that will enhance the enjoyment of wine and encourage the corkscrews to get winding, you will find it in these pages.

At the end are useful checklists: vintages, wine-making terms and vocabulary, and a guide to pronouncing some of the more common names.

BOTTLE SHAPES

The bottle has two functions. For the wine, it acts as a protective and portable container – in which it can acquire bottle age if this is desirable. From the point of view of the potential drinker, the bottle sends out a variety of signals that help to identify its contents. These signals may be explicit (the label), conventional (the shape of the bottle), or even subliminal (the advertising, packaging and presentation).

As a container, a glass bottle – teamed with its cork – remains the ideal material to contain wines for ageing; just enough interaction between the oxidizing influence of air and the contents of the bottle is permitted by the cork to allow the development of bouquet in wines made from certain grapes, notably Cabernet Sauvignon and Chardonnay.

Since it is odourless and inert, glass has no effect on the taste of the wine, even over prolonged periods. Considerations of quantity rather than quality in wine production have recently caused bottles to be superseded by plastic containers or even bags – and the true cork by plastic stoppers, clip-on or

Profile of a bottle

Neck
Cylinder of even shape, to take the long cork required for bottle ageing.

Ullage
Amount by which the bottle falls short of being full: the wine level should come half way up the neck. In old wines excessive ullage due to seepage through the cork may have caused the oxidation of the wine: beware.

Capsule
Made of lead (the best and most expensive), foil or plastic. Essentially for more attractive presentation, the capsule keeps the cork clean, but can also protect it from weevil.

Shoulder
Square shoulders are traditional to Bordeaux and many Cabernet wines; sloping shoulders are typical for Burgundy and often for other Pinot Noirs. Both shapes bin easily.

Bordeaux
The traditional Bordeaux shape has become the classic bottle for maturing fine Cabernet and Merlot wines all over the world. Red wines bought anywhere in this shape of bottle will usually be dry and may need ageing: some cheaper Cabernets will be in bottles without punts. In Bordeaux, dark green glass is used for red wines and some dry whites; clear glass for both dry and sweet whites. In France itself and in California, the capacity is 75 cl; elsewhere this may dwindle to 70 cl – check the label. The traditional Chianti Classico bottle is brown.

Punt
Indentation in the bottom of a bottle adds strength and helps catch sediment. Wines for quick consumption are often bottled without punts.

screw caps – for table wines intended for drinking soon after bottling.

The cork might disappear from bottles in many more mass-appeal wines, if market research did not continue to suggest that buyers remain attached to the 'business' of opening the bottle with a corkscrew.

The shapes of bottles have tended to evolve either for functional reasons, or as part of a marketing campaign (often based on a traditional regional shape) to help to identify a particular brand or area in the eyes of a buying public.

In bottle language generally, it is the more everyday wines, which need persuasive advertising campaigns to disseminate their names, that are usually found with the more eye-catching labels and bottle shapes. Top-quality wines tend to have classic, low-key presentation: they can rely on their reputation to promote them. Up-and-coming wines made in the same traditions and from noble grape varieties tend to imitate this bottling and labelling style.

Five of the classic bottle types are shown.

Burgundy
The shoulders are more sloping than in the Bordeaux bottle, and there is always a punt. Yellow-green glass is generally used for both red and white wines. In France and California the capacity is always 75 cl, but in other countries it may be 70, 72 or 75 cl. Rhône wines also use this bottle shape.

Flûte
The traditional bottle for German wines is a taller, more slender shape, with no punt. It usually contains 70 cl, though contents can vary from 68 to 75 cl. Conventionally Rhine wines are bottled in brown glass, Mosel in green. Clear glass is used for the Loire rosés. A green, taller version is used in Alsace.

Vintage Port
The pronounced shoulders help to catch sediment, and the shape is suitable for binning. A bulbous neck lets the cork expand during long bottle-ageing. The seal (often of wax) and lead capsule are heavy-duty to stop both seepage and cork-weevil attack. The glass may be dark brown or dark green.

Champagne
The cylindrical shape has a punt, and a distinct lip for the wire muzzle which retains the cork. The dark green glass is thicker than for still wines in order to withstand up to 6 atmospheres' pressure, and light-resistant to protect the susceptible contents, especially from neon or fluorescent light.

BOTTLE SIZES

The standard bottle capacity is now 75 cl, even in America, which saw metric measurements become standard for wines bottled after 1 January 1980. Some areas of the world have derogations before they have to comply with this regulation, and there are obviously enormous numbers of non-standard sizes still in use. However America, for example, will now only import bottles containing 75 cl, but Britain and Germany currently still accept 70 cl bottles.

The standard 75 cl bottle shape is sometimes found enlarged to twice that size (a magnum); there are also half bottles and even quarter bottles which are available on aircraft and trains for individual passengers to drink with their meals. Halves and magnums each have advantages and disadvantages in terms of availability and value.

Half bottles, beloved of lone diners, particularly in restaurants, are nowadays generally unloved and increasingly less available. The quality is not always as reliable as that in a standard bottle (they say in the trade that 'not such good wine goes into the halves'); and it is true that their bottle life is more limited, since the smaller quantity of wine matures more quickly. Their price will reflect the fact that two bottles, two corks, two capsules will be containing one bottle's worth of wine. Among the limited choice, the best buys are likely to be dessert wines such as Barsac and Sauternes.

But half bottles are offered by some merchants so that consumers may, economically, find out what they like.

Magnums contain twice the standard amount of wine, i.e. 1.5 L. In table wines, the cost should be *less* than twice the price of the standard bottle, since the unit price of bottling, corking and labelling will be more or less uniform whatever the bottle size. The 1.5 L bottle is also mass-produced relatively cheaply, in Italy, for example.

The favourable price comparison does not necessarily apply to fine wines, however, where the magnum bottle is a replica of the ordinary bottle but actually costs more to produce. And the contents of the bottle will further raise the price: good Bordeaux and Burgundy is often bottled in this size specifically for laying down, since the ratio of wine to cork is considered the optimum for maturation of the wine.

Magnum 1.5 L

Standard 75 cl

Half bottle 37.5 cl

> ● *Look closely at the quantity stated on the label of apparently standard-sized bottles: a measurement of the contents is the one thing that is universally compulsory in labelling.*
>
> *Most bottles from Eastern Europe and Germany, and many branded wines, contain 70 cl of wine. In France, the USA, Spain, Australia and South Africa, among others, most bottles contain 75 cl of wine, though France may, for the time being, export bottles containing 70 cl.*
>
> *In the past, a variety of different bottle contents was in use, which caused considerable confusion to the consumer. The situation has now been greatly simplified by the adoption of standard bottle sizes, and the general rule is that it is the bottle contents that are measured, not, as previously, a notional bottle size. A typical bottle would now have 75 cl branded on the glass at the base of the bottle, followed by 55 mm, which indicates that the bottle contains 75 cl when it is filled to within 55 mm of the top.*

How many glasses?

Guests at dinner will probably drink a total of half a bottle each – more if they are enthusiastic about tasting different wines and are offered a succession of interesting examples to accompany a varied menu.

The half-a-bottle estimate is most likely to be accurate at a buffet or informal meal where only one or two wines are being served: say, one red and one white.

Bear in mind that the first wines served are likely to be quaffed more deeply, and that the later ones may be more important, and more expensive. Be generous as the cellar-person, but not as the wine-waiter: it is better to have too much wine (and serve it judiciously) than to run short.

These formulae show the actual bottle capacity in terms of glasses filled with appropriate drinking measures.

Table wines
One 75 cl bottle gives:
8-9 ISO glasses
(drinking measure)
or:
up to 20 glasses
(tasting measure)

Vintage Port
One bottle – less sediment – gives:
10 Port glasses

Sparkling wines
One 75-80 cl bottle gives:
8 well-filled *flûtes*

- *If a bottle of red wine contains sediment and has to be decanted, you will get fewer glassfuls from it.*
- *Sweet after-dinner wines go further than table wines: allow one bottle for every eight guests.*
- *Filling a wineglass to the widest part of the bowl leaves space to swirl the wine and release the bouquet.*
- *You can fill a flûte almost to the top with sparkling wine: the CO$_2$ projects the bouquet out of the glass – no need to swirl.*
- *Complain at a restaurant if the waiter or sommelier fills a glass to the brim: you cannot swirl the wine, and he may be encouraging you to drink more – and order more bottles – than you meant to.*
- *When ordering a 'glassful' of wine, beware: such an amount is not everywhere defined by law. A wine bar that cares about good service (and probably looks after its stock) will provide a generous number of centilitres in a glass large enough for you to enjoy drinking the wine – rather than using the glass as a measure, and filling it to the brim.*

Bag-in-a-box

Today's alternative to bottles – for wines to be drunk quickly and not too seriously – is the bag-in-a-box. Anything from two litres up to a gallon of wine is packaged in a plastic bag encased in a cardboard box. As the wine is drawn off, through a plastic tap near the bottom, the bag collapses so that the remaining wine is not affected by air.

This is a cheap and convenient way of buying straightforward wine in bulk: its portability makes it ideal for picnics and barbecues, hence its evolution in California, Australia and South Africa. A coating to the plastic bag keeps the wine in good condition for several months, so this is also a practical way of having the odd glass of wine on tap, at home and for parties.

Before investing in a large bag-in-a-box, check that the contents are to your taste by begging a glass from someone else's, or by buying a standard bottle of the same brand.

And, as with bottles, check the volume of the contents carefully to make sure that you get value for money: boxes that look similar in size may contain different quantities of wine.

CORKS AND CAPSULES

Cork is the resilient, waterproof bark of the evergreen cork oak, *Quercus suber*, which is stripped at intervals of 12 years and upwards for manufacture into bottle stoppers and other items. The tree is a native of the Mediterranean, but is now cultivated elsewhere, e.g. in California; however, the trees with the thickest bark, which is capable of producing the best corks, are found in Catalonia. Portugal is also a good source of supply.

The best wines call for the best-quality corks: longer corks for wines to be laid down for some years; shorter corks for lesser wines intended for young drinking. A variety of laminated corks, stoppers made from compressed cork fragments and cork-covered plastic do for more everyday wines.

No man-made substitute compares with the all-round suitability of cork as a bottle stopper. Its unique cellular structure makes it impermeable; it compresses; it is supple enough to be inserted into a bottle neck, take the required shape exactly and yet be withdrawn relatively easily. Neither moisture nor changes in temperature affect its function (though dryness will eventually cause it to shrink), and prolonged contact with it does not affect the taste of wine.

The state of the cork

Take a look at the cork after removing the capsule and before applying the corkscrew: 'read' it for possible danger signals. These may turn out to be harmless.

A clean, springy cork is a sign that the wine has been recently bottled or rebottled. As a cork ages, it tends to darken and harden. If the label says that the wine is, say, 10 years old and the cork looks new, this is somewhat suspicious. However, an old Bordeaux bought at auction direct from the château may have a cork that seems younger than the wine. This is because top Bordeaux growths (*crus classés*) are recorked every 25 years or so to give maximum protection to the wine. If the wines on auction are from a cellar in Britain or Switzerland, for instance, they are unlikely to have been recorked, although the head cellarman of Château Lafite made a trip to Britain in 1981 to recork the old bottles of Lafite lying in private cellars.

Crystals Harmless: they indicate that the wine has simply not been over-refined; white wines may throw tartrates or crystals, if they have been subjected to cold at some time in their life.

Dryness Beware: the wine bottles may have been stored upright, allowing the cork to shrink and air to enter the bottle and cause oxidation. Taste carefully. At best, the corks may crumble and be difficult to extract.

Smell Sniff the cork when you have extracted it: if the bottle has been kept (as it should have) on its side, the damp end of the cork should smell sweetly of the wine in the bottle.

Mould Harmless: damp storage conditions may allow mould to grow on top of the cork and under the capsule. It is not damaging to the wine, but the top of the bottle should be carefully wiped after the cork has been drawn.

Oozing wine Beware: a substantial quantity of wine may have leaked out, admitting air and causing oxidation. Check the level of wine in the bottle, and taste carefully. Wines with high alcohol and/or sugar content are usually less fragile than light, dry wines.

Weevil damage This example of a Vintage Port cork infested by cork weevil is a rare occurrence in cellars today, since sawdust is used less extensively in the bins.

If you do find this pest in bottles from your cellar, don't resort to chemical treatments, which will damage your wine. Isolate any affected bottles and drink the contents without delay, before the cork is a write-off and the wine spoilt.

Capsules

The capsule encases the cork and the neck of the bottle. It gives the cork some protection against attacks by the cork weevil, and is pierced with a pattern of tiny holes to allow the cork to breathe.

Traditional capsules are made of lead. Some companies or estates colour-code theirs according to the type of wine, but there is no universal system for this. Tin-foil capsules look like lead from a distance, but are cheaper and much less robust. Modern wines, lower down the price scale, often have plastic capsules which carry their protective function so far as to seem virtually impregnable: the Waiter's friend corkscrew with its knife may be their only undoing.

Apart from their protective function, the name and crest embossed on the top of the capsule helps to identify bottles binned or cased in cellars, when the labels are not visible. (Indeed, the seal of a Port bottle may be its only identification until the cork is drawn to reveal the year and name of the shipper branded on it.)

Beware of a damaged capsule on a bottle of good wine from the cellar: examine the cork especially thoroughly in case it has deteriorated and caused the wine to oxidize.

Don't pour out wine over a lead capsule: cut it around the rim, or remove it altogether to avoid contaminating the wine.

● *Keep a clean stopper cork (as from a Sherry bottle) to restopper opened bottles when some of the wine remains. As a rule of thumb, sweet German wines (Auslesen, etc) drunk before they reach maturity, age as much in a day once opened as they would in a year in bottle. Full-bodied Rhône, Italian and Spanish reds last for a couple of days kept in the refrigerator door, as do sweet white wines from Sauternes and Barsac. (In general, the bouquet of a wine suffers more quickly than the taste if there is excessive contact with air.)*

● *If less than half a bottle of wine remains, decant it into a clean half bottle to prevent excessive contact with air. Keep a couple of clean empty half bottles handy for this purpose. Recork with a clean stopper cork. Soak the label off the original bottle and transfer it to the half for identification or, more simply, put on a sticky label.*

● *Wines sold in screw-cap bottles are likely to keep for several weeks if closed securely and stored at the right temperature – often in the door shelves of a refrigerator. Such wines are usually 'stabilized' before being bottled and once opened do not age as quickly as wines made by more traditional methods.*

● *Champagne stoppers are a boon at parties. A host who opens several bottles beforehand, stoppers them in this way and leaves them ready in the fridge will not have to interrupt the festivities to wrestle with potentially tricky corks.*

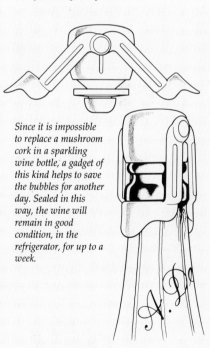

Since it is impossible to replace a mushroom cork in a sparkling wine bottle, a gadget of this kind helps to save the bubbles for another day. Sealed in this way, the wine will remain in good condition, in the refrigerator, for up to a week.

A CATALOGUE OF CORKS

The information on a cork

Unlike the label, which in every country is subject to rigorous legal requirements as to the information it shows, most corks need bear no specific information. In practice, the better the wine, the more words and numbers are likely to be printed on the cork: a top-growth Bordeaux will brand its cork with all the details, including the vintage; more common wines may simply have the name of the designated region (e.g. Rioja) or the location where it was bottled (*mis au domaine, mis en bouteilles dans nos chais/dans nos caves, erzeugerabfüllung*, etc). Many corks now have the code number of the bottler of the wine stamped on top: this can be seen when the capsule is removed, although most of the printing is visible only when the cork has been extracted.

Fine red wines for ageing in bottle take longer corks. Classic examples shown here are a Burgundy (Domaine Clair Daü's Clos Vougeot 1959) and three Clarets (Château Latour, Pauillac, 1955; Château Léoville-Las-Cases, St Julien, 1928; and Château La Tour de By, Bas Médoc, 1970)

Champagne corks

Especially good-quality cork is selected for Champagne corks, which must by law be branded with the word 'Champagne'. The characteristic mushroom shape is created when the long cork is inserted into the bottle: softened by soaking in water, the cork is driven for half its length into the bottle (it has to be squeezed to half its diameter to fit into the narrow neck). The projecting half of the cork is squashed down beneath a metal cap or disc which prevents the *agrafe*, or wire muzzle, from cutting into the cork. The wire is twisted securely around the flange on the bottle neck, and the whole is encapsulated in foil.

All five of the vintage Champagne corks pictured here were opened at the same tasting. There is a clear disparity in the size of the corks of the same age. Normally, a cork starts life wide and shrinks as it ages, although poor storage – such as being kept upright – can cause premature shrinkage.

A very shrunken, smooth cork probably means that the Champagne has considerable bottle age: the British call this 'old landed' Champagne.

In the profiles at the bottom of the page, the laminated layers of better-quality cork which come into contact with the wine itself are clearly visible. But composite cork – made of bonded fragments – serves to make the 'mushroom' tops of the corks.

1976 vintage 'Cordon Rouge' Champagne cork from G.H. Mumm of Reims

1975 vintage Champagne cork from Pol Roger of Epernay

Some fine white wines also merit bottle age: two *grands crus classés* are Château Coutet (Barsac), 1970 and Château Laville Haut-Brion (Graves) 1975.

Shorter corks are used for wines with a briefer life expectancy: whites are from South Australia's Barossa Valley, KWV of South Africa and Dr Bürklin-Wolf of Wachenheim in the German Rheinpfalz. Red Rioja from Spain can usually take a few years' bottle age.

Newer technology uses compressed cork fragments for everyday wines; synthetic, injection-moulded EVA promises non-tainting, dust-free, reliably stable stoppers.

1975 vintage Champagne cork from Krug of Reims

1976 vintage 'Extra' Champagne cork from Perrier-Jouët of Epernay

1975 vintage cork from Heidsieck Dry Monopole of Reims

A non-vintage cork, without its metal cap, from Charles Heidsieck of Reims

LABEL LORE

FRANCE

APPELLATION CONTRÔLÉE

Vintage

Name of wine-producing property
Château l'Estang is an archetypal *petit château* of Bordeaux.

CHATEAU L´ESTANG
1978

BORDEAUX SUPÉRIEUR
CÔTES DE CASTILLON
APPELLATION BORDEAUX SUPÉRIEUR · CÔTES DE CASTILLON CONTRÔLÉE

Region
Côtes de Castillon is one of the minor ACs of Bordeaux, usually good value.

Appellation Contrôlée

'*Mis en bouteilles par De Rivoyre & Diprovin Neg. à St. Loubes (Gde)*'
'Bottled by De Rivoyre & Diprovin, *négociants* at St Loubes (Gironde)'

ROBERT FILLIOL
PROPRIÉTAIRE A SAINT-GENÈS-DE-CASTILLON (GIRONDE)
PRODUCT OF FRANCE   75cl

Château-owner's name
Producer's address
Content by volume

VDQS

Name of wine/region
Côtes du Marmandais, SE of Bordeaux, are mostly soft, fruity reds made from the same grapes as the wines of Bordeaux: Cabernet, Merlot and Malbec.

'*Vin délimité de qualité supérieur*' or '**VDQS**'
'Wine of controlled superior quality': VDQS is an intermediate quality category between AC and *vin de table.*

Côtes du
Marmandais
VIN DÉLIMITÉ DE QUALITÉ SUPÉRIEURE
1978

Vintage

Producer's address:
'CCI Cocument – 47250'
'The cooperative cellars in the town of Cocument'

C.C.I. COCUMONT – 47250   73cl
MIS EN BOUTEILLE DANS NOS CAVES

Stamp showing the wine has been tasted, approved and officially designated VDQS.

'*Mis en bouteille dans nos caves*' 'Bottled in our own cellars'

VIN DE PAYS

'Country wine from the Ardèche region'

'Mise en bouteilles à la propriété'
'Bottled at the property'

Content by volume

vin de pays de l'ardèche
issu du cépage
GAMAY
Médaille de Bronze au Concours Général Paris 1974
Médaille d'Or au Concours Général Paris 1976
MISE EN BOUTEILLES A LA PROPRIÉTÉ
LES PRODUCTEURS DE SAINT-DÉSIRAT / CHAMPAGNE / ANNONAY
73 cl

'Issu du cépage Gamay'
'Made from the grape variety Gamay'

Awards won at France's most prestigious wine judging in 1974, 1976 and 1977

Producer's name

172

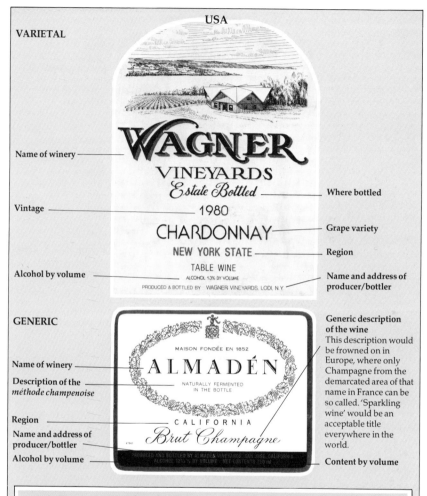

VARIETAL

USA

Name of winery

Vintage

Alcohol by volume

Where bottled

Grape variety

Region

Name and address of
producer/bottler

WAGNER
VINEYARDS
Estate Bottled
1980
CHARDONNAY
NEW YORK STATE
TABLE WINE
ALCOHOL 13% BY VOLUME
PRODUCED & BOTTLED BY WAGNER VINEYARDS, LODI, N.Y.

GENERIC

Name of winery

Description of the
méthode champenoise

Region

Name and address of
producer/bottler

Alcohol by volume

MAISON FONDÉE EN 1852
ALMADÉN
NATURALLY FERMENTED
IN THE BOTTLE
CALIFORNIA
Brut Champagne
PRODUCED AND BOTTLED BY ALMADEN VINEYARDS, SAN JOSE, CALIFORNIA
ALCOHOL 12½% BY VOLUME NET CONTENTS 750 ml

Generic description
of the wine
This description would
be frowned on in
Europe, where only
Champagne from the
demarcated area of that
name in France can be
so called. 'Sparkling
wine' would be an
acceptable title
everywhere in the
world.

Content by volume

● *In France, phrases such as* Grand Vin,
Grande Reserve *or* Cuvée Spéciale *on
the label have no strict, legal significance.
Similarly, 'Private Reserve' has no legal
definition in the USA.*
● Supérieur *usually means about 1 per
cent higher in alcoholic strength, not
necessarily any better in terms of quality.
However, in the South of France, a 12 per
cent alcohol wine is often preferable to one
of 11 per cent.*

● *Beware of German-looking labels whose
small print may be overlooked by innocent
buyers, but will reveal that the wine is the
blended produce of several EEC countries.*
● *Back labels with fairly technical
information that the wine-maker considers
interesting to potential drinkers are
customary on wines from California and
Australia, and appear increasingly on
wines exported from, say, Italy to English-
speaking countries. Supermarkets also now
provide helpful back labels, often with
serving suggestions.*

GERMANY

Village name (Deidesheim)
The addition of the suffix -er means 'of Deidesheim'.

'Qualitätswein mit Prädikat' or **QmP**
'Quality wine with particular distinction'.

Name of producer

The vintage does not appear on this label; it will probably appear on the neck label.

RHEINPFALZ

Deidesheimer Hofstück

Auslese

Qualitätswein mit Prädikat — A. P. Nr. 5 907 059 57 77

SCHLOSSBERG-KELLEREI, LEIWEN/MOSEL
Alc. ca. 11 % by Vol.   Produce of Germany   Contents 70 cls.

Region
Rheinpfalz is one of the 11 designated regions for quality wine.

Vineyard site or *Grosslage*

Type of wine: *Auslese*
Auslese is made from selected bunches of late-harvested grapes, so will taste medium-sweet to sweet.
If no grape variety is mentioned, it is probably a blend of several varieties.

Alcohol by volume

Content by volume

Quality control number or *Amtliche Prüfungsnummer*
Every QmP and QbA wine has a number.

SPAIN

Producer's name
Rioja wines are generally known by the name of the producer/ *bodega* rather than that of the vineyard/site.

Type of wine: Rioja

Producer's trademark

Name of estate

Vintage

Importer's name

PRODUCE OF SPAIN   75 cl.

MARQUÉS DE MURRIETA
Bottled by BODEGAS MARQUÉS DE MURRIETA · YGAY

Vinos de Rioja

YGAY

(LOGROÑO)

COSECHA 1975
Imported by Percy Fox and Co Ltd. London W 1

Content by volume

Bottling information
This is bottled by the producer at the *bodega* (winery).

Rioja denomination of origin seal
Rioja is among the most stringently regulated of Spain's production areas.

Name of the town where the *bodega* **is located**
Logroño is in the Rioja Alta.

Back label

RIOJA
GRAN RESERVA

Rioja denomination of origin seal

Gran Reserva
This indicates that at least some of the wine in the bottle has been aged in wood for 8 years or more. Alternative designations are *Reserva, Vino de crianza* and *sin crianza*.

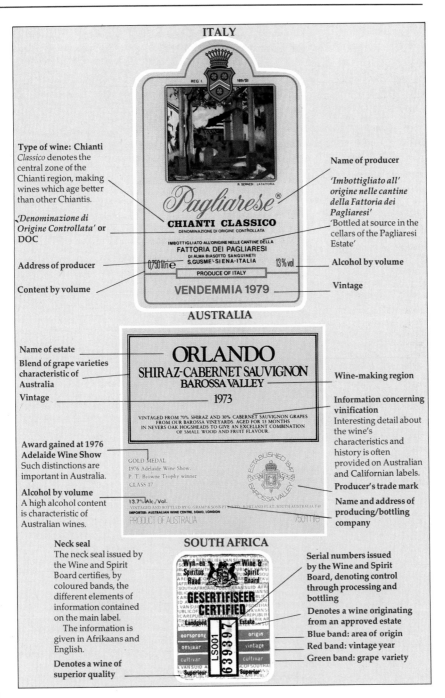

ITALY

REG. I.   189/51

R. SERNESI · LA FATTORIA

Pagliarese®

CHIANTI CLASSICO
DENOMINAZIONE DI ORIGINE CONTROLLATA

IMBOTTIGLIATO ALL'ORIGINE NELLE CANTINE DELLA
FATTORIA DEI PAGLIARESI
DI ALMA BIASOTTO SANGUINETI
S.GUSME · SIENA-ITALIA

0.750 litri e   13% vol

PRODUCE OF ITALY

VENDEMMIA 1979

Type of wine: Chianti *Classico* denotes the central zone of the Chianti region, making wines which age better than other Chiantis.

'Denominazione di Origine Controllata' or **DOC**

Address of producer

Content by volume

Name of producer

'Imbottigliato all' origine nelle cantine della Fattoria dei Pagliaresi' 'Bottled at source in the cellars of the Pagliaresi Estate'

Alcohol by volume

Vintage

AUSTRALIA

ORLANDO
SHIRAZ-CABERNET SAUVIGNON
BAROSSA VALLEY
1973

VINTAGED FROM 70% SHIRAZ AND 30% CABERNET SAUVIGNON GRAPES
FROM OUR BAROSSA VINEYARDS. AGED FOR 13 MONTHS
IN NEVERS OAK HOGSHEADS TO GIVE AN EXCELLENT COMBINATION
OF SMALL WOOD AND FRUIT FLAVOUR.

GOLD MEDAL
1976 Adelaide Wine Show.
P. T. Browne Trophy winner
CLASS 17

13.7% Alc./Vol.
VINTAGED AND BOTTLED BY G. GRAMP & SONS PTY LTD. ROWLAND FLAT, SOUTH AUSTRALIA 1.16
IMPORTER: AUSTRALIAN WINE CENTRE, SOHO, LONDON
PRODUCT OF AUSTRALIA   750 ml

ESTABLISHED 1847
BAROSSA VALLEY

Name of estate

Blend of grape varieties characteristic of Australia

Vintage

Award gained at 1976 Adelaide Wine Show Such distinctions are important in Australia.

Alcohol by volume A high alcohol content is characteristic of Australian wines.

Wine-making region

Information concerning vinification Interesting detail about the wine's characteristics and history is often provided on Australian and Californian labels.

Producer's trade mark

Name and address of producing/bottling company

SOUTH AFRICA

Wyn-en · Wine &
· Spiritus · Spirit
· Raad · Board
SOUTH AFRICAN
GESERTIFISEER
CERTIFIED
Landgoed   Estate
oorsprong   origin
oesjaar   vintage
cultivar   cultivar
Superior   Superior
LS001 639397

Neck seal The neck seal issued by the Wine and Spirit Board certifies, by coloured bands, the different elements of information contained on the main label.

The information is given in Afrikaans and English.

Denotes a wine of superior quality

Serial numbers issued by the Wine and Spirit Board, denoting control through processing and bottling

Denotes a wine originating from an approved estate

Blue band: area of origin

Red band: vintage year

Green band: grape variety

175

WINEGLASSES

On the premise that the wine is more important than the container, choose a glass that will enhance the pleasures of tasting and drinking. It is not a myth that the choice of glass affects appreciation of good wine: a poor design can distract your attention from the appearance, smell and taste of the wine. The right glass, on the other hand, creates the appropriate conditions for the wine, and is a pleasure to handle and to use.

Prerequisites for a good tasting or drinking glass include factors such as material, size and shape. Simplicity is a key: both coloured and cut glass obscure your view of the clarity and colour of the wine; clear, transparent glass, as fine as possible, gives maximum opportunity to appreciate and judge the wine's appearance. A glass should be large enough – especially in the bowl – to allow the wine to be swirled around before drinking; this process is no affectation, but airs the wine and enhances both bouquet and taste. A shape that narrows towards the top traps the aroma and bouquet inside and prevents them from evaporating too quickly – so you get the benefit of your wine's bouquet and it does not disappear into thin air.

The design suggested by these criteria is the ISO tasting glass.

The other shapes shown on these pages are classics. Avoid, if possible, the ubiquitous Paris goblet with a small, round bowl too shallow for swirling a reasonable amount of wine.

Caring for glassware
● *Wash glasses in warm water with washing-up liquid rather than detergent (and preferably neither); rinse thoroughly so that no hint of soap remains. Dry while still warm with a lint-free cloth (preferably linen), kept especially for glasses.*
● *To avoid the risk of breaking fragile glass put the cloth only – rather than fingers or thumb – into the bowl of the glass when drying or polishing.*
● *Dry glasses for Champagne especially thoroughly: damp inhibits the activity of the bubbles.*
● *Store glasses the right way up so that air can circulate in them, and to prevent them from being tainted by the smell of the surface they are resting on. Obviously, check for dust if the glasses are not often used.*
● *Make sure that the glasses are at a temperature appropriate to the wine to be served in them: e.g. room temperature for red wine.*

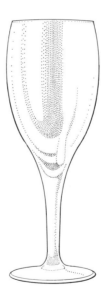

The tulip is the ideal all-purpose wineglass, sharing all the qualities of the ISO glass. Its long stem is elegant and easy to hold.

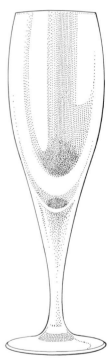

The Champagne *flûte* gives sparkling wine the depth it needs for the bubbles to develop (a shallow, wide shape lets them dissipate too quickly).

ISO tasting glass

Professionals in the wine world evolved the tasting glass endorsed by the International Organization for Standardization as the ideal design in which to judge a wine: its shape fulfils all the tasting prerequisites. The recommended quantity for tasting is 50 ml of wine (in a total capacity of 215 ml), but the glass is a pleasure to use for drinking any type of wine on any occasion – for both serious tastings and casual parties. And the tasting glass has the practical advantage of being safe in good dish-washing machines.

Bowl narrows towards top to retain bouquet

Fine glass enables warmth of hand to affect temperature if desired

Colourless transparent crystal glass shows wine's colour

Curved bowl permits wine to be swirled without spilling

Stem permits glass to be held without warming chilled wine or obscuring contents from sight (with either fingers or fingerprints)

Foot gives stability and can be held to swirl glass

The *ballon,* a shape associated with brandy, shows good Burgundy well. The short stem invites you to cup the bowl and bring out the bouquet of red wine with the warmth of the hand.

This fine-looking glass suits good red Burgundy well as it has plenty of space for swirling. Its large capacity means that a normal measure (one-eighth of a standard bottle) fills it only one-third full.

This wider-mouthed version of the classic tulip is often used in the Bordeaux region for serving fine Claret.

OPENING BOTTLES

Open wine bottles with as little palaver as possible: use an efficient corkscrew and devote your attention to the well-being of the wine in the bottle, rather than to the extraneous ceremonies that many books on the subject of wine recommend. Don't complicate matters by feeling obliged to wrap the bottle in a snow-white and odourless napkin (often top restaurants don't bother with this unnecessary practice). The chances of a bottle breaking while being opened are infinitesimal nowadays. And far from showing due respect for a prestigious wine, the napkin deprives it of its identity by hiding the label from view. Spend time caring for the wine rather than worrying about the laundry. (Of course, some sort of cloth is necessary to catch the drips if you use an ice bucket to chill your white wines.)

Corkscrews Hundreds of ingenious devices have been invented to reduce the amount of muscle-power that you need to extract a cork. The most effective of these is the Screwpull, a startlingly simple recent invention: you just keep winding. This and the Butterfly lever are ideal for people whose hands are not particularly strong.

Not recommended: a gimlet screw with a solid core: such screws often have sharp edges which cut into the cork, splitting it and making it difficult to draw cleanly.

Recommended: a worm thread, i.e. a spiral of wire with a sharp tip (which is not centred in the spiral). Widely spaced twists to the spiral give better purchase on the cork when it is being drawn out of the bottle. The essence of a corkscrew is the spiral bore, which must drive easily and in a perfect vertical down into the cork, damaging it as little as possible in the process, and must then provide good resistance in order to draw the cork out of the bottle. The spiral should always be at least 7 cm (2¾ in) long to grip the longer corks of fine wines.

Screwpull
The plastic frame sits on the bottle neck, locating the screw centrally in the cork and ensuring that it bores into the cork vertically as the handle is twisted clockwise. Continued twisting of the handle in the same direction (the principle of the oil drill) drives the frame against the bottle neck and draws the cork out. This method is virtually always successful, even on venerable, crumbly corks.

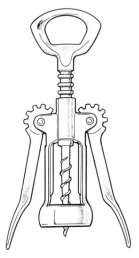

Butterfly lever
Begin with the levers pointing downwards, parallel with the screw. Locate the frame over the neck of the bottle with one hand to ensure that the screw is centred on the cork and bores into it vertically. Twist the handle with the other hand, letting the levers rise to a 'ten-to-two' angle as the screw penetrates the cork. Place the bottle on a table-top and use both hands to push the levers downwards, thus forcing the cork out.

Opening still wines Cut around the capsule just below the rim of the bottle, using a knife or the tip of a corkscrew: some bottles have a row of perforations as a guide. It is vital that wine should not come into contact with a lead capsule, but pouring out over the ragged edge of any capsule can be messy.

The capsule can be removed altogether, though in some instances (e.g. château-bottled Bordeaux or estate-bottled German wines), retain it as part of the presentation.

Take a look at the state of the top of the cork and wipe off any mould or dirt. Then remove the cork with your chosen corkscrew.

> ● *Sticking cork Hold the neck of the bottle for a few seconds under warm running water so that the glass expands; don't wet the cork. OR insert a simple corkscrew at an angle for greater leverage, or if cork has broken off half way down.*
> ● *Crumbling cork Lever the fragments of cork out with the tip of a corkscrew.*
> ● *Crumbs of cork in wine Strain into a decanter, carafe or jug. A silver strainer is preferable to steel or plastic. Otherwise, use a coffee filter paper, or perfectly clean and detergent-free muslin or cheesecloth.*

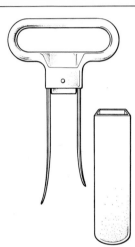

Wooden counterscrew
Begin with the wooden screw driven home. Locate the frame over the neck of the bottle with one hand, and twist the *upper* of the two handles clockwise to drive the worm well down into the cork. When the spiral has disappeared into the cork, begin to twist the *lower* of the two handles clockwise. The wooden screw emerges, forcing the frame against the neck of the bottle and drawing the cork out.

Waiter's friend
This incorporates a knife blade to cut the capsule. Choose a model with a long, thin worm thread. Screw the worm as accurately as possible vertically into the centre of the cork until the claw-shaped foot can be clipped over the side of the bottle neck: then lever the handle upwards to draw the cork part-way out. Screw the worm a little farther into the cork, then repeat the process until the cork is drawn out.

Butler's friend
This two-pronged extractor or cork-puller does not pierce the cork; the undamaged cork can, therefore, in theory be replaced in the bottle undetected – hence the nickname. Slide the prongs down into the neck of the bottle on either side of the cork, using a to-and-fro movement. Then pull upwards, twisting, to extract the cork. This is a good method for fragile, friable corks.

OPENING SPARKLING WINE

If sparkling wine has been properly chilled and gently handled, the cork should come out of the bottle with a whisper of 'smoke' rather than a violent 'pop', and without spilling wine everywhere. However, the outcome is always unpredictable, so be prepared with a handy glass to save any wine that would otherwise be spilt.

Hold the bottle at an angle close to the horizontal – at least 45° – while removing the cork, and avoid pointing it at anyone or at anything breakable, just in case the cork does shoot out uncontrollably.

But although the mechanics of opening a bottle of sparkling wine are important, the best way to be sure the results are foolproof is to treat the wine

correctly while it is in your care, for however long a time, *before* you open it.

Always store sparkling wine bottles horizontally. All corks dry out unless they are kept in contact with the wine, resulting in damage to the contents of the bottle: moreover, a dry cork loses its elasticity and is harder to remove without breaking. Keep a case of wine on its side so that all the bottles are horizontal: otherwise, half the bottles point downwards but the other six are upright.

When stacking bottles for storage, the Champagne manufacturers recommend making sure that the air in each bottle is not trapped up in the neck, right next to the cork. The routine to follow is to hold the bottle horizontally, and to dip

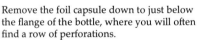

Remove the foil capsule down to just below the flange of the bottle, where you will often find a row of perforations.

Untwist the wires holding the cork in place and remove the wire muzzle. Once this is off, always keep the fingers of one hand over the top of the cork to prevent it from flying out prematurely, and to feel when it begins to loosen.

Tilt the bottle gently to an angle of 45° to the horizontal, and have an empty glass – preferably a *flûte* – standing ready near by.

Keeping the left hand in position over the cork, use the right hand to rotate the bottle gently.

(Rotating the bottle rather than the cork means that the 'mushroom' top is less liable to break off.)

As you turn, you should detect the cork gradually beginning to 'give'. You can then ease it gently out of the bottle with the finger and thumb.

the cork downwards through an angle of 45° so that the bubble of air floats back up into the bottle. Return the bottle to the horizontal and place it in position in the bin.

The contents of a bottle that has rested undisturbed in a cool place will be least likely to gush out violently when the cork is extracted: movement stirs up the carbonic acid gas. A bottle that has just had a bumpy car ride, for example, will be impossible to open without the loss of some wine.

But although chilling sparkling wines is the order of the day, don't serve them so cold as to numb the taste buds, and don't keep your unopened bottles indefinitely in the refrigerator: 48 hours is the limit.

If using Champagne pliers to help with a tricky cork, grip the bottle neck with the fingers of the left hand, keeping the index finger over the cork for safety.

Take the pliers in the right hand and grip the mushroom top with them. Ease the cork upwards until the index finger feels it begin to 'give'. Put down the pliers and finish removing the cork by hand.

Gradually ease the whole of the left hand over the cork so that the pressure is taken in the palm. Gently ease out the cork with the thumb and fingers of the right hand.

- *Don't buy sparkling wine from a shop display where the bottles have been standing upright, so drying out the corks, or from a shelf where they have been exposed for any length of time to the harmful effects of fluorescent lighting.*
- *Remember to avoid shaking the bottle as far as you can while opening it, and that a bottle that has been chilling undisturbed is the easiest to open without spilling.*
- *Avoid pointing the cork at anything vulnerable: however carefully you open the bottle, there is a risk of the cork shooting out suddenly and causing damage.*
- *Always have a glass handy to take the first measure of wine.*
- *Champagne pliers may be helpful for tackling a stubborn cork which refuses to budge under finger-power alone. If your fingers are not particularly strong, you may prefer to start out by using one of these gadgets anyway.*

- *If the mushroom breaks off the top of the cork, pierce the cork gently to release some of the pressure, and open – carefully – with a corkscrew.*
- *If a little wine bubbles out, place the palm of the hand over the mouth of the bottle for a moment, and the effervescence should subside.*
- *A Champagne stopper will take care of any wine left in an opened bottle.*

Left-handed people, when opening sparkling wines, may find it easier to reverse these instructions laterally, and to read left for right and *vice versa*.

FOOD WITH WINE

Happy marriages between food and wine are not made in heaven. They need a basic compatibility between the partners, and a little imagination. And just as there is usually more than one ideal partner in the world, so there is almost always more than one wine to complement a particular dish.

Country cooking, especially, has evolved many a time-honoured combination: the regional dishes of France and Italy are often perfect partners for their local wines. But this does not exclude appropriate alternatives.

Some food 'kills' wine: with hot, spicy dishes, drink lager instead. The mildly spiced food of northern India, and Chinese food – apart from that of Hunan and Szechwan – is excellent with the aromatic white wines, like Gewürztraminer and Sauvignon. Avoid red wines, though.

Very salty food is difficult to match. While Beluga caviar goes well with Champagne, eat the saltier Sevruga with schnapps or aquavit. Salty Roquefort cheese spoils the taste of red wine: try Sauternes or Barsac for a delicious salty-sweet combination.

Smoked food is a different department. With smoked salmon, serve the aromatic whites, a Fino Sherry, or a rich, full Californian Chardonnay such as those from Napa, Sonoma or Alexander Valley. Top white Graves, e.g. mature Château Laville Haut-Brion or Domaine de Chevalier, also suit well.

Smoked trout and mackerel go well with most of the Alsace grape varieties, or a Fumé Blanc from California. Surprisingly, smoked fish is also excellent with German wines which have a touch of sweetness, since this is always balanced by a refreshing acidity. A Mosel Spätlese, or even an Auslese in a year with good acidity, is marvellous with a smoked trout or haddock mousse.

Barbecue food calls out for straightforward, definite-tasting wines which appeal at first impact rather than with subtle flavour. Chops, steaks and spareribs go wonderfully with zingy Zinfandel, mouthfuls of good Cabernet and clearly defined European tastes like Rioja and the reds of Catalonia. If you begin your barbecue with dips like guacamole, go easy on the spices and choose a crisp, aromatic white wine such as Sauvignon (or Fumé Blanc) or Gewürztraminer.

Seafood takes the whole range of white wines, from full, buttery Chardonnay – Burgundy or Californian – with Maine lobster to Pinot Grigio with clams. Fresh-water fish such as trout go more easily with a delicate, flowery wine, such as a light Californian or Mosel Riesling.

The plainest food suits the finest wines. Thus, roast beef, cold or hot, is the perfect foil for your top Bordeaux, Burgundy or Californian Cabernet wines. Roast lamb, or chops or cutlets, also throws these wines into relief.

Game can take something more robust – the longer the game is hung, the more assertive the red wine should be. Well-hung hot roast pheasant, partridge and grouse, as well as saddle of hare, are perfect with red Rhône, Gattinara or other Nebbiolo wines, or a big Côte de Nuits Burgundy. When game is cold, it is more delicate (all cold meat appears this way), and then goes well with red Bordeaux. However, this category is a wide one, and the plump, full, exotic-tasting top Pomerols can take rich well-flavoured hot game, whereas a more delicate St Julien would be better with cold meat.

In fact, when considering wines from an area as large as Bordeaux, it is wise to plan the menu with vintage chart in hand, because a Claret from a light year will go better with a more delicate dish, while a big, concentrated year, such as 1961 or 1975, can take a 'bigger' dish.

Red Rhône wines (Gigondas, Châteauneuf-du-Pape), robust Californian reds, and Cabernet Shiraz combinations from Australia are wonderful with dishes like *daube, boeuf Stroganoff,* goose, venison and wild boar. Unexpectedly, the last three well-flavoured game dishes are also excellent with the spicy white wines of the Rheinpfalz. This is what local gastronomes choose.

With regional 'oddities' a good rule is to go for the wine the locals drink: Alsace Riesling with sauerkraut; Hungarian red with goulash; Cahors, Madiran or Corbières with *cassoulet.*

RELIABLE RELATIONSHIPS

Aromatic dry whites go with: smoked fish (e.g. mackerel, eel); grilled mullet; *bouillabaisse;* hams and salami; *pâté; tacos;* onion *quiche;* little, hard goat cheeses.

Light dry whites go with: fresh-water fish; mussels, whitebait; fish or shellfish pasta.

Medium-bodied dry whites go with: fish *terrines;* cold fish salads; seafood pancakes; *risotto* of most types.

Full-bodied dry whites go with: crustaceans (e.g. lobster, crab); fish (e.g. turbot, halibut); *nouvelle cuisine salades composées* (e.g. with scallop, crayfish, shrimp, prawn); chicken in white sauce.

Fruity whites with a touch of sweetness go with: canapés at a cocktail party or light buffet; little fresh shrimp. Offer these wines, too, as aperitifs and between meals.

Medium-sweet to sweet whites go with: fruit desserts (e.g. pear Charlotte). Wines with suitable balancing acidity, like Mosel, providing interesting contrast with smoked fish *pâté* or *mousse.*

Very sweet whites go with: desserts made from peaches or pears; strawberries and cream. Between meals, serve with cake or almond biscuits.

Luscious dessert whites go with: ripe pears and peaches. Between meals, serve with walnuts.

Fresh lively reds go with: grilled fresh salmon steaks; pink salmon trout; grilled sausages or *saucisses;* herby roast rabbit; liver; hamburger; roast young pigeon or *poussin;* cheese (e.g. Dolcelatte, Bresse blue, fresh cream cheese or *fromage blanc*).

Medium-bodied reds go with: dishes made with minced or ground meat (e.g. meatballs, meat sauces for pasta); roast lamb; beef in any form; braised meats; roast game birds (especially if not well hung); cold game.

Full, assertive reds go with: casseroles and stews *(daube, cassoulet, goulash);* roast pork with prunes.

Powerful, robust reds maturing with age go with: well-hung game birds (roast or in *salmis*): wild duck; roast turkey with chestnut stuffing; venison; wild boar; hare (roast or in *civet*); mature Cheddar cheese.

Dry Rosés go with: fish soup with *rouille; salade niçoise,* all Mediterranean dishes.

PERFECT PARTNERS

Vinho Verde grilled sardines, *salade niçoise*

Dry Vouvray *rillettes, pâté*

Premier Cru Chablis oysters

Sancerre, Pouilly Blanc Fumé, Sauvignon de Haut Poitou, Quincy, Reuilly, Menetou-Salon dry goat cheeses, snails

Lugana, Montecarlo, Orvieto Abboccato, Pinot Grigio melon and Parma ham

White Côte de Beaune plain lobster or crab

Sweet Vouvray strawberries and cream

Muscat-de-Beaumes-de-Venise Christmas pudding, pecan pie

Sauternes, Barsac, Quarts de Chaume, Bonnezeaux *foie gras,* desserts based on pears

Rheinpfalz Spätlese roast goose

Chinon, Bourgueil, Beaujolais fresh salmon

Madiran, Bandol *confit d'oie*

Barbera, dry Lambrusco (from Modena, Bologna, Parma) pasta with meat sauce

Beaujolais, Tavel Rosé *saucisse de Lyon*

Barbaresco, Crozes-Hermitage rabbit with mustard sauce

Youngish Dão and Portuguese reds swordfish

Zinfandel, Cirò roast pork

Valpolicella little Lake Garda salmon trout

Chianti Classico *bollito misto,* liver, *osso bucco,* pigeon

Cabernet from Friuli or Alto Adige veal dishes

Red Rioja moussaka, *paella* (White Rioja if the *paella* consists mainly of fish)

DECANTING

For wines with sediment, decanting is a necessity. It is essential, too, for fine wines long trapped in bottle: the aeration helps them develop bouquet and lose the natural reticence of a long maturation. For other wines, decanting is not vital – but it can help the liquid in the glass reach its full potential. The action of 'pouring over', done an appropriate time before drinking, simply gives all the wine's components an opportunity to reach the air and open out to the maximum capacity for that particular wine. The time spent in the decanter in the dining-room gently brings a wine from cellar temperature to the appropriate temperature for drinking. Decanting an everyday wine straight from the wine shop's shelves in a warm kitchen will also achieve this aim, but more speedily.

Decanting into clear glass has its aesthetic aspect as well as its functional ones. Part of the enjoyment of wine lies in appreciating the colour, no longer veiled from sight in green bottle glass. This is one of the reasons for decanting red wines. White wine has no sediment and less need to be 'aired'. The only reason for decanting a white Burgundy, say, might be for people to 'guess the wine'. But you could equally well hide the label, and pouring white wine from the bottle is normal procedure.

Aerating wine

Esters and aldehydes develop during a wine's bottle life: when these volatilize on contact with the air, the bouquet – and with it the whole character of the wine – is released. With red wines this happens at a higher temperature than with whites; with older wines the process is often slow. Hence the benefits of decanting.

Any straightforward red wine that is healthy and robust such as basic Claret, Rioja, Bull's Blood or Côtes du Rhône will like to be decanted. The really big, assertive, 'up-front'-style Californian Cabernets and the Australian Cabernets and Cabernet/ Shiraz blends demand decanting to enable them to develop dimension and complexity. Youthful, vigorous wines benefit from the 'pouring over' action and time in decanter, which gives the compacted flavour a chance to soften and become more round.

Even young wines of no great body, such as Beaujolais, Valpolicella and good commercial blends, will taste just a little better for being 'aired'.

Just how much better is a loaded question. Blind tastings to compare decanted wines with identical ones served from the bottle have come up with no clear consensus for or against decanting. For most wines, however, it certainly does no harm, and in many cases, it seems to do positive good.

What to decant into?

Glass decanters are obviously the most aesthetically pleasing containers for fine wine, but decanting is worth doing into any jug or carafe – even an empty bottle – that is it the action of pouring over that aerates and opens out the wine. With the aid of a funnel this can be done into another wine bottle; a jug or carafe will suit a straightforward wine; and an earthenware jug makes a pleasant decanter for a simple country wine to be served at, say, an alfresco meal. However, the container should not be open if the wine is to stand in it for any length of time, particularly if the top is wide. The conventional decanter's narrow neck and stopper provide the best conditions for fine wine: the pouring over process will have provided all the oxidation necessary, and during its time in decanter the wine can 'rest' without losing its bouquet into the air.

There is no special decanter shape traditional for either Bordeaux, Burgundy or Port. Square decanters are usual for whisky; it would be fine to use one for wine (although it might offend purists) – provided you had rinsed out the last drop of whisky.

Decanting off sediment

Sediment is a good sign in a bottle: it shows normal development in an aged wine that started life tannic and with deep colour. However, you don't want it in your glass: it makes the wine look murky, and it affects the taste, hence the purpose of allowing sediment to gravitate to the bottom of the bottle, or to accumulate along one side if the bottle is binned for a great length of time without being moved (as with Vintage Port). And hence the need to handle the bottle gently to avoid disturbing the sediment.

A basket serves to bring the wine from the

● *Very occasionally, a wine will refuse to pour off and separate from the sediment, which will be more like tiny suspended particles. When this happens, it is usually a sign that the wine has some bacterial trouble or other technical fault, and it may taste tainted, even bitter. Fortunately, however, this is a rare occurrence.*

● *When the sediment has become stirred up into the wine, your hands are unsteady, or the job has to be done fast, decant through a coffee filter paper in a funnel. But don't tell anyone, and don't do it for your better wines: switch to a more modest wine if you are caught unawares.*

● *If you have to wash a decanter for red wine just before use, don't use ice-cold water.*

● *Clean stained decanters by letting them stand overnight containing a weak solution of water and vinegar or a proprietary denture cleaner; then scrub stains with a bottle brush. Rinse half a dozen times in clean water before draining and using or storing.*

● *Remember to wash the stopper, too, after each use: a stale taste can affect the next wine you pour into the decanter.*

● *Store decanters upright, without stoppers, after first making sure that they are perfectly clean and dry.*

Basket holds the wine bottle horizontal.

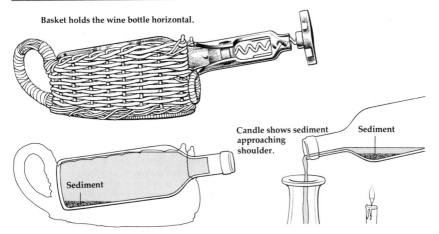

Candle shows sediment approaching shoulder.

Sediment

Sediment

cellar in the horizontal position in which it has been stored. Standing the bottle upright to remove the cork and then laying it down again in the basket makes no sense, since the sediment will already have been stirred up into the wine.

However, the basket has two advantages in the process of pouring the wine off its sediment. Use it to keep the bottle level while carrying it from the cellar to the decanter. And use it to keep the bottle steady while you use a counterscrew corkscrew to extract the cork as gently as possible.

A lit candle helps to show you when the sediment nears the shoulder of the bottle, when you should stop pouring. Draw the cork, wipe the bottle lip – and light the candle. Lift the bottle out of the basket and hold above the candle so that the light shines

through the shoulder of the bottle. Gently and steadily pour the wine into the decanter. When you see the cloudiness or sediment moving up into the shoulder of the bottle, stop pouring. Remember to stopper the decanter while the wine is resting.

A silver or glass funnel may help, but a steady hand is usually sufficient.

Decanting without a basket is perfectly possible, provided that the bottle has been allowed to stand upright for several days in the room where you will decant it, so that the sediment has resettled in the bottom. Tilt the bottle very gently when pouring the wine into the decanter – using the candle to spot when the sediment approaches the shoulder. Up-ending the bottle can, however, make stray bits of lees float up into the main body of the wine again, so watch it carefully.

All is plain sailing at informal meals with only one wine. At a dinner party with several wines, on the other hand, a little organization is necessary – just as you time the cooking so that vegetables are not soggy and meat undercooked.

It is fine if all the wines can be decanted several hours beforehand to avoid a last-minute rush; sometimes, however, this is simply not possible. Old or fragile wines may need decanting immediately before the meal. Two white wines (a dry one for the first course and a sweet one for the dessert) may each have to be taken out of the refrigerator and opened just before serving. Dividing the serving of the food and the last-minute preparation of the wine between two hosts always helps.

Often, however, the reds and the Port

WHEN TO DECANT?

You decant old wines and you decant young ones. Whether you do this just before the meal, just before the course they are to accompany, two hours before sitting down or the morning before dinner depends on the type of wine: on its weight, the grape variety, its geographical origin, the type of vintage (tannic and robust or light and delicate), and its age. The timetable must take into account a good many variants.

Bordeaux

Treat very old Claret, e.g. pre-1920, as you would Port: take a look at the wine just before dinner and decide after tasting whether to decant it at the beginning of the meal or just before the relevant course.

With Bordeaux, much depends on the *type* of year. 1928s, having started life hard and tannic, often need a few hours of decanting before being drunk; 1929s need less time, since they are softer and some are showing their age. 1945s, tough and dense, need several hours in decanter before serving. 1947s take the same treatment, since they are rich, but 1949s are more delicate and can take less time. 1961s and 1966s need several hours. 1964 Pomerols and St Emilions, being richer, take longer than Médocs of the same year. Give the 1970s longer than 1971s, and 1975s longer than 1976s.

However, sometimes the very tannic vintages do not need a lot of contact with air,

will be in their decanters before the guests arrive. Then the first thing to do is to welcome people with a *planned* aperitif: offer, for example, a sparkling wine, a German white wine or a special Sherry with no further ado.

In a well-ordered world, the table should have been set a couple of hours earlier, so that the temperature of the glasses for red wines poses no problem.

The sequence of the wines to be served need cause no worry: apart from the consideration of which wines go best with which foods, a few guiding principles help determine the planning order.

The basic premise is that one wine should not 'kill' another: that is, the first wine served should not have such a dominant flavour that it envelops a since this simply dries them up further. Over-exposed, they can become 'stringy'. Vintages with a lot of 'fat' or richness take decanting time well – they open out more and more. And there are always exceptions which break the rules on timing and succeed.

Even *petits châteaux* benefit from being poured into a carafe an hour or two before drinking. But heed warnings about keeping modest châteaux too long: no decanting will help a wine that is already tired.

Burgundy

The justification for decanting is as valid for Burgundy as for Bordeaux, though the process is not traditional in the region. One top Burgundy *négociant* used to decant, but found that some of his American visitors doubted the age of his wines if they were not poured out of cobwebby bottles. Unless your friends are as cynical, decant your Burgundies with the same rules and exceptions as for Bordeaux. Remember that a *grand cru* from the Côte de Nuits will have more body, backbone, structure and richness than a *premier cru* from, say, Volnay on the Côte de Beaune – and can therefore take longer in the decanter than the lighter wine.

1961s, 1962s, 1964s, 1966s, 1969s, some 1970s, 1971s all take an hour or two of sitting in the decanter before they reach their best. Give 1972s a long period, perhaps a couple of hours; 1973s a shorter period, say, 40 minutes; and decant 1976s several hours ahead of drinking. Wines of the 1940s and

more subtle one following. For this reason, aromatic wines are difficult to follow. At an all-white-wine meal, it is risky to serve a Gewürztraminer before a white Burgundy, or a Sauvignon before a Riesling. Either a Gewürztraminer or a Sauvignon is all right, however, is you are going on to red wine for the next course.

As a general rule, serve young wines before old, because the taste sequence is better – but beware of choosing a really strong, beefy young wine before a delicate, old one. For instance, avoid serving a 1978 Californian Cabernet Sauvignon straight before a 1953 Mouton-Rothschild with no stepping-stone in between. The contrast could be too violent for harmony, in spite of the fact that in both wines Cabernet

Sauvignon predominates.

A grape-variety theme provides another guideline. Probably the most felicitous and reliable sequences are of wines from similar regions, but international mixtures, with type and grape variety in common, can be interesting. A total mixture of grape varieties can be too disquieting to the palate. Better, perhaps, to have a 'Nebbiolo evening', to try some good Italian wines, with a Barbaresco leading into a Barolo; or a 'Pinot Noir evening', with a Hunter Valley Pinot Noir leading into a Côte de Nuits; or a 'Cabernet evening', with a vivid Cabernet from the Alto Adige or the Friuli leading into a Bourgeois Growth Claret, and maybe finishing up with a Classified Growth if it is a special occasion.

1950s may be a bigger 'style' that will take decanting time. If you have reason to suppose that your old Burgundy is not of the 'big' type, check and taste first, and proceed as for venerable Ports and Clarets.

Port
Late-bottled, Ruby and Tawny Port have no sediment, so decant only to see them in an elegant decanter. Vintage Port needs decanting off its sediment; it will also benefit from aeration after its long years in bottle.

Decant 15- to 30-year-old Vintage Port from a strong vintage the morning before the meal. Stopper the decanter, and leave it in the dining-room: the Port should be sublime.

A 1927, to be drunk in the 1980s, should be decanted only a couple of hours before dinner. With something as venerable as a 1912, draw the cork immediately before dinner and taste: if it seems at all fragile and

delicate don't decant until just before drinking. If it seems lively and robust, decant before dinner. These older wines show variation between bottles, each of which has developed in its own way at its own pace.

Other wood-aged wines Battle will always rage on decanting times for Barolo and Barbaresco. Some swear it should be done the night before the great dinner party – 24 hours before the blast-off. However, this can be too much: the touch of volatile acidity that these long wood-aged wines often possess is greatly accentuated after such prolonged contact with the air. Some wonderfully opened-out wines remain 'healthy' after 4-5 hours in decanter, and some top Chianti Classico wines benefit from virtually a whole day in a decanter; but for a wine to survive this treatment, it must have been handled perfectly during vinification and maturation, and its wood-ageing must not be excessive.

● *Decant later rather than sooner to play safe. A fine wine that is decanted too long before the meal can lose some bouquet, become rather flat, and will never recover, whereas a wine that has not had enough time in decanter can still open out in the glass. If you feel your wine is still 'holding back', have patience and swirl it around gently in the glass to release that bit more to come on bouquet and palate.*

● *Simply drawing the cork and leaving the bottle to stand for an hour or two before drinking it – 'allowing the wine to breathe', some people call it – does virtually nothing towards aerating the wine. The tiny amount of air allowed into the bottle by the removal of the cork will reach only the topmost part of the wine. (Removing the cork like this does, on the other hand, get rid of any bottle stink.)*

SERVING TEMPERATURES

Temperature is the prime consideration in serving wine so that it can be appreciated at its best. Fashion and taste at both national and personal levels disagree about the ideal serving temperature for some wines; some American restaurants, for example, serve Champagne and white wine far too cold for the subtleties of flavour to be discerned, while in southern Italy in summer the red wines can be so warm as to be almost soupy.

In general, red wines need to be drunk at a temperature warm enough for their bouquet and aroma to be volatilized, while white wines should be cool enough to be refreshing. On the other hand, the finer the white wine, the less its subtleties should be masked by cold, while some of the reds that are meant for young drinking have little complexity to yield in the form of bouquet, and are quite happily consumed at cellar temperature.

As a rule, older wines have to be treated much more gently than younger, more robust wines. Good white Burgundy of some age (10 years or more) is extremely fragile, and 1/2-1 hour in the refrigerator should be enough. Longer can harm the nose, or even make a wood-aged wine such as a top Côte de Beaune white seem maderized, or 'over the top'. A young, brisk Mâcon Blanc, however, can take several hours in the refrigerator.

SERVING TEMPERATURES

These temperatures are recommendations, not hard-and-fast rules: a degree or two on either side of the temperature indicated may suit individual taste and circumstances. Always remember that older wines are fragile and moderate the temperature accordingly: drink fine whites slightly less cold and fine reds less *chambré*.

Take into account the ambient temperature and the climate: young Bordeaux Rouge, for example, drunk a year or two after the vintage on a stuffy day in Bordeaux, would be delicious at the lower end of the scale for reds. The same wine drunk on a winter's day in London or Boston would taste raw this cold, but rounded and warming at around 18°C. The dining-room might be comfortably warm, but a cold day needs the psychological element of warmth of the higher temperature.

FORTIFIED WINES

Sherry
Chill Fino, Manzanilla and dry Montilla. Serve Oloroso and cream Sherries at room temperature, which will also bring out the nutty flavour of good Amontillado.

Port
Chill White Port, as they do in Portugal. Serve Vintage, old Tawny and Late-bottled Port at room temperature.

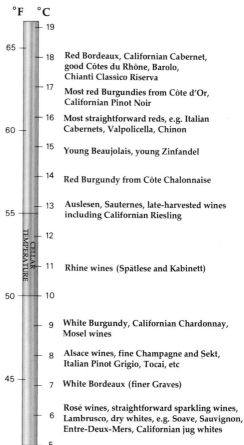

°F °C

19

65 — 18 Red Bordeaux, Californian Cabernet, good Côtes du Rhône, Barolo, Chianti Classico Riserva

17 Most red Burgundies from Côte d'Or, Californian Pinot Noir

16 Most straightforward reds, e.g. Italian Cabernets, Valpolicella, Chinon

60 — 15 Young Beaujolais, young Zinfandel

14 Red Burgundy from Côte Chalonnaise

13 Auslesen, Sauternes, late-harvested wines including Californian Riesling

55 — 12

CELLAR TEMPERATURE

11 Rhine wines (Spätlese and Kabinett)

50 — 10

9 White Burgundy, Californian Chardonnay, Mosel wines

8 Alsace wines, fine Champagne and Sekt, Italian Pinot Grigio, Tocai, etc

45 — 7 White Bordeaux (finer Graves)

6 Rosé wines, straightforward sparkling wines, Lambrusco, dry whites, e.g. Soave, Sauvignon, Entre-Deux-Mers, Californian jug whites

5

A wine which has undergone maturation in a wooden cask or barrel usually has more complexities to give up than one which has seen only the inside of a concrete or stainless steel vat before being bottled. The interaction of the flavour of the wine itself with the influence of the wood is a delicate question of balance and harmony, which extremes of temperature can upset. Old Clarets and Burgundies should thus receive no sudden warming or cooling, just a gentle trip from cellar to dining-room and time to acclimatize there. Swirling in the glass and the heat of the hands will warm the wine – as will the presence of a number of people in the room, and maybe even the warmth generated by burning candles.

Remember, though, that rigorous attention to the temperature of the wine in bottle is not enough. Wine glasses should be of the appropriate temperature – don't serve chilled wine in glasses still warm from the dishwasher; make sure those for red wines are not icy-cold.

And watch the room temperature, too. The temperature of a chilled wine can rise by several degrees Fahrenheit in as many minutes in a warm room. 'Room temperature' itself is a phrase that needs examination. It was coined in temperate climates in the days of draughty houses before central heating was the norm: 15-18°C is what is meant.

TO CHILL WINES

Refrigerator Put bottle (kept upright if it contains any sediment) in the refrigerator for 1-2 hours. The door of the fridge is less brutal than the interior.

Freezer In extreme emergency, put wine in the freezer for NOT MORE THAN 10 MINUTES. Certainly not a treatment for the better wines.

Ice bucket One efficient method for cooling wine and keeping it cool at table or outdoors at picnics is to stand it in a container filled with cold water and about a trayful of ice cubes (iced water is more effective than ice alone). If sediment poses no problem, the unopened bottle can be inverted in the iced water for a short time to cool the neck.

Vinicool This attractive plastic holder keeps ready-chilled wines at the same cool temperature for 2-3 hours without the mess – and the expense, when large quantities are required – of ice.

TO WARM WINES

Too-rapid heating makes wine cloudy and ultimately vinegary and undrinkable. Bring wine to a room temperature as gently as possible, preferably away from a source of strong heat. Just stand the bottle in the room where you are going to have your meal, which will presumably be at a pleasant temperature which is neither too warm nor too cold.

Warm decanter As an emergency, transfer the wine into a carafe, decanter or spare wine bottle which has first been warmed slightly with tepid water. Not for the better wines.

> ● *Beware: once* chambré, *or warmed through to drinking temperature, good red wine should be drunk. It will not benefit from being returned to the cold cellar: the process cannot be repeated.*
> ● *Don't keep unopened bottles of wine indefinitely in the refrigerator: they can lose flavour and bouquet and become rather flat.*
> ● *Better serve wine too cool than too hot. It will quickly warm up in a centrally heated house or with the warmth of the hands, but it can be irretrievably damaged if it becomes too hot.*
> ● *It is snobbery to think you should never add ice cubes to wine – red, white or rosé – provided it is ordinary table wine (better wines deserve better treatment), although it is a tactic you should only resort to at a terrace or beach lunch in hot sunshine.*

RESTAURANT WINE LISTS

High mark-ups on restaurant wine lists are a fact of life most people have to contend with. It is a rare restaurateur who dares to keep the wine prices low to encourage increased consumption.

The fundamental purpose of any wine list is to ensure that the diner has all possible information regarding each wine. Clarity is important in presentation: a list can even be handwritten, as long as it is legible – if this is not at the expense of detail.

It is essential to list not only the name of the wine (and the price, which is somehow never omitted), but also the shipper or producer-grower where relevant; only then can a diner recognize a wine previously enjoyed, or identify a producer who inspires confidence. The name of a top Bordeaux château speaks for itself, but every property should be cited with its region: e.g. St Julien, Fronsac. In Burgundy, one man's Gevrey-Chambertin is not exactly the same as another's. All Italian Cabernets and Merlots from the Friuli are not identical, nor are all Valpolicellas; the same goes for the wines of the Rhône, the Loire and Alsace. Californian wines should always be listed with the name of the producer and the grape variety, and the individual vineyard name where relevant. German wines should be listed with their estate and shipper.

Other signs of a lack of energy on the part of the restaurant proprietor come from a list that is too conservative: the 'classic' list with all the Bordeaux First Growths – but all the inferior vintages. On a more modest level, the restaurateur may rely on the 'old faithfuls' of the international wine trade (e.g. overplayed, overpriced Nuits St Georges, instead of a more enterprising, lesser-known Monthelie; or Sauternes, rather than good-value Loupiac); or heavily advertised branded wines of mass distribution (the customer pays for the advertising), or a list that is identical to a dozen others because it is compiled by the same wine merchant or wholesaler. Sometimes, a specialized regional wine list (e.g. a comprehensive choice of Italian wines in an Italian restaurant) is far more rewarding than an inept attempt to represent the world.

This example shows a selection of white wines in a page from the beautifully presented *carte des vins* of a restaurant in France. Wines on French restaurant lists are nearly always exclusively French; in Italy, too, only Italian wines tend to be shown; Germany, though a wine producer, would be likely to include a selection of non-German wines. In importing countries such as the USA and Britain, restaurant wine lists are usually more international.

It is the way that the list here is set out, rather than the specific wines included on it (although the choice is broad), that makes it a model for restaurants anywhere. The wines are clearly divided according to colour, and subdivided into the region of origin. A good range of vintages caters for people who like young wines, as well as those who prefer something more mature. An excellent spread of price enables everyone to find something within reach of their pocket. A reasonably good cross-section of half bottles is offered. Where more than one type of wine is produced in a region – such as among the white wines of Bordeaux – they are clearly described as dry *(vins blancs secs)* or, in the instance of Barsac, sweet *(vin blanc moelleux et liquoreux)*.

Emphasis in this list is on the Beaujolais and Mâconnais, because the restaurant is actually in Mâcon, and the menu includes some regional dishes which will go perfectly with such local wines. Yet there is no regional chauvinism, and the other wine-making areas of France are not neglected. Elsewhere, the wine list incorporates a note on suggested marriages between the dishes on the menu and wines on the list: e.g. sweet Barsac to accompany *foie gras* and Roquefort cheese; dry whites with a touch of fruit (e.g. Mâcon-Villages or Alsace Riesling) to accompany grilled fish; and full-bodied, fatter whites (like the great white Burgundies); or piquant wines (like those of the Jura) for fish served in a sauce.

Above all, the list gives exact details of the grower/producer and bottler. It is not a 'lazy' list, where the restaurant proprietor has simply gone to a few big suppliers – nor is it (worse still) an 'all-purpose' list, where the Burgundies are identified by no more than a series of names such as Meursault and Pouilly-Fuissé, with no source of supply divulged. Such vagueness leaves the proprietor of the restaurant at liberty to pick up 'bargains' or remnants as and when he finds them. Great wine lists are made by tasting, not convenience buying.

Vins Blancs

RÉGION DE BOURGOGNE - MÂCONNAIS - BEAUJOLAIS

			1/1	1/2
MÂCON-VILLAGES	« Vignoble de Soméré », Pierre Santé, Propriétaire à la Roche-Vineuse	1979	54	
MÂCON-VILLAGES	« Clos des Tournons », mis en bouteille au Clos des Tournons par E. Chevalier, Négociant à Charnay	1979	55	32
MÂCON-VIRÉ	Mis en bouteille par Piat, Négociant à Mâcon	1979	56	
MÂCON-IGÉ	« Château London », Carpi-Gobet, Propriétaires à Igé	1979	46	
BEAUJOLAIS-BLANC	« Château de Loyse », Sté Civile d'Exploitation - Thorin, mis en bouteille au château	1979	65	35
SAINT-VÉRAN	« Domaine des Crais », Roger Tissier, Viticulteur à Leynes	1979	57	
Primé au Concours Général Foire de Paris 1980				
SAINT-VÉRAN	Groupement de Producteurs de Prissé	1979	57	
Médaille d'Or 1980 au Concours des Grands Vins de France à Mâcon				
POUILLY-FUISSÉ	« Les Crays », Michel Forest, Viticulteur à Vergisson	1979	95	50
POUILLY-FUISSÉ	Mis en bouteille par Mommessin, Négociant à Mâcon	1979	100	
POUILLY-FUISSÉ	« Domaine de la Chapelle de Pouilly », mis en bouteille par Piat, négociant à Mâcon	1977	105	
MEURSAULT (1er Cru)	« Château de Blagny », Comtesse Pierre de Montlivaut, mis en bouteille par Piat, Négociant-Eleveur à Mâcon	1972	120	
MERCUREY	« Château de Chamirey », Marquis de Jouennes d'Herville, Propriétaire à Mercurey, mis en bouteille au château	1978	120	

RÉGION D'ALSACE

RIESLING	Mis en bouteille par A. Willm, Négociant à Barr	1975	60	
GEWURZTRAMINER	Mis en bouteille par Kuentz - Bas, Négociant à Husseren-les-Châteaux, Réserve personnelle	1979	69	
Prix d'honneur au Concours des Vins d'Alsace à Colmar (millésime 1979)				

RÉGION DU JURA

L'ÉTOILE	« Château de l'Etoile », Vandelle et Fils, Viticulteurs à l'Etoile, mis en bouteille au château	1978	60	
ARBOIS	« Domaine de Grange Grillard », H. Maire, Propriétaire à Arbois	1979	70	

RÉGION DU VAL DE LOIRE

MUSCADET DE SÈVRE ET MAINE	« Château de l'Aulnaye », mis en bouteille au château	1979	42	25
SANCERRE	« Cave des Chanvrières », mis en bouteille par Fournier à Verdigny	1978	81	45
SANCERRE	Lucien Thomas et Fils, Viticulteurs à Chaudoux, mis en bouteille à la propriété	1980	69	
		1979		35
POUILLY-FUMÉ	« Les Moulins à Vent », Caves de Pouilly-sur-Loire, mis en bouteille à la propriété	1979	67	37

RÉGION DE PROVENCE

BELLET	« Château de Crémat », Vigne Saint-Jean, mis en bouteille au château, par G.F.A. J. Bagnis et Fils à Saint-Roman-de-Bellet (Alpes-Maritimes)	1980	100	

RÉGION DES CÔTES-DU-RHÔNE

CONDRIEU	Georges Vernay, Viticulteur à Condrieu, mis en bouteille à la propriété	1979	150	
Cépage viognier				

RÉGION DE BORDEAUX

VINS BLANCS SECS

MOUTON-CADET	Bordeaux A.O.C., Blanc de Blancs, mis en bouteille par Baron Philippe de Rothschild S.A.	1979	49	28
CHÂTEAU MOULIN DE SÉGUR	Graves Blanc sec, Michel Boyer, Propriétaire à Cérons, mis en bouteille au château	1978	59	
CHÂTEAU TOUMILON	Graves Blanc sec, Jean Sévenot, Propriétaire à St-Pierre-de-Mons	1978	42	23

VIN BLANC MOELLEUX ET LIQUOREUX

CHÂTEAU COUTET	Barsac, A.O.C., mis en bouteille au château par la Société Civile du Château Coutet à Barsac	1976	120	
(classé 1er Cru en 1855)				

Vins Rouges

RÉGION D'ALSACE

PINOT NOIR servi frais	André et Gérard Hartmann, Propriétaires-Viticulteurs à Voegtlinshoffen, mis en bouteille à la propriété	1978	55	

RÉGION DU SUD-OUEST

CAHORS	Les Côtes d'Olt à Parnac, mis en bouteille à la propriété	1977	55	

RÉGION DE PROVENCE

BANDOL	« Château Pradeaux », Comte Portalis, Exploitant-Propriétaire à St-Cyr-sur-mer, mis en bouteille au château	1974	110	

RÉGION DU MÂCONNAIS-BEAUJOLAIS

MÂCON	Mis en bouteille par Mommessin, Négociant-éleveur à Mâcon	1981	41	20
BEAUJOLAIS	● Sélection Pierre Ferraud, Négociant à Belleville	1980	41	
	● Mis en bouteille par Grandjean-Lanery, Négociant-éleveur à Mâcon	1980	36	20
BEAUJOLAIS-VILLAGES	● « Creuze Noire », R. Duperron, Récoltant à Leynes, mis en bouteille à la propriété	1980	50	
	● Union des Coopératives Vinicoles de Bourgogne à Charnay-lès-Mâcon	1980	41	24

WHY A CELLAR?

'The cellar' is a grossly exaggerated name for the place in which most people store their wine. Yet since it is in a cellar that wine is traditionally stored to reach the peak of its maturity, it is by definition an environment with all the attributes necessary to help a wine to develop. It is, thus, useful to examine these qualities and look at what they contribute to the process. The ideal may be unattainable, but it sets standards by which you can judge the most congenial (and avoid the most unsuitable) part of your home for storing your wine.

Temperature is a key factor. Being at least partly underground, a cellar is well insulated by the surrounding soil and the building overhead – and so is protected from excessive heat and (more important) from sudden fluctuations in temperature.

The ideal temperature for storing wine is between 7 and 12°C. If the temperature rises *gradually*, with seasonal changes, to over 15°C, this is unlikely to harm the wines, but it probably means that they will mature more rapidly than those kept at an absolutely steady temperature. Avoid sudden rises and drops in temperature; a steady temperature even higher than 15°C is preferable to abrupt fluctuations since this, too, will simply tend to shorten the life-span of wines and cause them to age more rapidly.

In a cellar where the temperature is towards the top of the range, there is an argument for storing the white wines below the reds, since the warm air which rises will do less harm to the red wines.

Humidity is a characteristic of most underground cellars. Except for Sherry and Madeira, wine bottles are always stored on their sides to keep the cork in contact with the wine so that the cork does not dry out and shrink, admitting air. Excessively dry storage conditions can also gradually dry out the tops of the corks and cause them to shrink. In the natural environment of an underground cellar, the cool temperature often has, as its concomitant, moist air. In a well-built home closet or wine cupboard, a humidifier is the technological answer; its effect can be simulated by sprinkling gravel on the floor of a cellar and occasionally dampening it, or simply by keeping a bowl of damp sand or gravel in the storage cupboard.

Excessively damp conditions can damage the labels on wine bottles. This may not matter for home consumption, provided a record is kept of the identity of the contents, but it may reduce the value of wine that is to be sold.

Damp is also an encouragement to a vast variety of fungal infestations. Most of these are not harmful to the wine, and the bottles can be wiped off, one by one – but it is messy. Don't use wooden racks or cases in places where mould can flourish; bin the wine in brick divisions or stack it in metal frames instead, and NEVER treat anything in the cellar with chemical fungicides: their odour will penetrate both capsule and cork, and affect the taste of the wine. By the same token, don't store strongly smelling substances or chemicals anywhere near your wine.

Stability is a normal attribute of a wine cellar, and is all-important for the perfect maturation of the wine. Any movement stirs up the sediment thrown off by maturing red wines. For this reason, wine storage should preferably be in a place unaffected by any kind of vibration – from either a near-by road or railway line or an adjacent staircase. Ripples or concentric rings on the surface of a glass of wine (or water) stood on a level surface will indicate whether constant vibrations are present.

Darkness tends to be a natural feature of underground cellars and light is particularly harmful to wines stored in clear glass bottles, e.g. white Graves, Sauternes/Barsac and Roederer Cristal Champagne.

Cold storage units The modern technological answer for the wine-drinking apartment dweller, which seems most closely to approximate to a real cellar, is a thermostatically controlled cabinet. These are commercially available in a variety of sizes. Many have a vertical graduation of temperature, with the coolest shelves – for your sparkling white wines – at the bottom, and the warmest – for your reds – at the top.

This is fine in theory, but can be dangerous in practice, unless used with discretion. The designers tend to confuse serving temperatures with storage temperatures and try to achieve both at the same time. This may work well in a restaurant or household with a rapid turnover in wine, but most people run the risk of keeping wine too long at the wrong temperature: the cold sections of these cold cabinets are to my mind *too* cold, and ultimately 'flatten' good white Burgundy altogether. Their range of temperatures – from 7 to 16°C – seems unnecessarily wide. However, if you choose a cabinet with a more moderate overall temperature, and if you use it wisely, it could be the perfect short-term storage system, particularly if the alternative places in your home offer widely fluctuating temperatures or an otherwise uncongenial environment.

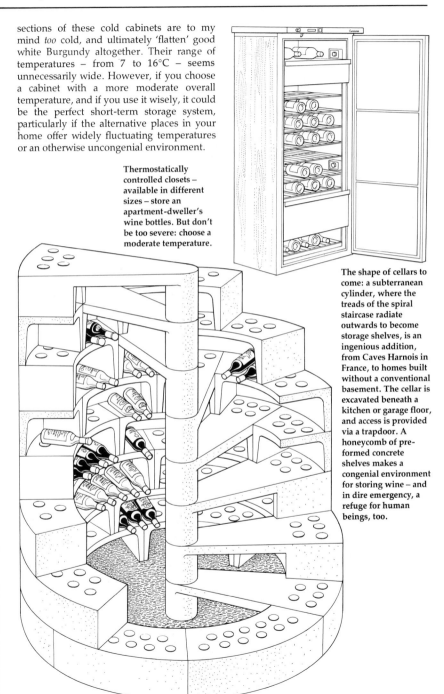

Thermostatically controlled closets – available in different sizes – store an apartment-dweller's wine bottles. But don't be too severe: choose a moderate temperature.

The shape of cellars to come: a subterranean cylinder, where the treads of the spiral staircase radiate outwards to become storage shelves, is an ingenious addition, from Caves Harnois in France, to homes built without a conventional basement. The cellar is excavated beneath a kitchen or garage floor, and access is provided via a trapdoor. A honeycomb of pre-formed concrete shelves makes a congenial environment for storing wine – and in dire emergency, a refuge for human beings, too.

THE SHORT-TERM CELLAR

If you were to buy a number of cases of top château or *domaine* wine and mature them yourself, you would need the ideal storage conditions described on the preceding pages, otherwise the result could turn out to be an expensive failure. However, the fact that you have neither the financial resources, the space – nor the patience – for this type of investment does not mean that it is not worth storing *some* wine at home. After all, the main reason for having a good cellar is availability of the wine you like at the stage at which you like to drink it.

A further reason is that it does any wine good to 'rest' for a month or two before you drink it: mature wines, in particular, are not at their best if moved around just before being drunk. This goes for the shaking they receive both in car rides home from the merchant's and in transit from storeroom or cellar to dining-room table.

The location of your short-term cellar should conform as far as possible to the ideal conditions – at least, it should *not* be somewhere too hot, too variable in temperature, too draughty, or subject to any kind of constant vibration.

A cellar in a case

The wines you choose as your stand-by will depend on whether you eat a good deal of fish and shellfish; whether your cooking involves a predominance of, say, Italian recipes; whether you are an habitual barbecue cook, or need something to wash down your take-away and carry-out meals.

CASE 1

● *1 bottle German Kabinett wine (An all-purpose, fruity white suitable as an aperitif)*

● *1 bottle Muscadet (An aperitif for people who like a dry white; also good with fish)*

● *1 bottle Sauvignon from California or France: either cheaper, e.g. Sauvignon de Touraine, or more expensive, e.g. Pouilly Blanc Fumé (Good with fish or Chinese food)*

● *1 bottle Chardonnay from California or France: either cheaper, e.g. Paul Masson, Taylor's California Cellars, Mâcon Blanc, or more expensive, from a smaller Californian winery, or from the Côte de Beaune or Chablis (Suitable for fish or white meat)*

● *1 bottle all-purpose, soft, fruity white: e.g. South African Steen or the drier Italian Soave*

● *1 bottle dessert wine: a reasonable Cérons or Loupiac from Bordeaux, a Muscat-de-Beaumes-de-Venise from the Rhône; or a bottle of Port*

● *1 bottle robust red: e.g. a good Australian Shiraz from Coonawarra, or a lighter Côtes du Rhône*

● *1 bottle light, fruity red: e.g. Valpolicella or Beaujolais*

● *1 bottle assertive red: e.g. Barbera or Zinfandel*

● *2 bottles good Cabernet: either Californian or a petit château from Bordeaux of a good vintage*

● *1 bottle Spanish red: a Rioja, or a Torres wine*

CASE 2

● *1 bottle aromatic white: Gewürz-traminer from Alsace, California or Austria – where it might be sweeter*

● *2 bottles soft, fruity Riesling: either Californian or German*

● *1 bottle Champagne*

● *1 bottle sparkling wine: Californian, Spanish, or French, e.g. from Alsace, the Loire or Burgundy*

● *1 bottle Italian dry white: e.g. Pinot Grigio or Verdicchio*

● *2 bottles medium-weight red: e.g. Chianti or Chilean Cabernet*

● *1 bottle Italian Cabernet, to compare with:*

● *1 bottle Cabernet from the Loire, e.g. Chinon, Bourgueil, Saumur-Champigny*

● *1 bottle mature, strong red wine, e.g. Crozes-Hermitage or Australian Hunter Valley Cabernet/Shiraz*

● *1 bottle Sherry or Madeira*

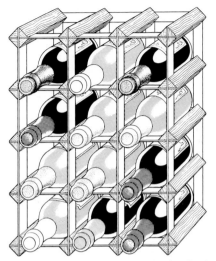

In a cool but draught-free corner, racks of steel and wood are useful to hold 12 or 16 bottles of wine that you intend to drink in the short-term. This kind of system can also be made to fit the dimensions of any appropriate corner or closet where the conditions are right for the wine.

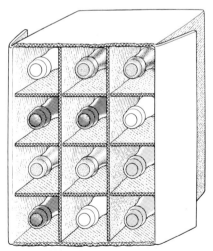

Cardboard wine cartons from the wine merchant's are robust enough to store wine for a good while in the right circumstances. But beware of using them in a proper cellar, where the humidity will eventually soften the card and make it liable to collapse when you lift the case of wine.

Racks and bins

Racks hold each bottle of wine individually in place; in bins, bottles are simply laid one on top of another. You can, therefore, fit about one-third more bottles into the same amount of space if you bin rather than rack.

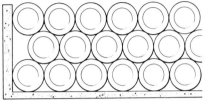

Bottles in bins may be stacked one on top of another (above). This optimizes space, but makes it difficult to extract a bottle from low down in the bin. Separating the layers with laths (below) makes it easier to remove the odd bottle, and is the better method for bins containing different wines.

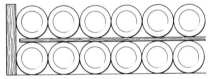

● *Bin or rack wine bottles with the tops facing outwards, so that they are easy to identify from the capsules.*

● *Built-in bins need to be substantial. A single case of wine weighs almost 15 kg; a well-stocked cellar, with dozens or even hundreds of bottles, will need strong bins to contain it safely. Use bricks for large numbers of bottles; for bookshelf-style bins, use planks at least 2.5 cm thick, and stagger the position of the upright supports to add strength.*

● *Remember that heat rises: the top of a cupboard or closet may be the warmest place in a room.*

● *Should you be lucky enough to have the original wooden case in which a classified Bordeaux wine or a Vintage Port was supplied, keep it in good condition, since it can contribute to the resale value of the wine. Original cardboard cases do not have the same value, and anyway are less durable – trying to carry wine in a damp or damaged case is to risk dropping and breaking the bottles.*

STOCKING A CELLAR

Ideally, the contents of a cellar will correspond to the owner's tastes and needs – as well as to the available space and money. Red wines are likely to predominate, since they are best value bought young and comparatively inexpensive; but be sure you have the conditions in which they will mature properly if they are a long-term investment. Fewer white wines benefit from such ageing, though some honourable exceptions are recommended below.

The following wines are *not* worth laying down. They should be bought as and when needed, rather than tying up space and capital with wines which essentially should be drunk young and which are always available: Muscadet, Sancerre, Pouilly Blanc Fumé, Anjou rosé, anything labelled Sauvignon, straightforward Chenin Blanc, Soave, Verdicchio, Valpolicella, Bardolino, Vinho Verde, Liebfraumilch, Beaujolais or anything marked Gamay, *vin de pays* from France and virtually anything marked 'table wine' in any language.

The only exception to this last rule is a small group of excellent Italian wines which, largely for bureaucratic reasons, are labelled *vino da tavola* rather than DOC; examples are Sassicaia from Tuscany, Spanna from a house like Vallana in Piedmont, Venegazzù from Veneto, and Foianeghe from Trentino.

What you put in your cellar should be determined by what you like to drink. Many people might not think it worth while, for instance, laying down Champagne, although both vintage and non-vintage Champagne improve with some bottle age. Vintage Champagne is delicious at 6-7 years old, and non-vintage will develop well for 6 months to a year after buying. Keep magnums or bottles, not half bottles.

Port is the fortified wine that most repays keeping: buy it young, and keep it until it is about 15-20 years old. Lay down only Vintage and single-*quinta* Vintage Port, e.g. Croft's Quinta da Roêda, Taylor's Quinta de Vargellas, Cockburn-managed Quinta da Eira Velha, Graham's Quinta de Malvedos.

Lay down special anniversary Bual or Malmsey, if you like Madeira; top houses, such as Cossart Gordon, may occasionally issue exceptional blends to commemorate special events.

Special Sherries brought out by the top houses are usually already old, but some repay further keeping. Ask for the top range of wines from houses like Gonzalez Byass, Domecq, Williams & Humbert and La Riva. Fino Sherries, however, should be drunk as young and as fresh as possible.

Most people will think that young red wines of class are the ideal candidates for their cellar. The first decision is whether to lay down in case lots, or in smaller units. Case lots are generally far more satisfactory. In the first place you can buy at a better rate (often wholesale rates) when the wine is younger. Furthermore, a case really allows you to see a wine develop. If you have only a few bottles, you might use them all at a dinner party, even if you think the wine needs more time.

When buying for laying down, use a merchant who has a good reputation, and who may have 'first offers' of a newly released Bordeaux vintage at advantageous prices; go for the good years (refer to Vintage notes) and take advice, saying whether you are looking for long- or medium-term drinking.

Red wine: basic types that repay keeping in bottle are good-class Cabernet/Merlot wines, Cabernet/Shiraz wines, Syrah wines from the Northern Rhône, and *premier* or *grand cru* Pinot Noir from the Côte d'Or. To a lesser degree, Chianti Classico Riservas from fine years need keeping, and Nebbiolo wines, such as Barolo and Barbaresco – but if the latter have had prolonged ageing in wood before bottling, they will not need so much time in the cellar. This also applies to Brunello di Montalcino.

White wines that repay keeping are high-quality Chardonnay wines (be they from Burgundy, California or Australia), Sémillon-based wines – whether sweet and luscious from Sauternes/Barsac, vinified dry from the Hunter Valley in Australia, or dry and mixed with Sauvignon as with top Graves (Château Laville Haut-Brion and Domaine de Chevalier). Late-harvest Riesling wines, whether from Germany, Alsace or California (and now, occasionally, Australia too) also need time to open out.

THE FIVE-CASE CELLAR With limited means, and money for five cases of wine for laying down, choose:	● *1 case fine red Bordeaux from an excellent year, e.g. a Classified Growth from the Médoc, Graves or St Emilion/Pomerol.* ● *1 case Cabernet Sauvignon from the Napa Valley in California.* ● *1 case red Burgundy: a* **premier** *or* **grand cru** *(bought from an impeccable source – i.e. a top négociant/domaine-owner or top estate).*	● *1 case top Chardonnay from the Côte de Beaune: e.g. a* **premier cru** *Puligny-Montrachet or Meursault (also from an impeccable source), or from Sonoma or Alexander Valley in California.* ● *1 case Mosel Riesling Auslese.* *Or substitute for one of the above:* ● *1 case Rhône red: Hermitage, Crozes-Hermitage, or Côte Rôtie.*
THE TEN-CASE CELLAR With double the capacity, both financial and physical, invest in ten cases of top wine. Add to the five-case list:	● *1 case Bordeaux: add a top Bourgeois Growth to the collection (keep it for a little less time than the Classified Growth); or add a second Classified Growth, from a different area – e.g. if the first selection is a top Médoc, add a Graves, St Emilion or Pomerol.* ● *1 case young Châteauneuf-du-Pape from a top estate, e.g. Domaine du Vieux Télégraphe, Domaine de Beaucastel, Clos de l'Oratoire des Papes, Château Rayas, Fortia, Château des Fines Roches, Domaine de Mont Redon.* ● *1 case Napa Valley Cabernet Sauvignon to supplement the first: the best examples in California of this grape variety disappear if not bought really young.*	● *1 case Australian Cabernet/ Shiraz blend: compare the development of the last two. Both are unknown quantities over long distances.* ● *1 case white wine: try a Riesling Auslese from the Rheinpfalz, Rheingau or Nahe regions; or a rare late-harvest wine from Alsace; or an exciting example of what the Riesling does when really ripe in Monterey (e.g. Jekel) or the Santa Ynez Valley (e.g. Firestone). Napa and Sonoma also produce superb examples of this type of wine, but they will be expensive. If you prefer your luscious white wines to be made from Sémillon/Sauvignon, go to a top Sauternes or Barsac château.*
THE TWENTY-CASE CELLAR With the possibility of buying 20 cases of wine, explore some of the alternatives already suggested, or elaborate on the basic ten from the following recommendations:	● *Buy two Médocs from different areas (e.g. Château Cos d'Estournel from St Estèphe and Château Grand-Puy-Lacoste from Pauillac).* ● *Buy a* **premier cru** *red wine from the Côte de Beaune, and:* ● *a* **grand cru** *from Côte de Nuits.* ● *Buy a* **grand cru** *Chablis, to match your Côte de Beaune white.* ● *Match your Sonoma or Alexander Valley Chardonnay with one from Napa (Mondavi, Trefethen, Freemark Abbey), Monterey (Chalone) or Santa Clara (Mount Eden).* ● *Take a superb dry Sémillon wine from the lower Hunter Valley of New South Wales (The Rothbury Estate Individual Paddock) or a Barossa Valley late-harvest Rhine Riesling (Orlando).*	● *Age one of the Cabernet wines of Italy (Venegazzù, Sassicaia, or one from Trentino-Alto Adige), a Chianti Classico Riserva (Badia a Coltibuono, Castello di Vicchiomaggio, Castello di Uzzano, or a smaller Riecine or Le Pici), and a Barolo, Barbaresco (Franco Fiorina) or robust, spicy Spanna.* ● *Go international with a case of Catalan red (Torres' Gran Coronas 'Black Label'), or a case from one of the South African estates that are using Bordeaux-type grape mixtures (e.g. Meerlust).* ● *Or go exotic, and age a Ridge Zinfandel – the winery is in the Santa Cruz Mountains, but the grapes come from a variety of areas: try the Paso Robles from San Luis Obispo.*

WINE TASTINGS

In the cellars of Bordeaux, wine tastings are more a duty than a pleasure, as the wine-makers and their potential customers guess the future of a harsh, tannic young wine and try to predict its long-term career. Spitting is the order of the day – no one wants to swallow.

Even the professional taster with the apparently enviable task of trying out drinkable wines to recommend to the public has to represent the range of wines available and cater to the general taste, as well as seeking out personal favourites.

But most of us undertake wine tasting purely for pleasure. We taste wines in their prime, to learn more about the subject or to size up the ones we might want to buy. And with only ourselves to please we can taste many wines or few, swallow or spit, as we like.

- *NO SMOKING in the tasting room.*
- *Don't wear pale colours or delicate clothes at a 'real' wine tasting: a good deal of wine gets spat out all around you.*
- *A woman can wear a flavourless, unscented lipstick that does not affect her own taste impressions – provided she knows it is the type of tasting where people are given their own glass. At a tasting where everyone shares the same glass, smudges of lipstick are offensive.*
- *No one should wear scent, after-shave, hair spray or similarly scented preparations: these may not disturb the nose and palate of the wearer, who is used to their presence, but will be devilish for other people.*
- *Make notes to record your impressions of each wine: you will want to remember your favourites, and to know which to avoid in future. Score cards may be provided: they serve as a checklist of the different elements of taste and a record for you to refer to later on.*
- *Don't crowd around the wines at a tasting so that other people cannot reach them. If you want to chat to friends, move away from the wines and the serious tasters.*
- *If you are worried about your spitting prowess, try practising (with water?) in the kitchen sink at home. Aim improves with practice.*

Commercial tastings

Wine merchants will often give tastings for good customers, or for people who they hope will become good customers – which may include personal buyers or people buying wine for, say, a corporate dining room. The wines shown are nearly always those available on the current list, and sometimes discounts are offered for orders made as a result of the tasting.

Occasionally you will be shown wines that are not yet ready (very young top Bordeaux, for example) but for which the merchant is taking orders in order to get the most advantageous price. Ask your merchant what to look for. A wine which has a long life before it will not taste as soft and supple as a wine that is ready to drink; if the acidity and tannin are to the fore, it is nearly always a good sign in a great wine that needs maturing.

The way these tastings are organized varies little from one merchant to another. You arrive, and are given a glass and a tasting card, showing the name and price of each wine with space beside it to write your comments.

You start tasting at your own pace. If there are a lot of wines, decide which ones interest you most and taste only those. The maximum number you can evaluate at a time varies with experience – some people find a dozen quite enough; others feel they can judge twenty. After that, you are in the realm of the professionals, who will normally choose surroundings quieter and more serious than a wine merchant's tasting to do their job properly.

Educational tastings

Educational tastings, or 'workshops', are organized by merchants, clubs or wine societies, and are often 'led' or tutored. This means that there will be a speaker, probably on a theme (a region, or a grape variety, for instance), and it is highly likely that you will be seated at a table, with several glasses, in order to compare the wines.

These workshops are an excellent way to broaden the vinous horizons, to try wines you might not otherwise have considered, and to decide what you like and what you do not, at comparatively little cost. The speaker's opinions and experience are useful in helping to form your own, and there is nearly always ample opportunity to ask questions.

You also meet other people who like wine,

which can sometimes result in pleasant arrangements such as sharing cases of wine, if you are ordering wines after the tasting. Membership of wine clubs, associations and societies is nearly always worth while both for the wine and for the social side.

Do-it-yourself tastings

If you decide to hold your own tasting at home, it is wise to choose a theme. Otherwise, people contribute such varied wines that you will not know what to look for, and the variety of tastes can be confusing. Begin with a theme like 'Italian whites', or 'Rhône reds', then have, for instance, a Cabernet tasting, or a Muscadet tasting.

A more 'advanced' tasting might take a good vintage in Bordeaux – perhaps 1975 or 1978 – starting with a few red *petit château* wines, e.g. Côtes de Bourg, a Bordeaux Supérieur and a Montagne St Emilion, going on to a couple of bourgeois growths from the Médoc, and finally a couple of classified growths, choosing from the Médoc, Graves, or St Emilion/Pomerol. 'Graduation day' could be a tasting of German *Spätlesen*.

Have no more than eight wines at a home tasting. Provide suitably shaped glasses, and buckets for spitting and pouring away, if people are tasting seriously.

If you want to taste wines without the help of food, nothing more than plain dry biscuits should be provided at the tasting itself, but follow a tasting with a meal – tasters are always hungry after these events, and it is nice to see the wines again when you drink them with the meal afterwards.

Water should also be provided during the tasting, as lots of tannin can dry the mouth, and a white cloth somewhere is useful for really judging the colour of a wine – tilt the glass against a white background and you get the exact shade. But if you use a white cloth on the table with the wines, be warned: red wine stains are very difficult to remove.

If the tasting is a comparative one, say, looking at a group of Valpolicellas to decide which one you like best, find out if people would prefer to do this 'blind', with the label hidden or covered, so that they are not prejudiced by knowing the origin.

The wines themselves will always teach you something when you taste, and it is fascinating to build up what is called a 'palate memory', so that one day you say 'I have had that one before!'

Hold the glass by the stem or – preferably – the foot: this makes it easy to swirl, and your fingers neither obscure the colour and clarity nor affect the temperature.

Tasteful behaviour

The way to avoid getting drunk is, of course, to spit out the wine once you have sniffed its bouquet, taken it into your mouth and swirled it around the whole palate. You will get just as much 'taste' as if you swallowed it, since there are no taste buds in the throat: the only effect you miss is the influence of alcohol.

You spit into the receptacles provided – metal spittoons, or wooden wine cases filled with sawdust. Pour any wine remaining in your glass into the large bottles with funnels provided for this purpose, then go on to the next wine.

Pour just a tasting amount into your glass – perhaps less than one third if the glass is big. But you do need a large enough quantity to swirl and let the wine breathe.

Wines are usually arranged so that heavier ones follow lighter ones. It is natural to assume that whites should be tasted before reds, as at a meal, but some people prefer to start with the more tiring, tannic reds and then go on to the cool whites as a reviver.

Most tastings are held in the morning when the tasters are fresher: it is almost impossible to judge a wine after a large lunch. The light is often better in the morning, too, for appraising the colour of a wine.

SCORING THE TASTE

Whether you call it aroma, bouquet, odour or nose; whether you refer to flavour or taste; whether or not you enter into minute analysis of the sugar-acid balance, the tasting ritual is the same: appearance, smell, taste.

On the other hand, there are different ways to record your impressions. At some tastings, score cards are provided for you to rate each wine on a scale of one to 20, simply according to how well you like it. Other tastings provide checklists which itemize the different facets of a wine: you assess each factor separately and tally up the totals to obtain your score out of 20.

Checklist systems create a more detailed profile of a wine's taste. Some background knowledge is needed to take into account the type of wine you are tasting: 'typical' or 'right for type' means that factors like colour, body and acidity are appropriate in the context.

An example is the DLG system which evaluates German white wines, but in principle is adaptable to different kinds of wine. Note how the points accorded to appearance and smell – both significant factors in forming your impression – rate less highly than taste, by far the most important aspect.

The broad categories of the DLG checklist are fine if you are tasting half a dozen wines. The Davis system is perhaps more useful for a larger number of wines, and also provides a record for future comparisons. The more detailed analysis calls for familiarity with the components that make up the taste – i.e. more tasting experience.

Either one of the systems described gives you a score out of 20. Then you are back with your personal terminology. Whether you would say of a wine rating 16 points that you 'like it very much', call it 'excellent' or simply 'good' depends on your own vocabulary as much as on your taste buds.

Three different sets of descriptions below show how you might phrase your comments on your score. And whatever your words, the wine with the highest points is the one to seek out again.

Since all judgements are relative, how you react depends to some extent on the status of the wine. If you know you are being presented with a range of expensive Californian Cabernets at a blind tasting, you might be more rigorous in your criteria than if you were encountering a range of more everyday supermarket wines – in which instance your expectations would be lower and your pocket less affected. When wines presume to the heights, they must be judged by the highest standards.

Score card (points out of 20)		Impressions of taste		
Wine	20			
	19	like extremely	superb	outstanding
	18			
Winery	17			
	16	like very much	excellent	good
	15		very good	
Vintage	14	like moderately		
	13			
Comments	12	like slightly	good	acceptable
	11	neither like not dislike		
	10		acceptable	
	9	dislike slightly		
	8			
	7	dislike moderately	mediocre	unacceptable
	6			
	5	dislike very much		
	4			
	3	dislike extremely	undrinkable	
	2			
	1			

DLG scoring system

The features evaluated by the Deutsche Land-wirtschafts-Gesellschaft system are especially appropriate for judging German white wines.

Feature and its evaluation
(attainable maximum per wine: 20 points)

Colour (max 2 points)
Typical: 2 Bright yellow: 1 Pale or dark: 0

Clarity (max 2 points)
Crystal-clear: 2 Bright: 1 Cloudy: 0

Odour (max 4 points)
Fruit and perfume: 4 Fragrant-flowery: 3
Clean: 2 Lacking character: 1 Unsound: 0

Taste (max 12 points)
Well-matured and noble: 10-12
Matured and harmonious: 7-9
Clean and vinous: 4-6 Sound: 1-3 Unsound: 0

Wine		
Winery		Vintage
Feature	Max points	Score
Colour	2	
Clarity	2	
Odour	4	
Taste	12	
Total	20	

Davis 20-point system

Ten factors are scrutinized in the system evolved at the viticulture/enology department of the University of California at Davis.

Factor and its evaluation
(maximum points possible per wine: 20)

Clarity (max 2 points)
Brilliant: 2 Clear: 1 Cloudy: 0

Colour (max 2 points)
Perfect: 2 Slightly off: 1 Off: 0

Aroma/bouquet (max 4 points)
Distinct varietal: 4 Slight varietal: 3
Vinous: 2-1 (off-odours: *subtract* 1-2)

Volatile acidity/acescence (max 2 points)
Not vinegary: 2 Slightly vinegary: 1
Obvious vinegar: 0

Total acid (max 2 points)
Right: 2 Slightly low/high: 1 Too low/high: 0

Sugar/acid balance (max 1 point)
Good: 1 Too low/high: 0

Body (max 1 point)
Right for type: 1 Too light/heavy: 0

Flavour (max 2 points)
Right for type: 2 Slightly off: 1 Off: 0

Astringent/bitter (max 2 points)
Normal: 2 Slightly high: 1 Too high: 0

General quality (max 2 points)
High: 2 Average: 1 Low: 0

Wine		
Winery		Vintage
Factor	Max points	Score
Clarity	2	
Colour	2	
Aroma/bouquet	4	
Volatile acidity	2	
Total acid	2	
Sugar/acid balance	1	
Body	1	
Flavour	2	
Astringent/bitter	2	
General quality	2	
Total	20	

It was once the custom to leave a foot of stalk on the melon freshly picked for lunch. The gardener would insert the amputated end into a bottle of vintage Port so that the melon's dying gasp was an intake of wine to diffuse the flesh with flavour and colour.

It has to be *good* Port; the fundamental rule about wine in food is that if the dish is to be good enough to eat, the wine must be good enough to drink; and it is generally true that the wine appropriate to drink with a dish is the best wine to assist its cooking. The dry whites that accompany fish are the ones to add to the poacher; the big reds to tope with game casseroles and steak and kidney pie are right for the pot (plus any sediment left after decanting them; keep Port sediment for this, too).

In the kitchen, wine's first task is as a tenderizer in marinades, particularly for hearty meats. The chosen marinade will also call for oil to carry the other flavours – of herbs, onion juice, garlic, the wine itself – into the wine-softened tissues. An hour of such treatment will have an effect, but a longer time is better.

Soups The idea of liquid with liquid offended the classicists, who did not take wine with their soup. The rule was bent by adding the last of the aperitif wine to the bowl, or a touch of the wine that was to accompany the next course.

When the carcases of hare, pheasant, chicken and duck are the basis of soups, Sherry, Madeira or Port are worthwhile additives, stirred in, pre-warmed, just before the end of the cooking.

Fish and shellfish Fish is naturally tender and needs little marinating, and the marinade will be too fishy to use as the cooking liquid. In the absence of sea-water for the cooking, make a court bouillon: to just enough water to cover the fish, add a quarter as much dry white wine, sliced carrot and onion (celery and leek are optional extras), a bouquet garni and salt; simmer for 30 minutes. Fennel and dill are potential flavourings, but may overwhelm a delicate fish. Strain the liquid and cook the fish in it from cold.

Meat If a cut of meat is totally immersed in a marinade (which should not contain salt or the colour and juices will disperse), its life in

	Soups	Stews, casseroles (including marinade)	Sauces (including marinade)
Sparkling wines	onion soup	use as a still white wine in fish and chicken dishes	
White wines	dry: fish soups	dry: fish and chicken; all fish and shellfish, especially mussels and scallops; Riesling: *coq au Riesling*	
Red wines	Bordeaux: cherry soup	medium-bodied: chicken *en cocotte*; robust: hare, venison, wild boar	medium-bodied: in cherry *compote* for roast duck; robust: saddle of hare
Port	Ruby: game soups	sediment from decanted Port: all game dishes	
			Cumberland sauce
Sherry	dry: chicken and game soups	steak and kidney pudding	
Madeira	Sercial/Verdelho: chicken liver soup, kidney *consommé*		Sercial/Verdelho: *sauce madère* for ham
Marsala	dry: clear soups		

the refrigerator is longer – a week or more. If the final cooking process is to be by direct heat, drain and dry the meat well, or what was to sear will merely stew. If basting is called for, use the marinade. The sought-after benefit of wine in cooking is not the alcohol but the flavour; the alcohol would give a harsh edge to the taste. It will evaporate if the cooking vessel is uncovered. An alternative is to boil the wine until it is half the starting quantity. Then add it to the dish, *warmed* so as not to interrupt the cooking.

Keep wine reduced in this way in stoppered bottles in the refrigerator for deglazing pan juices after meat has cooked. First, though, *flambé* the pan residues with a little warmed brandy and douse the flames with the wine. If, finally, the colour of the sauce is less than appealing, stir in a small spoonful of tomato purée.

Desserts Champagne poured over almost any soft, sugared fruit turns a meal's finish into a festival. A chilled Mosel makes a pleasant alternative. Making a Champagne sorbet or sherbet is only for the brave; sweet white wines are easier to work with.

Egg yolks and sugar whisked into Marsala make *zabaglione*; white wine or Sherry blended with lemon, sugar and cream becomes a syllabub – two desserts with wine in the leading role. And fortified wines – Madeira, sweet Sherry – certainly fortify trifle.

Red wine, too, has a place in dessert-making, particularly for poaching firm fruit like pears.

Savouries and allsorts Wine and cheese work well together. The wine is the binder in molten cheese dishes and should be used in very small quantities – white wine (and a touch of Kirsch) in the fondues based on Swiss cheese; Sherry in Welsh rarebit.

Use old (but not off) red wine to replace some or all of the vinegar in salad dressings, but not those for use on lettuce. To turn wine into vinegar requires a 'vinegar mother' – a piece of thick, crinkly skin that produces acetic fermentation.

To make *oeufs en meurette*, poach eggs in Burgundy that has first been the boiling liquid for onion, garlic and herbs. Then reduce the strained liquid, thicken with a *beurre manié* of butter and flour, and use as a sauce for the eggs.

Terrines and *pâtés* put a dash of dry white wine or Madeira or Port to effective use.

Desserts	Miscellaneous
macerating berry fruits; in sorbet	use as white wine when no longer sparkling
sweet: macerating fruit, in sorbet; Cérons or Loupiac: syllabub	Swiss fondue; in *pâtés*, terrines; Riesling: in sauerkraut
medium-bodied: stewing pears; macerating strawberries, peaches; Bordeaux: Claret jelly	Burgundy: *oeufs en meurette*
Port jelly; macerating dried fruit, e.g. prunes	*melon au porto*
sweet: trifle	Welsh rarebit; in *pâtés* and terrines; in Chinese cooking
Bual: in fruit pies, e.g. apricot; Malmsey: trifle	in *pâtés*, terrines
sweet: *zabaglione*	

● *For marinating and casseroling robust meats, different kinds of wines can be used together. Save the dregs of drinking wines in the refrigerator, in airtight jars filled to the brim.*

● *If you decide to add wine to a recipe, reduce the other cooking liquid by the same amount. A little goes a long way.*

● *Remember that in a recipe 'a glass of wine' usually means 75-100 ml of wine, rather than a generous drinking measure.*

● *Cooks of Chinese food need never run out of ginger root if they slice and peel the whole thing and keep it in the refrigerator, pickled in Sherry.*

WINE AND HEALTH

Doctors have always been aware of the benefits of moderate drinking as well as the hazards of excess. Happily, the current medical evidence gives a comforting 'yes' to two questions raised by an increasingly enlightened public: is it an acceptable health practice to drink moderate amounts of alcohol? And does wine offer any advantages?

Long-term influences of wine
Longevity An impressive 10-year study of alcoholic drinks and mortality by Dr Arthur Klasky of the Kaiser-Permante Medical Center in Oakland, California, matched four groups of 2,015 people for age, sex, race and cigarette smoking: the only variable was the number of alcoholic drinks per day. After ten years, people who reported two or fewer drinks a day fared best; compared to these, the six-plus drinkers had a doubled mortality rate, and both the non-drinkers and the three-to-five-per-day drinkers had about 50 per cent more deaths. That is bad news for abstainers, but it means that a drink or two a day should do most people no harm.

The death rate from cardiovascular problems was the highest in non-drinkers and lowest in people who drank two or fewer drinks each day. Dr John Kane of the University of California Cardiovascular Research Institute believes this is due to the increase of high-density lipoprotein (a type of fat in the blood) caused by alcohol consumption. The current opinion is that high-density lipoprotein is correlated with a lowered incidence of heart disease. Other factors that increase these protective blood fats are exercise and dietary unsaturated fatty acids such as those found in corn oil and avocados. Perhaps the ideal health regime would be a vigorous workout followed by a light snack of avocado salad and a glass of wine.

Diet When poor appetite is a problem, a glass of wine taken twenty minutes before a meal is a natural aperitif: it increases salivation, stimulates stomach activity and secretion of digestive juices, increases bile flow and assists the natural evacuation of the colon. These natural processes are aided by the fact that the pH of wine is near the pH of the stomach juices, around 3.5, thus helping maintain the optimal environment for digestion.

Paradoxically, a glass of wine *with* the meal can double the weight loss of obese people, possibly because of its satisfying variety and tranquillizing effect.

Wine is an excellent addition to the bland low-salt diet of heart or blood-pressure patients. The goal of these diets is to decrease sodium and increase potassium intake, especially for people on diuretics (fluid pills). The mean value of all wines is 91 mg of potassium and 8 mg of sodium per serving. Table wines have a better sodium/potassium ratio – and are thus safer for the heart patient – than Sherry, Port or white dessert wine.

Wine is an important dietary source of iron but, unfortunately, not nearly sufficient to treat iron-deficiency anaemia. Likewise, wine is a poor source of vitamins, although red wine does have more vitamins than white. In fact, the B-complex metabolism is interfered with by alcohol, and heavy drinkers may suffer from B-vitamin deficiency.

In terms of trace minerals the non-alcoholic content of wine (congeners) have been shown to increase absorption of the important minerals calcium, phosphorus, magnesium and zinc. These same congeners have been shown to inhibit the growth of many bacteria, including those commonly responsible for travellers' diarrhoea. So the oft-heard advice about the protection afforded by wine with meals in foreign lands may well be true.

Diabetics may safely increase the pleasure of meals and enhance the quality of life with a glass of wine per day. Alcohol does not require insulin for its metabolism, so dry wines are better. Either sweet wines or more than a glass a day will make weight control more difficult, raise the blood sugar and increase the likelihood of the painful polyneurites complications.

The aged Repeated studies have shown that older people who take wine with meals and in small amounts at bedtime find that it improves appetite, makes sleep more restful, increases morale and reduces the amount of tranquillizers and sleeping pills needed. Not only the time-honoured sedative, alcohol, is at work here: wine also contains various gamma-butyrolactones which have been shown to be 10-100 times more effective as an anti-anxiety agent than alcohol. This may well explain why wine tends to make people mellow, whereas spirits sometimes have the opposite effect.

Short-term effects

Medication Ours is a drug-taking society. It is estimated that 80 per cent of civilized populations take some drug each day. Alcohol often interacts with such drugs. A common problem is in the increase of sedation if alcohol is added to narcotics, antihistamine and tranquillizers. A particularly insidious interaction is sometimes seen in people drinking and smoking marijuana. Apparently, the onset of the alcohol effects are delayed, leading to dangerous miscalculations as to how capable a person is to drive, swim or operate machinery.

Even the seemingly harmless analgesics, acetaminophen and aspirin, can cause problems. Mixing alcohol and acetaminophen may lead to liver damage. Regular drinking when taking a large amount of aspirin greatly increases aspirin's tendency to cause gastro-intestinal bleeding. Check with the doctor before drinking when taking any drug.

Headaches By far the most common headache associated with alcohol is the one associated with the hangover syndrome. Since alcohol dilates blood vessels, it can trigger off migraine or cluster headaches and worsen those due to premenstrual tension. Individual people may have specific vulnerability to various types of wine (red or white), but no general rules seem to apply.

Allergy When you are troubled by allergies, alcohol will make the symptoms worse. Alcohol stimulates the mast cells to release the histamine which in turn causes the familiar allergy symptoms; moreover, some red wines contain histamines. In addition, allergic people may be bothered by the yeast or moulds inherent in making wine. Finally, the proteins used in 'fining' wine – casein, gelatine, egg white and isinglass – are all allergens in themselves.

In spite of this, wine allergy reactions are mild and of short duration. Taking an antihistamine before drinking can help.

Hangovers Hangovers are the subject of many jokes, but it is no laughing matter to suffer from headache, fatigue, nausea, tremor, thirst and muddled thinking. Studies have shown that the more you drink, the worse the symptoms.

Alcoholic drinks contain tannins, acids, esters and higher alcohols in addition to the common ethyl alcohol. The more of these additional substances in a drink, the more likely the hangover. Wood-aged wines and scotch and whisky have more of these and are thus more conducive to hangovers.

So, if prone to hangovers, try drinking wine that has not been wood-aged. If you do over-indulge, drink several glasses of water (to combat dehydration), take a high B-Complex + C vitamin pill (alcohol lowers these water-soluble vitamins) and several aspirins (to reduce oedema) before retiring.

Alcohol and the liver

Blood alcohol level is dependent upon absorption and metabolism. Not all alcoholic beverages are alike in terms of absorption: on an empty stomach, beer and wine give half the blood level of a spirit drink. If wine is drunk with a meal, the blood level will be one-third of that produced by a cocktail or aperitif drink. If the meal contains much fat, absorption will be even slower due to delayed gastric emptying. Finally, for reasons that are not clear, red wine gives a lower blood alcohol level than white.

Metabolism of alcohol by the liver is at a constant rate – usually 30 g per hour; so if one drank slowly at the rate of a large glass of table wine per hour, blood alcohol levels would not build up to intoxicating proportions.

Alcoholics and heavy drinkers, however, metabolize alcohol at a somewhat faster rate – until they develop liver disease.

The liver is the chief site for the metabolism of alcohol. Excessive alcohol intake can overwhelm the liver and produce a variety of problems such as cirrhosis. The contribution to alcoholic liver disease made by drinking habits, inheritance, vitamin deficiency and diet, is complicated and unresolved. At present, it seems wise to limit one's intake to roughly a bottle of table wine a day; above that the risk of cirrhosis is greatly increased. Protective measures include drinking with meals, substituting wine for spirits, vitamin supplements and a balanced diet.

VINTAGE NOTES

Vintage charts invariably have more relevance and use in areas of the world where the climate is not always kind. Germany, for example, has more 'highs' and 'lows' than, say, the Hunter Valley of New South Wales. But even in the finest of climates there are always nuances to fascinate the keen wine drinker.

The differences between the years are compounded by the hand of the wine-maker, who may vary his usual procedure one year; he could pick earlier, keep the juice on the skins longer, or add some stems to the must instead of completely de-stemming. So, blanket assumption about vintages are inadvisable. There are certainly vintages in which much more fine wine is made than in others, but always remember that a poor wine-maker will not suddenly mend his ways when a good vintage comes along, and a brilliant wine-maker can do wonders with not very prepossessing material.

Vintages are not so important for the wine drinker who usually sticks to a good, well-blended varietal, and prefers quaffing to discussion. Modern technology has made it possible to drink well year in and year out. But for the finest wines, the most intriguing tastes, the drinking experiences, it is wise to know a little about vintages – and fun to watch how they develop.

FRANCE

Bordeaux

Red wines More is talked about vintages in Bordeaux than anywhere else, because they differ, sometimes considerably, giving interestingly varied styles of red wine. Classed growths from great and very good years can last for 50 years or more, although this kind of ageing obviously gives a mature taste and delicacy that is more subtle than robust, young fruit does. It is a pity to drink a top growth from a great year at under 12 years, and some would say they peak at about 20-25 years. Bourgeois growths need less time, usually starting to drink well at about 6-8 years in very good years, perhaps peaking at 15. In lighter years, both classed and bourgeois growths become softer much more quickly, and are usually delicious at between 5-12 years. *Petits châteaux* of the most robust kind rarely improve after 5 years. Always remember, though, that the massive, tannic years are not necessarily the ones that last best – those years of perfect balance, although not so overpowering, can mature the most gracefully.

Great years, with the tannin and body to require laying down: 1970, 1975, 1978, some 1979s, maybe 1981.

Past great vintages: 1945, 1947, 1949, 1961, 1966.

Good to very good vintages,

sometimes with more charm and elegance than sheer body – the best wines will last well: 1971, 1973 (for moderate ageing), 1976, a few 1980s.

Past vintages of this delicious quality: 1953, 1959 (bigger than most), 1962. 1948 falls in a category of its own, and is very good.

Some vintages particularly favoured St Emilion and Pomerol, e.g. 1964, 1971 and 1979, while 1955 particularly favoured Graves.

White wines Drink dry white Bordeaux very young, a year or two after its vintage. This applies to Bordeaux Blanc and Entre-Deux-Mers, both now made with a lot of Sauvignon, a grape variety for young drinking. The AC Graves is now also Sauvignon-dominated, so the same rules apply, except for the very expensive but superb Château Laville Haut-Brion and Domaine de Chevalier, which become exquisite with bottle age – these two drink better after 10 years.

Sauternes and Barsac Classed-growth Sauternes and Barsac are better drunk after 10 years, and keep for decades. Lesser wines are well developed after 5 years.

Great years: 1967, 1971, 1975, 1976.

Great years of the past: 1945, 1947, 1961.

Good to very good years or years of promise: 1962, 1970, 1979, 1981.

Burgundy

Red wines People say that Burgundy is not as long-lasting as it was, but the same rules apply as for red Bordeaux – in years of fruit, acidity and tannin balance, wines mature well. *Grand cru* wines of the best vintages do not begin to open out before 10 years of bottle age, and last for decades more. *Premiers crus* open out a little earlier and do not last quite as long, while village or *commune* wines are delicious from about 4 years and should be drunk within the decade. So, when buying Burgundies to lay down, concentrate on the *grand* and *premier cru* wines, rather than village or *commune* wines, e.g. Gevrey-Chambertin-Clos St Jacques rather than simple Gevrey-Chambertin. And always buy from impeccable sources: the most reputable *négociants* and estates. Great years with the potential to age beautifully: 1969, some 1971, 1976, 1978, some 1979.

Past excellent vintages: 1945, 1947, 1948, 1949, 1961, 1962, 1964, 1966.

Good to very good vintages, with wines of great drinkability, but with a more limited lifespan: 1970, 1973. 1972 is more solid. Both 1980 and 1981 are very patchy, but there are some good 1980s from the best estates.

White wines These always are better than the reds in the less good years. Nearly always a safe, if expensive bet. 1978s are excellent.

Beaujolais Drink Beaujolais within 1-2 years of its birth, Beaujolais Villages from 1-3 years. The nine *crus* are delicious from 2-4 years. *Crus* like Moulin-à-Vent and Morgon from fine years occasionally need longer, tending to lose their Gamay grape flavour and becoming almost 'Pinot Noir' and Côte d'Or in taste. 1976 untypically made big wines with tannin (almost unheard of in Beaujolais); some optimists say the *crus* will last splendidly, like the fabled 1947s. 1977 was thin and dry. 1978, 1979 and 1981 are delicious vintages. 1980 is fair.

Chablis Vintages do not necessarily correspond to those for the rest of Burgundy: e.g. 1975 was poor on the Côte d'Or, with much rot in the vineyard, but made splendid wines in Chablis. 1971

was a classic. 1973 was charming and some have lasted well. 1974 improved in bottle. 1975 and 1976 (the latter with rather 'fat' wines which almost resemble those of the Côte de Beaune) were both very good indeed. 1977 was rather 'green', although there were some exceptions. 1978 was superb. 1979 is delicious, but not long lasting. Both 1980 and 1981 produced far better wines than at first expected.

The *grands crus* can last beautifully in great years – at 10 years old they are splendid, and can amaze for 5-10 years more. *Premiers crus* taste delicious when between 3 and 6 years old (8 in the case of very good vintages). Straight Chablis is best when 2-5 years old, and Petit Chablis (which is rarely seen now) should be drunk within 1-2 years.

Rhône

The great red wines of the Rhône do not last as long as top Bordeaux. Rhône wines drunk at 20 years old and more tend to have 'dried up', and are preferable younger (say at 10-15 years, from the greatest vintages), when the tannin is balanced by vivid fruit. However, there are people who like the vegetal nose and dry tannin of really old Syrah, from the Northern Rhône, and the mixed grape varieties of Châteauneuf-du-Pape. The latter is attractive when it still has a youthful 'cherry' quality to match the body of the wine. Aged white Rhônes tend to oxidize, or go 'flat' and lack freshness in taste.

Southern Rhône (Châteauneuf-du-Pape area)

Very good recent years: 1978, 1979, 1980.

Great years of the past: 1945, 1947, 1961, 1967.

Northern Rhône (Hermitage area)

Very good recent years: 1970, 1978, 1979, 1980.

Great years of the past: 1945, 1947, 1961.

Loire

Muscadet Should always be drunk within 1-3 years of its birth. It rarely has a poor year.

Touraine and Anjou Dry white wines, rosés and light reds should be drunk when a few years old. The exceptions are the sweet or medium-sweet Vouvrays from Touraine, together with wines such as Quarts de Chaume, Bonnezeaux and Coteaux-du-Layon in Anjou, where bottle age enhances the honey flavour. Drink between 10-30 years in very good vintages; great wines from really top years will last longer. 1971 was a great year for these white wines, as was 1976. **Sancerre, Pouilly Blanc Fumé** Drink within 1-3 years. The 'poor' vintages here usually refer simply to small quantity.

Alsace

Virtually every year produces very pleasant wines, illustrating the fact that vintages are less important for white than for red wines. In some years a shortage of some grape varieties causes prices to rise. 1971 and 1976 produced *vendange*

tardive wines which keep beautifully, even for 10-20 years. The rarely made great, sweet wines, called Sélection de Grains Nobles, can last even longer. Lesser vintages are usually drunk at 2-5 years, although Réserve Personnelle wines, or other specially selected *cuvées* can last for much longer. The rare Alsatian wine with a site name (e.g. Schoenenberg or Rangen) is of top quality. Recent vintages have all been good, with 1979 the best among them, but there was virtually no Gewürztraminer or Muscat in 1980.

Champagne

As with Port, the Champagne houses decide independently whether or not to 'declare' a year a vintage. Most houses made Vintage Champagne in 1970, 1971, 1973, 1975, 1976 and 1979.

SPAIN

The vintage situation in Spain is easier to describe than that of some countries, because the area of Rioja is usually the only region where a little background knowledge is useful. This is not because in Spain every year is one of unremitting sun – indeed, rain at the wrong time frequently causes rot, although spray treatment against this is slowly improving – but because most wines are made to be savoured when a few years old and released when ready to drink.

Rioja

The best overall recent years are 1964, 1966, 1968, 1970, 1973, 1975, 1976 and 1978. 1977 was probably the only poor vintage of the 1970s. 1971 was very good.

A Monte Real 1956 drunk in 1981 tasted admirable, but was probably an exception. Riojas of over 10-12 years of age can begin to dry up and have a less fruity taste. Certain *bodegas* do tend to make wines that last longer than others – Marqués de Murrieta, Muga, Ardanza from La Rioja Alta, and Monte Real from Bodegas Riojanas. Old white Rioja can have a nutty, rich taste if it is not oxidized.

Penedès

The white wines should be drunk within a few years of their birth to obtain maximum charm and freshness. The reds are mostly sold when they are ready to drink, and even the splendid Torres wines Gran Coronas and the 'Black Label' are usually released when they are attaining their peak – this is generous of the producer, for that means that *he* is financing the maturing in bottle rather than you in your cellar.

Other wines

Vega Sicilia is a famed rarity from the province of Valladolid. None of it is sold at under 10 years old, when it is ready to drink. In some opinions, the ageing in wood tends to be too long and almost eliminates further potential for harmonious maturation in bottle. However, another wine from the same province, Protos from Bodegas Ribera Duero, is superb when drunk at 8-12 years old.

Valdepeñas should be drunk within a few years of its harvest, and is already good in the spring following the vintage.

GERMANY

Great years: 1945, 1949, 1953, 1971 and 1976.

Years when fine to very fine wines were made: 1959, 1961, 1964, 1967, 1975, 1979. Good wines were made in 1969, 1970, 1973, 1980 and 1981.

The German wine-maker possesses a high degree of technical ability, and it is rare that a year produces unpleasant wine: green, unripe acidity is the enemy here, with 1972 an example. In a year when most of the wines can be of medium quality, those growers on the best sites will always produce wines of higher natural sugar, and therefore, in German terms, higher quality.

Some years favour a particular area more than others, e.g. 1961 and 1964 for the Mosel; 1967 for the Rheinpfalz; 1969 for the Mosel; 1970 for the Rheinpfalz; 1971 for the Mosel and the Rheingau; 1975 for the Mosel; 1980 for the Pfalz.

ITALY

Piedmont (Red wines)

Barolo asks for some bottle age, although not too much, since it has already spent a good many years in cask. On the whole, good Barolo vintages should be drunk at about 8-10 years old, and great vintages will be at their best at 10-20 years.
Great years: 1971 and 1978.
Very good years: 1970 (could be termed great), 1974, 1979. 1981 looks good – a bit like 1974.
Disappointing years: 1973, 1975, 1976 and 1977. 1972 was declassified and did not appear as Barolo.
Barbaresco falls into line with Barolo. Barbera can be made light and fresh, when it is not DOC. Barbera d'Asti, Barbera d'Alba and, to a lesser extent, Barbera del Monferrato, need a few years in bottle, but never as much as Barolo or Barbaresco.
Gattinara, Ghemme and Sizzano have a usual span of 6-12 years.

Tuscany (Red wines)

Keep Chianti Classico; enjoy straight Chianti young. Classico Riserva deserves maturation, as this wine is from both the very good years and the best sites. Recent very good or excellent vintages, for Chianti Classico, Brunello di Montalcino and Vino Nobile di Montepulciano: 1967, 1968, 1969 (especially Chianti), 1970, 1971 (not Montepulciano), 1975, 1977, 1978, 1979 and 1980. 1973 was exceptionally good for Montepulciano.

Friuli-Venezia Giulia and Collio

The white wines for which these regions are famous are usually drunk within a few years of their birth. The Cabernet and Merlot red wines are also at their best when they retain lots of youthful fruit – from 2-5 years of age. As there are a great many grape varieties grown in the region, years may favour some more than others. Throughout the 1970s fine wines were made, especially in 1974, 1977, 1978 and 1979. 1980 was light but good.

Veneto

Soave, Valpolicella and Bardolino are for drinking within a few years. The only wines to keep for as much as a decade are the rich Amarones. The 1970s produced very good wines, with the exception of 1975 for Valpolicella and 1972 for everything. 1977 and 1979 were excellent all round. 1981 is good average quality.

Other wines

Always drink white wines young: 2-5 years is the general rule. This goes for Verdicchio from the Marches; Frascati from Latium; Orvieto from Umbria; the delicious Riesling Italico or Pinot wines from Trentino; the very fine whites (Riesling, Gewürztraminer, Sylvaner) from Südtirol/Alto Adige, although Riesling Renano can age with style.

Red wines made from the Schiava grape (Trentino-Alto Adige) and Sangiovese (most especially in Emilia Romagna) are lightish, and should like Beaujolais be drunk young. Lambrusco falls into this category. Rubesco di Torgiano from Umbria needs a few years longer. The great Teroldego from Trentino can take 5-10 years' bottle age, as can some of the wines of the south, such as Copertino, Cirò, Aglianico del Vulture, Taurasi.

USA/CALIFORNIA

Vintage charts are particularly difficult for California. In each widely differing area, there are properties and companies often making a whole range of wines – a 'winery' rarely makes one wine, but is more likely to make five or six; the big companies may even make a score of wines. These will be from different grape varieties, and a successful year for one is not necessarily so for another. The whole area of California is a relative newcomer to fine wine-making, and so estimates at longevity are sometimes mere guesses, and not based on sound experience over decades. When winery, wine-maker and even area (in the wine-making sense) are new, the drinker is travelling through uncharted territory.

Monterey

An area comparatively new to producing fine wine, and which largely specializes in good-quality 'blends' by the big companies. Vintages from 1975 onwards all good, except 1976.

Santa Barbara

A very new wine area. The late 1970s, 1980 and 1981 all produced some splendid wines.

	Napa	Sonoma
1970	Great reds: superb Cabernet Sauvignon, Zinfandel.	Superb reds for ageing; good whites.
1971	Reds and whites: average quality.	Generally rather disappointing.
1972	Cabernet Sauvignon very poor; Chardonnay best bet.	Poor reds; whites better, especially Chardonnay.
1973	Very good Cabernet Sauvignon and Zinfandel; Chardonnay the best of the whites.	Good all round; some excellent examples.
1974	Huge reds: some massive, rich Cabernet Sauvignon and Zinfandel. Chardonnay very good.	Very good Cabernet Sauvignon and Zinfandel; whites less good but interesting and high-quality.
1975	Some very classy reds; some Cabernets may turn out to be better balanced for ageing than the famed 1974s. All whites very good indeed.	Reds which look set for long life; good whites, with some very good Johannisberg Riesling late-harvest wines.
1976	Great, concentrated reds; some very good, full whites.	Very rich, concentrated Cabernet Sauvignon and Zinfandel to cellar. All whites of high standard.
1977	Second year of drought, but all grape varieties did magnificently.	All varieties produced fine wines, fit to age. Johannisberg Riesling perhaps greatest success.
1978	First-class whites, especially Chardonnay and Sauvignon Blanc; full, big reds.	Year of Chardonnay, with some wonders for future drinking. A successful year overall.
1979	Whites have remarkable balance and will last.	Whites outclass reds, especially Chardonnays.
1980	Chardonnay and Pinot Noir will last beautifully.	Slightly variable: whites seem more successful than reds.
1981	Looks good, especially for whites.	Very promising.

AUSTRALIA

Vintages are only important for fine Estate wines, usually made from familiar grapes like Cabernet, Shiraz (or Syrah), Chardonnay, Riesling and Sémillon. The very well-made big brands, benefiting from advanced technical knowledge, often do not show a vintage and appear on the market when they are ready to drink. And, since the turnover is good (Australians drink seriously), the wine is virtually always 'in condition', with no tired, oxidized bottles loitering for months on the shelves.

Hunter Valley (New South Wales)

Vintages throughout the 1970s and 1980 were all good, except for 1971, which was wet and disastrous. Some years favour red, and some white. There were some outstanding whites in 1974, reds and whites were very good in 1975, whites have the edge in 1976, reds took the prize in 1977, 1978 made quite fast-developing wines, 1979 produced big wines, 1980 was elegant for both colours and 1981 was very good and stylish.

Barossa Valley (South Australia)

1974 was the poor vintage here. Excellent whites in 1973; 1976 produced excellent reds and late-harvested whites (sweet), elegance in 1977, 1978 good to a bit more, 1979 good (very good in the Eden Valley), 1980 produced wines with excellent balance and 1981 was very good, particularly for whites.

Milawa (Victoria)

1974 and 1975 produced wines that were light and thin, while in 1977 storms destroyed anything significant. 1971 and 1972 produced wines which were big and broad, 1976 was most successful both for quantity and quality, 1978 and 1979 produced wines with finesse, with 1980 a very honourable year for both colours and 1981 especially good for whites.

VINTAGE PORT

If possible, wait 15-20 years, depending on the weight of the vintage, before drinking Vintage Port. Don't necessarily drink in chronological order – light years before massive years is the rule.

Great vintages of history include 1908, 1912, 1924, 1927, Noval 1931, 1934 and 1945 (a classic year).

Recent vintages

1947 is lighter than 1948. 1950 is light. 1955 produced big, full, strong wines, which are superb drinking from 1980 onwards. 1958 is light and attractive. 1960 is quite soft and absolutely ready in the 1980s. 1963 is a classic year of the first order, which will go on and on. 1966 should be drunk before the 1963, and it has a lot of fruity flavour. Cockburn's produced a 1967 of breed and style. 1970 will be excellent; 1975 a bit lighter; it is early days to pronounce fully on the 1977s and Noval is the famous wine of 1978. Some houses declared the 1980.

Individual-*quinta* wines that are very good are: Taylor's Quinta de Vargellas, Croft's Quinta da Roeda, Cockburn-managed Quinta da Eira Velha (from 1978), Graham's Quinta de Malvedos and Delaforce's Quinta da Corte. They tend to be made in years not declared as Vintage by the houses that own them.

PRONUNCIATION GUIDE

abboccato (It) ah-bo-**kah**-toe
Alella (Sp) ah-**lay**-lyah
Aligoté (F) ah-lee-go-**tay**
Aloxe-Corton (F) ah-loss cor-tawn
Alto Adige (It) ahl-toe ah-dee-jay
amabile (It) ah-**mah**-bee-lay
Amontillado (Sp) ah-mon-tee-**yah**-doe
Anjou (F) ahn-joo
Appellation Contrôlée (F) ah-pel-lahss-yon
con-troe-lay
Auslese (Ger) **ow**-slay-zuh

Barbaresco (It) bar-bah-**ress**-coe
Barbera (It) bar-**bear**-ah
Bardolino (It) bar-doe-**lee**-noe
Barolo (It) bar-**oh**-loe
Barsac (F) bar-sack
Beaujolais (F) boh-joh-lay
Beaune (F) bone
Beerenauslese (Ger) **beer**-en-ow-slay-zuh
Bereich (Ger) buh-**rike**
Bernkastel Kues (Ger) **bearn**-cahs-tel **koo**-us
Blanc de blancs (F) blahn duh blahn
Blanc Fumé (F) blahn **few**-may
Bocksbeutel (Ger) **box**-boytl
bodega (Sp) boe-**day**-gah
Bordeaux (F) bor-doe
Bourgogne (F) bor-**gon**-yuh
Brouilly (F) broo-yee
Brunello di Montalcino (It) broo-**nell**-oh
dee mon-tahl-**chee**-noe
brut (F) broot
Bual (Por) boo-**ahl**

Cabernet (F) cah-bear-nay
Cahors (F) cah-or
cave (F) cahv
Chablis (F) shah-blee
chai (F) shay
Chambertin (F) shahm-bear-tan
Chambolle-Musigny (F) shahm-bol mew-seen-yee
Chardonnay (F) shah-doe-nay
Chassagne-Montrachet (F) shah-san-yuh
mon-rah-shay
Chasselas (F) shass-lah
Château (F) shah-toe
Châteauneuf-du-Pape (F) shah-toe-nuhf-doo-pahp
Chénas (F) shay-nahss
Chenin Blanc (F) shay-nan blahn
Chiroubles (F) shee-roobl
Cinsault (F) san-so
clarete (Sp) klah-ret-ay
climat (F) clee-mah
Clos Vougeot (F) cloh voo-joh
colheita (Por) cul-**yay**-tah
consorzio (It) con-**sorts**-ee-oh

Corbières (F) cor-byair
Corton (F) cor-tawn
cosecha (Sp) co-**say**-chah
Coteaux Champenois (F) coat-toe chahm-pen-wah
Côte Chalonnaise (F) coat shah-lo-nayz
Côte de Beaune (F) coat duh bone
Côte de Nuits (F) coat duh nwee
Côte d'Or (F) coat dor
Côte Rôtie (F) coat roe-tee
Côtes du Rhône (F) coat doo **rone**
crémant (F) cray-mahn
cru (F) crew
cru classé (F) crew clah-say
cuvée (F) coo-vay

Dão (Port) downg
Debröi Hárslevelü (Hun) **deb**-ruh
har-shlay-vuh-loo
Dolcetto (It) dol-**chet**-toe
Douro (Port) doo-roe

Echézeaux (F) eh-shay-zoh
Edelfäule (Ger) **ay**-del-foil-uh
Egri Bikavér (Hun) **egg**-ree **bee**-kah-vair
Einzellage (Ger) **ine**-tsuh-lah-guh
Eiswein (Ger) **ice**-vine
élevage (F) ay-leh-vazh
Entre-Deux-Mers (F) ahntr-duh-mair
Erzeugerabfüllung (Ger) **air**-tsoy-guh-**ahb**-foo-lung
estufagem (Por) ish-too-**fah**-gum

Fendant (Sw) fahn-dahn
fiasco (It) fee-**ahss**-koe
Fino (Sp) **fee**-noe
Fleurie (F) fluh-ree
Frascati (It) frahss-**cah**-tee
frizzante (It) freet-**zahn**-tay
Friuli (It) free-**oo**-lee

Gamay (F) gam-may
Gattinara (It) gah-tee-**nah**-rah
Gevrey-Chambertin (F) zhev-ray shahm-bear-tan
Gewürztraminer (Ger) guh-**vurts-trah-**mee-ner
goût de terroir (F) goo duh tair-wah
Graves (F) grahv
Grenache (F) greh-nahsh
Grignolino (F) gree-nyol-ee-no
Grosslage (Ger) **gross**-lah-guh
Gumpoldskirchner (Aus) **goom**-polts-ker-khnuh

haut (F) oh
hautes (F) oat
Hérault (F) ay-roh
Hermitage (F) air-mee-tahj
Heurige (Ger) **hoi**-ree-guh

212

Jerez de la Frontera (Sp) hair-**eth** deh lah
fron-**tair**-ah
Johannisberg (Ger) yoh-**han**-iss-bairk
Juliénas (F) zhoo-**leay**-nass

labrusca (Lat) la-**broos**-cah
Lacryma Christi (It) la-**cree**-mah **kriss**-tee
Languedoc (F) lang-dock
Mâcon (F) mah-kohn
Manzanilla (Sp) man-zah-**nee**-ya
Margaux (F) mahr-goe
Médoc (F) meh-dock
Merlot (F) mehr-loe
Meursault (F) muhr-soe
mis en bouteilles (F) meez ahn boo-tay
Montilla (Sp) mon-**tee**-yah
Montepulciano d'Abruzzo (It)
    mon-tay-pool-**cha**-no dah-**brood**-zoe
Moscatel de Setúbal (Sp) moss-cah-**tel** deh
    seh-**too**-bol
Moulin-à-Vent (F) mooh-lahn-ah-vahn
mousseux (F) moo-suh
Müller-Thurgau (Ger) **moo**-lair-**toor**-gow
Muscadet (F) muhss-kah-day

Nahe (Ger) **nah**-uh
Nebbiolo (It) neh-**byoh**-loe
Neuchâtel (Sw) nuh-shah-tell
Nierstein (Ger) **neer**-shtine
Nuits St Georges (F) nwee-san-jawj

Oechsle (Ger) **uhk**-sluh
Oloroso (Sp) oh-loe-**roe**-soe
Oltrepò Pavese (It) ohl-treh-**poe** pah-**veh**-seh
Orvieto (It) or-**veay**-toe

Pauillac (F) paw-yack
Pays (F) **pay**-yee
perlant (F) per-lahn
pétillant (F) pet-tee-yahn
petit (F) puh-tee
Phylloxera (Lat) fil-**lox**-uh-rah
Piesport (F) **peez**-pawt
Pinot Grigio (It) pee-noe **gree**-joh
Pinot Noir (F) pee-noe nwah
Pomerol (F) pom-uh-rohl
Pouilly-Fuissé (F) poo-yee fwee-say
Pouilly-Fumé (F) poo-yee few-may
pourriture noble (F) poo-ree-toor **nobl**
premier cru (F) prem-yay crew
Premières Côtes (F) prem-yair coat
Puligny-Montrachet (F) poo-lee-nyee
    mon-rah-shay
puttonyos (Hun) **puh**-tawn-yosh

Qualitätswein mit Prädikat (Ger)
    kvah-lee-**tets**-vine mitt **pray**-dee-kaht
Quincy (F) kan-see
quinta (Por) **keen**-tah

Recioto (It) ray-**shot**-oh
Retsina (Gk) ret-**see**-nah
Rheingau (Ger) **rine**-gow
Rheinhessen (Ger) **rine**-hess-en
Rheinpfalz (Ger) **rine**-faltz
Ricasoli (It) ree-**cah**-so-lee
Riesling (Ger) **reece**-ling
Rioja (Sp) ree-**oh**-ha
rosé (F) roh-zay
Roussillon (F) roo-see-yon
Ruwer (Ger) **roo**-vuh

Saar (Ger) sahr
Sancerre (F) sahn-sair
Sangiovese (It) san-joh-**vay**-zeh
Sauternes (F) soh-tairn
Sauvignon Blanc (F) soh-veen-yon blahn
Schaumwein (Ger) **shohm**-vine
secco (It) **say**-co
Sémillon (F) say-mee-yohn
Soave (It) **swah**-veh
solera (Sp) so-**lair**-ah
Spätlese (Ger) **shpet**-lay-zuh
spumante (It) spoo-**mahn**-tay
Szamorodni (Hun) soe-moe-rod-nee

Tafelwein (Ger) **tah**-fel-vine
Tavel (F) tah-vel
Teroldego (It) teh-**rol**-dey-go
Trentino (It) tren-**tee**-no
Trockenbeerenauslese (Ger)
    trok-en-beer-en-**ows**-lay-zuh
Tokay Aszú (Hun) **tow**-koy ah-soo

Ugni Blanc (F) oon-yee blahn

Valdepeñas (Sp) val-day-**pain**-yass
Valpolicella (It) val-poh-lee-**chay**-lah
Vaud (Sw) voh
Veltliner (Aus) velt-**lee**-nuh
vendange (F) ven-dahnj
Verdelho (Por) vehr-**dee**-yoh
Verdicchio (It) vair-**dee**-kee-oh
Vinho Verde (Por) veen-yoh **vair**-day
vin jaune (F) van zhone
Vitis vinifera (Lat) **vee**-tis vin-**if**-uh-rah

Wachau (Aus) vah-kow
Wehlen (Ger) **vay**-len

Yquem (F) ee-kem

213

GLOSSARY

Alcohol Ethyl alcohol (C_2H_5OH), a chemical compound formed by the action of natural or added yeasts on the sugar content of grapes during **fermentation.**

Alcoholic content Measurement of the alcoholic strength of wine varies with local regulations: in most countries it is now expressed on the bottle label in terms of a percentage of the total volume, e.g. a table wine might be between 10 and 14 per cent alcohol by volume.

Back-blending New Zealand term for adding *Süssreserve* for sweetening.

Botrytis cinerea A fungus which attacks grapes, forming a mould. In cold, wet weather, or on black grapes, *Botrytis* is harmful. In fine, warm harvests it gradually withers white grapes, concentrating their flavour and sugar so that they produce sweet wines, high in alcohol and with a unique bouquet. This is the 'noble rot' or 'noble mould' responsible for the world's great sweet white wines, e.g. Sauternes and Californian late-harvest Rieslings.

Botrytized Grapes or wine affected by *Botrytis cinerea.*

Bottle ageing The gradual maturing and mellowing of fine wines containing a high proportion of tannin and other extract matter, due to very slow oxidation and interaction of the components in the wine.

Bottle sickness A passing indisposition to which newly bottled wines are subject, sometimes due to the stabilizing treatments a wine undergoes before bottling, such as the addition of sulphur dioxide. The transfer of the wine from cask to bottle is also a process that 'tires' or 'shocks' a wine. Laying down the wine bottles for a couple of months eliminates the problem.

Carbonic maceration Process of fermenting uncrushed grapes in a closed vat containing a carbonic gas atmosphere, producing light, grapy red wines for young drinking.

Chambré (Fr) At room temperature (of bottles of red wine, in preparation for drinking).

Chaptalization The addition of sugar to grape **must** during fermentation to increase the wine's alcoholic content: the extra sugar is converted into alcohol. The practice is not permitted in Italy, but in France and Germany may be allowed in stringently controlled circumstances.

Corked Wine with a distinctly 'off' smell, reminiscent of rotting wood or fungus. Unlike bottle stink, it gets worse rather than better on contact with air. The cause is **oxidation** due to a bad cork; fortunately, this is a rare fault.

Crush US and Australian term for the grape harvest or vintage; it also measures – in tonnes – the total quantity of grapes harvested.

Cultivar South African term synonymous with 'grape variety'.

Dosage Concentrate of sugar, wine and/or brandy added to sparkling wine before final bottling, to flavour and sweeten.

Enology *see* **Oenology**

Fermentation Biochemical process by which the sugar in grape juice is converted into alcohol and CO_2 by the action of yeast enzymes. Most fermentation stops naturally when the alcohol reaches 15 per cent, but some yeasts continue working at even higher levels.

Flor (Sp) a film of yeast cells which forms naturally on some types of Sherry during **fermentation** and for some months after the vintage.

Fortified wines Wines (e.g. Port, Sherry, Madeira, etc) to which brandy or rectified alcohol has been added, sometimes halting **fermentation** before all the sugar is converted into alcohol.

Generic Wine named according to the general type to which it belongs, e.g. 'rosé' or 'fortified wine'. Also, wine named after the type characteristic of a particular region, e.g. 'Burgundy'. In EEC countries, a generic description may be applied only to wines which come from the original designated area, e.g. the term 'Californian burgundy' would be not be permissible.

Light wine In the USA, a wine which is low in alcohol.

Malolactic fermentation A secondary **fermentation,** usually subsequent to the alcoholic one, by which tart malic acid is converted into milder lactic acid and CO_2. Usually desirable in red wines, sometimes in whites if the total acidity is high.

Must Unfermented grape juice or crushed grapes.

Négociant (Fr) A shipper or wine merchant who buys wine in bulk from different sources and prepares it for sale: by maturing, treating, perhaps blending, and bottling it.

Noble rot see *Botrytis cinerea.*

Oenology The knowledge and study of wines and wine-making.

Oxidize, oxidation Bacterial deterioration due to excessive interaction of wine with air; a limited amount of oxidation is part of wine's maturing process, and helps the bouquet to develop.

Phylloxera Louse which attacks vine roots; most European varieties are susceptible and are therefore grafted on to resistant American root-stocks.

Sommelier (Fr) Wine-waiter.

Sparkling wine Wine which has undergone a secondary **fermentation** in vat or in bottle and has thus become effervescent through the formation of bubbles of CO_2 gas.

Still wine Non-sparkling wine, i.e. the majority of table wines.

Süssreserve (Ger) Concentrated, unfermented grape **must**, sometimes added to wine to sweeten it before bottling.

Tannin A stringent-tasting organic compound found in red wines, and deriving from grape stems and skins and/or the oak barrels in which wine is matured, particularly when these are new.

Tartrates Harmless crystals of potassium bitartrate that may form in cask or bottle from the tartaric acid naturally present in wine. Cold stabilizing treatment prevents their formation.

Ullage The amount by which a container (cask or bottle) falls short of being full – i.e. the air space above the wine.

Varietal Wine named after the (principal) grape variety from which it is made. After 1982, in the USA, the named grape variety has to constitute at least 75 per cent of the wine's volume; in Europe, the proportion is usually 100 per cent.

Vinification The science of making wine from grapes. 'Vinified' may be a synonym for 'fermented'.

Vintage The year's grape harvest, and the date given to the wine fermented from those grapes.

Viticulture The science of cultivating the vine and producing grapes.

Vitis vinifera The species of grape from which most European and Californian wines are made. Since it is susceptible to **phylloxera**, most European *vinifera* vines are grafted on to resistant American root-stocks.

Wood-ageing Maturation of wine in casks or barrels which permit minute amounts of air to interact with the components in the wine. The age and the kind of wood used contribute character to the wine, e.g. oak barrels, especially when new, impart tannin and a vanilla taste.

FRENCH TERMS
Blanc de blancs white wine (especially Champagne) made exclusively from white grapes
Blanc de noirs white wine made from black grapes
Brut dry (Champagne)
Cave cellar, underground wine store
Chai building for storing wine
Château wine estate, especially in Bordeaux
Claret English name for red Bordeaux wines
Climat individual vineyard, particularly in Burgundy, Alsace
Clos walled vineyard, especially in Burgundy
Côte(s), **Coteau(x)** hillsides, slopes covered with vineyards
Crémant sparkling wine made in Champagne, Burgundy, Alsace, Loire; *crémant* has less pressure than Champagne
Cru growth or crop of grapes
Cuvée contents of a vat or *cuve*, or batch of blended wine
Demi-sec semi-sweet
Domaine property or estate, particularly in Burgundy
Élevage 'bringing up' or maturing of wine, sometimes done by *négociant-éleveur*
Goût de terroir earthy taste deriving from soil
Marque déposée trade mark
Mis(e) en bouteille(s) . . . bottled . . .
Moelleux sweet
Mousseux sparkling
Négociant wine merchant or shipper
Perlant with a very slight sparkle
Pétillant slightly sparkling, 'prickly'
Primeur early wine
Propriétaire owner
Pourriture noble noble rot, *Botrytis cinerea*
Récolte crop, vintage
Sec dry
Vendange vintage
Vendange tardive late-vintage, late-harvested
Vigne vine
Vin de Pays country wine
Vin de Table table wine
Vin Doux Naturel fortified sweet wine
Vin gris 'grey' wine, made from slightly pressed black grapes – in fact, pale rosé colour
Vin jaune 'yellow' wine, found in the Jura
Viticulteur vine-grower

GERMAN TERMS
Abfüller bottler
Amtliche Prüfungsnummer (APNr) official quality testing number
Anbaugebiet a specified region
Auslese wine from selected bunches of grapes
Beerenauslese high-quality sweet wine made from selected single grapes
Bereich wine-producing district
Deutscher Tafelwein (DTW) 100 per cent German table wine
Edelfäule noble rot or *Botrytis cinerea*
Einzellage individual vineyard site

Eiswein wine made from grapes frozen on the vine and when pressed. Must be accompanied by a distinction such as *Auslese*, etc
Erzeugerabfüllung bottled by the grower
Grosslage collection of individual vineyard sites
Halbtrocken medium dry
Kabinett a category of QmP wine
Keller cellar
Perlwein sparkling table wine with a pressure of up to 2.5 atmospheres
Qualitätswein eines Bestimmten Anbaugebietes (QbA) quality wine from a specified region
Qualitätswein mit Prädikat (QmP) quality wine with distinction
Schaumwein sparkling wine, often made from imported wine
Sekt or **Qualitätschaumwein** good-quality sparkling wine
Spätlese wine from late-harvested ripe grapes
Tafelwein table wine
Trocken dry
Trockenbeerenauslese very rich wine made from grapes dried on the vine and attacked by *Edelfäule*
Weingut wine estate growing all its own grapes
Weinkellerei winery
Weinstrasse scenic road through vineyards
Winzergenossenschaft, Winzerverein winegrowers' cooperative

ITALIAN TERMS
Abboccato semi-sweet
Amabile slightly sweeter than *abboccato*
Amaro bitter
Bianco white
Cantina cellar, winery
Cantina sociale cooperative
Casa vinicola wine house or wine company
Chiaretto light red
Classico central 'kernel' of DOC area, hence implicitly the most select wine
Dolce sweet
Frizzante semi-sparkling
Liquoroso strong, often sweet wine; may be fortified
Muffa nobile noble rot
Riserva wine aged for specified period, possibly in cask, depending on DOC
Rosato rosé
Rosso red
Secco dry
Spumante sparkling
Vecchio old; wine matured for specified period
Vendemmia harvest, vintage
Vino da tavola non-DOC wine; sometimes fine, but more often pleasant, everyday drinking

SPANISH TERMS
Abocado sweet
Años age in years when bottled
Blanco white
Bodega cellar, winery
Cava cellars for making Champagne-method sparkling wines; the wines themselves
Clarete light red
Cosecha crop, vintage
Dulce sweet
Embotellado de origen estate-bottled
Espumoso sparkling
Reserva mature quality wine, aged in wood
Rosado rosé
Seco dry
Tinto red
Vendimia vintage
Viña vineyard
Vino de mesa table wine

PORTUGUESE TERMS
Adamado sweet
Branco white
Clarete red
Colheita vintage
Doce sweet
Engarrafado na origem estate-bottled
Espumante sparkling
Garrafeira wine from a private cellar or stock; implies better quality
Quinta farm estate
Região demarcado demarcated area
Rosado rosé
Seco dry
Tinto red
Velho matured (red wine)
Verde young
Vinha vineyard
Vinho de consumo ordinary wine, often served 'open' or in carafes

AUSTRIAN TERMS
Ausbruch rich, sweet wines
Heurige new, 'green' wine; also cellar or wine garden where it is drunk
Ried defined site within larger vineyard
Spitzenwein top-quality wine
Tischwein 'table' wine, everyday wine
Weinbaugebiet legally defined wine-growing area
Weingutsiegel Osterreich neck label which signifies government approval

MEASUREMENTS

LIQUID CAPACITY

1 centilitre = 10 millilitres
1 litre = 100 centilitres
1 hectolitre = 100 litres

Metric	US measures	UK measures
	33.8 fluid ounces	35.2 fluid ounces
1 litre	2.11 pints	1.76 pints
	0.264 gallons	0.220 gallons

BOTTLE SIZE EQUIVALENTS

Metric (litres)	USA (pints)	UK (pints)	
3	6.339	5.280	
1.5	3.169	2.640	'magnum'
1	2.113	1.760	
0.75	1.585	1.320	'standard bottle'
0.50	1.056	0.880	Tokay bottle
0.375	0.792	0.660	'half bottle'
0.187	0.395	0.329	'quarter bottle'

AREA

1 square kilometre = 0.386 square mile
2,590 square kilometres = 1 square mile
1 hectare = 2.471 acres
100 hectares = 1 square kilometre
259 hectares = 1 square mile

YIELD

In red wines, yield is linked with quality – usually, the less produced, the better the wine. A Bordeaux vineyard with over 5,000 vines per hectare will eventually produce under 40 hectolitres – less than 5,000 bottles – for sale to the consumer.

With white wines, yield is not so important: fine white wines can be made from vineyards yielding 80-100 hl/ha, although in Burgundy the figure would be less.

Botrytis severely limits production further, so wines from grapes affected are necessarily expensive.

Château Ausone, for instance, one of the greatest Bordeaux properties, will bottle 60 barriques (18,000 bottles) of wine from the 1981 vintage. This means that each hectare of vineyard actually resulted in only 2,570 bottles. (Remember that wine is lost during barrel ageing due to evaporation, tastings and samples.)

By not aiming for such high quality, with vines younger than at Ausone, encouraging high quantity by lighter pruning, and perhaps even eliminating cask ageing with its evaporation in favour of élevage in vat, it is possible to get over 10,000 bottles from a hectare of vineyard in Bordeaux in a good year such as 1979.

TEMPERATURE

To convert degrees centigrade to degrees Fahrenheit
Multiply °C by 9, divide result by 5 and add 32.

To convert degrees Fahrenheit to degrees centigrade
Subtract 32 from °F, multiply by 5 and divide result by 9.

ABBREVIATIONS

AC Appellation Contrôlée
AOC Appellation d'Origine Contrôlée
BOB Buyer's Own Brand (of Champagne)
Bul Bulgaria
Ch Château
d centilitre(s)
DO Denominação de Origem
DOC Denominazione di Origine Controllata
DTW Deutscher Tafelwein
EEC European Economic Community
F France
g gram(s)
Ger Germany
Gk Greek
ha hectare(s)
hl hectolitre(s)
Hun Hungary

It Italy
kg kilogram(s)
km kilometre(s)
KWV Ko-operatieve Wijnbouwers Vereniging
Lat Latin
LB Late-Bottled (of Port)
ml millilitre(s)
NV non-vintage (of Champagne or Port)
Por Portugal
QbA Qualitätswein eines Bestimmten Anbaugebietes
QmP Qualitätswein mit Prädikat
RD recently disgorged (of Champagne)
Sp Spain
Sw Switzerland
VDQS Vin Délimité de Qualité Supérieure
Yugo Yugoslavia

BIBLIOGRAPHY

ADAMS, Leon D.: *The Wines of America*, revised edition, Houghton Mifflin, New York, 1978

AMERINE, Maynard A. and ROESSLER, Edward B.: *Wines: Their Sensory Evaluation*, W. H. Freeman, San Francisco, 1976

AMERINE, Maynard A. and SINGLETON, Vernon L.: *Wine: An Introduction*, revised edition, University of California Press, Berkeley, 1978

ANDERSON, Burton: *Vino: The Wine and Winemakers of Italy*, Little, Brown and Co, Boston, 1980; Hutchinson, London, 1980

ARLOTT, John and FIELDEN, Christopher: *Burgundy, Vines and Wines*, revised edition, Davis-Poynter, London, 1978

BALZER, Robert L.: *Wines of California*, Abrams, New York, 1978

BESPALOFF, Alexis: *The New Signet Book of Wine*, New American Library, New York, 1980

BEZZANT, Norman and BURROUGHS, David: *The New Wine Companion*, Heinemann, London, 1980

BRADFORD, Sarah: *The Englishman's Wine: The Story of Port*, Macmillan, London, 1979

BROADBENT, Michael: *The Great Vintage Wine Book*, Alfred A. Knopf and Christie's Wine Publications, New York, 1980; *Pocket Guide to Wine Tasting*, Mitchell Beazley in association with Christie's Wine Publications, London, 1982

CHROMAN, Nathan: *The Treasury of American Wine*, Crown Publishers, New York, 1982

COOPER, Derek: *Wine with Food*, Artus Books, Marks and Spencer, London, 1980

EVANS, Len, *Australia and New Zealand: Complete Book of Wine*, Paul Hamlyn, Sydney, 1974

FAITH, Nicholas: *The Winemasters*, Hamish Hamilton, London, 1978; Harper and Row, New York, 1978

FLETCHER, Wyndham: *Port: An Introduction to its History and Delights*, Sotheby Parke Bernet, London, 1978

FORBES, Patrick: *Champagne: The Wine, the Land and the People*, Gollancz, London, 1972; Reynal, New York, 1968

GONZALEZ GORDON, Manuel M.: *Sherry: The Noble Wine*, Cassell, London, 1972

HALLGARTEN, F. L. and S. F.: *The Wines and Wine Gardens of Austria*, Argus Books, London, 1979

HALLGARTEN, Peter: *Guide to the Wines of the Rhône*, Pitman Publishing, London, 1979

HALLGARTEN, S. F.: *Alsace, Wine Gardens, Cellars and Cuisine*, Wine and Spirit Publications, London, 1978; *German Wines*, Faber, London, 1976

HALLIDAY, James: *Wines and Wineries of New South Wales*, University of Queensland Press, St Lucia, 1980

HALLIDAY, James and JARRATT, Ray: *The Wines and History of the Hunter Valley*, McGraw-Hill Book Co, Sydney, 1979

HARVEY, John and Sons: *Harvey's Pocket Guide to Wine*, Octopus, London, 1981

HOGG, Anthony: *Guide to Visiting Vineyards*, Michael Joseph, London, 1981

JEFFS, Julian: *Sherry*, 3rd edition, Faber, London, 1982

JOHNSON, Hugh: *Pocket Encyclopaedia of Wine*, Mitchell Beazley, London, 1977; Simon and Schuster, New York, 1977; *Wine*, Nelson, Sunbury-on-Thames, 1973; Simon and Schuster, New York, 1975; *The World Atlas of Wine*, revised edition, Mitchell Beazley, London, 1977; Simon and Schuster, New York, 1978

LICHINE, Alexis: *(New) Encyclopedia of Wines and Spirits*, 4th edition, Alfred A. Knopf, New York, 1974; Cassell, London, 1979; *Guide to the Wines and Vineyards of France*, Alfred A. Knopf, New York, 1979; Weidenfeld and Nicolson, London, 1979

LIVINGSTONE-LEARMONTH, John and MASTER, Melvyn: *The Wines of the Rhône*, Faber, London, 1979

OLKEN, Charles E., ROBY, Norman S., and SINGER, Earl G.: *The Connoisseurs' Handbook of Californian Wines*, Alfred A. Knopf, New York, 1980

PENNING-ROWSELL, Edmund: *The Wines of Bordeaux*, Penguin Books, London, 1979

PEPPERCORN, David: *Bordeaux*, Faber, London and Winchester, Mass., 1982; *Drinking Wine*, 2nd edition, Macdonald, London, 1982

READ, Jan: *The Wines of Spain and Portugal*, Faber, London, 1973; Monarch Books, New York, 1974; *Guide to the Wines of Spain and Portugal*, Pitman Publishing, London, 1977; Monarch Books, New York, 1978

ROBINSON, Jancis: *The Wine Book*, A & C Black, London, 1979

RONCARATI, Bruno: *Viva Vino, DOC Wines of Italy*, Wine and Spirit Publications, London, 1976

SCHNEIDER, Steven: *The International Album of Wine*, Holt, Rinehart and Winston, New York, 1977

SCHOONMAKER, Frank: *Encyclopedia of Wine*, Hastings, New York, 1979; A & C Black, London, 1979

SIEGEL, Hans: *Guide to the Wines of Germany*, Pitman Publishing, London, 1978

STABILISIERUNGSFONDS FÜR WEIN: *German Wine Atlas*, Davis-Poynter, London, 1977

SUTCLIFFE, Serena: *André Simon's Wines of the World*, Macdonald, London, 1981; McGraw-Hill, New York, 1981; *Great Vineyards and Winemakers*, Macdonald, London, 1982; Rutledge Press, New York, 1981

THOMPSON, Bob: *The Pocket Encyclopedia of California Wines*, Mitchell Beazley, London, 1980; Simon and Schuster, New York, 1980

THOMPSON, Robert and JOHNSON, Hugh: *The California Wine Book*, Morrow, New York, 1976

YOXALL, Harry W.: *The Wines of Burgundy*, Pitman Publishing, London, 1979; Stein and Day, New York, 1979

Decanter Magazine Ltd, 16 Black Friars Lane, London EC4, UK

The Wine Spectator, M. Shanken Communications Inc, 305 East 53rd Street, New York, NY 10022, USA

The Friends of Wine (for members of Les Amis du Vin), 2302 Perkins Place, Silver Spring, Maryland 20910, USA

INDEX

219

CREDITS

Photography
1-7 Clive Corless; **14-15** F. Jalain/Agence Top; **16-77, 168, 170, 171** Malkolm Warrington; **82-3** Rosine Mazin/Agence Top; **87** Adam Woolfitt/Susan Griggs Agency; **90** Alain Choisnet/The Image Bank; **95, 146-7** Fred Lyon/Rapho; **99** Even/The Image Bank; **103** J. Guillard/Agence Top; **106 Carlos Santos/Rapho; 110** S. Weiss/Rapho; **114, 118** Jon Wyand; Amedo Vergani/The Image Bank; **122-3** Bob Croxford/Zefa; **127** Bruno Barbey/John Hillelson Agency; **131** Monique Jacot/Susan Griggs Agency; **134** Zefa; **135** Art Directors Photo Library; **143** Michael Freeman; **154** Sebastiao Barbosa/The Image Bank; **159** Ted Spiegel/John Hillelson Agency; **162-3** Paulovsky/Rapho.

Artwork
Hayward & Martin Ltd
Maps
Clyde Surveys Ltd
Typesetting
Technical Editing Services, London
Origination
Adroit Photo Litho Ltd, Birmingham